COCH

# COCHRANE

## BRITANNIA'S SEA WOLF

### DONALD THOMAS

**Cassell Military Paperbacks**

Cassell & Co
Wellington House, 125 Strand,
London WC2R 0BB

Copyright © Donald Thomas 1978

First published by André Deutsch 1978
This Cassell Military Paperbacks edition published 2001
Reprinted 2001, 2002 (three times)

A CIP catalogue record for this book is available from the British Library

ISBN 0-304-35659-X

Printed and bound in Great Britain by
Cox & Wyman Ltd., Reading, Berks.

*For my Father and Marion*

# Contents

—

# List of Plates

—

# Maps

—

# Preface

THE life of Thomas, Lord Cochrane, later 10th Earl of Dundonald, is more extraordinary than that of Nelson, and more far-fetched than anything which the late C. S. Forester permitted Horatio Hornblower. With a brig-sloop, which *The Times* later described as half the size of the smallest Victorian naval tug, he harried the French and Spanish shipping of the Mediterranean, seizing over fifty vessels, one of them a powerful frigate, many times the size of his own warship and carrying over three hundred seamen and marines. As a frigate captain himself, he kept the French coast in turmoil and, with his single ship, halted the main French advance into Catalonia for over a fortnight. With his explosion vessels and fire-ships at the Basque Roads, he reduced the French fleet to an array of stranded hulls, helpless before the guns of the British squadron.[1]

Such exploits might, perhaps, make him little more than a Hornblower who had stepped from the pages of fiction into the centre of Napoleonic sea warfare. Unlike his fictional counterpart, however, Cochrane entered parliament and became a Radical reformer, a quarter of a century before the Reform Bill of 1832. As a democrat and an opponent of wholesale official corruption, he fought the Admiralty administration and the naval system as determinedly as he fought the French. By his account, these enemies revenged themselves on him by means of forged charts to secure his naval disgrace, and by a carefully organised prosecution to convict him as one of the principal movers of the greatest Stock Exchange fraud of the century.

That he should have survived imprisonment as a felon, then established his innocence, and ended his long life as admiral of the fleet is more than most works of fiction could accommodate. They would hardly risk including in addition the account of his campaigns as a mercenary admiral, in the service of liberty, in the Pacific, the Atlantic, and the Mediterranean, or his achievements in setting free more territory than Napoleon conquered. After so much, it seems hardly surprising that he should also have devised plans for poison gas and saturation bombardment, offering them to the Prince Regent in 1812, the year in which the waltz was first introduced into the ballrooms of London.

His personal enmities were fierce and prolonged, their nature being indicated by the presence of two senior admirals, the senior admiralty civil servant, and a lord chief justice as his principal antagonists. A century after the events had taken place, the grandson of Lord Chief Justice Ellenborough was still trying to demonstrate that despite the public vindication of Cochrane's innocence he was, after all, guilty of the great Stock Exchange fraud.

Even in our time, reactions to Cochrane remain strong. John Gore, the most recent editor of Thomas Creevey's papers, describes Cochrane in that work as "one of the most splendid naval commanders that ever paced a quarter-deck". This was very much the view of Cochrane's later contemporaries in the Victorian period. At the other extreme, Doris Langley Moore in *The Late Lord Byron* describes him as "mercenary and dilatory" and as "the grasping admiral, whose numberless postponements of action are a curiosity of naval history". No one could have been more surprised by this last judgement than Cochrane's contemporary critics, whose general complaint was that he was all too ready to attack precipitately and take unacceptable risks. It was discipline rather than impetuousness, which Cochrane lacked in the view of his Victorian biographer J. W. Fortescue, who rather quaintly suggested that many of his hero's problems might have been solved if only he had had a public school education.[2]

As in the case of so many biographical subjects, each age has seen in Cochrane what it has wanted to. His immediate contemporaries regarded him as a splendid national advertisement for superior British seamanship. The Radicals cheered him as a champion of democracy, Scott and the Romantics saluted him as the liberator of nations oppressed by foreign rule. To the Victorians, he was the supreme example of the hero of a boys' adventure story brought to life. It is no coincidence that Captain Marryat, who served as a midshipman under his command, used Cochrane's exploits as the subject-matter of some of his fiction. His guilt or innocence of the Stock Exchange fraud remains ultimately beyond proof or disproof, but his Victorian admirers thought such a crime morally impossible in so fine a man. The controversy was not settled, however, since a later generation still found the figure of the flawed hero more psychologically interesting than the unblemished variety.

In modern terms, Cochrane is perhaps most illuminating when seen against the social panorama of his age and in the full dimensions of his naval, political and personal life. Directly or obliquely, his story lives in the poetry of Scott or Moore, the diaries of Creevey, the letters of William Beckford, the novels of Marryat, as much as in the despatches of the time, the court reports, or the contemporary press. One of the most important documents is the *Autobiography of a Seaman*, written in the last months of his life. As an old and dying man, he used a professional writer, G. B. Earp, to assist him. Inevitably, the question was raised as to how much of the book was Cochrane's and how much Earp's. Fortunately, the more important sections can be checked against the logs of the *Pallas* and the *Imperieuse*, the reports of the *Naval Chronicle*, naval despatches, transcripts of trials, and independent contemporary accounts. By this test, the *Autobiography* is fair and accurate in its account of the naval career. For the disputes with the Admiralty, and particularly the controversy over the Stock Exchange trial, it is inevitably a partisan document, whether Cochrane wrote it himself or it was written by Earp from his dictation or notes. In the case of Cochrane's *Narrative of Services in the Liberation of Chili, Peru, and Brazil*, there is corroboration of its events in the memoirs of William Miller, W. B. Stevenson, and other witnesses of the campaign against the Spanish in Chile and Peru.

In writing the present account of Cochrane's life, I have been most grateful for the assistance given by a number of libraries and institutions. My thanks are particularly due to the Bodleian Library, Oxford; Bristol Central Library; the British Library, Departments of Manuscripts and Printed Books, and the Newspaper Library, Colindale; Cardiff Central Library; the London Library; the Ministry of Defence Library; the National Library of Scotland; the National Maritime Museum; the Public Record Office; the library of University College, London; the University Library, London, and the library of the University of Wales Institute of Science and Technology.

Finally, I must acknowledge the advice and help of Mr Piers Burnett, Mr Michael Thomas, and Mr Alan Williams at various stages of the writing of the book, and my wife's enthusiasm during its long completion.

# I

# The Lords of Culross

—

In the last years of the eighteenth century, when the vogue for picturesque and romantic scenery coloured the middle-class view of nature, the bay of Culross was reckoned to be well worth a visit. Some of its admirers swore that it matched anything to be found on the Rhine. A dozen miles above Edinburgh, the northern shore of the Firth of Forth broke into a series of wooded bays, set in the hills of Kinross. In deep green billows, the foliage rose like a leafy, undulating wall from the dark rocks of the foreshore. Sloping gardens and rustic cottages, which were more romantic to view than to inhabit, marked the road where market carts and occasional carriages rumbled between Kincardine and Rosyth.

Above the bay of Culross, the ridge of the hill was distinguished by the fine south front of Culross Abbey. Its Renaissance façade and corner turrets, in so leafy a setting, suggested one of the smaller châteaux of the Loire. The house had been begun in 1608, from designs by Inigo Jones, and had been commissioned by Edward Bruce, lawyer, diplomat, and Master of the Rolls. True, it was not a real abbey of the sort made so thrillingly fashionable by the Gothick novels of the 1780s and 1790s. Yet it adjoined the ruins of the original Cistercian monastery, which Malcolm, Earl of Fife, had founded in 1217. Young ladies and gentlemen of sensibility, seeing Culross on a stormy night, the wind chasing the clouds across the sky, the moon glimmering fitfully on water, dark trees, and mediaeval ruins, were transported from reality to the fantasies of Mrs Radcliffe and her followers, whose three-volume "horrid novels" were the current sensation of circulating libraries in Edinburgh and London.

However, behind the charming view there lay a changing and often disagreeable reality. Like so many great houses, this one had been built at the height of a family's fortunes and had descended to those who could ill support its expenses.

The splendour of the Inigo Jones house was not disputed. Among the fine drawing rooms of the first floor, with their spacious long gallery, was an apartment hung with Gobelins tapestries. Here the King, who was both James VI of Scotland and James I of England, was royally entertained in 1617. The Bruce family in the sixteenth and seventeenth centuries had been men of business and figures of political influence, the creators of wealth and the arbiters of policy. But their line dwindled until only one daughter remained at Culross, Lady Elizabeth Bruce. She married William Cochrane of Ochiltree and bore him a son who inherited Culross. Indeed, he inherited more than that. His Cochrane kinsmen had been Earls of Dundonald since 1648 when the title was conferred on Sir William Cochrane, a loyal supporter of Charles I, by the hard-pressed King. In 1758, the 7th Earl had gone to Canada on General Wolfe's staff, in the campaign to drive the French from the St Lawrence settlements. A few months later, news came to Culross that the Earl had been killed in the preliminary assault on Louisberg. Major Cochrane of Culross was now the 8th Earl of Dundonald.

When the Bruces were succeeded by the Cochranes, the men of business and law gave way to those who for five centuries or more had known little but the arts of war, by land and sea. In previous reigns, their abilities had been highly esteemed, bringing them rewards or favours from their royal masters. But in the age of the House of Hanover, as the power of patronage passed into ministerial hands, such rewards were few and the favours short-lived. Still the Cochranes lived and died in the old profession of their ancestors, as though the new era of commerce and parliamentary influence had not come into being. Three of them died in Marlborough's wars, then the 7th Earl fell at Louisberg and Colonel Charles Cochrane, son of the 8th Earl, was killed at Yorktown in the last stages of the American War of Independence, having been aide-de-camp to Cornwallis.

For the most part, the Cochranes attained modest rank and little fame. Their choice of life, as Samuel Johnson termed it, was unfortunate. Commerce, industry and invention were creating the new wealth of the eighteenth century. The profession of arms might be admired in moments of national peril, tolerated when necessary, but was mostly regarded with priggish contempt.

After enjoying his earldom for twenty years, Major Cochrane of Culross died in 1778. The abbey and its estates passed to his son, Archibald Cochrane, as 9th Earl of Dundonald. The new Earl was thirty years old. His son, whose naval career was to begin so inauspiciously in 1793, was almost three. The 9th Earl also brought to

Culross his beautiful but delicate wife Anna, who bore him four sons, the survivors of her seven pregnancies.

The misfortunes of the new generation at Culross began early. Anna died in 1784, after ten years during which she had been pregnant more often than not. The widowed Earl, increasingly preoccupied by expedients to save the estate from bankruptcy, handed over the care and education of his four sons to a series of hired tutors. Pedagogues of all sorts came and went with disconcerting rapidity. As a rule they were remembered more for their personal oddities than for any learning which they imparted. Young Thomas Cochrane was much impressed by a French tutor, Monsieur Durand, who was a Catholic and refused to set foot inside the kirk. Worse still, he caused outrage among the suspicious Presbyterians by interrupting their Sunday devotions with the sound of gunfire, as he opened hostilities from the churchyard against the magpies who were stripping the Culross cherry orchards while the owners prayed. Other tutors were less engaging and were remembered without affection. There was one pedant whom Thomas Cochrane could only recall as the man who had boxed his ears for asking the difference between an interjection and a conjunction. Seventy years later, Cochrane admitted that this response had permanently extinguished all his remaining interest in philology.[1]

The young Thomas Cochrane, who assumed the courtesy title of Lord Cochrane, as his father's heir, had little systematic education. On the other hand, he was well informed in history and practical science. He showed a natural aptitude and enthusiasm for learning, with a mind whose strong alliance of intellectual power and quick imagination was to make him an equally formidable opponent in war or politics. His sense of history and locality was naturally developed by an interest in his own ancestors and in the events which had made Culross both famous and infamous. The journey to Rosyth was enlivened by the sight of the remote crossroads where John Blackadder, Laird of Tulliallan, had lain in wait for the Abbot of Culross, Sir James Inglis, in 1530, and had treacherously murdered him. In Culross itself was the spot where, in 1038, King Duncan of Scotland had fought a desperate defensive battle against the invading Danes. Defeated at last, the King withdrew towards Perth, accompanied by the one man whose loyalty had never yet failed, his commander-in-chief, Macbeth.[2]

The Cochranes of the eleventh century perhaps fought on the other side at Culross. According to family tradition, they were "sea rovers"

from Scandinavia whom the fortunes of war brought to Scotland. It
was not until the thirteenth century, however, that their name first
appeared in official Scottish documents as "Coveran", and then as
"Cochran". A hundred years later, while England was ruled by the
Plantagenets, the family assumed a new importance in Scotland's
affairs in the person of Robert Cochran. His taste for fine architecture
was combined with an ability to hew his opponent to pieces with a
broadsword in a remarkably short space of time. It was the latter
quality which recommended him to James III of Scotland. Thomas
Cochrane later remarked that his ancestor played the same role to
King James as Cardinal Wolsey was to do to Henry VIII, though with
a different conclusion.

Unscrupulous in most things, Robert Cochran was loyal to his
master, crushing the power of the Scottish nobility in order to reinforce the authority of the King. James duly rewarded him with the
Earldom of Mar. Exasperated by this, the disgruntled knights and
noblemen met to plan their vengeance, which was to take effect at a
ceremonial military gathering. They fell upon Robert Cochran there
and brought him to the bridge at Lauder. The bodies of other court-
iers lynched by the plotters were already dangling from the bridge.
Cochran coolly suggested that if they proposed to despatch him in the
same manner, then his rank as Earl of Mar entitled him to die by a
silk cord from his own pavilion. By way of answer, one of the knights
wrenched off the gold chain about Cochran's neck, and slipped the
noose over him. A moment later, King James's trusted servant
dropped over the side of the bridge, and died as the rope sprang
taut.

Surprisingly, in view of their way of life and the troubled times, no
other Cochrane died by the hangman's art. A near exception was Sir
John Cochrane, younger son of the 1st Earl of Dundonald. When the
Protestant Duke of Monmouth raised the west of England against
the Catholic James II, Sir John joined the Earl of Argyll's simultaneous rebellion in Scotland. After its failure, he was taken prisoner
and sentenced to death. It required only the arrival of the death
warrant from London to seal his fate. But his daughter, showing the
traditional spirit and audacity of the Cochranes, dressed herself as a
man and "twice attacked and robbed the mails (between Belfor and
Berwick) which conveyed the death-warrants". At the same time,
she persuaded Father Petre, King James's confessor, to forward a
bribe of £5000 for Sir John's life. A pardon was accordingly obtained.
Bishop Burnet, staunchly Whig and Protestant, preferred another

story. According to this, the King pardoned Sir John after a private interview, during which the prisoner betrayed details of secret negotiations between the rebels and William of Orange, who was to depose the King three years later and reign as William III. Not that Burnet was prepared to forego the story of the bribe entirely, remarking that Sir John had "a rich father, the Earl of *Dundonald*: And he offered the Priests 5000l. to save his son. They wanted a stock of money for managing their designs: so they interposed so effectually, that the bargain was made."[3]

Whatever the precise truth, Sir John had had a very narrow escape. His cautionary experience persuaded the rest of the Cochrane family to spend most of the next century in loyal, if humdrum, service to the crown.

Eventful and vivid though his family history might be, the young Thomas Cochrane was quite as apt to be influenced by the present as by the past. His background, in this respect, differed markedly from that of English political patrons and their favourites, who knew that lucrative administrative posts as "placemen" of the ministry, no less than the political reward of sinecure employments, were theirs by right to manipulate or enjoy. As late as 1833, Lord Macaulay, writing of Sir Robert Walpole in the *Edinburgh Review*, could remark equably, "That he practised corruption on a large scale is, we think, indisputable. . . . Walpole governed by corruption because, in his time, it was impossible to govern otherwise . . . the House of Commons was in that situation in which assemblies must be managed by corruption or cannot be managed at all." The attitude of men of affairs in the eighteenth century could hardly be more accurately mirrored. Despite the scorn of later generations, the recent memories of "corruption" were not unduly disquieting to Macaulay, either as essayist or as minister of the crown. When Cochrane, with his clear sense of honour and political decency, encountered the easy-going ministerial politics of his time, he showed neither respect nor mercy to his opponents.[4]

His childhood world made him ill-equipped for the great moral compromise of public life. Culross was idyllic, though not remote, bounded by the hills of Kinross, the smooth waters of the Forth, and the city of Edinburgh a dozen miles downstream, already fulfilling its claim to the cliché, "The Athens of the North". To Cochrane, Edinburgh was always the natural seat of learning and jurisprudence, of fine art and high society. The noble buildings of the defunct

Scottish parliament served as a reminder that at the beginning of the century Scotland had still been free of the borough-mongering and ministerial bribery of Westminster politics.

Worse still, Westminster showed its scorn for the Scots, the "Sawneys" and "North Britons", as an inferior breed whose very religion was despised. A group of Presbyterians sought an interview with Lord Thurlow, the Lord Chancellor, to ask that they should not continue to suffer civil and political disqualifications merely for being Presbyterians. "Gentlemen," said the Lord Chancellor, "I'll be perfectly frank with you. Gentlemen, I am against you and for the Established Church, by God. Not that I like the Established Church a bit better than any other church, but because it *is* established. And whenever you can get your damned religion established, I'll be for that too. Good morning to you."[5]

However great their distaste for English public life, the decline of the family estates left the Cochranes with little choice but to seek their fortunes through it. As patterns for the young Lord Cochrane's future, his childhood world was haunted by the dim and often downright shady figures of his paternal uncles. Uncle Charles, of course, had died for King and Country at Yorktown, but his surviving brothers were energetically involved in different public pursuits.

The Honourable Basil Cochrane had chosen the service of the East India Company, where his nephew might one day make money in considerable quantities. Unhappily, when the boy was eight years old, news reached Culross of a great misfortune in Uncle Basil's life. In his zeal for justice, he had been so unfortunate as to flog two Indians to death, or so it was alleged. They had been guilty of falsifying the account books at Negapatam, where Basil Cochrane was in charge of John Company's affairs. The keeper of accounts, Vydenadah, refused to produce the books so Basil Cochrane had him tied to the balustrade and flogged by a team of sepoys to persuade him of his error.[6]

Of the two "murdered" Indians, one Ramah Naig, was found to be alive and well. But Vydenadah had certainly died several days after the beating, from whatever causes. The East India Company in Madras was obliged to hold an inquiry. The next year, 1786, the Court of Directors in London read the report and dismissed Basil Cochrane from their service. They would have preferred to see him removed from India altogether but he remained as a merchant, victualling the ships of the Royal Navy at Madras on the basis of a one per cent commission. He knew too much about the secrets of the East India trade for the directors to risk public warfare with him. He was ready to tell the world, for example, the story of "condemned provisions". These cases of rotten food were put ashore from ships and written off. They were then resold to other ships, as fresh supplies, and in due course put ashore somewhere else. Dumped and sold repeatedly, the putrifying cargoes sailed the Indian Ocean "at the expense of the public".[7]

The East India directors made their peace with Basil Cochrane, who spent the next forty years screwing every last penny from the Victualling Board of the Admiralty, on whose behalf he operated. Once, at least, they thought they had the measure of him, reckoning that he owed them over £9000. They should have known better. There was a ten-year dogfight in the Court of Exchequer, in Parliament, where Cochrane presented petitions against them, and in the press. When it was over, the Victualling Board had not seen a penny of their money and found themselves, by the vagaries of Exchequer, condemned to pay Cochrane almost £1000.[8] It was unlikely that the East India Company would receive Basil Cochrane's nephew with much enthusiasm.

A more hopeful avenue was opened by the career of a more distinguished uncle who was to win high naval honours, Alexander Cochrane, then a captain in the Royal Navy. The 9th Earl of Dundonald disliked the navy, having tried it for a short while himself, so Uncle Alexander acted independently. He had fought with distinction under Admiral Lord Rodney and his influence was sufficient to allow him to enter little Thomas Cochrane's name, as midshipman, on the books of four Royal Navy ships: the *Vesuvius,* the *Caroline, La Sophie,* and the *Hind.* Of course, it was not intended that the child should go to sea at an unreasonably tender age. Uncle Alexander was merely ensuring that if his nephew was allowed to choose the navy, then his seniority as a midshipman would date from the time his name was entered on the ships' books.

Apart from such figures as Basil and Alexander, the six Cochrane uncles contained one man who was the "black sheep" of the family in the grand manner. As a scoundrel and a fraud, Colonel Andrew Cochrane-Johnstone, as he called himself, was to play the most important role in his nephew's life. He was a profiteer and slave-trader who had entered the army and risen to the rank of colonel by 1797. Then he was appointed Governor of Domenica, a post which he reasonably regarded as carrying a licence to pilfer and embezzle to his

heart's content. As for his slave-trading interests, the government
could not have been more helpful. The 8th West India regiment was
put under his command and he quickly set them to work for his
private use, building a fine estate to house the harem of girls whom he
collected as a hobby. He seemed the archetype of the Victorian
"bounder" or "cad". As he watched the parade of slave women with
a connoisseur's eye, or observed the flogging of a recalcitrant subject,
it might seem that this easy existence could not last. For this con-
tingency, he had a well-laid plan. When, in 1803, the great investigation began, the acts of embezzlement and misappropriation had been
so arranged that they all appeared as the work of his subordinate,
Major Gordon.

The court-martial, however, was a match for Cochrane-Johnstone.
Its members heard the evidence, acquitted John Gordon, and indicted
the ex-Governor of Domenica himself. Still he eluded their vengeance.
As time went by and the law delayed, it grew more difficult to prove
the case. To the disgust of George III, the prosecution failed. Yet in
the general brevet promotion of army officers in 1803, Cochrane-
Johnstone was passed over. Indeed, he was made to resign his commission. He wrote to the Prince of Wales saying that he had heard
his resignation was to be cancelled and that he was to be made a
major-general. A cold official reply informed him that if he had heard
anything of the kind, he was sadly in error. Cruelly misjudged, he sat
in the comfort of his Harley Street house, describing himself, moist-
eyed, to all who would listen as "an innocent man, who had devoted
his life and fortune to the service of his King and Country". In order
to be immune from arrest for debt and to turn unreservedly to
"speculation", he bought the parliamentary seat of Grampound. The
constituency was so notoriously corrupt that even an anti-reform
House of Commons made an exception and abolished it a decade
before 1832. When the authorities chose to topple Thomas Cochrane
from a hero's pinnacle, the rogue uncle was a handy instrument.[9]

The 9th Earl himself exercised the most direct influence over his
son's development. Quick-tempered, anxious, unpredictable, he was
crotchety with good reason, tight-fisted because he had nothing
to give. He harped querulously on the "res angusta domi", that
convenient Latin tag conditioning his family to frugality and
parsimony. In politics he was a Whig, approving progress and
emancipation at a future date which seemed to recede infinitely. When
he ventured out of Culross, to visit Edinburgh or London, he returned
complaining tetchily, "This is an age of sentiment, novels, and

overstrained refinement." He despised those who tried to sail "with the tide of the *popular*". While disliking political oppression, he deeply suspected men like William Wilberforce whom he saw parading their "misguided phrenzy or opinion, making a bustle about Slave Trade, *Freedom*, and emancipation of Negroes, while they will turn their eyes from scenes of domestic and national misery". In fact the young Wilberforce's evangelical enthusiasm embraced the suppression of Sabbath-breaking, drunkenness, and indecent literature at home, as well as slavery overseas. To the Earl, he seemed just the type to become the dupe of violent revolutionaries. "He surely does not foresee the consequence of *ill-timed* alterations."[10]

Even before the death of his young wife, the Earl himself turned away from politics to the immediate question of the "res angusta domi". It was both a corroding anxiety and, at the same time, the spur to achievement. He vowed to redeem the family fortunes, perhaps to hand on to the young Lord Cochrane a flourishing estate whose wealth would be greater and more enduring than that of his ancestors who had built Culross. The new fortunes of the Cochranes would not lie in war, nor in the corrupt ministerial favouritism of Westminster and the "places" found for political sycophants. The riches would be those of the new age which was dawning in Europe, the wealth of reason and the rewards of enlightenment. The 9th Earl of Dundonald would be remembered as a great scientist, inventor and manufacturer of his day.

It was less absurd than it might seem. As a young man, the Earl had spent a short while in the navy. During this period, he had noticed the ravages of worms on the bottoms of ships, where they ate into the structure of the hull. The replacement of so much rotten timber was a considerable drain on the resources of the Admiralty. A few ships were "hobnailed", the bottoms covered with large-headed iron nails, but this was far too expensive a method to be undertaken often. The 9th Earl, pondering this problem, thought of the coal on the Culross estate. It was only mined in a small way, the Earl's philanthropic principles forbidding the use of colliers' wives and daughters as "beasts of burthen" in hauling the coal to the surface. He had undertaken some simple experiments of his own with coal, in a kiln. When it was "reduced" to coke, a thick black substance was given off, known as coal tar. The coke was readily bought by the new ironworks. But might not the coal tar be refined in such a way that it could be used to coat the hulls of ships?[11]

When his son and heir was six years old, the Earl turned almost

exclusively to the pursuit of his scientific dream, being granted a
patent for his "coal tar". In the following year, 1782, he pacified his
creditors with promises of future riches and set up "The British
Tar Company" at Culross. He was not alone in the venture. Matthew
Boulton, who had successfully marketed James Watt's steam·engine
was a family friend. Joseph Black, "the father of modern chemistry"
and Professor of Chemistry at Edinburgh, was a friend and
enthusiast. Sir John Dalrymple, a parliamentary lawyer, surveyed
the company's financial obligations and reported favourably to the
Earl's creditors. By 1783 there were four furnaces at Culross, pro-
cessing twenty-eight tons of coal a week. The Earl was delighted and
thought only of expanding the project. Adam Smith as well as Black
and Dalrymple became an admirer of the new process. Now was the
time to raise vast sums of capital and the Earl wrote hopefully to his
uncle Andrew Stuart urging him to invest at such a propitious moment. "We are encouraged to proceed in establishing the manufacture upon a very large scale in different parts of Great Britain . . .
but a capital of thirty to forty thousand pounds will in the course of a
few years need to be expended." Such an outlay was staggering, it
was far more than all the accumulated debts of all the Cochranes in
history. £22,400 was invested with a promise of an annual clear profit
of £5000.[12]

The delighted Earl was within reach of his ambition. He had, after
all, achieved an easy and cheap answer to the problems of worm-
eaten vessels. Dalrymple hardly exaggerated when he claimed that
"from a Naval Nation Lord Dundonald deserves a Statue of Gold".
The Earl travelled to Birmingham, taking young Thomas Cochrane
with him, and talked to the great James Watt of this and other inventions which had either been proposed or were thought desirable.
Young Lord Cochrane remembered how they discussed the problem
of finding some source of lighting for the streets of towns and cities.
The man who could invent and patent such a process was assured of
wealth and honours. The solution seemed far away. On the Culross
estate the Earl was preoccupied with the distilling of coal tar and
had no leisure to consider other men's problems. He was concerned
over the vapour which was given off in the process, since it was in-
flammable and possibly injurious. Near the house itself, he had an
experimental kiln which he decided to adapt in order to get rid of the
unwanted fumes. In darkness, he fitted a gun barrel to the outlet
pipe, carrying the vapour to a safe height. Then, as the process of
extracting coal tar began, he held a light to the muzzle. Three miles

away, on the other shore of the Firth, the inhabitants stared in amazement as the dark waters and distant coast blazed with light. But the Earl's head was bent to examine the dark and glossy coal tar on which he had set all his hopes. Above him, the gas lighting, which he had invented without realising it, blazed unheeded. It was William Murdoch, an employee of James Watt who saw the possibility latent in the one invention which might have saved Culross. He developed it and it was later patented by Frederic Winsor in 1804.[13]

But the Earl still had his coal tar and, taking young Lord Cochrane with him once more, he set off for London. He was about to present his great discovery to the Admiralty and their ship-repairers. It was not too much to hope that wealth and honour would be his at last.

The Admiralty seemed disinclined at first to take any notice of the coal tar invention. But they relented and agreed to coat one side of a buoy at the Nore with the Earl's patent mixture. However, they insisted that it was to be done at the Earl's own expense, the Navy Board was not to be committed to any financial outlay. The inventor agreed and the buoy was prepared. He waited impatiently during the trial period and then went to receive the verdict of the Admiralty. Yes, the experiment had been a complete success, protecting the side of the buoy against the worm while the other side had rotted. No, the Admiralty was not interested in the invention.

The Earl was dumbfounded by this reply. He had pacified his creditors, borrowed a further £22,400 and was irretrievably in debt unless coal tar were adopted. Why should it not be? Still with young Lord Cochrane in tow, he began to visit shipbuilders, to see if there was some special technical problem involved in using coal tar, some minor defect which he might be able to overcome. He received his answer at last from a shipbuilder in Limehouse.

"My lord," said the man, "we live by repairing ships as well as by building them, and the worm is our best friend. Rather than use your preparation, I would cover ships' bottoms with honey to attract worms."[14]

Similar objections, wrote Lord Cochrane, were "everywhere encountered" among the shipbuilders. "Neither they, nor any artisans in wood, would patronise a plan to render their work durable." As for the Admiralty and the Navy Board, it was common knowledge that many of the clerks in the King's dockyards also acted as agents for the private contractors. They were hardly likely to recommend

to the Board a substance which would lead to a recession among those
on whose behalf they acted and whose profits they shared.[15]

Father and son returned, suitably chastened, to Culross. But
though the Earl's fortunes had taken such a turn for the worse, he
was confident that some other scientific development might yet
secure the future of his family. To make assurance doubly sure, he
began to work on a host of projects simultaneously. Perhaps it was
his election to the Royal Society of Scotland which gave him the
confidence to launch out in this manner, but the other members of
the British Tar Company grew uneasy. Its future might be unpromising but at least it was not actually losing money. Joseph Black went
to Culross and was alarmed to find that the Earl had lost his enthusiasm for coal tar and was now pottering about with experiments for manufacturing salt or attempting to produce sal ammoniac.
"I endeavoured to dissuade him from the pursuit of these for the
present, and advised him to attend to the branches of his manufacture
which had already succeeded and were bringing in money."[16]

It was certainly true that the coal tar process was a scientific
success, but the refusal of the Admiralty and the reluctance of shipbuilders to use it had put an end to its commercial use. Without such
patronage, a return of £5000 a year on the £22,400 investment was
impossible. Perhaps, then, the salvation of Culross lay in the manufacture of salt. The Earl published *The Present State of the Manufacture of Salt Explained*, only to find his time and enthusiasm expended
in the literary snarling of a pamphlet-war with men who disagreed
over his figures for the populations of Britain and France, or for the
amount of salt imported. Meanwhile, the shadow of total ruin spread
over Culross and its inhabitants.

As he pottered about his experimental "salt-pan", the Earl noticed
that the process produced a quantity of soda. But for the time being
he was obsessed by salt-manufacture and the production of alkalis
was an irrelevance. He had, without realising it, revolutionised the
manufacture of soap and glass, as he discovered when other men took
his soda, used it instead of scarce barilla, and made their fortunes.
While his financial position grew worse, he spread his intellectual
resources as widely as his borrowed capital. The bankrupt estate at
Culross began to produce alumina for silk and calico printing, British
gum as a substitute for imported gum senegal, sal ammoniac, and
white lead. The Earl himself began to experiment in making bread
from potatoes, as an aid to the poor.

Not one of these activities was on a scale sufficient to cover its own costs and, as the noble inventor dissipated his energies and abilities, his behaviour grew progressively odder. He certainly drank more heavily as his commitments grew more oppressive, but he also assumed something of the character of a scientific Micawber, hoping every day that a sudden miracle in technology would manifest itself to retrieve the family fortunes.

The Earl's four sons can have expected little from the estate and they were the least surprised of anyone when in 1793, when Thomas Cochrane was seventeen, Culross Abbey and the family lands had to be put up for sale to satisfy the creditors. The Earl had a special brochure printed and opened it with an appeal "To his Countrymen". He admitted that "There are few situations in which it may be thought proper for an individual to bring himself or his private concerns forward to the public eye." In the present case it had been done "with reluctance". However, the reluctance and a habitual reference to the "res angusta domi" which had handicapped the author's genius, were quickly followed by a well-balanced promotional address for the sale of Culross. There was no sentimental grief for a lost family home, no picture of the scenic beauties of the place. The Earl summed up Culross Abbey as an industrial asset, listing the quantities of coal and fire-clay which might be mined there, once the woods, which had been so much admired by lovers of the Romantic scene, were chopped down and the ground cleared. Not that the woods were without significance, of course. Timber was fetching a high price as conflict with France threatened and obliged the Admiralty to build more ships.

The financial catastrophe which had overtaken the Earl in no way diminished his enthusiasm for scientific investigation. While he and his creditors were in prolonged negotiation for the disposal of Culross, he produced his largest and most important publication, *A Treatise Shewing the Intimate Connection that Subsists between Agriculture and Chemistry*. But once again, he was in advance of his time. What was dismissed as eccentricity in the Earl of Dundonald was to be hailed as the genius of discovery in Sir Humphrey Davy. Indeed, the most bitter irony of all was still far in the future, when the Earl was an old and dying man, struggling to support his ailing mistress and her child in Parisian squalor, to which he had been driven by the most remorseless of his creditors. From the miseries of this exile, where drink had become his last consolation, the old man heard that their Lordships of the Admiralty had conceived an interesting new idea. In 1822, they had asked a committee of the Royal Society, under the chairmanship of Sir Humphrey Davy, to investigate the possibility that coal tar might be an effective and cheap preservative for ships' bottoms. The committee reported favourably and their Lordships congratulated themselves on their acumen. Not only was their suggestion vindicated but the cantankerous Scottish earl who had taken out a patent in the 1780s, had neither heart nor money to renew it in 1806. The Admiralty, by biding its time, got the process for nothing.

The Earl was preoccupied with the dispersal of his family. He also remarried in 1788, choosing a handsome widow, Isabella Raymond. She died in 1808, her dark and aquiline beauty preserved in her portrait by Gainsborough. On marrying Mrs Raymond, he parted with young Lord Cochrane and his brother Basil, who spent six months at Mr Chauvet's military academy in Kensington Square, London, with a view to subsequent careers in the British Army. One member of the family who had done well in the world, at that time, was the scapegrace uncle, Andrew Cochrane-Johnstone. He was very nearly a full colonel and well placed to persuade the Horse Guards to provide a commission for Lord Cochrane in the 104th Foot, a regiment well down the seniority list of the army. There was a family row when the boy returned from Chauvet's and swore that he hated military life and would prefer the navy. The Cochranes, he was made to understand, were no longer rich enough to indulge such fads. So the two youngsters were seen off to London again by stage-coach, that being the most economical conveyance. The Earl's agent watched them go, observing, "It is true they have not had very much education, but they are strong and fine to look at and very sensible and will get on anywhere."[17]

It seemed that Lord Cochrane, at least, was about to prove the agent wrong on this last point. The great drama raged over an improbable pair of items – a bilious yellow waistcoat and matching trousers. The colour happened to be that of the Whig party, to which the Earl was firmly attached, and he had conceived the novel idea of sending his son off to join his regiment in the party colours. "I was admonished never to be ashamed," wrote Cochrane, describing the ordeal, for the Earl regarded party and loyalty as matters for proud display. Moreover, his son must look like a young officer of fashion. This, too, the Earl interpreted somewhat oddly. He had the youth's head cropped and its remains plastered down with "a vile composition of candlegrease and flour". The net result was that Lord Cochrane, in clothes cut absurdly for his height, and outrageously coloured, appeared in the London streets looking more like a pantomime clown than an infantry officer. Hoots of laughter followed his progress and the gang of ragged boys near Charing Cross jeered him until he almost wept. The misery of these weeks determined him that he would take his chance anywhere rather than in the loathsome profession of the army. Summoning up his courage, he returned home to inform his father.[18]

The Earl was first speechless with surprise and then furious. When the boy begged to be saved from "the degradation of floured head, pigtail and yellow breeches", the Earl, seeking some rational basis for his anger, accused Lord Cochrane of insulting him personally and the Whig party in general. He proceeded to box the boy's ears in a very spirited manner. But as the latest of innumerable rows between father and son subsided into sullen separation, the most important question remained unanswered. The Cochranes had been sometimes imprudent and often unfortunate, but they had never flinched from their adversaries and they had borne adversities of many kinds with a courage which was wholly admirable. Robert Cochran, facing execution, had treated his murderers with haughty contempt, but here stood the latest of his line, a gangling ninny who ran home to his father because some rough boys shouted rude words at him near Charing Cross. The Earl's anger must have masked his dismay as he wondered what more could be done for his son and heir.[19]

The solution to this and many more problems was at hand. While the hopeful young cadets attended Mr Chauvet's military cramming course in Kensington Square, another building in that same group of handsome dwellings standing in semi-rural parkland close to the London road might have caught their attention. It was a residence of the French ambassador, the Marquis de Chauvelin, who since the revolution of 1789 had embraced the more fashionable title of "Citizen Chauvelin". But for all his revolutionary protestations, the young Marquis matched the type of the aristocratic nincompoop quite as well as any young nobleman of the old order. He was incompetent in negotiation and tactless in diplomacy, despised by the ministers of George III and suspected of bourgeois inclinations by the apostles of pure revolution in Paris.

It was not Chauvelin who attracted most attention but another, older man whose position was that of a mere attaché. In the mornings he worked among his books, writing his memoirs it was said. In the afternoons he went out to keep his private and secret diplomatic appointments. The young men of Mr Chauvet's military academy watched him limp towards his carriage, a man in early middle-age with a puffy, rounded face and full figure, wearing leather breeches with top boots, a round hat and short tail-coat, his hair arranged in a little queue. He was known to the Prime Minister, William Pitt, and to the Foreign Secretary, Lord Grenville, as a "deep" and "dangerous" man. The other inhabitants of the square heard that he had once been Bishop of Autun, until he cast his allegiance on the side of the revolution. His name was Charles Maurice Talleyrand, the future Foreign Minister of Napoleon, and perhaps the greatest name in European diplomacy.[20]

Talleyrand's mission in the spring of 1792 was to form an alliance with England or, at least, to persuade Pitt's government to remain neutral in the republic's war against Austria and Prussia. Talleyrand was an anglophile with many friends in English cultural life and in the Whig opposition. The Tories were less well-disposed to him, the Foreign Secretary writing to George III on 28 April 1792 that Talleyrand was not to be considered as more than an attaché. The printshops of Piccadilly exhibited "strong" caricatures of a smooth-tongued and two-faced ex-bishop. When Chauvelin, Talleyrand, and other members of the French embassy went to Ranelagh one evening, where ladies and gentlemen of fashion sipped cool drinks or walked among the pleasure gardens, listening to the music, the "fasionables" gathered themselves up at the sight of murderers in their midst and fled precipitately.[21]

Talleyrand failed to get his alliance, but he persuaded Pitt to announce England's neutrality, which was a valuable consideration when the Duke of Brunswick's army drove back the French towards Paris in a few months' time. He returned to Paris in July 1792, where his "wisdom" and "circumspection" had already been proclaimed by the *Chronique de Paris* on 11 June.

He was still in Paris on 10 August when the mob invaded the Tuileries, as the Duke of Brunswick neared Paris, and command of the revolution passed from its intellectual leaders to the butchers who were prepared to do the work at which finer sensibilities shuddered. The Swiss guard was massacred, prisons where enemies of the revolution were held became slaughterhouses, associates of the royal family were lynched. Marie Antoinette's friend, Madame de Lamballe, was torn apart, her "executioners" wearing the most private parts of her anatomy as decorations.

The news reached England on 14 August with reports of 11,000 men and women having been massacred. Charles James Fox and the members of the Whig opposition, who had watched the progress of the revolution with interested benevolence, were dismayed. J. B. Burges wrote from Whitehall to Lord Grenville that the mob had advanced on the British embassy, but the Swiss Guard there had been hidden and so escaped the massacre. Quite apart from horror at the events, the government must decide what to do about the ambassador, Lord Gower. "I tremble for the safety of Lord Gower and family," wrote Burges. So did Pitt, who insisted to the Foreign Secretary that it was "absolutely necessary to lose no time in bringing Lord Gower from Paris".[22]

The withdrawal of the British ambassador was inevitable, Lord Gower arriving back in London on 3 September. It was the first movement of the diplomats' danse macabre, preceding a great war.

A fortnight after Lord Gower's return, the limping figure of the ex-Bishop of Autun was seen again in Kensington Square. At the insistence of Danton, he had become the apologist of the new phase of the revolution, still striving to keep peace with England. He presented a memorandum explaining that the "downfall of the King of France" did not mean that the new republic presented "an insult and a menace to all kings". On the contrary, France professed nothing but "friendship" and "esteem" for England. Yet just as France had not interfered when England beheaded Charles I, but had recognised the new régime, so England must cease to meddle in the affairs of the infant republic.[23]

Such was the philosophy which Talleyrand expounded. It was small wonder that his audience at St James's was a trying encounter. George III, in place of his quirky, exclamatory manner on social occasions, received the envoy with glacial correctness and in almost total silence. Queen Charlotte, like a stately-rigged ship, ostentatiously turned her back on Talleyrand's apologies and refused either to speak to or look at him again.

Citizen Chauvelin was even more detestable. In August it was thought that he had bolted for France and a watch was kept for him at Dover and Margate, the likely ports of embarkation. But it proved that he had only gone down to Brighton for a couple of days. Presumably he had met a messenger from the National Convention, but the news which he had to send to Paris was not encouraging. The August massacres had turned the people of England against France. They felt a natural human interest in the fate of Louis XVI and Marie

Antoinette. The political injustices of royalist France were eclipsed
by a concern for the imprisoned family. The Whigs, who had opposed
war on the grounds that it would be waged to interfere in the internal
affairs of France, now washed their hands of the revolution. There was
no longer an extreme anti-war faction in England which a few months
previously had daubed the walls of London with such slogans as,
"No war with France or we rebel".

During the autumn of 1792, the peacemakers like Talleyrand
continued their efforts, but they did so without conviction. There
was no inescapable reason driving France and England into conflict.
Rather, the public mood which had been so strong for peace was
drifting into approval of war.

The crisis came on the evening of 23 January 1793. In St James's
and the City, Westminster and Southwark, small groups of men and
women gathered to read the bills which had been freshly posted. As
the crowds gathered, there was a mood of stupor and then indignation, the news being passed back from one person to another. Two
days before, Louis XVI had been taken from captivity and guillo-
tined. The shock was followed by suppressed anger. Every theatre
closed and at one in which the performance had already begun, the
audience demanded that the curtain should be rung down and the
play stopped as a mark of respect. Men went home and reappeared
in black coats. The court, parliament, and the great mass of the
people went into mourning. By this final act of barbarity, the French
republic had put itself beyond the conventions of diplomacy.

The next morning there was a hurried correspondence between the
King, Pitt, and Lord Grenville. The royal drawing room to be held
that afternoon was postponed and, instead, there was a meeting of
the Privy Council at the Queen's House. On the King's insistence, the
meeting drew up "the necessary order that Monsieur Chauvelin may
instantly leave the kingdom". As for Talleyrand, he had already
written to Grenville denouncing the "crime" of his countrymen in
executing their King. He was permitted to stay for the time being
and eventually made his way to America. It was a wise decision,
since he had been secretly denounced to the Convention by Achille
Viard on 7 December as a collaborator with emigrés.[24]

George III left his Privy Council. As he drove through the London
streets, he was heartened by the crowds who cheered and roared,
"War with France! War with France!" The diplomatic minuet was
almost complete. Even as the King greeted his enthusiastic subjects,
Lord Grenville was writing to Lord Auckland, British ambassador at

The Hague, "the next despatch to you, or the next but one, will announce the commencement of hostilities. Probably the French will commence them".[25]

As a matter of fact, hostilities had already begun. Captain Robert Barlow was off the north-west coast of France, commanding the Royal Navy brig-sloop *Childers*, a diminutive warship with a single gun-deck and eight small guns on either side. He was standing in towards the entrance of Brest harbour, the mouth of the port being guarded by two artillery forts. There was hardly a breath of wind and the flood tide was carrying the *Childers* towards the harbour entrance. When the ship was less than a mile away there was a white puff of smoke from one of the forts, the hiss of a cannon ball overhead, and then a plume of spray just beyond the brig-sloop. Assuming that there was some error of identification, Barlow ran up his ensign. At this the fort on the other side of the harbour opened fire as well and he found himself caught in a resolute crossfire. His only advantage was that the *Childers* was so small as to be a difficult target at that range. None the less, a 48-pound shot hit the upper deck, exploding into three fragments and doing superficial damage. The tide was not due to change for some hours and Captain Barlow owed his escape to a light breeze which sprang up and enabled him to carry his ship clear of the port. He returned home with the questionable honour of being the first man to engage the enemy.[26]

On 1 February 1793, the French Convention put hostilities on an official footing by declaring war on England and Holland. The news reached London on 4 February and five days later George III wrote from Windsor to Lord Grenville, describing it as "highly agreeable to me".[27]

It was not, perhaps, highly agreeable to the Earl of Dundonald but it certainly opened up opportunities for placing his remaining sons in the army or the navy. Young Lord Cochrane had made a sufficient ass of himself to rule out the army, however much his father might have preferred that to a naval career and his uncle, Alexander Cochrane, had at least entered his name as a midshipman on the books of several small and undistinguished vessels. It was not much, but it was the only expedient at hand. The 9th Earl had not even the money to buy his son's uniform but the first weeks of war were a time of great patriotic feeling and the nation's leaders were more ready than usual to encourage martial ambition among the young. Lord Hopetoun was approached, and the Earl managed to borrow

£100 from him. Part of this was laid out in the purchase of a gold watch, which Cochrane received with the remains of the money and a dour warning that it was the only inheritance he need expect.

The frigate *Hind*, lying off Sheerness, was the first available ship on whose books the young man's name had been entered. Lord Cochrane's grandmother happened to be going to London at the time and, since he had yet to prove his capacity for looking after himself, he was entrusted to her care. With the final lecture on the spartan virtues of the "res angusta domi" echoing in his mind, he watched the vistas of Culross, Edinburgh, and Scotland, fade behind him. On 27 June, in charge of an uncle who saw him safely from London to Sheerness, Cochrane and his luggage were ferried out to the frigate, which lay at anchor in the river estuary, the sails reefed on her tall masts.

Even the general air of public indignation against France could not disguise the deep preoccupation with hard cash which dominated naval affairs. It was a fact of war that enemy ships were far more often captured than sunk. In the first year of the new war, for example, the British captured thirty-six French ships of which twenty-seven were incorporated into the Royal Navy. The French took nine British ships in return. Subject to the ruling of the Admiralty prize courts, the value of the ships captured from the enemy was shared, however unequally, between captains, officers, and men, as well as the admiral who happened to hold general command of the area in which the seizure had occurred. Though it was not mentioned in the patriotic ballads, it was a commonplace observation among those who knew naval life at first-hand that British seamen thought of cash rather than glory as they sailed into battle. From long experience, Captain Marryat observed that sailors "always begin to reckon what their share of prize money may be, before a shot is fired". An ordinary seaman, under an enterprising captain, found that his real income was higher than that of many officers on more easy-going ships. As for the commanders, they included such men as Captain Digby, who was to command H.M.S. *Africa* at Trafalgar and who had amassed £60,000 in prize money before he was thirty years old, which put him well on the way to being a millionaire by modern values.

To most Royal Navy crews there was no incompatibility whatever between glory and cash. Glory was excellent for national morale and personal reputation, but it had proved a notoriously unnegotiable commodity for heroes and their dependents. Once the elation and gratitude of their countrymen began to cool, the heroes of the hour were easily regarded as the "surplus population" of the long years of peace.

To a young man in Cochrane's position, the life of a naval officer was rich in promise. From the day on which he joined H.M.S. *Hind*, there was to be almost continuous war for twenty-two years. Few periods in history could have presented a better opportunity for the acquisition of wealth by conquest. Whatever interludes might occur in the land campaigns, the war at sea was likely to be unremitting.

Such, at least, was the golden prospect offered to hopeful young officers. In more general terms, the nation was possessed by two alternative views of naval life. The first was that of a stout-hearted, élite fighting service, unrivalled in the world. As the Royal Marine bands piped "Hearts of oak are our ships, jolly tars are our men", they caught this sentiment with trite precision. The second and opposing image was of a navy of surly, press-ganged crews, kept to their duty by homicidal floggings and the fear of being hanged. Starved, diseased, and cowed, these men rose in occasional desperate mutinies, which were put down by brutal repression.

Like all travesties, each of these pictures reflected an element of truth. Though its officers were less wealthy and its social prestige stood below that of the more famous regiments of the army, the Royal Navy was an élite fighting force. "You can always beat a Frenchman if you fight him long enough," Cornwallis assured Nelson. Such sentiments were arrogant as expressions but accurate as matters of record. It was not superior moral character but more thorough training in the techniques of battle which, for example, enabled many British gun crews to deliver two broadsides against a passing French ship in exchange for the one they received. Moreover, while the French Navy had been allowed to dwindle during the eighteenth century, Britain's maritime interests had dictated the opposite policy. Her most impressive ships had been laid down during that period. The *Victory* was forty years old at Trafalgar, the *Defiance* was forty-one, and the *Britannia* was forty-three, having been launched in 1762.

Despite the dark legends of the press gangs, the lure of prizes was potentially the more effective weapon in recruiting seamen. The attraction was simply that piracy had been made legal for the duration of hostilities. In pursuit of their prey, the most respectable commanders of English ships resorted to devices which would have caused international dismay half a century later. Royal Navy captains flew American, Danish, or even French colours to dupe their opponents, hoping to come close enough to ships or shore-batteries to do untold damage before their victims awoke to the deception. When Sir Sydney Smith sailed almost into Brest harbour in 1795, flying French colours and hailing his enemies in their own language, no one thought he had acted otherwise than honourably. The French, in turn, went hunting in English colours. Though there was a difference in build between English and French ships, identification was by no means easy. Ships were frequently captured and incorporated into the opposing navy without even a change of name. The *Bonne Citoyenne* and the *Revolutionnaire* fought in the Royal Navy under their original names. There was an *Achille* on both sides at Trafalgar.

To hide a ship's guns, or to show sailors on deck dressed in the French style, were minimal deceptions by the Royal Navy. In return, the French set traps for avaricious crews. When Napoleon annexed Italy, all shipping in Italian waters became fair game. Captain Abraham Crawford described in his *Reminiscences* the delight of his comrades on H.M.S. *Sultan* at finding two merchant ships anchored and abandoned off the Ligurian coast, their crews having retired to a nearby town for the night. Boarding parties swarmed up the sides and cut the cables. But neither of the ships could be moved. The British sailors had fallen for the lure of ships moored by an extra line from the masthead to the cliffs above them. Concealed on these heights, the watching sharpshooters opened a flashing hail of musketry, which scythed among the boarding parties on the open decks. Any man who climbed the mast to sever the line would have been an easy target in the moonlight. But so long as the rope was not cut, there was no escape from the musket fire. The boarding parties were saved at last by the presence of mind of a lieutenant. Dressing a dummy in sailors' clothes, he hoisted it aloft. Every musket on the cliffs opened fire, and the dummy fell. During the moment when the sharpshooters were occupied with reloading, the most agile of the British sailors shinned up and cut the ropes.[28]

But there was a code of honour in such matters. The British despised the French practice of having sharpshooters in the rigging to pick off individual officers and men during close skirmishes. It was one thing for a row of cannon to fire a general broadside at an enemy ship, when no one man fired specifically at another. But for a marksman to take deliberate aim at his opponent and shoot him was not an honest form of combat. Such had been the feeling in the army during the eighteenth century and so it was to remain for many captains and their crews. Prudence, as well as chivalry, endorsed the sentiment, since marksmen and their weapons had a disconcerting habit of setting fire accidentally to their own rigging.

The same prejudice operated against the use of delayed-action devices or "submarine" warfare. Metal carcases were sometimes packed with gunpowder and floated into enemy ports or anchorages under cover of darkness. "Not a fair proceeding," said Admiral Otway during the Walcheren expedition. "Unmanly," announced Captain Crawford, "assassin-like". Even the heating of shot before firing was regarded as a despicable French subterfuge. More than a decade after the Napoleonic wars, the naval historian William James still thought that, "The employment of hot shot is not usually deemed honourable warfare." But, like the sharpshooters in the rigging, the practice also involved serious risk of setting fire to the ship which employed it.[29]

However, a young officer in Cochrane's position, joining the navy with a hope of enriching himself by prizes, faced a more powerful enemy than France or Spain, and one whose weapons were a good deal more sophisticated: the Admiralty and its prize courts. In the view of many serving officers, these courts were at best unsympathetic and, all too often, cynically corrupt. It was relatively common for a hopeful young commander and his men to find that, after a hard-won capture, the Admiralty proposed to appropriate the entire value of the prize. It was always open to the heroes to fight for their claim in the prize court. But even if they won their case, they might hear that the cost of the proceedings had swallowed up more than the sum due to them, so that they were now in debt to the court as well as having been robbed of the proceeds of their valour.

A man might complain publicly or privately against the prize system. But before he set himself up as a "sea lawyer", he was well advised to remember that this very employment, let alone his promotion, lay in the hands of the Admiralty itself. In consequence, there was a good deal of private grumbling and very little public campaigning.

Even in time of war, appointment and promotion continued to be the great preoccupations of aspiring heroes. John Wilson Croker, who became Secretary to the Board of Admiralty in 1809, was dismayed by the "avalanche of applications", which fell upon his desk, day after day and year after year. He may have reflected that Lord St

Vincent, as First Lord of the Admiralty from 1801 to 1804, had refused to favour protégés, even when they came from his own family,
and had returned blunt refusals to the Duke of Kent and the Prince
of Wales when they sought preferment for one of their favourites.

An easy pretext for rejection, in the case of a young man for whom
a first naval appointment was sought, was to show that he was too
old. As Croker informed one persistent suitor, "a man turned nineteen years of age is more than six years too old to begin a sea life".
Nelson had been a midshipman at twelve, and his friend George
Parsons at eleven. Other "Young Gentlemen" went on active service
at ten years old or less, until 1794 when the Admiralty laid down that
candidates for commissions must be at least eleven. After several
years of being dressed like a hero and beaten like a child, the boy
might "pass for lieutenant". He would still be young, in many cases.
Indeed, Admiral Rodney had appointed his son to the command of a
British warship at the age of fifteen. But the path from junior lieutenant to first lieutenant of a ship more frequently depended on the
removal of senior lieutenants by death or misfortune. Many young
officers must have shared the dream of William Price in *Mansfield
Park*, as he imagined the annihilation of these human obstacles to
glory, and his own splendid heroism once he had stepped into their
shoes.[30]

On promotion to a ship of his own, the lieutenant would become a
commander. When appointed to a ship of over twenty guns, he rose to
post-captain, or captain as it was more generally known. But all such
promotions were liable to cause bitterness. When there was a vacancy
for the command of a ship, the best placed lieutenants were those
serving on the admiral's flagship. Some of these were beneficiaries of
"parliamentary promotion", in which the protégés of a member of
parliament were promoted, in exchange for his support of the government. Lieutenants on smaller and less distinguished ships might live
and die in their more lowly rank.

Once a lieutenant or a commander became a post-captain, there
was no impediment to the highest rank except for a very long list of
senior officers. Captains themselves were listed in order of seniority.
When there was a vacancy for a rear-admiral, it was filled from the
head of the list. Beyond that, there were prospects of becoming vice-
admiral, and even admiral of the fleet. In 1794, there were 425
captains, each waiting long and hopefully to move into the place of
the man above him. By 1815, the captains' list had grown to double
that length, making promotion a long and discouraging process.

However, a man might console himself by scanning the names of casualties after each glorious victory, and then doing a little simple arithmetic.

Hope deferred and prizes withheld inevitably tarnished the enthusiasm with which many officers had gone to war. Sir John Barrow wrote angrily to the Admiralty in 1810 that French ships were coming inshore at night and seizing English merchant vessels just off the coast of Kent. The commander of the Royal Navy brig, who was supposed to afford them protection, had evidently had his fill of war by dinner time. He was in the habit of anchoring his ship, retiring to his house at Birchington for a comfortable night's sleep, and leaving the French to do as they pleased. His motive was something more than cowardice or indolence. An entire Royal Navy squadron actually witnessed one seizure, under the eyes of the local population, and did nothing to prevent it. As the French ship made off with her prize, wrote Barrow, "it is mortifying enough to hear people publicly crying out, 'Aye, this is what we get for paying taxes to keep up the navy; a French privateer is not worth capturing, she will not pay the charges of condemnation.'"[31]

The commander of the squadron, like the captain of the single brig, had learnt the hard lesson that French raiding vessels were too expensive to capture. A small privateer would not even cover the costs in the Admiralty court, so that the victors themselves would have to pay for their valour out of their own pockets. However, the captain who slept ashore may also have fortified himself with the example of Admiral Thomas Matthews, half a century before, who had contrived to spend eighteen years on his country estate without once going to sea.

The reputation of the navy in the war of 1793–1815 reached peaks at the time of great individual victories and then declined as the public mind grew more preoccupied by the horrors of the press gang and the lash. Pressing, as it was called, had become the only means by which a nation of fifteen million could sustain an expanding naval war to contain Napoleon. Yet the consequences of the system led to encounters between British ships, in full view of their countrymen, during which they fought one another as vigorously as they fought the French.

In one such incident, just off Gravesend, the Royal Navy's *Immortalité* sent two boatloads of men, fully armed, to seize enough men from the East India Company's *Woodford* and *Ganges* to make up their complement. As the men of the *Immortalité* attempted to scale the steep, curving sides of the other ships, they were met by a fusi-lade of shot and missiles, and threatened by the cutlasses of the East India crews if they advanced further. When the lieutenant of the party sent against the *Woodford* saw that one of his men had had his foot nailed to the bottom of the long-boat by a pike, he ordered his marines to open fire. Two of the *Woodford*'s crew were shot dead, but the resistance to the boarding parties continued until the Royal Navy at last withdrew with its wounded. The lieutenant of the long-boat was indicted for murder, though acquitted at Maidstone Assizes. Even so, such public skirmishes in the Thames estuary were hardly calculated to boost the nation's enthusiasm for its senior service.[32]

In the navy which young Lord Cochrane now joined, there were even more bizarre aspects of the pressing system. When, for instance, the bands of the *Victory* played, "Britons, Strike Home!" as she sailed into battle at Trafalgar, the sentiments must have sounded a little incongruous to those eighty-two foreigners who made up an import-ant part of the flagship's crew. There were twenty-eight Americans on the *Victory* on that occasion, as well as Frenchmen, Africans, and Indians. It was commonplace for men from neutral ships to be pressed. The American government was foremost in condemning the British for pressing its sailors, while the British swore that American ships were spiriting away shirkers who wished to avoid their patriotic duty as true-born Englishmen.

Many French and Spanish seamen also chose to serve with their captors rather than to spend the rest of a long war rotting in Dart-moor or one of England's other prisons. But Lieutenant Thomas Hodgskin was determined to enlighten the "apparent ignorance" of the public by revealing that foreigners, American or European, were by no means the most unlikely conscripts for the Royal Navy. "I knew Africans, who had been stolen from Africa, taken in a slave-ship, afterwards cloathed, on board a guard-ship, and, without being able to speak a word of English, sent to man the British fleet. . . . Such a thing is a burlesque upon a national defence."[33]

Thomas Cochrane, like almost all contemporary naval officers, accepted that pressing was a necessary evil during the critical years of the war against France. Even after 1815, there were many figures of influence who took offence when the system was criticised. In 1822, Captain Marryat had rashly published his *Suggestions for the Abolition of Impressment*. Some years later, he had occasion to seek permission from William IV to wear a French order conferred on him by Louis XVIII and, at the same time, to seek promotion. The King, having been Lord High Admiral as Duke of Clarence, took a keen interest when the request was forwarded to him.

"Marryat! Marryat!" said the old King suspiciously. "By-the-by, is not that the man who wrote a book against the impressment of seamen?"

"The same, your majesty."

"Then he shan't wear the order, and he shall have nothing!"[34]

The popular view of the naval discipline awaiting the victims of the press gang was conditioned by the grim reputation of figures like "Old Jarvie", as Lord St Vincent was known. In one cameo, his hard-set and weatherbeaten old face watched with stern satisfaction the expiring struggles of a mutineer dangling at the yard-arm. As the struggles ceased, St Vincent turned to his companion, raised his hat in salute to the ceremony rather than to the man who had died, and said confidently:

"Discipline is preserved, sir!"[35]

Surgeon Cullen, one of his critics, denounced him as "haughty and imperious, rigidly and unnecessarily strict . . . which made him very much disliked by his captains and officers". But the dour old admiral had also sailed through the famous battle of Cape St Vincent, im-movable on the poop of the *Victory*, unshaken even by the blood and brains of a marine blown in his face, as he continued sucking an orange.[36]

For all his harshness, St Vincent showed a resolve and an independence of mind which was lacking in lesser men. Admiral Sir John Duckworth, for instance, was regarded as brute and sycophant by men who served under him. "Old Tommy", as he was called, was loathed without reservation. William Richardson, a gunner on H.M.S. *Tromp*, recalled Lieutenant Byam of that ship being so habitually drunk that "he staggered so that the quarterdeck was hardly large enough to hold him". Duckworth summoned him to the flagship, where he learnt that Byam was related to a family of considerable political influence. He at once gave the drunken lieutenant command of a ship and, to no one's surprise, Duckworth received a knighthood in his turn.[37]

Duckworth's brutality appeared when, after prolonged and re-peated reefing of the sails on H.M.S. *Castor*, the men dared to descend to the deck, cheer ironically, and go below. Duckworth tried the four ringleaders of this "mutiny", sentencing three to be flogged and the other to be hanged. Christmas Day 1801 being at hand, he chose that for the execution. The knot was placed under the man's chin, prolonging his sufferings until he struggled so wildly that it slipped round to the side of his neck and ended his life. The season of good will continued on Boxing Day with two floggings of three hundred lashes and one of five hundred.[38]

A dramatic consequence of such discipline was seen in the loss of Royal Navy ships like the *Africaine*, the *Hermione* and the *Danae*. The crew of the *Hermione* murdered their officers in 1797 and sought sanctuary in Spain, while the men of the *Africaine*, when boarded by the enemy, refused to fight anyone but their own captain, who was cut down in the skirmish. Before sailing, they had petitioned the Admiralty for his removal, offering to serve for a year without pay under some other commander.[39]

However, these incidents were as exceptional as they were sensational. The attention of most men was taken up by such mundane matters as food and drink. Corned beef and biscuits, wine and water, made up much of the diet in ships of the Atlantic squadrons. The beef, reported young Bernard Coleridge, had been ten or eleven years in the corn. The biscuits felt like cool calves' foot jelly or blancmange when swallowed because of the number of maggots in them. The water was the colour of pear tree bark "with plenty of little maggots and weevils in it", while the wine tasted like a mixture of sawdust and bull's blood. For all these shortcomings, Bernard Coleridge was still lucky not to be on a ship which ran short of water, however unpalatable the supply might seem. When the level fell low, the butts were closed up except for a hole at the top with a musket barrel in it. Any man wanting a drink was obliged to suck it up through the barrel. A further deterrent to unnecessary drinking was to keep the butt at the masthead. A man had first to go aloft, carry the butt down to the deck to drink, and then replace it at the masthead once more.[40]

Officers fared better than their men in matters of diet, particularly on the larger ships of the line, the battleships of the Napoleonic period. Yet officers and men alike had an interest in the safety of the ship. As war approached, there were astute men of business, with no particular interest in shipping, who would buy up the most unseaworthy vessels as cheaply as possible. They knew that when hostilities commenced, these could be hired out to the Admiralty for £400 a month, their owners recouping the purchase price two or three times in a year by this practice.

Whether England's warships were hired or purpose-built, many of the nation's heroes found themselves in what were euphemistically described as "wet ships", a term applied to vessels which let the sea through their timbers at a disquieting rate. During the blockade of Toulon in 1796, St Vincent informed the Navy Board that many of his ships were "a complete sieve, from the poop to the orlop deck, both in the decks and the sides; repaired as they are with planks of Pomeranian and Holstein growth, the water runs through them like a porous dripping-stone". William Richardson, who lived as an ordinary seaman on the orlop deck, confirmed this. "Our ship was so leaky ... that we had seldom a dry bed to lie on, and frequently shipping a great deal of water the decks were never dry." Proof of this was clear when the ship returned to Spithead. "The ship being so continually wet the green grass was growing on her sides and on her decks under the gun-carriages."[41]

The pervasive damp turned bruises into ulcers and brought all manner of ailments to Richardson's comrades. But still there were other men who suffered worse fates in order that the shipbuilders might profit. The new war meant good business for the Royal Dockyards and, particularly, for the private yards to which about two-thirds of the contracts went. A careful builder could charge £9 or £10 a ton for a ship which only cost him £3 or £4 a ton to build. There were, of course, drawbacks. Poor quality timber had to be used to make such economies and, in bad cases, while the final work was being completed on the slipway, the first timbers had already rotted. Far more dramatic, however, were the economies made on the main bolts which, literally, held a ship together. When the vessel was inspected, all the bolts appeared to be in place, but in some cases it was only "the tops and points" of the expensive copper shafts which ornamented the hull. Some crews escaped the consequences of this, but other ships disintegrated at sea, the loss of the *York*, the *Blenheim*, and the near-loss of the *Albion* being attributed to this fraud. St Vincent, writing to Lord Spencer from his flagship in 1797, remarked, "You may rest assured, the Civil Branch of the Navy is rotten to the very core." He later insisted that "Our dockyards stink of corruption." To the victims or their comrades, they also stank of murder.[42]

The scale of administrative corruption in the navy which young Thomas Cochrane entered was so vast that it seems remarkable that England ever got a fleet to sea. At critical moments, such as trying to heave a stranded ship off a shoal by means of a kedge-anchor, it would be discovered that the cables provided were anything up to 90 feet short of the stated length because of economies practised by the dockyard manufacturers. When confronted with this, the officers of the rope-yard replied in pious unanimity that it was nothing to do with them. The cables must have "shrunk" when they were coiled up.[43]

More generally, the same work was charged for many times over, and wages drawn for men or children who did no work and, for that matter, rarely went near the dockyard. In less than eighteen months, the cooperage at Woolwich dockyard charged £3670 for work whose value was £264. Among the skilled craftsmen who were paid for these labours was a blind and elderly man who received £120 a year for allowing himself to be led to the dockyard from time to time.[44]

Far from diminishing one's admiration for the victors of the Nile, or Trafalgar, or the Glorious First of June, the revelation of such practices enhances their reputation still further. They triumphed not only over the enemy abroad but over the enemy at home as well. To keep pace with war and embezzlement, the money voted for the navy rose from four million pounds in 1793 to fifteen million in the year of Trafalgar, and to twenty million by the time of Waterloo. St Vincent, as First Lord of the Admiralty, won the reluctant approval of the government for a Commission of Naval Enquiry into frauds and abuses. But the Commission's reports merely confirmed what most people had already guessed. Up to a quarter of the annual budget for the navy had disappeared into the pockets of those who contrived the frauds and abuses.

Predictably, men who had political influence or held offices of state were milking the revenues quite as assiduously as their rivals in private commerce. An admiral would retire with a pension of £410 a year, a post-captain with £210. But the fortunate sycophant who held the post of "clerk of the ticket office" at the Admiralty retired with £700 a year. The total sum paid to thirteen widows and orphans of admirals and captains killed in battle was less than the pension paid to one widow of one Admiralty commissioner. Cochrane himself noticed with interest that for eight years after the death of his grandmother, she having been the widow of a naval captain and in receipt of a widow's pension, "some patriotic individual had been *drawing her pension, as though she were still living!*" Dean Inge's description of politics as the art of transferring the contents of one's opponents' pockets to those of one's supporters was seldom truer than during this period. It was calculated, for instance, that the sinecure payments to the Duke of Buckingham would have financed the entire supply departments at Chatham, Dover, Gibraltar, Sheerness, the Downs, Heligoland, Cork, Malta, the Mediterranean, the Cape of Good

Hope, Rio de Janeiro, and would still have left more than £5000 in the Treasury. The majority of Royal Navy officers put such things firmly from their minds and steered hopefully for glory. None the less, it must have occurred to many of them to wonder what would happen if ever there should be a young commander of audacity and tactical brilliance who chose to fight the enemy at home as well as the enemy at sea. With the advent of Lord Thomas Cochrane, the answer to such speculation was about to be provided.[45]

# 2
# Steering to Glory

—

H.M.S. *Hind* was a far cry from the ships which gripped the patriotic imagination in 1793. The popular image was of the mighty leviathans of 90 or 120 guns, the bronze mouths of the cannon towering in successive ranks to guard the black fortress of the hull. There was an almost baroque splendour in the upper decks, ornate with white and gold, and the curve of the great sails against the sky.

Ships like the *Hind* were a different matter. She carried a single tier of guns, twenty-eight in all, and they were 9-pounders, against the 32-pounders of the great battlefleets. Even by the standards of the frigates, she was not powerfully armed. Instead of the ornate white and gold, her hull was topped off with acid-yellow. Regardless of appearances, however, it was the *Hind* or ships of her type which carried on the day-to-day business of war against France for the next twenty-two years.

For most contemporaries, the sight of England's warships, anchored offshore in deeper water, was their closest acquaintance with naval life. The distance was a necessary one and was made more significant by the boats which rowed in careful circles round the anchored vessels. With their scarlet tunic'd Royal Marines, long-barrelled muskets at the ready, these were the guard-boats, intended to dissuade volunteers and pressed men alike from trying to slip through an open port and swim for home.

When Cochrane and his luggage were rowed out from the shore in a bum-boat, it was the duty of the midshipman of the watch to direct the little harbour craft to the entry port of the *Hind*. The captain of the frigate happened to be his uncle, Alexander Cochrane, which was the young man's only asset in joining her. Captain Cochrane was not on board at that moment, but his nephew was required to report himself to the quarterdeck like any other newly-arrived midshipman.

More than sixty years later, his first moments on the *Hind* re-

mained one of the most vivid impressions of his life. He reached the
quarterdeck, its surface holystoned to a wooden pallor and smelling
strongly of pitch with which the caulkers repaired the decking of a
ship in port. Having been told to report to the lieutenant of the
*Hind*, Jack Larmour, he naturally expected to find him there. There
was no one there but a common seaman, "with marlinspike slung
round his neck, and a lump of grease in his hand". The man was
"busily employed in setting up the rigging". The young Lord
Cochrane interrupted him and asked where he might find Lieutenant
Larmour. The seaman with the lump of grease and the marlinspike
explained that he *was* Lieutenant Larmour, improbable though it
might seem. "His reception of me," wrote Cochrane, "was anything
but gracious."[1]

There were reasons for Larmour's hostility, as Cochrane discovered.
"A tall fellow over six feet high, the nephew of his captain, and a lord
to boot, were not very promising recommendations." It was worse
than that, because though Cochrane was a lord, his father was nothing
but a crotchety and bankrupt old Scottish earl, in the eyes of the
world. A young lord without money was the worst proposition of all
for his comrades. It also seemed that Larmour had heard of the
regimental fiasco and of the way in which the aspiring naval hero had
run home to his father because he had been laughed at by rude boys
near Charing Cross.

Larmour was irritated by the interruption, according to Cochrane,
and annoyed at having been "saddled with a hard bargain". He gave
the young man his first naval order.

"Get your traps below!"

The ship's boys carried the new midshipman's luggage down to the
twilight of the gun-deck, where the marines also stood guard by the
open ports to frustrate any of the pressed men who tried to stow away
in the returning harbour-craft and supply-boats. For a young man of
Cochrane's height, the headroom below deck was so little that he was
never to be able to stand upright. But his berth was further down in
the hull, below the gun-deck, in the communal accommodation for all
midshipmen.

At that level, there was almost total darkness, the little light that
there was filtering down through the gratings of the decks above. The
midshipmen, like the seamen, lived below the waterline, where even
in the brightest summer day it was impossible to see clearly without a
"purser's moon", as candles were known.

The single berth of the midshipmen was lined with shelves on to which all personal possessions, food and clothing, were crammed. It was commonly stocked with plates, glasses, cutlery, combs, hats, quadrants, salt-butter and whatever other supplements to the ship's diet the men had managed to bring with them. During the day, the berth was almost filled by the table at which the midshipmen dined. By night, the "cots" of canvas stretched on wood were slung from hooks in the beams. There was, of course, no such thing as bed linen or blankets unless the new arrival had brought some of his own.

Cochrane's innocence of living conditions on board ship was such that he had brought a considerable quantity of luggage with him. Among this was a sea chest, so imposing that it would literally not fit into the berth. As an old man, he still remembered the voice of Lieutenant Larmour behind him, at the door of the berth where the uniformed marine stood guard.

"This Lord Cochrane's chest? Does Lord Cochrane think he is going to bring a cabin aboard? The service is going to the devil! Get it up on the main deck!"

The sea chest disappeared and, presently, Cochrane followed it to see what had happened. He saw to his astonishment that under Lieutenant Larmour's orders, one of the seamen was sawing open an end of it and that some of his possessions were already scattered about the deck. As Cochrane appeared, Larmour explained brusquely to him that it had been found necessary to saw the chest in half owing to "the lubberliness of shore-going people in not making keyholes where they could be most easily got at".[2]

If it seemed to Cochrane that he had entered a world ruled by lunatic logic and peopled by grotesques, there were further and stranger surprises in store. As the midshipmen assembled by candle-light for their afternoon tea, he discovered that all of them were not younger than he was. If a midshipman failed to pass for lieutenant, he remained a midshipman. In one crowded berth there were boys of ten and men in early middle age, known as "oldsters", who would be midshipmen until death parted them from their profession. The shore-bound moralists who feared that the drunkenness and debauchery of the "oldsters" might corrupt the young boys were entirely correct. Reticence and decency were not characteristics of life among a couple of hundred men cooped up for months at a time on a ship hardly more than a hundred feet long. Even men who were wasted to skeletons by venereal disease still boasted of what they would do if they lived until the next port of call. "I'll get well soon," shouted one dying man, "time enough at any rate by the time we go to Malta, and then I'll have another rattle at a bitch of a whore!"[3]

The bullying of "youngsters" by "oldsters" in the midshipmen's berth was more fearful than the moral example. It generally took the form of "cobbing" in which the victim was held down and beaten black and blue with a stocking filled with wet sand. Cochrane, as the captain's nephew, was a risky subject for such treatment. Instead he shared the ordeal of the menu, eaten at a table whose cloth was rarely changed and bore the marks of several weeks' dinners. At the worst, the diet might be small beer and ship's biscuit, at the best there would be potatoes and beef. While the ship was at anchor off Sheerness, the meals could be supplemented by bread, butter, and fruit sold by a woman who came out with the bum-boat and sat with her wares around her on the main deck. Midshipmen removed their coats to eat and rolled their sleeves up, so that both the coats and shirt-cuffs would remain unmarked when they next appeared on deck.

In the summer heat, conditions on the orlop deck, below the water-line, were appalling. The officers slept above but the orlop contained the crew, as well as the midshipmen. A hundred men or more slept at intervals of just over two feet, while even the gun-ports on the deck above them were kept strictly closed. Long before morning, the air was fetid and hot. Even those who might, none the less, have fallen asleep from exhaustion were apt to be woken at midnight and 4 a.m. by the shouts and clattering as the new watch turned out.

Cochrane's close acquaintance, as a midshipman, with the men he was later to command, instilled in him an understanding and admiration for them. None of them, however, made a greater impression on him than Lieutenant Jack Larmour, one of those rare officers who had risen from the ranks. A few days later, at the command "All hands to unmoor ship!" the *Hind* slipped away from her anchorage into the obscurity of the North Sea, seeking out French privateers who might harry Britain's Baltic trade by sallying out from the fiords of Norway. It was a fruitless reconnaissance, except for Cochrane who set himself to learn from Larmour the practical crafts of seamanship, which most officers considered beneath their dignity to investigate. Cochrane, like Larmour himself, despised those young officers wished on the navy by "parliamentary influence". Such men became first the sycophants of an admiral's flagship and then, more disastrously, commanders of ships in their own right. But, as Larmour pointed out, parliamentary influence had never got a ship off the rocks of a lee shore.

When the *Hind* returned from her reconnaissance, Larmour and the new midshipman were transferred to the *Thetis*, bound from Plymouth to North America with Admiral Murray's squadron. Cochrane's apprenticeship continued. "We soon became fast friends," he then recalled, "and throughout life few more kindly recollections are impressed on my memory than those of my first naval instructor, honest Jack Larmour."[4]

For a young man whose advancement depended on prize money, North America was as unpromising as the North Sea. But Larmour's tuition had given Cochrane a skill which marked him out from the other midshipmen. Admiral Murray was impressed and, though Cochrane had not yet been in the service long enough to "pass for lieutenant", the admiral appointed him an acting-lieutenant on the *Thetis* in January 1795. A cruise as acting-lieutenant on H.M.S. *Africa* followed this and by the beginning of 1796, at twenty years old, Cochrane was eligible to be examined for substantive promotion. The time had come round quickly in his case because of the early date at which his uncle Alexander had entered his name on the books of several ships.

The examination took place while Murray's force was patrolling off Nova Scotia. Launches from the other ships, bearing young men whose blue coats and cocked hats were carefully brushed and whose breeches were immaculately white, converged on the flagship *Resolution*. A candidate was required to bring his log books and certificates of conduct, and would probably have a copy of *Moore's Navigation,* or a similar volume for last minute consultation while waiting to go before the examining board.

The oral examination was carried out by three senior captains. They assembled in the stern cabin of the flagship, sitting in judgement at their table with a clerk to one side of them. If some midshipmen felt more like criminals facing prosecution than candidates in an examination, the setting certainly reinforced the impression.

Like other candidates, Cochrane handed over his log books and certificates of conduct for the board's perusal. There followed standard questions in trigonometry and navigation, which were no real problem to a midshipman who had read his textbooks. It was the second part of the examination which unnerved and defeated most of them. The young man was told to imagine himself in command of

a vessel in a particular location and under certain weather conditions. Various hazards were then thrown in his way by the question-
ers, and he was required to give instant answers as to the action he
would take. Delay meant theoretical shipwreck and actual failure in
the examination. But when the captains, sitting at their table, came
to Cochrane they were dealing with a young man who had more than
a year's practical experience as acting-lieutenant. This, at least, was
some defence against them as they strove to dismast him, run him
aboard another vessel, or wreck him on their own carefully contrived
rocks.[5]

Thanks to Jack Larmour's practical instruction and his own ability
to think quickly, young Lord Cochrane survived the perils of the
examiners' imagined storm. Other midshipmen emerged crestfallen
from the great cabin, their reputations smashed on the rocks of
Beachy Head or stranded on the Goodwin Sands. Cochrane, instead
of being told to do six more months at sea and try again, left the
*Resolution* with a lieutenant's commission.

It was Admiral Vandeput, Murray's successor, who appointed
Cochrane as a lieutenant on the *Resolution* for a brief period. Cruising
the waters from the St Lawrence to Chesapeake Bay, Vandeput found
little sign of the French or the war and the *Resolution* settled down to
an agreeable social routine.

Cochrane's first dinner was in the captain's dining cabin, a spacious
room in the stern of the vessel with large square-paned windows overlooking the sea. Its elegant furnishings and studied ritual seemed a
world away from the life of the orlop deck, twenty feet below. As the
braided and cock-hatted officers walked the deck before dinner, the
Royal Marine band piped "The Roast Beef of Old England" to
summon them to their food. The sunlight, reflected through the stern
windows by the shifting sea, caught the polished silver and finely-
wrought glass. Dinners of this sort began at about 3 p.m. and lasted
for the best part of two hours, several courses and a number of wines
being consumed.

Cochrane noted, however, that the "leading motive" of a seaman
was "prize money", and it was never more true than in his own case.
The social pleasantries on board the *Resolution* hardly masked his
ravenous need of this extra income. To make matters worse, Vandeput
and his well-heeled officers decided that, when winter came, there
was no point in resuming patrols until the spring. The admiral
dropped anchor in Chesapeake Bay and went ashore to a large house
which he had rented. Parties of officers joined him for shooting and

hunting. As Cochrane remarked, it was fortunate for the admiral that the Virginians "retained their affection for England, her habits, and customs. Even the innkeeper of the place contrived to muster a tolerable pack of hounds". Admiral Vandeput, whose particular fetish was very tall girls, was also in pursuit of the Misses Tabbs, each more than six feet high.[6]

During the boisterous dinner parties and the enforced gaiety, Cochrane brooded over the war he was missing and denounced the government of toadies and placemen who had lost England's colonies for her. He believed that the United Colonies meant what they said in 1775, "that on the concession of their just demands, 'the colonies are to return to their former connections and friendship with Great Britain'". Might not a more democratic and reformist government in Britain have prevented the great schism?[7]

Among such thoughts came the announcement that H.M.S. *Thetis* was to return to England. His companions behaved with tolerant amusement towards the tall anxious "Sawney" with his mop of red hair and his unpredictable sentiments. But since he seemed so desperate for a chance to fight, he was sent back across the Atlantic with the *Thetis*. His orders were to proceed with Admiral Keith's flagship from Plymouth to Gibraltar, for the great battle of the Mediterranean had just begun.

The Mediterranean had not been the scene of many British victories between 1793 and 1797. To blockade the major ports of Toulon, Cadiz and Brest, in order to prevent the escape of French battle-fleets and wholesale slaughter among British convoys to the West Indies, had proved an intolerable strain on the Royal Navy's resources. By 1796, the British had abandoned the bases at Leghorn, and Corsica, pulling back to Gibraltar and concentrating along the Atlantic coasts of France and Spain. Corsica had been occupied at the start of the war. There had even been the portentous possibility that, on his father's advice, the young Napoleon Buonaparte was to volunteer for the Royal Navy.

The turning point in the history of the Mediterranean war came on 14 February 1797 in the Atlantic battle of Cape St Vincent. Admiral Jervis dealt a costly blow to the Spanish, prevented their rendezvous with the French to support an invasion of Ireland, and won himself the title of Earl St Vincent. Among the cheers of victory, the British commanders returned to the Mediterranean, St Vincent in command with Nelson and Keith as his assistants. Minorca was taken in 1798 and the base at Malta re-established. Brest and Cadiz were mere blockades, but the Mediterranean promised a running fight.

Cochrane's superior, Lord Keith, was a youngish commander, inclined to keep his thoughts and opinions to himself. He appeared to encourage Cochrane's enterprise and daring, though he attacked his character without mercy in private correspondence. Lord St Vincent, who was so often to be Cochrane's opponent, was still at Gibraltar, a caricaturist's portrait of advancing age, the flushed and pear-shaped head settling forward on the breast, the body crippled and swollen by dropsy. He received Cochrane with courtesy, however, and confirmed his appointment on Keith's flagship, H.M.S. *Barfleur*.

Soon after, St Vincent retired to seek a cure at Bath, haunted by Sir John Orde who had been passed over in favour of Nelson and now demanded "satisfaction" from the aged lord with pistols or swords. Cowardice was not one of St Vincent's failings. It took a court order and a direct command from the Admiralty to prevent him from "obliging" Sir John.

The *Barfleur* and Keith's other ships were at first detained by the necessity of maintaining the blockade against Cadiz. Blockading was both the most important and most dreary of the Royal Navy's tasks. The French needed only a momentary lack of vigilance on the part of the blockaders to slip away from the anchorage and be lost indefinitely. Cochrane spent over four months anchored seven or eight miles off Cadiz waiting for the enemy to attempt a break-out. The break-out never came. From time to time, as he surveyed the port through his spy-glass, there were signs of the ships preparing for sea. It was the standard bluff, carried out by a few men who did not even have to be sailors. Here, as at Toulon and Brest, scores of British ships, their marines and crews, were kept idle by the tricks of a few untrained enemy civilians.

Tempers grew short on the *Barfleur*. Then Cochrane first brought himself to the notice of the Admiralty and his immediate superiors in the simplest and most dramatic way. He got himself court-martialled.

A lieutenant's life on a flagship was in many ways enviable. He ate well in the wardroom and better still when invited to dine with the captain. He had a cabin to himself, even if it was only eight feet square and its "walls" consisted merely of painted canvas stretched on wood. But the formal etiquette and judicious flattery of superiors which contented the young men appointed through "parliamentary influence" made Cochrane increasingly irritable. He had joined the navy to fight, both as a profession and because he desperately needed the rewards of prize money to continue in his career. Neither the Spanish fleet in Cadiz nor his own superiors seemed in any hurry to oblige him.

Deprived of a chance to match himself against the French or the Spanish, he opened hostilities against the first lieutenant of the *Barfleur*, Philip Beaver. It was an odd choice, since Beaver despised the useless "parliamentary" officers quite as much as Cochrane did. "We have so many for promotion," he burst out one day, "that few are left for plain duty. We had just now nearly run over a brig, but where from, or whither bound, the Lord knows – a pretty look-out for a smart ship." The junior lieutenants were respectful to his face and laughed at him behind his back. There was an occasion for great hilarity when someone contrived that Beaver should be hauled before the admiral for having sent his own correspondence at the reduced seaman's rate. It was a trivial enough matter and Beaver was soon proved innocent of it, but the air of pompous gravity which he displayed on his return must have caused further ill-suppressed snorts of mirth. "No man can be too careful of character," he announced over the matter of the postage stamp. "Such an accusation might have been whispered at a future time, but its utter falsehood is now placed on record."[8]

As a matter of fact, Beaver's record was good but not distinguished. He had joined the navy at eleven and fought under Rodney against D'Orvillers at twelve. After seven years as a midshipman and fifteen as a lieutenant his promotion seemed ominously long-delayed. Apart from an attempt to found a colony of high-minded men and women on an island off Sierra Leone, which had ended in disaster, the Royal Navy had been his life.

But there was a flaw in Beaver's character, as Cochrane saw it. On several occasions the *Barfleur* left the blockade force to collect supplies from the North African port of Tetuan. Instead of taking on cattle already slaughtered, the animals were embarked live and slaughtered on board. Beaver permitted this, though he knew it was done to allow certain officers to run a lucrative trade in hides. These were stowed in empty casks. The result, as the noses of Cochrane and his companions soon detected, was that throughout the months of the blockade the *Barfleur* reeked like an ill-ventilated glue factory. Other ships of the squadron caught a hint of it, cheerfully hailing their leader as "The Stinking Scotch Ship", a compliment to Keith's nationality rather than Cochrane's.[9]

The wardroom storm broke after a visit to Tetuan. Cochrane and Captain Cuthbert of the Marines had been ashore duck-shooting. They returned in the launch just as the *Barfleur* was about to sail, both of them covered in mud. Deciding that it would be "disrespectful" to report to the quarterdeck in that state, the two men went to change. Lieutenant Beaver had watched them come aboard, so there was no urgency. By the time that Cochrane emerged from his cabin into the wardroom, the *Barfleur* had weighed anchor and set sail for the Spanish coast. Almost at once, he was followed into the wardroom by Beaver, who began to berate Cochrane and Cuthbert in front of the other officers.

"You have both made me appear exceedingly ridiculous, for I have just reported you to the captain as left on shore, not having heard of your return to the ship!"

This outburst, from a man who had watched them come aboard, was calculated to bring out the worst in Cochrane. His temper was violent but, as his adversaries discovered, its expression was controlled and withering.

"I cannot help it," he said casually, "if you appear ridiculous to the captain." The "parliamentary" lieutenants goggled.

Beaver, totally unaccustomed to such language from a junior officer, stopped abruptly. But his was the ultimate weapon.

"Unless I am acquainted with your return to the ship," he said sharply, "while I am first lieutenant, you shall not go out of this ship."

"Aye," said Cochrane softly, as Beaver sat down at the wardroom table. Then he added, "Lieutenant Beaver, I do not wish to hear more on the subject now, but you shall hear from me on the subject another time."

And having said this, Cochrane turned his back on Beaver, looking towards the windows in the stern, and began to whistle. Beaver sat upright, got to his feet, and strode from the wardroom to the quarterdeck, where he complained that the arrogant young Lord Cochrane, when reprimanded, had challenged him to a duel. The warm and sickly odour of rotting hide was hardly noticed in the new wardroom atmosphere of insulted honour and abused authority.[10]

It was in everyone's interest that the matter should die a quiet and speedy death. They reckoned without Lieutenant Beaver's dour sense of duty. Within a few days, Lord Keith received the first lieutenant's official application for a general court-martial on Lord Cochrane. There was no means of denying it. Cochrane lived under open arrest until the *Barfleur* and ships of the fleet were next assembled at the anchorage of Tetuan. There the trial was to take place.

At eight o'clock in the morning, the ritual began, the *Barfleur* firing a signal gun and flying the Union Jack from her mizzenmast, the nearest of the three masts to the stern, from which signals were flown. The ship was prepared as if for a general inspection, decks scrubbed white, hammocks stowed, guns run out, and a party of Royal Marines, in scarlet with white pipe-clayed belts, under the command of a lieutenant, ready to receive each member of the court as he came aboard.

Full dress uniform was not worn unless an admiral was on trial. But by nine o'clock the members of the court had assembled, with Lord Keith as president. The court-martial was to be held in the great cabin, normally occupied by the captain. The long dining table was covered with traditional green baize, on which pens, ink, paper, prayer books and the Articles of War were laid for the members of the court who sat there. "Open the court," said the president, and Cochrane was marched in, his sword placed before the president himself.

Lieutenant Beaver called the witnesses to prove his case, while officers and men of the *Barfleur*, as was their privilege, pressed into the cabin to stand and watch the proceedings. Lieutenant Robert Jackson was examined. "Was you at the wardroom table on the evening of the ninth instant?" demanded Beaver. "Do you remember my coming into the wardroom, and saying to Lord Cochrane and Captain Cuthbert of the Marines that they had both made me appear exceedingly ridiculous?"

How could any of the witnesses forget it, in the light of what had followed? It was soon clear that there was no dispute as to what had taken place, but Lord Keith was looking grimmer with every moment that passed. Napoleon had invaded Syria and Sir Sydney Smith was under desperate siege at Acre. The French advance into Italy had reached Tuscany. At any moment, enemy fleets might break out of Brest, Cadiz and Toulon, falling like wolves upon the helpless flocks of the West India convoys and escorting an army of French troops and native rebels to invade Ireland. And here was the *Barfleur* and a host of other warships, lying peaceably at anchor while it was decided whether Lord Cochrane had spoken rudely to Lieutenant Beaver in the wardroom.

Lord Keith contained himself until Beaver had finished, and then his impartiality vanished.

"I hope this will be a lesson to officers how they apply for courts-martial in future, without first speaking to their captains or admirals. The first intimation I had on the subject was from the letter of application for the court-martial being put into my hand. Here are all the flag-officers and captains called together, at a time when the wind is coming fair and the ships ought to be under way. I think I am made the most ridiculous person of the whole!"

Cochrane tactfully announced that he would not "occasion delay" and that he would call no witnesses. He contented himself with pointing out that it was Beaver who had provoked the rudeness by his own foolish and unreasonable behaviour. The cabin was cleared while the court considered its verdict and the members voted, the junior officer voting first so that no member was intimidated by the expressed decision of his superior. Presently, the court was opened again and Cochrane was marched back in.

"The court," announced Lord Keith, "is of opinion that the charges are not proved, and do therefore acquit the said Lord Cochrane."

Despite this announcement of the court's verdict, the proceedings were not over. Lord Keith resumed.

"Lord Cochrane, I am directed by the court to say that officers should not reply sharply to their superior officers, and a first lieutenant's situation should be supported by everyone. A ship is but a small place where six or seven hundred persons are collected together and officers should in every part of it avoid any flippancy."[11]

There was a ripple of braided cocked-hats being replaced and Cochrane's sword was returned. Perhaps there was some satisfaction in the *Barfleur*'s wardroom at the discomfiture of Lieutenant Beaver. But Cochrane was not such a fool as to believe that he had got away with his indiscretion. The judge-advocate at the trial was Lord Keith's secretary and the admiral's final reprimand to Cochrane was included in the minutes, to be forwarded to the Admiralty in London. The first official notice taken of the young lord was, in consequence, as of a junior officer given to insubordination and disrespect towards his superiors. It might seem to matter little at the time but it was to matter greatly in another year or two.

As for Lieutenant Beaver, the authorities looked more kindly on his impetuous zeal. In a few months more, he was appointed to the command of the *Dolphin*, a 44-gun frigate, with the rank of post-captain.

.          .          .          .

Cochrane, never one of Keith's particular protégés, was now regarded with suspicion by the admiral, who began to seek pretexts for getting rid of him. With St Vincent's retirement Keith assumed the command of the war in the Mediterranean, shifting his flag to the *Queen Charlotte*, where Cochrane still remained one of his junior officers. In the course of these changes, the French fleet escaped to sea and joined a Spanish force off Cartagena, a development which did nothing to increase Cochrane's respect for his own superiors.

It was Nelson who was the unlikely means of enabling Keith to dispose of Cochrane. The *Queen Charlotte* was at anchor off Palermo in the summer of 1799, while Nelson was living ashore as the idol of Neapolitan court and society. His defeat of the French in southern Italy had restored the position of King Ferdinand, who had none the less left Naples for his alternative capital in Sicily. Nelson received Cochrane at Palermo on several occasions and discussed naval affairs with him in a tone of remarkable frankness. One phrase stuck in the young lieutenant's mind. When they talked of tactics and manoeuvres, Nelson seemed to lose patience with the niceties of Cochrane's exposition, which seemed a little too much like the examination answers of a midshipman. "Never mind manoeuvres," growled the great hero, "always go at them!" It was almost identical to Wellington's maxim in land battles against the French, and Cochrane regarded it as the soundest piece of advice on the matter that he had ever received. On the other hand, he later understood why many officers complained of Nelson that if he had not been killed at Trafalgar, he would certainly have been court-martialled for hazarding the fleet.[12]

Just before their meeting, Nelson had overtaken and captured a number of French ships between Italy and Sicily, including a 74-gun ship of the line, the *Généreux*. Having talked with Cochrane since then, and knowing something of his disposition and spirit, Nelson may have recognised a reflection of his own panache and zeal. Perhaps it was this which prompted a suggestion to Lord Keith of making Cochrane prize-master of the *Généreux* for the voyage from Sicily to Port Mahon, Minorca.

To have command of a 74-gun battleship at the age of twenty-four, even for a single voyage, was an exhilarating experience. But Cochrane was somewhat less exhilarated when he went aboard. Lord Keith had provided a very special crew, made up of men from all the other ships in the fleet who were too badly injured or sick to carry out normal duties. The rigging of the ship was also in some disorder, as might be expected from a recent prize to which little had been done by way of repair. Indeed, the general state of the ship was barely seaworthy. The one concession was in allowing Cochrane to take his younger brother Archibald as midshipman.

The *Généreux* was midway between Sicily and Minorca when the wind freshened, and those on the quarterdeck saw the spray beginning to fly from the caps of the waves. During the next few hours, the troughs of the green surges deepened and the breeze gathered strength until it was blowing a full gale. The *Généreux* was across the path of the storm, rolling violently, the leeward ports almost under water. But Cochrane was looking up at the towering mastheads. There had been no leisure to reset the rigging before the ship was ordered to sea and it was evident that something had gone badly wrong with the sails. As the ship rolled to leeward, the wind went out of them and they hung in limp festoons. Then, as the *Généreux* heeled upright, they filled out with a sudden crack, so abruptly that they were in danger of splitting or being torn clean away from the masts by the tremendous force of the gale.

At any moment the *Généreux* was likely to be dismasted. Once that happened the hull would be pounded by the seas, broadside-on, until the gun-ports or timbers were driven in. Even if there were men to work the pumps, they would be no match for the flood that swirled into the hold. The only hope was to reset the rigging. Yet, as Cochrane remarked, the ship rolled so heavily that any man who went aloft would find himself at a dizzy angle, the sea boiling immediately under him, the ropes and spars slippery from driving spray. A fit, well-trained crew would find it difficult. With a complement of sick and wounded it was an awesome labour. His first independent command seemed likely to end in the loss of a 74-gun battleship on a routine voyage from Sicily to Minorca. His only consolation was that he would be unlikely to survive for the inevitable court-martial.

As the ship heeled precipitously under another driving squall, it seemed as though she might capsize even before she could be flooded. Cochrane made his decision, beckoning his younger brother and striding towards the mainmast. The two tall, youthful Scots were, after all, fitter than anyone else on board, and Cochrane's boyish idealism forbade him to give orders which he himself would not be prepared to carry out. As the canvas thundered and billowed against the darkening sky, the gangling figure began to climb with surprising agility. He shouted to the men below him that the mainsail must be furled. Even that was not guaranteed to save them, but it would reduce the violence of the ship's rolling. Seeing that Cochrane was prepared to go aloft, the men began to follow, clinging as he did to the slippery wetness of ropes and spars, while the wind shrieked about them, the cold spray stinging like a lash and the foam surging below the angled mast.

For a while, in the darkness, they struggled with the thick and heavy shroud but gradually the canvas was close-reefed and the ship's progress grew calmer. At last it was possible to manoeuvre her. As if acknowledging defeat, the storm died down and essential repairs could be carried out. Battered but still afloat, the *Généreux* dropped anchor off Port Mahon.[13]

By his seamanship on many such occasions, Cochrane proved his ability. Moreover, the flag-officers decided that if the unruly red-haired young man was to be a nuisance, he might as well be a nuisance to the enemy instead of to his superiors in the wardroom. To promote him to commander was the price of his removal, since he was not to be given a ship of much significance. A French corvette, the *Bonne Citoyenne*, nothing as grand as a frigate, had lately been captured from the enemy. A year after the *Généreux* episode, at twenty-five years old, Cochrane was told he could have the command of the little raiding-vessel.

This promise upset Lord Keith's secretary, who had a brother looking for a command just then. Lord Keith agreed that it was absurd, in that case, to give the *Bonne Citoyenne* to Cochrane. The appointment was cancelled and the impatient young commander was informed that they would find him another ship. When they did, it was the sort of vessel at which men looked and then guffawed loudly on being told that, despite its appearance, it was actually intended as a warship.

H.M.S. *Speedy*, lying at Port Mahon, was neither a frigate nor a corvette. She was euphemistically described as a "sloop" by the Admiralty. In fact, she was a coasting brig of 158 tons, suited to light work in calm water. Her rigging was such that Cochrane found one of the smallest sails from the *Généreux* was larger than the mainsail of his new "sloop". On paper, however, she sounded formidable enough, having a crew of eighty-four men and six officers, as well as fourteen guns.

Cochrane went aboard and examined the ship. The glory of occupying the captain's cabin was diminished by the headroom below decks being no more than five feet. A table, surrounded by lockers which doubled as seats, filled the accommodation. Space was so confined, Cochrane discovered, that he could only sit by crouching and rolling on to the lockers first. There were other problems which seemed still more intractable. How does a man over six feet tall shave in a cabin no more than five feet high? His answer was to open the skylight, place the shaving mirror on the deck outside and shave with his head poking through the skylight.[14]

Then there was the matter of the *Speedy*'s armament. There were indeed fourteen guns but they were 4-pounders, which looked more like the sort of gun carried by a man going hunting than the artillery of a man-of-war. Cochrane collected up every ball that would be fired in a complete broadside and found that they fitted easily into his pocket as he walked the deck. He persuaded Lord Keith to let him have a pair of 12-pounders, so that he could mount them as bow and stern chasers. After several experiments he returned them to the ordnance wharf. There was not room on the *Speedy*'s deck for the gun crews to work large guns effectively. More alarming still, he discovered that the force of the explosion shook the little ship's timbers so violently that she was in danger of springing several leaks. There was nothing for it but to make do with the "popguns" already on board.[15]

Among his compensations, he was able to appoint his younger brother Archibald as midshipman, and he had an excellent deputy in Lieutenant William Parker. Best of all, there was what he called "my first piece of luck", which befell him within a few hours of the *Speedy* sailing as convoy escort from Cagliari on 10 May 1800. French privateers were active in these waters and it was difficult for the sloop to keep a close watch on the fourteen merchantmen in straggling formation. At 9 a.m., Cochrane recorded, "observed a strange sail take possession of a Danish brig under our escort". To abandon the rest of the convoy and turn back to aid a straggler was a risk, but Cochrane took it. At eleven-thirty, he entered in his private log, "rescued the brig, and captured the assailant". The French privateer was the 6-gun *Intrepide*, no match even for the *Speedy*. It was mere formality to overhaul her, fire a warning shot, and put a prize crew aboard. Against the background of the Mediterranean war, the *Intrepide* was insignificant. For Cochrane, however, she was his first prize after seven years in the navy.

On 14 May, almost midway during the voyage to Leghorn, five armed boats closed on the convoy. "At 4 p.m.," Cochrane reported, "the boats boarded and took possession of the two sternmost ships."

Again, he took a calculated risk, turning back to the two captured merchant ships. Fortune habitually favouring the bold, provided a
sudden and propitious wind. "The breeze freshening, we came up
with and recaptured the vessels with the prize crews on board,"
Cochrane noted in his log. The armed boats had left the scene, but
both French prize crews were themselves prisoners. On 21 May, he recorded "At anchor in Leghorn Roads. Convoy all safe." Best of all,
his first fortnight of command had also brought him one captured
French ship and over fifty prisoners.[16]

This was the opportunity for which he had longed. Though detained in May by the bombardment of Massena's French army at
Genoa, he and his crew captured three prizes in June, and three more
in July. That natural talent for piracy, which made up an important
part of his character as a seaman, had found its true employment in
the service of his country. On 3 August 1800, he anchored off Leghorn
with his small fleet of prize vessels. "Lord Keith received me very
kindly," he wrote. Lord Keith could afford to, since he received a
substantial share of the prize money as the admiral commanding the
area.[17]

On Keith's orders, Cochrane spent the rest of the year operating
from Port Mahon against the Spanish coast, whose defenders soon
knew about the brig and its captain. To counter this, Cochrane had
the *Speedy* repainted to resemble the *Clomer*, a neutral Danish brig
which traded up and down the Spanish Mediterranean coast. On 21
December, Cochrane was cruising off the Spanish coast when he
sighted a ship which had the appearance of "a well-laden merchantman". The prize was too good to miss and the *Speedy* gave chase to
the large but unarmed vessel. On coming parallel, the ports of the
"merchantman" swung open to reveal a row of heavy and powerful
bronze cannon.

Cochrane, on the quarterdeck of the little brig, muttered something
about having "caught a Tartar", and then ordered his men to run
up Danish colours. But there was worse to come. The large ship had
appeared to be only lightly manned, whereas now a couple of hundred armed men had appeared from below decks and the first boat
was being lowered. If the *Speedy* attempted to run, she would be
blown from the water. If she remained, then the Spaniards would
board her. She had, as Cochrane remarked, "fallen into the jaws of a
formidable Spanish frigate".

As the Spanish boat pulled closer, Cochrane ordered out of sight
everyone who was wearing a recognisable British uniform. Then he

revealed their defender. From below decks came a man in Danish uniform. He not only looked Danish, he spoke Danish as well and had been taken on by Cochrane in Minorca for that reason. As the Spanish boat came within hail, the Dane began to parley with its occupants, who still seemed insistent on boarding the *Speedy*. But Cochrane had further elaborated his masterstroke, following the pattern by which he customarily unnerved his opponents. When they thought that the worst had happened, there was, as a rule, one more thing for which they were totally unprepared.

In this case, the Dane spoke dolefully in his guttural Spanish and indicated the foremast of the brig. Cochrane's seamen had been busy and there now flew a single yellow flag: the *Speedy* was in quarantine with several cases of plague on board. It all fitted the Dane's story of having come from Algiers, where plague had indeed broken out, and it was perfectly adapted to the Spanish fear of importing the contagion into their own country. A boarding party which remained on a plague-stricken brig would have small chance of survival. Even after a brief visit they might well take the pestilence back to their own crowded ship.

The Spaniards hesitated. Then the boat's crew bent to their oars and began to pull back towards the frigate. It was not worth the risk. The Spanish ship "filled and made sail".[18]

Cochrane's ingenuity in the face of superior weapons was sometimes as elaborate as this and sometimes very simple. Three months later, on 18 March 1801, the *Speedy* had just put to sea from Port Mahon when, towards evening, Cochrane saw that she was being followed by a large and powerful frigate. He signalled the frigate, using the Royal Navy code in operation at the time, and received no reply. The only hope for the *Speedy* lay in escape. Cochrane crowded on his sails but the force of the wind was such that one sail parted company from the rigging. At dawn the next day, the frigate still had them in sight and gained steadily on the little brig until that evening. There could be only one end to the chase. During the second night, as on the first, the frigate was guided by the glimmer of light which was inevitable on any ship. An hour before dawn she was almost on top of her prey. And then the sky lightened. Just ahead of the frigate there was a large wooden tub with a candle burning it. Of the *Speedy* there was no sign.[19]

Both at sea and on shore the legends about the new commander began to spread. When some exiled French royalist officers gave a fancy-dress ball during the *Speedy*'s visit to Malta, Cochrane decided to go in the dress of an ordinary British seaman, complete with marlinspike and a lump of grease in his hat. It did not occur to him that the French officers would take him for a real British seaman who was trying to force his way into the genteel company of themselves and their ladies. At the door of the ballroom he found his path barred. Such costumes, he was told, were not permitted. Cochrane accused the French royalist of slandering British sailors and announced that, having bought a ticket for their ball, he would come in any costume that he chose.

The French officer who acted as master of ceremonies came to the door and reached for Cochrane's collar, in order to drag him out of the ante-room. Cochrane replied with a powerful punch to the royalist's nose and an obscenity, carefully spoken in French. There was a confusion of flying fists and falling bodies, the angry young Scot felling all those who approached, until the picket-guard came running and Cochrane was carried off to the French regimental guard-room.

When his identity was discovered, the master of ceremonies demanded satisfaction for his swollen nose. The two men and their seconds met behind the island ramparts at dawn. The long-barrelled pistols were raised and the two shots rang out almost simultaneously. Cochrane felt a blow to his chest, but the bullet had been stopped by his coat and waistcoat, merely bruising him. To his horror, he saw the Frenchman stagger and fall. But, he assured Cochrane, he was "not materially hurt", merely wounded in the thigh. None the less, Cochrane was shaken by the episode and gave his word never again "to do anything in frolic which might give even unintentional offence".[20]

On the first anniversary of his command, he was at sea, off Barcelona. On 5 May 1801, the *Speedy* gave chase to Spanish gun-boats, which hastily put into Barcelona. They behaved in every way like decoys, but Cochrane was undeterred. At daylight on 6 May, he set course through the early mist for Barcelona again, only to find himself sailing straight towards a powerful frigate, as the morning cleared. He recognised the *Gamo*, a 32-gun Spaniard with a complement of over three hundred sailors and marines, and just four times the size of the *Speedy*. Cochrane's own crew was depleted by his very successes, since almost half of them had been put aboard captured vessels as prize crews in the past few weeks. He now had fifty-four men, instead of ninety, barely enough to sail the ship. To these rather startled seamen, he announced that he was going to engage the Spanish warship. All hands were piped to action and the *Speedy* steered towards the enemy.

In the moment before battle, each man knew his place. On the gun-deck the cannon were lined up at the ports, the row curving out slightly towards the centre. Powder-boys sat expectantly on the boxes brought from the magazine, while shot and wads were placed by each gun on its wooden trolley. Captains of the gun-crews wore priming-boxes buckled to their waists as they watched the locks fixed upon the guns and the lanyards laid around them. Officers with swords drawn stood by their divisions of men, while the last furniture from the captain's cabin and the wardroom was carried down into the hold. The entire ship might become the scene of hand-to-hand fighting and it was important that the decks should be cleared "for action". An efficient crew would clear even a battleship in five minutes or so.

As the two ships raced towards one another, Cochrane stood on the little quarterdeck with Lieutenant Parker, his brother Archibald, and as many of the crew as could be spared to carry small arms or cutlasses for the fight. There was no point in firing a broadside yet, since the shot would not carry half the distance to the Spanish ship. On the other hand, the *Gamo* now had the *Speedy* within range of her powerful guns.

The one factor in Cochrane's favour was the improbability of what he was about to do. The officers of the *Gamo* would never believe that anyone but a lunatic would try to attack them with a brig whose mastheads hardly reached much above their own quarterdeck. The frigate fired a shot which hissed above the *Speedy*'s deck and plunged into the water beyond. At the same time she ran up the Spanish colours. Cochrane watched this and then ordered his signaller to run up the American flag. The *Speedy* was now passing the windward side of the *Gamo* at 9.30 a.m., the mouths of the Spanish guns at the open ports silent but menacing. The American flag caused enough confusion and indecision among the Spanish officers to allow the brig to slip past unscathed. Then Cochrane turned his ship, came round on the leeward side of the *Gamo*, lowering the American flag and running up the British ensign.

Flame spouted from the *Gamo*'s ports, followed by a rolling bank of smoke, as the first broadside roared out. The *Speedy* survived it, overtaking the frigate and coming in upon her fast. Cochrane ordered his men to hold their fire but to double-shot their guns. This reduced the range still further but turned a broadside into a lethal hail of small, sharp fragments of metal. The boom and billow of a second broad-side from the *Gamo* echoed across the water but the *Speedy*, having got the leeward position, came through it undamaged. Lord Rodney had long since established that a ship to leeward was a difficult target, since her attacker tended to heel towards her with the wind, depress-ing the guns and making them liable to fire into the sea rather than into the enemy.

As the Spanish gunners reloaded, Cochrane brought the *Speedy* in, almost as though he were going to ram the frigate, and there was a crash as the little brig's masts locked with the lower rigging of the *Gamo*. The frigate's guns roared out again, but the cannon balls passed over the heads of Cochrane and his crew, tearing their sails and splintering some of the spars but unable to touch the hull. He ordered the *Speedy*'s own 4-pounders to be angled upwards and fired. The result was devastating. The shot came ripping upwards through the *Gamo*'s gun-deck, causing appalling casualties among the gun crews and killing both the captain and the bosun. The bizarre and gruesome contest lasted for about an hour in this form. On three occasions, the Spanish marines from the *Gamo* tried to board the *Speedy*. Each time, Cochrane let them muster on the edge of the frigate's deck, and then swung his own ship away, opening up a watery gap and leaving them immobilised. Before they could with-draw, the musket-fire and shot from the brig cut through their ranks. Improbable as it might seem, he had fought the heavily-armed Spanish frigate to a standstill. "From the height of the frigate out of the water," he noted, "the whole of her shot must necessarily go over our heads, whilst our guns, being elevated, would blow up her main-deck." He had, of course, no intention of settling for less than total victory. His two killed and four wounded left him with forty-eight men against three hundred Spaniards. As he wrote in his des-patch, "The great disparity of force rendering it necessary to adopt some measure that might prove decisive, I resolved to board." He informed his men of this, adding that they must "either take the frigate or be themselves taken, in which case the Spaniards would give no quarter". By this time, however, his men were flushed with enthusiasm at what they had achieved so far. In the words of one witness, they shouted that they would follow Cochrane to hell itself, if that was where he proposed to lead them.

Leaving Surgeon Guthrie at the wheel, he sent half his men with blackened faces to climb stealthily up the *Gamo*'s bows, hidden from view by the curve of the hull. Cochrane himself led the remaining score of men amidships, scaling the frigate's side and bursting on to the deck. In the confusion of smoke and musket-fire, one seaman fell dead at the rail, and Lieutenant Parker struggled on, wounded through chest and thigh. Cochrane's tall figure and red hair under a cocked hat was an unmistakable rallying point, as he watched the careful working out of his plan. The "cool determined conduct" of his men with fist and cutlass amidships had already engaged the attention of the Spaniards when the first black-faced devils came leaping and shrieking from the bows. Caught on both sides, the defence began to fall into confusion.

It was hard for the Spanish to use their full weight in such a skirmish on the crowded deck. Equally, it was unthinkable that forty-eight men should defeat three hundred. Cochrane, driven back to the rail, roared down to Guthrie, the only man left on the *Speedy*, since someone had to hold the wheel. The words were clearly heard by the Spaniards as he ordered the next wave of attackers to be sent across. Guthrie concealed his surprise and acknowledged the command. The men of the *Gamo* began to recoil from the apparent trap of an innocent brig crammed with Royal Marines. The heart seemed to go out of the Spanish resistance. Their captain and bosun were dead and over fifty more men had been killed or wounded in the carnage of the gun-deck as the *Speedy*'s broadsides tore upwards through the planking. The men who had followed Cochrane aboard looked and fought like devils with cutlass and small arms. Leaderless and bemused, the superior Spanish force began to edge towards the stern of the *Gamo*. As they did so, there was a pause and the eyes of men on both sides turned to the mast. The Spanish colours had been struck, the flag coming slowly down. There was no longer even a pretext for resistance as the *Gamo* surrendered to the little brig alongside her. In fact it was one of the British seamen who, on Cochrane's orders, had slipped through the skirmish and lowered the Spanish flag.

The *Gamo* should have been able to blow the *Speedy* out of the water before the British ship came near enough to fire a shot. The Spanish troops should have been able to overwhelm the depleted crew of the brig as soon as she came alongside. A man who was so foolish as to lead forty-eight seamen on board an enemy ship with a crew of more than three hundred ought to have found himself and his men prisoners within a few minutes. As it was, Cochrane's main problem was how to cope with a prize of such magnitude. It was almost necessary to abandon the *Speedy*, since thirty of her crew were needed to get the *Gamo* to Port Mahon, leaving hardly more than a dozen men to manage the brig. The Spanish seamen and crew were bundled into the frigate's hold, 263 still unwounded. Realising the puny power which had defeated them, it seemed as though they might try to overpower the British prize crew, whom they outnumbered almost ten to one. But Cochrane had thought of that too. He ordered the most powerful guns on the *Gamo*, the two 24-pounder carronades from the bows, to be manhandled until they pointed down into the hold. Throughout the voyage British seamen with lighted tapers were stationed by the loaded guns to discourage thoughts of counter-attack by the prisoners. In this manner the *Speedy* returned to the British base on Minorca, escorting the prize which towered above her.[21]

Cochrane's immediate superior, Captain Manley Dixon, wrote excitedly to the Secretary of the Admiralty on 9 June, describing "the very spirited and brilliant action", which Cochrane had led. Cochrane himself attributed success, in his official despatch, to Lieutenant Parker, Archibald Cochrane, and to the "exertions and good conduct of the boatswain, carpenter, and petty officers". Neither the Admiralty in general, nor St Vincent as First Lord, reciprocated this enthusiasm. St Vincent, assuming office with the new government of Henry Addington, was not likely to make the mistake of flattering a brash young commander whose recent court-martial had shown such disrespect for his superiors. The old man had a reputation to maintain, the scourge of rebellious officers and mutinous seamen alike. It was left to Captain Edward Brenton, who was ironically St Vincent's biographer, to proclaim after the war that, in single-ship actions, those of Cochrane "stand pre-eminent". Indeed, outside the Admiralty, the *Gamo* incident caught the public imagination. There was a steady procession of viewers to the public rooms in Lower Brook Street, where a new painting of the engagement by the fashionable marine artist Nicholas Pocock was proudly exhibited.[22]

Traditionally, Cochrane would be made post-captain and given command of the prize when it was enrolled in the Royal Navy. As for prize money, a xebec-class frigate, shared among so few men, even allowing for Admiral Lord Keith's portion, was a lucrative prospect. There was some astonishment, and then anger, when the Admiralty announced that the *Gamo* would not be bought for the navy. She was to be auctioned off as merchantman or hulk at a fraction of the price, perhaps little more than the costs of the prize court proceedings. As for Cochrane, he would have no frigate to command, so there was no need to promote him post-captain. Such a rank would be ludicrous for a man who was ordered to continue in command of a brig-sloop.

Other men took up Cochrane's case. His uncle, Alexander Cochrane, wrote two letters to St Vincent, soliciting his nephew's promotion. The Earl of Dundonald wrote later, criticising the effect that delay would have upon his son's seniority in the navy list. There was so much feeling on Cochrane's behalf that "it became almost a point of etiquette with the earl *not to make him a captain*". One of St Vincent's colleagues was reported to have said, "My lord, we must make Lord Cochrane 'post'." To which the old man growled, "The First Lord of the Admiralty knows *no must!*"[23]

Ignoring the official snub to himself, Cochrane fought determinedly for recognition of his second-in-command, Lieutenant Parker. Parker had continued to lead his men with exemplary courage, though a Spanish sword had run through his thigh and a musket ball had hit him in the chest. Cochrane vowed that Parker must be promoted and the Admiralty were equally resolute in their decision to ignore him.

Cochrane wrote direct to St Vincent on three occasions, urging Parker's promotion, before the First Lord replied that "the small number of men killed on board the *Speedy* did not warrant the application". If Cochrane had thought prudently about his future prospects in the Royal Navy he would have dropped the matter. Instead, he wrote to St Vincent, reminding him that his own earldom had been awarded for an action in which there was only one man killed on his flagship. The innuendo was calculated to heat the First Lord to apoplexy. He knew full well that his enemies swore the casualties had been light on the flagship because St Vincent kept well out of danger, leaving Nelson and the inshore squadron to do the fighting.[24]

Having infuriated the First Lord, Cochrane then turned upon the Commissioners of the Admiralty collectively. He wrote them a letter on 17 May, enclosing another for Evan Nepean, the Secretary to the Board, remarking bitterly to him, "if their Lordships judge by the small number killed, I have only to say that it was fortunate the enemy did not point their guns better". Nepean replied smoothly that it was "perfectly regular" for Cochrane to write to him, "but that it is not so for officers to correspond with the Board". Cochrane wrote back furiously, saying that he cared nothing for this but demanded to be "favoured with an answer" to his application on behalf

of Parker. Nepean wrote a dismissive note, informing Cochrane that
he had "nothing in command from their Lordships to communicate
to you". Lieutenant Parker's recognition was to be delayed until
Cochrane was in a position to extort it from the Admiralty.[25]

In the view of his brother officers, Cochrane had wrecked his career
by this contretemps with men of political and professional influence.
He and the *Speedy* were relegated to more humdrum tasks, indeed he
admitted that his name was now "placed on the black list of the
Admiralty, never again to be erased". The brig was downgraded to
packet-escort or to run errands to Algiers. By a typical irony of
war, it was in the North African port that she met the *Gamo*
again. The Admiralty had deprived Cochrane and his crew of
their expected reward by selling the frigate to the Algerians "for a
trifle".[26]

Cochrane cared little whether or not his name was on the Admiralty
"black list". He had out-fought the Spaniards and now he proposed
to out-fight the Commissioners by much the same methods. It was
not pure altruism, since the outrage to an innate sense of honour was
almost equalled by the affront to his mercenary values. His country
urged him to fight bravely, which he did, but he expected to be paid.
Additional feats of bravery, in his view, merited additional financial
reward. Close acquaintance with the "res angusta domi" had taught
him the value of money, and the simple lesson that a price could be
put upon acts of valour.

Lord St Vincent was unlikely to agree with Cochrane in public,
but even he attacked privately "the frauds in the receipt of forfeited
prize money". That Cochrane and his crew were robbed of some of
their rewards is a matter of record. In one case they received nothing,
and Cochrane was told that he was personally in debt for £100 as the
cost of proceedings. It was true that his ordinary seaman earned,
through prizes, more than the pay of officers on other ships but that
hardly consoled them for injustices done.[27]

In July 1801 the *Speedy* was packet-escort between Port Mahon
and Gibraltar with little opportunity for taking prizes or for any sort
of independent action. The letter bag was put aboard the brig at Port
Mahon and she sailed in company with the packet-boat until they
arrived off Gibraltar. There the bag was transferred to the packet-
boat which sailed into Gibraltar alone and then returned. This extraordinary ritual had been ordered by the commandant of Port Mahon,
a friend of the merchant who had the contract for carrying mails.
The contractor knew that the packet-boat he had hired, for the

lowest possible price, was far too unseaworthy to be entrusted with the mails. He had therefore reached a private agreement with his friends in the Royal Navy that the letter bag should go aboard the *Speedy* and be transferred off Gibraltar, so that it would look to the authorities there as if it had come all the way in the packet-boat.

Cochrane escorted the boat along the Mediterranean coast of Spain, keeping a wistful eye on any possible prizes. It was just beyond Alicante that he saw some small merchant vessels anchored in a bay. As soon as the *Speedy* turned inshore towards them, they weighed anchor and their captains ran them ashore to avoid capture. Not only would Cochrane have had to land his men on a hostile coast but he might have had to wait several hours until the tide had risen sufficiently to float any of the vessels off. "To have stopped to get them off would have been in excess of our instructions," he decided. "To set fire to them was not."

The *Speedy* dropped anchor in the bay, leaving the packet-boat and its crew waiting nervously offshore. The broadside of the little 4-pounders boomed across the water and, to Cochrane's satisfaction, there was an explosion and a billow of fire from one of the vessels, which was carrying oil. Soon they were all alight and for many miles around the glow of fire filled the night sky.

On the following morning, as the *Speedy* sailed out of the bay, the top-sails of three splendid ships appeared on the horizon. "Spanish galleons from South America," said Cochrane instinctively. The day was only just dawning but there was enough light for the *Speedy* to give chase. As the sun bathed the sea with the brilliance of a Mediterranean summer, the shape of the three great ships grew clearer. They were the *Indomitable*, the *Formidable* and the *Dessaix*, three of the most powerful ships of the line in the French fleet. It was unusual for them to be so close inshore but they had been attracted by the light of the burning merchant vessels.

Even the *Speedy* could hardly take on three battleships at once, indeed most commanders would have hauled down the ensign and surrendered without further ado. A well-aimed broadside from the *Dessaix* would sink the brig in an instant. Cochrane decided that it might just be possible to outmanoeuvre the three battleships and escape to the open sea. He put the *Speedy* under full sail to take advantage of the wind and told his men to trundle the fourteen 4-pounder guns overboard. They would be useless in any action against the three great ships and their weight would only slow the brig down. Then he ordered his men to the sweeps, the long oars which were

worked by sailors to move a ship when becalmed or to give her extra
speed in an emergency.

The three French ships had moved apart to block every way of
escape. Cochrane's first concern was to manoeuvre the *Speedy*
rapidly and unexpectedly so that she seldom faced the menacing
broadsides of the battleships as their rows of guns towered above her.
But by avoiding the broadsides he inevitably exposed the ship to the
chase-guns in the bows or stern of the French battleships. As the shot
ripped through the sails of the brig, fragments of wooden spars fell
away and clattered on the deck.

So long as she remained pinned between the French battleships
and the Spanish coast, the *Speedy* would inevitably be destroyed.
But if she could gain the open sea, there was a chance that lightness
and greater manoeuvrability would enable her to elude the French
until darkness fell and she could escape. Cochrane ordered all the
stores to be thrown overboard to lighten the ship still further, as the
French men-of-war closed in. Then, under full canvas, he brought the
little brig on a course between the *Dessaix* and one of the other ships.
The French were taken aback at first, since they expected Cochrane
to sail away from them rather than towards them, but the captain of
the *Dessaix*, Christie Pallière, was in time to order a hasty broadside
as the brig sped past. When the rolling gun-smoke thinned and
cleared, the *Speedy* was still afloat and heading for the horizon.

Pallière immediately tacked in pursuit, while the brig dodged and
turned to avoid capture. For an hour, the chase continued but with
each salvo from the guns in the *Dessaix*'s bows more holes appeared
in the tattered rigging of the *Speedy*. As she lost canvas, the *Dessaix*
was soon within musket shot of her and then, overhauling her, turned
broadside on and fired. It was as well for Cochrane and his men that
the speed with which the battleship turned carried her too far, so that
the heavier shot plunged into the sea just ahead of the *Speedy*'s
bows. But the full force of scattered grape-shot struck the rigging,
cutting apart the sails until they hung in shreds, and tearing away
spars and sections of the masts. Without guns or rigging, there was
no more to be done. Cochrane ordered the colours to be hauled down.

He was escorted aboard the *Dessaix* and stood face to face with his
late adversary Pallière on the French quarterdeck. As was customary, he took off his sword and offered it to his captor. Pallière shook
his head.

"I will not accept the sword of an officer who has for so many
hours struggled against impossibility," he said courteously.

Cochrane was indeed a prisoner, but he was permitted to continue wearing his sword.[28]

The *Speedy* had sailed for the last time under Cochrane's command but, as he was taken on the *Dessaix* to Algeciras, he was able to reckon up the prizes of thirteen months in command. He had captured over fifty other vessels, 122 guns, and 534 prisoners. On his arrival at Algeciras, he was still treated more like a guest than a prisoner by Captain Pallière. The two men were on the *Dessaix* when Sir James Saumarez attacked Algeciras with his squadron. "It shall not spoil our breakfast," said Pallière coolly, as they sat in the stern cabin of the battleship. The meal continued until a British round shot crashed through the stern timbers of the *Dessaix*, showering the breakfast table with broken glass from a wine bin which had been under the sofa.[29]

As a matter of fact, Cochrane's unusual experience of the Royal Navy's gunnery lasted for no more than a couple of weeks, before he was exchanged and returned to Gibraltar. He owed this exchange to the arrival of a squadron of Spanish ships on 12 July. The garrison band of Gibraltar assembled on the foreshore, playing "Britons, Strike Home!" as Sir James Saumarez and his squadron put to sea again, the Royal Marine band on the poop of his flagship *Caesar* piping, "Come, cheer up, my lads, 'tis to glory we steer!" The two fleets met at twilight, Captain Keats of the *Superb* dashing between the two columns of the Spanish ships, firing to right and left of him. In the darkness and the smoke, he caused such confusion that two Spanish ships, the *San Hermenegildo* and the *Real Carlos*, each mistook the other for a British attacker and exchanged heavy broadsides. The sails of the *Real Carlos* began to burn and soon the hull caught fire. In this state she collided with the *San Hermenegildo*, whom she was still fighting, and set fire to her as well. As both ships blew up, Captain Keats boarded and captured the *San Antonio*. It was the second captain of this ship for whom Cochrane was exchanged.

Because he had lost the *Speedy*, Cochrane was automatically court-martialled, the trial taking place on board the *Pompée* in Rosia Bay on 18 July. There was no doubt that he would be acquitted. He had done all that could be expected of him when the brig was confronted by three battleships. Most commanders would have given up far more easily. On the other hand, if his case had been inquired into too strictly, the use of the *Speedy* to carry the packets in order to facilitate the profits of a merchant who happened to be a friend of the commandant of Port Mahon was bound to come to light. He was hurriedly and formally set free.

From St Vincent's correspondence, it seems that he rather hoped that Cochrane would be removed from his consideration by remaining a prisoner of the French or the Spanish. But Cochrane had returned as the twenty-six-year-old commander who had won a victory over the *Gamo* which was already passing into legend, and who had fought a heroic, if hopeless, action against three French battleships. To refuse him either promotion to post-captain or a new command might stir up a hornet's nest. St Vincent delayed as long as he could, and then compromised. Cochrane was promoted post-captain with effect from 8 August 1801, the date on which the Admiralty received confirmation of his acquittal by the court-martial of 18 July. Those who alleged that his promotion had been too long withheld were duly silenced. But the new rank carried no new command with it. Smarting under this ingenious punishment by the First Lord, Cochrane returned to Edinburgh. He was a captain without a ship, and a hero without a battle to fight.

It mattered less than it might have done. Just as the war had been precipitated by a change of public mood as much as by the logic of policy, so now there was a general but ill-defined inclination for peace. Neither side in the war had gained a decisive advantage after almost a decade of military and naval struggle. The British had seized a few overseas territories, while France had established her influence in Italy. But Pitt and others concluded that Buonaparte having gained supreme power in France, was a reasonable man who would be content with what he had won. The revolutionary horrors of 1793 had long ceased to be sufficient pretext for continuing the war.

In the autumn of 1801, Lord Cornwallis and Talleyrand met at Amiens to draw a treaty restoring the two nations, in effect, to their *status quo* of 1793. France would leave Naples and southern Italy. England would evacuate Malta and return all conquests except for Trinidad and Ceylon. The Cape of Good Hope, seized by England as a precaution, was returned to Holland. The affairs of Europe itself were to be left aside. Negotiations dragged on until the following March, when the major European questions still remained unresolved. But peace had been decided on, and so the Treaty of Amiens was signed. Sheridan called it a peace which everybody was glad of and nobody was proud of. The elder Lord Palmerston dismissed it sourly as "the peace which passeth all understanding". Such sentiments were quite contrary to popular taste. When General Lauriston brought the terms to London, the delighted crowds whose predecessors had roared, "War with France! War with France!" on that winter day in 1793, dragged his carriage through the streets in triumph. But before the agreement of Amiens was signed, those whom it concerned most closely had already begun to prepare in their minds the renewed war that must come. The young Lord Cochrane had no idea when it would come or whether there would be a part in it for him. He needed desperately the chance to win his fortune in battle, but the enemy at home who robbed heroes of the pounds, shillings and pence of courage had also to be defeated. In such warfare, a man could not afford to show the chivalry which he might accord to an enemy who was French or Spanish.[30]

# 3

# "A Sink of Corruption"

—

BECALMED by the new peace, the hero of fifty sea fights, the victor of the *Gamo* incident, and the gallant defender of his little brig against three French battleships, returned home. Like all the best heroes, he appeared modest and self-contained. At twenty-six years old, with his mop of red hair, awkward height, and beak of a nose, he was beginning to acquire a certain physical distinction which the caricaturists could put to good use. But the shallow waters of naval politics and parliamentary intrigue concealed worse perils than the Catalan coast and Cochrane was well aware that he must begin a new apprenticeship. One of those with whom he allied himself was the Radical country gentleman William Cobbett. It was at Cobbett's house, in a soft and leafy Hampshire valley, that Mary Russell Mitford first saw the young naval hero. She found him "as unlike the common notion of a warrior as could be. A gentle, quiet, mild young man, was this burner of French fleets as one should see in a summer day. He lay about under the trees, reading Seldon on the Dominion of the Seas, and letting children (and children always know with whom they may take liberties) play all sorts of tricks with him at their pleasure."[1]

The mild bookishness was no mere pose. Cochrane felt the need to complete that education which had been imparted during his boyhood so randomly. Gathering up the remains of his prize money, he travelled to Edinburgh to enter himself as a student of the great Professor of Moral Philosophy, Dugald Stewart. Like so many nineteenth-century academics renowned for their teaching rather than for publications, Dugald Stewart's name passed into obscurity. But to the progressively-minded sons of the ruling class at the turn of the century, he was the great educator. His pupils included Walter Scott, Lord Palmerston, Francis Jeffrey, later editor of the *Edinburgh Review*, Lord Cockburn, a future solicitor-general, Henry Brougham, one day to be Lord Chancellor, and James Mill, political philosopher and father of John Stuart Mill.

Though he was the great tutor of the Whigs and the patrician Radicals, Dugald Stewart's enemies swore that he was indoctrinating the country's future leaders with the politics of revolutionary France. His students found him a thin pale man, as Lord Cockburn recalled, with intense grey eyes, shaggy brows, and the high bald dome of intellect. He combined tenacious argument with the vocal agility of a great actor or preacher, as he demonstrated irrefutably the nature of constitutional wisdom and the virtues of the ideal republic. His more earnest followers declared that to hear Dugald Stewart was to sit at the feet of a new Demosthenes. More worldly spirits thought him every bit as good as Mrs Siddons.

Cochrane worked a good deal harder than the younger students, partly because "it was necessary to be economical", and work was cheaper than pleasure. His compensation was the physical and architectural splendour of Edinburgh in the early nineteenth century. A new series of vistas had been added by the classicism of Robert Adam, rivalling the mediaeval city and the castle on the hill. Corinthian columns, mellow gold, and ceiling frescoes brought interior grandeur to such buildings as the Advocates' Library. Sir David Wilkie swore that the city combined the noblest of Prague and Salzburg, the most romantic of Orvieto and Tivoli. Edinburgh, remarked Chopin, speaks to the imagination.[2]

Poverty and the discipline of war taught Captain Lord Cochrane to subordinate personal comfort and private inclination to the stern demands of public duty. Marriage and domestic attachments were still an unattainable luxury to a man in his position. A wife was not an asset to a naval officer looking for advancement. Indeed, marriage was the one pretext which St Vincent needed to put an end to Cochrane's career altogether. "Sir," he had written to one of his favourite lieutenants. "You having thought fit to take yourself a wife, are to look for no further attentions from your humble servant."[3]

But Cochrane's time at Edinburgh was important in his development. He went there with a personal grievance, he emerged with a political philosophy. Called upon to advise a junior officer treated as he had been, Cochrane's answer was unequivocal.

"If you have, in the exercise of your profession, acquired a right which is wrongfully withheld – demand it, stick to it with unshaken pertinacity – none but a corrupt body can possibly think the worse of you for it; even though you may be treated like myself – you are doing your country good service by exposing favouritism, which is only another term for corruption."[4]

But with the coming of peace, Lord St Vincent had also chosen to make his mark as a reformer by investigating dockyard corruption. Such revelations would hardly have served national morale while the war was in progress but just before the Treaty of Amiens was actually signed, the gouty First Lord wrote to the Commissioners at the dockyards of Plymouth, Portsmouth, Chatham, and Woolwich, ordering them to put their books and papers under seal at once, pending an official inspection. When the Public Thanksgiving on 1 June 1802 was safely over, the necessary arrangements were made. From August until October, the Board of Admiralty toured the dockyards, reporting from Sheerness on 16 October, "the Public has been suffered to be defrauded to a very considerable extent, and delinquencies passed unpunished". St Vincent himself had already written to Addington, the Prime Minister, from Plymouth, "We find abuses to such an extent as would require many months to go thoroughly into, and the absolute necessity of a Commission of Enquiry to expose them appears to the Admiralty Board here in a much stronger light than ever."[5]

As St Vincent soon discovered, there were men at every level who resisted any such investigation. There were sailors who enlisted on ships at sea and dockyard hulks simultaneously, thus drawing double pay. At the other social extreme, there was the Deputy Commissioner who enjoyed a house, servants, salary, private yacht and crew, all paid for from the funds of his dockyard, which he had not even visited for the past four years. Government ministers grew uneasy over what might be made public by their First Lord's proposed "Commission of Inquiry". By the autumn of 1802 it was evident to them that the French had no more intention of fulfilling the terms of the Treaty of Amiens than they had. Renewed war seemed inevitable. It was all very well for St Vincent to insist on commissions of inquiry, but whatever "sink of corruption" lay in the dockyards was likely to be exhumed in the middle of a new and more desperate struggle against the power of Buonaparte. There were already popular movements growing in England which opposed a renewal of war. They and their more influential sympathisers might do untold damage to Britain's military resolve with such ammunition as St Vincent would unwittingly provide.[6]

The prospect of war made an autumn sitting of parliament necessary, though there was no indecorous haste and the session began on
22 November with the shooting season over. The cabinet and the
First Lord argued, until St Vincent refused to take his seat in the
Lords. Faced with inevitable public scandal sooner or later, Addington chose to placate St Vincent and delay the crisis. The commission
was agreed to, though the government managed to reduce some of its
proposed powers as the price of consent. Five commissioners were
appointed, two naval officers and three lawyers. Three of the five were
also Members of Parliament.

The Commission issued fourteen reports, the first, on naval store-
keepers at Jamaica, on 12 May 1803; the last, on the Royal Hospital
at Greenwich, on 30 June 1806. Most of the old accusations were
documented and many more were proved. In private shipyards, 300
men could build seven ships a year. In naval yards 3000 men could
barely manage to repair seven ships a year. The Navy Board had
never checked what money in the yards was paid to whom, or why.
That was left to the dockyard clerks. "It is scarcely to be credited,"
said the Commissioners in their Sixth Report. Worse still, the Navy
Board had never checked any of the paybooks. Three of its four
members had no idea whether anyone else checked them either.[7]

But the ministers need not have worried. Even these revelations,
when they came, were lost in the greater drama of the new war. By
the beginning of 1803, Buonaparte was raging at the British ambassador, Lord Whitworth, over England's failure to withdraw from Malta.
Britain replied, suggesting that the withdrawal be postponed for ten
years and that the island of Lampedusa should then be made an
alternative base. Addington forwarded counter-accusations of French
interference in Italy and the preparation of an invasion force on the
Channel coast, near Boulogne. In the Commons, on 11 February, a
Bill was introduced extending militia training to twenty-eight days.
News of this brought a summons from Buonaparte to Lord
Whitworth. The great Consul harangued the ambassador, swearing
that he would as soon see the English in possession of the Faubourg
St Antoine as of Malta. England must choose either to join him and
share the spoils of Europe, or oppose him and be crushed. The invasion force at Boulogne was mentioned. So long as there were two
parties in England, Buonaparte explained, one for peace and one for
war, France must prepare for either eventuality. Orders for the raising of 500,000 troops were therefore to be given. If England chose
war, Buonaparte promised to lead the invasion himself.[8]

On 8 March, the King informed the Commons that England was under threat of invasion from the French and Dutch Channel ports. Militia regiments throughout the kingdom were mobilised. The speed with which the two nations flew to war contrasted strongly with the diplomatic pas-de-deux of 1792. But this time it was not fear of revolutionary contagion nor outrage over butchery disguised as "the stern justice of the people" which forced Addington to issue his ultimatum. England now faced the simple military reality of a great European power, armed and led by a man in whose shadow the rest of the Continent trembled.

An attempt to form a national war cabinet failed when Pitt refused to join Addington. None the less, dramatic plans were devised for continued government of the country after Buonaparte's army should have landed. The King and the Prime Minister would move to Chelmsford or Dartford, to direct the counter-attack against French beach-heads in either Essex or Kent. The Queen would be evacuated to Worcester with the duplicate bank books and the crown jewels. The press would be controlled by the Secretary of State, and acts of government would be issued from London by the Privy Council.[9]

England's ultimatum embodied demands for the ten-year occupation of Malta, thus ensuring its own rejection. Lord Whitworth, after a final row with Buonaparte at a Tuileries reception, demanded his passports and left Paris on 12 May. The French ambassador left London at dawn four days later. On 18 May, war was declared. The revelations of Lord St Vincent's Commissioners of enquiry led to prosecutions for over-charging, or not building H.M.S. *Ajax* to specifications. But after all the apprehension, these one-day trials made little impact on a public whose fearful preoccupation was with the enemy across the water.[10]

As early as 8 March the press gangs had been out at Portsmouth, Gosport, Cowes, and on the Thames. "Every merchant ship in the harbour and at Spithead was stripped of its hands, and all the watermen deemed fit for His Majesty's service were carried off," *The Times* reported three days later. Six hundred men were pressed on that occasion, leaving merchant ships to be manned by foreign nationals who were, in theory, immune from conscription. The press on the Thames gathered in a thousand more sailors, but the United States consul, G. W. Erving, was soon at the Admiralty, protesting at the number of American sailors pressed into the Royal Navy. Their Lordships agreed reluctantly that all men who could produce "satisfactory testimonials of their being citizens of America" were to be discharged. But proof of citizenship was a fruitful topic of discord between America and Britain. When United States citizens were still held on Royal Navy ships, the Lords of the Admiralty ingenuously explained that they had not been released because they had been heard to express "a wish that they may have the opportunity of meeting the common enemy". In fact, their Lordships found it hard to adjust to the idea, after quarter of a century, that those who looked and spoke like Englishmen, and in some cases were English-born, were not fair game for the press gang.[11]

When war was declared, Cochrane wrote to St Vincent, seeking command of a ship to "operate inshore and harass the French coast in the Atlantic", as the *Speedy* had done the Spanish coast in the Mediterranean. St Vincent replied that no ships were available. He had not forgotten the tall young captain with his slow, insolent manner and his expressed contempt for governments and their servants. He had made Lieutenant Beaver the laughing stock of the flagship. He had reminded St Vincent of the rumours which alleged that his lordship had led from the rear in the great battle which won him his title. He had taunted the Admiralty Board with suggestions that they would have been better pleased with the *Gamo* if the *Speedy*'s casualty list had been longer. By St Vincent's standards, the contemptuous young Scot had yet to learn the lessons of naval discipline.[12]

Cochrane listed the ships in preparation and sent it to the First Lord. St Vincent replied coldly that they were promised elsewhere. Cochrane sent a second list of ships just under construction. They could hardly have been promised yet. St Vincent wrote angrily that they were all too large for a junior captain to command. But Cochrane was not without sympathisers. The Earl of Dundonald wrote to St Vincent on his son's behalf, and received a dull answer. The Marquis of Douglas wrote. "I have not forgot Lord Cochrane," replied the First Lord, "but I should not be justified in appointing him to the command of an 18-pounder frigate when there are so many senior captains of great merit without ships of that class."[13]

Cajoled by these protesters, St Vincent meditated his revenge. Cochrane himself was pacing the famous "waiting room" of the Admiralty, among other hopeful commanders, demanding audience with the First Lord. At length, St Vincent received him and Cochrane, in his slow deliberate lowland manner, played what seemed to be the winning card.

"If the Board is evidently of the opinion that my services are not required, it will be better for me to go back to the College of Edinburgh and pursue my studies, with a view of occupying myself in some other employment."[14]

Cochrane later recalled, "His lordship eyed me keenly, to see whether I really meant what I said." But there was no doubt that the preposterous young captain, who dared to address the First Lord in a tone bordering on contempt, was in earnest. St Vincent knew that to send Cochrane back to Edinburgh was, effectively, to dismiss him from the Royal Navy without charge or trial. He could well imagine the storm which would break over their Lordships' heads in that event. As Cochrane recalled, St Vincent's displeasure was visible in his face as he dismissed the young captain.

"Well, you shall have a ship. Go down to Plymouth, and there await the orders of the Admiralty."[15]

Cochrane went straight to Plymouth. Almost at once he was informed that his new ship was ready for him, and that the Admiralty had appointed him to command H.M.S. *Arab*. He dreamt, as he later recalled, of "a rakish craft, ready to run over to the French coast, and return with a goodly batch of well-laden coasters". With this in mind, he toured the dockyard in search of her and was finally led to the place where she lay. His first recorded observation on seeing her was, "She will sail like a haystack."[16]

H.M.S. *Arab* was not a warship at all but a battered old collier. With the coming of war, some enterprising businessman had bought her, almost from the scrapyard, in order to hire her out at £400 a month to an Admiralty which was hard-pressed to find ships. Cochrane may have seen himself getting the better of St Vincent, but he had been deftly snared. He had demanded a ship and orders. Now he had got both. His supporters would hear of his new command and, never having seen H.M.S. *Arab*, would relax their efforts.

It was apparent that there could be no question of getting the *Arab* to sea in her present state. She had been stripped down to her "bare ribs". Indeed, he found it was impossible to refit her at all except by using old timbers scavenged from other hulks recently broken up. When he had done the best he could with her, he was ordered to take her out on trials, round Land's End, into St George's Channel, and then back to Plymouth. This was his first voyage for many months and, at the sight of several ships which looked like possible prizes, he set a course to intercept them. But the *Arab* handled, according to her appearance, like an overladen tub. While her new captain fulminated on his little quarterdeck, the ancient collier wallowed at a humiliating and increasing distance from the quarry she was intended to pursue.

Despite this, when the *Arab* returned from her trials she was given immediate orders to join the flotilla of ships, under Lord Keith's general command, which was endeavouring to blockade Napoleon's invasion force in Boulogne. This was proving less easy than the Admiralty had hoped. Boulogne harbour was dry at low tide and its principal channel of navigation was the course of the little river Liane which ran through it. The original intention had been to sink blockships in this channel and so avoid the necessity of a full-scale blockade. But as Captain Crawford observed, watching these futile attempts from the deck of the *Immortalité*, it was almost impossible to get a favourable wind and tide so that the block-ships would be in the right positions for scuttling. After a month of "calms and contrary winds" the ingenious idea was abandoned and the entire squadron settled down to the dreary weeks of a conventional blockade.[17]

There was no lack of excitement on board the *Arab*, though it was not of the kind which Cochrane had envisaged. The problem with the vessel, as with most colliers of the day, was that she would sail quite well but only in one direction. With the wind behind her, there was no difficulty in crossing from Ramsgate and the Kent coast to Boulogne. But nothing, it seemed, would persuade her to sail back against the wind. While the other ships of the blockade force prudently withdrew, Cochrane and his crew were left struggling with their ungainly craft, endeavouring by rigging and sweeps to sail or row her out of danger, until the tide changed and began to carry them clear of the French coast.

As Lord St Vincent's revenge, the *Arab* could hardly have been improved upon. Most forms of offensive action were out of the question while, as Cochrane remarked, the first strong wind from north or north-west was going to wreck the vessel on the French shore. No one who knew anything about ships or their handling would have ordered a collier to take part in the Boulogne blockade, as he complained to Lord Keith. His complaint was forwarded to the Admiralty, where Cochrane imagined it would cause considerable satisfaction.

There was, however, one method of dealing with their Lordships which might still prove effective in getting the *Arab* removed from the Boulogne blockade. The time had come to stage an international incident in the Straits of Dover, choosing the United States as the opposing party. There was a special reason for the choice. The

American ambassador in London, occupying the residence in Wimpole Street, was James Monroe, who had already served as congress-
man, senator, and governor of Virginia. Later and better known as
President Monroe, he had shown strong sympathy with revolutionary France during his period as envoy there and was almost the last
man alive to tolerate interference with American shipping on the
high seas.

By great good fortune, Cochrane was able to manoeuvre the *Arab*
with sufficient speed to intercept the United States merchant ship
*Chatham*, bound from New York to Amsterdam. In his most outrageous manner, he stopped and boarded the *Chatham* in the Dover
Straits. He informed her master, Captain Chur, that there was a
British blockade of the river Texel and that, consequently, the
*Chatham* must turn back. Chur was surprised at the news, which was
natural enough since Cochrane had just invented this particular
"blockade" for his own purposes. Indeed, when the American captain seemed about to ignore the warning and sail on, Cochrane advised him that if he did so he would be sunk. The *Chatham* dropped
anchor in the Downs, and Chur sent an anxious message to Wimpole
Street.

Monroe's enemies found him lacking in certain of the finer intellectual qualities, but he was ideally qualified to blast their Lordships
of the Admiralty with his protests over this outrage. He accused them
of allowing the *Chatham* to be "impeded in her voyage" and her captain to be threatened by Cochrane. "I am led to presume that this is
some mistake," he added, in describing the alleged blockade. The
Admiralty hastily admitted that Cochrane's action was "unauthorised". They had no wish to add an American war to all their existing
commitments. As a general precaution, the *Arab* and her commander
were sent to protect fishing fleets beyond the Orkneys. In these lonely
northern waters, where the collier now patrolled, there were no
prizes, no signs of the enemy, and not even a fishing fleet to protect.
Cochrane's punishment by the Admiralty was by no means over.
For more than a year he endured this "naval exile in a tub, regardless of expense to the nation". Lord St Vincent was content, noting
in Cochrane's case, "not to be trusted out of sight", and adding for
good measure, "mad, romantic, money-getting, and not truth-tell-
ing". Admiral Keith hastened to support the First Lord and, temporarily forgetting the prizes which he had enjoyed through
Cochrane's efforts, reported the young post-captain as "wrong-
headed, violent and proud".[18]

The cruise of the *Arab*, from 5 October 1803 until 1 December 1804 was described by Cochrane as "a blank in my life". It was fortunate for him that political life at Westminster had been somewhat more eventful. William Pitt and Charles James Fox, the two dominating figures of the opposition, had privately agreed to bring down the Addington government. One of the unlikely targets which they chose was Lord St Vincent, the very symbol of the fight against naval corruption. While Pitt led the attack in the House of Commons, newspapers like the *True Briton* and pamphlets such as Francis Blagdon's *Naval Administration: A Letter to the Earl of St Vincent*, accusing him of "incapacity" and "misconduct", maintained a shrill denunciation before the general public. Another of Blagdon's pamphlets, *Audi Alteram Partem*, went further, assuring its readers that St Vincent had paid £3000 out of public funds in an attempt to get the earlier pamphlet suppressed. St Vincent may be an unsympathetic figure but it is only fair to add that when the proposition for suppressing the first pamphlet was put to him, he replied characteristically that he "would not give sixpence to suppress or stop the circulation of that, or of all the pamphlets in the world".[19]

When the renewed war had broken out with France, Addington had tried to induce Pitt to serve under him. Attacked on all sides during the spring of 1804, he gave up the struggle to govern alone and reconciled himself to serving under Pitt. His administration resigned on 10 May 1804, Pitt becoming Prime Minister for the last time in his life. Addington was created Viscount Sidmouth when, in 1805, he became President of the Council in the new ministry. Indeed, Pitt's government contained six of Addington's twelve colleagues who, a few weeks before, had sworn that Pitt was a danger to his country and the curse of its politics. Sheridan, surveying the Treasury Bench across the floor of the Commons, remarked scornfully, "The six new nags will have to draw not only the carriage but those six heavy cast-off blacks along with it."[20]

There was no place for St Vincent in the new administration. He had stirred up too much mud in the murky depths of naval affairs and had been the main target in Pitt's attack on the Addington government. Worse still, libel actions against Blagdon and others had been begun on his behalf by the former ministry. The new Attorney-General was obliged to continue them, thus putting Pitt and his colleagues in the invidious position of prosecuting men who had written at their own instigation while they were in opposition. For St Vincent there could be no hope. He was replaced as First Lord of the Admiralty by Henry Dundas, 1st Viscount Melville, later to be impeached for fraud.

Melville, although over sixty, was described by his acquaintance Joseph Farington the painter as "very hearty & has great spirits. . . . He drank wine liberally". For better or worse, he was a total contrast to the grim figure of St Vincent. Melville disliked formal interviews with officers and conducted virtually all his business by correspondence. "The intercourse I had with Naval Officers was at my *dinner table*." Dinner parties were, for the new First Lord, the prime source of information about the navy and the war. Melville had been a loyal colleague of Pitt, rewarded by simultaneous incomes as Treasurer of the Navy, President of the Board of Control, and other offices. Sheridan suggested that in a time of national crisis, decency required the surrender of at least one sinecure, but Melville could not see it.[21]

The favours shown to him, he showed to others in turn. When the Duke of Hamilton wrote, complaining that one of the most promising Scottish seamen, young Lord Cochrane, was exiled on a collier somewhere between the Orkneys and Greenland, Melville took notice. The Duke, at least, was not a man to be ignored, however much the other members of the Board of Admiralty might wish the exile to continue. When Cochrane returned from fifteen months of desolation, he learnt that Melville had given him a command: the *Pallas*, a new fir-built frigate of thirty-two guns.

The appointment occurred just in time. Though St Vincent was out of office, the work of his Commission continued with the appearance of a 10th Report. Lord Melville was accused of "malversation", as it was quaintly termed, or embezzlement on a grand scale, as Treasurer of the Navy. The crimes alleged against him covered a period as far back as 1782. He was obliged to resign as First Lord and was impeached before the House of Lords on a motion of the Commons. A year later, he was acquitted, though this would have been too late to do Cochrane any good.[22]

The *Pallas* was precisely the "rakish" craft of which he had dreamed. She was 667 tons with thirteen guns in a graceful curving line on each side of her main deck, as well as half a dozen chase-guns. But despite this, there was no rush of volunteers to serve under Cochrane. It was a long time since men had heard of any prizes taken by him and they had no intention of going to sea with a booby who had forgotten that war was, in the first place, a matter of cash. Having no better alternative, Cochrane resorted to the press gang. When two constables got in the way, his men beat them up in a running fight. A summons was issued for Cochrane's arrest on charges of assault. In turn, Cochrane brought an action against the Mayor of Plymouth for assault upon men employed in the King's service. He lost the case.

But when the *Pallas* sailed out of Plymouth on the grey winter sea of 21 January 1805, the mood of the conscripted men began to change. As compensation for his exile in the *Arab*, Melville had allowed Cochrane to cruise for several weeks off the Azores before joining convoy duty in the Atlantic. During those few weeks, the plunder of the trade between Cadiz and the West Indies was to be his for the taking. As the captured vessels, under prize crews from the *Pallas*, dropped anchor in the Hamoaze, the papers reported Cochrane's new wealth with pop-eyed incredulity.

> February 24 – Came in the *Caroline* from Havannah with sugar and logwood, captured off the coast of Spain by the *Pallas*, Captain Lord Cochrane. The *Pallas* was in pursuit of another with a very valuable cargo when the *Caroline* left. . . .

> March 7 – Came in a rich Spanish prize with jewels, gold, silver, ingots, and a valuable cargo, taken by the *Pallas*, Captain Lord Cochrane. Another Spanish ship, the *Fortuna*, from Vera Cruz, has been taken by the *Pallas*, laden with mahogany and logwood. She had 432 000 dollars on board, but has not yet arrived.

> March 23 – Came in a most beautiful letter-of-marque of fourteen guns, said to be a very rich and valuable prize to the *Pallas*, Captain Lord Cochrane.[23]

In warmer waters off the Azores and the Spanish coast, Cochrane was displaying the same mixture of audacity, initiative, and humanity which had characterised his Mediterranean exploits. On 15 February, the *Pallas* captured the Spanish merchantman *Fortuna*, homeward bound for Corunna. In great distress, the rather elderly Spanish captain and his partner came aboard the *Pallas*. Both men had lost everything when their first ship had been taken by a British cruiser in 1779. They had built up their fortunes slowly and were now about to lose them for the second time. Cochrane consulted his officers, who agreed that each of the two men should be handed five thousand dollars of the cargo which the *Fortuna* was carrying. As a matter of democracy, Cochrane then ordered the bosun to pipe all hands. Addressing the crew, he described what had happened and his proposal to return the sums of money to the two elderly Spaniards. By this stage of the voyage, the crew were happy to do whatever their golden-fingered commander suggested. They shouted, "Aye, aye, my lord. With all our hearts," and roared out three cheers for their captives.[24]

Not all the prizes were brought home. On one captured ship Cochrane found some promising bales, which when cut open contained merely a collection of Papal bulls, destined for what he called "the Mexican sin market". They consisted of dispensations for eating meat on Fridays and "indulgences for peccadilloes of all kinds with the price affixed". Supply had exceeded demand, however, and they were being returned to Spain. Since there would be still less demand for them in the sin markets of England, Cochrane ordered his men to throw them overboard.[25]

By the end of March, the *Pallas* had sent home four captured vessels with prize crews on board and was herself heavily weighed down by plunder. As the laden frigate prepared to turn for home the sea off the Azores was covered by a low heat-mist, the mastheads of the *Pallas* standing clear of it. Though Cochrane could see nothing from the quarterdeck, the look-out suddenly called out, reporting the maintopgallant masts of three ships of the line closing upon the *Pallas*. Cochrane altered course immediately but, as he strained to make out the shapes of the approaching battleships through the bright dazzle of the haze he identified them clearly as French. The weeks of happy plundering had come to an end.

The situation was closely akin to the ultimate fate of the *Speedy*. While it was true that the *Pallas* was a frigate rather than a brig, she was no match for a battleship, let alone for three. Moreover, as she altered course, the wind freshened and a heavy sea began to run. The ports were closed across her main-deck guns, which were otherwise under water, and even the guns of the quarterdeck, where Cochrane stood, dipped into the waves as the frigate heeled over in the rising sea. The heavy surges also made it impossible for the three battleships to use their guns at this stage, but they were coming up fast on the *Pallas*.

To hoist more sail in the face of the storm was contrary to most rules of safety, but it was Cochrane's only chance of getting clear. He ordered the *Pallas*'s hawsers to be got to the mastheads and hove taut, securing the masts as firmly as possible, and then for every stitch of canvas to be spread. The lumbering frigate ploughed into the sea which burst in plumes of spray over her bows as the forecastle plunged underwater and sent the waves sluicing back along the deck as it rose again. But still the battleships were gaining and, looking back, Cochrane logged several yellow flashes of the priming pans as the French gunners tried unavailingly to get a steady aim at their target.

Until there was a lull in the storm, it would be difficult for the French to take advantage of their broadsides, but the battleships drew level with the *Pallas* one on either bow at a distance of less than half a mile, while the third was more remote. Their guns were in position and they had only to wait for the sea to grow calmer in order to confront Cochrane with the choice of annihilation or surrender. For the time being, the storm was Cochrane's ally as the four ships plunged along with sails taut under the full force of the gale. In the two months of the cruise he had trained his men to perfection to do things which some of them saw little use in. He now ordered them to man the rigging and, at a given signal, to haul down every sail at precisely the same moment. As he gave the signal, the helm of the *Pallas* was to be put hard over and the frigate turned across the path of the storm. The effect of this manoeuvre, and of the lowering of sails, was that she was "suddenly brought up" and, as Cochrane felt, "shook from stem to stern".

The three French battleships, with the wind in their sails, shot past at full speed, quite unprepared for anything of this kind. Indeed, they were several miles farther on before they could shorten sail or trim on the opposite tack. Meanwhile it was the *Pallas* which spread full sail and again set off in the opposite direction at a speed of more than thirteen knots. But the French captains brought their ships round at last and the chase was resumed grimly. They pursued the frigate for the remainder of the day and the night that followed. But the history of the *Speedy* was destined to be repeated, in one respect at least. As dawn broke, the three great ships found themselves closing in on a ballasted cask with a lantern bobbing upon it. All around them otherwise, there stretched a vast and empty sea.[26]

On 3 April, in the Western Approaches, the *Pallas* was sighted by H.M.S. *Brilliant* making for Plymouth under full sail. Two days later, as the citizens lined the Hamoaze to satisfy their curiosity, she sailed gracefully in and dropped anchor. As a symbol of victory, and of Cochrane's innate sense of showmanship, three captured candlesticks had been lashed triumphantly to the masthead of the *Pallas*. They were each five feet tall and made of solid gold.

Cochrane never needed a press gang again. His own share of the prize money from the cruise of the *Pallas* was said to have been £75,000. If this was the case, even the humblest and most reluctant member of the crew was now likely to have more money in his pocket than he had ever seen in his life before. But there was, as usual, bitterness over Cochrane's rewards. Sir William Young, the admiral commanding at Plymouth, was awarded half of Cochrane's prize money, on the grounds that he had copied out the orders for the sailing of the *Pallas* after they had come from the Admiralty. He was thus technically in command of the operation.[27]

Cochrane's anger was kept private for the time being, since he wanted a rapid favour from Admiral Young, leave of absence to stand as a parliamentary candidate in the coming election. One moving spirit in the matter was his scapegrace uncle, Andrew Cochrane-Johnstone, who had frequent occasion to record such journeys as, "On my return to town yesterday, from a visit to my nephew, Lord Cochrane, at Plymouth . . ." Cochrane-Johnstone had already bought his seat in parliament for the rotten borough of Grampound, thus enjoying immunity from arrest for his habitual refusal to pay his creditors. But two Members of Parliament in the family would offer opportunities for financial adventure beyond even his dreams.[28]

Cochrane saw the matter differently. The man who precipitated him into active politics was William Cobbett, the stalwart farmer's son, ex-sergeant-major, and former enemy of revolution who had now turned against the corruption of parliamentary life. Cobbett appealed for an honest man to contest the most corrupt borough in England at the coming election. The borough was Honiton and the man who answered the appeal was Cochrane. The challenge of the impossible was no less invigorating, in its way, than when the *Speedy* had engaged the *Gamo*.

Cochrane-Johnstone went to the Admiralty to press for his nephew's leave of absence. Apart from the election there was the matter of what Cobbett euphemistically described as "some business between them", by which the uncle no doubt hoped to induce his nephew to invest part of the prize money in certain "speculations". The three unlikely campaigners in Honiton were, therefore, Cochrane, his devious uncle, and the forthright Radical hero, William Cobbett.[29]

The *Gamo* had been easy by comparison. Honitonians regarded their votes as part of their property. A man who wanted them must pay the price. They accused Cobbett and Cochrane of trying to bankrupt them by destroying the system of electoral bribery. "They tell you," Cobbett reported, "flatly and plainly, that the money, which they obtain for their votes, is absolutely necessary to enable them to live; that, without it, they could not *pay their rents*; and that, from election to election, the poor men run up scores at the shops, and are trusted by the shopkeepers *expressly upon the credit of the proceeds of the ensuing election*." They assured him that he and Cochrane "had their *hearts*", but that the ministerial candidate, Bradshaw, who was paying five guineas a time, had their votes.[30]

Cochrane left Plymouth and arrived in Honiton on 8 June 1805 for the election hustings. The *Naval Chronicle* approved of his arrival "in a true seaman-like style, accompanied by two lieutenants and one midshipman in full dress, in one carriage . . . followed by another, containing the boat's crew, new rigged and prepared for action". On the platform, amid rival flags and bunting, he was supported by Cobbett and Cochrane-Johnstone.[31]

The hustings seemed more like a fair or market while the ministerial candidate, Cavendish Bradshaw, addressed the crowd. Under flat, farmers' hats, the rubicund faces of the electors shone with well-fed enthusiasm. Among these voters and their wives in summer dresses and bonnets, moved the boat's crew of the *Pallas* and a horde of unenfranchised rustics eager for the fun. Bradshaw spoke briefly and was heard with the respect due to a candidate who paid his way. The crowd cheered dutifully as he sat down.

When Cochrane rose, tall and impressive in his captain's royal blue and gold, the voters waited to see what he could offer them. They heard a cool, restrained speech against naval corruption. Some began to shift impatiently. Voices urged him to "spend his money sailor-fashion". He replied that he would stand "on patriotic principles", and there was shocked silence. Patriotism was appealed to like this by men who were not prepared to pay their way. The hecklers reminded him that he could not take a man's vote for nothing, any more than he would expect to take his cattle or barley.[32]

There was a welcome diversion when Cochrane sat down, and Bradshaw and Cobbett got up, shouting abuse at one another. Whether it was the boat's crew of the *Pallas* or Bradshaw's men who struck the first blow, the excitement spread, the crowd erupting as a struggling, brawling mob. In this Hogarthian mêlée, men who were first aboard enemy ships gave a good account of themselves in the streets of Honiton. While Bradshaw and Cobbett bawled their insults, the words "windbag" and "libeller" clear above the tumult, Cochrane rose and roared at his men for order. But when peace was restored, the hustings were deserted, the bunting trampled, the political debate over. Cochrane was urged to canvass "independent voters", but it was a discouraging process. One such independent soul grinned up eagerly at him, when approached, and whispered, "You need not ask me, my lord, who I votes for. I always votes for Mister Most." When reproached for such cynicism, the Honitonians replied that Members of Parliament "took care to get *well-paid*", and the voters "had a right to do the same if they could". But while they reprimanded Cochrane, the electors jeered Cobbett, adapting the cry, "Bread and cheese, and no empty cupboard", so that the streets of Honiton echoed to, "Bread and cheese, and *no empty Cobbett!*"[33]

It is a tribute to Cochrane's personal appeal that, though he lost, some people actually voted for him. The rest took their five guineas from Bradshaw and elected him. But after this, a crier appeared in the streets, ringing his handbell and chanting, "All those who voted for Lord Cochrane may repair to his agent, J. Townshend, Esquire, and receive ten pounds ten." The ballot was not secret and the names of these voters were known. Bradshaw's supporters were dumbfounded. To bribe one's men beforehand was common enough: to reward men afterwards, without warning, was another matter. Worse still, Bradshaw's voters had actually lost money by electing him.[34]

The young man whom the electors had dismissed as a political simpleton drove out of Honiton on the Plymouth road. He left behind him a constituency in which even the most corrupt men now felt that they had, somehow, had the worst of the encounter.

Some, of course, comforted themselves by regarding his Quixotic gesture as a mere spiting of enemies. They were wrong. It was part of a calculated strategy to set him at the centre of British politics. As the *Pallas* put to sea again, and he reflected on the lessons of the campaign, his reforming zeal in respect of the Royal Navy grew to embrace the entire political and electoral system of Great Britain. He decided to stand for parliament again at the next opportunity, as an "independent" candidate and a sympathiser with parliamentary reform.

During the rest of 1805, the *Pallas* was assigned to convoy duty between Portsmouth and Quebec. On the first crossing, it was discovered that during the Honiton election someone in the dockyard had removed the valuable copper bolts securing the ship's compass and had replaced them with iron. In consequence, the compass would never work accurately and the *Pallas* owed her escape from disaster to a sudden clearing of fog on the Canadian coast. On the long weeks of the crossing Cochrane also had ample experience of the difficulties of keeping a convoy together. The frigate displayed a lamp at night for the other ships to follow but merchant captains preferred to rely on the blaze of light in the stern windows of other vessels ahead of them. This led to confusion from time to time as some of the slower, laden merchantmen got the wrong course and were separated from the convoy.[35]

Cochrane had devised a powerful and distinctive convoy lamp which would shine like a beacon from the frigate and guide the convoy by its unambiguous glare. He offered the idea to the Admiralty who rejected it. Soon afterwards, however, their Lordships announced a competition with a prize of fifty pounds for the best design for such a convoy lamp. Knowing that it would be useless to enter the idea under his own name, Cochrane persuaded his agent, Brooks, to put it forward as his own entry. It won the competition. With some satisfaction, its inventor then revealed his true identity. In consequence, he wrote, "not a lamp was ever ordered, and the merchantmen were left to the mercy of the privateers as before". Lord St Vincent might have gone, but Cochrane recognised that his true enemies were the "administrative powers of the Admiralty". These were the secretaries and the civil servants, the placemen and their hirelings, who survived wars and treaties, ministers and changes of government, alike. They had recognised their adversary from the start and were assiduously plotting his downfall.[36]

By the time that Cochrane returned from convoy duty at the end of the year, Trafalgar was over and the great pageant of Nelson's burial was in preparation. Napoleon, having failed to gain command of the Dover straits for the necessary six hours had turned to the conquest of Austria. His success at Ulm, despite the British victory at Trafalgar, had proved a final insupportable blow to Pitt. His face a sickly yellow and haggard by mortal illness, the great Prime Minister had entered the last weeks of his life.

In the new year of 1806, the *Pallas* under Cochrane's command was sent with Admiral Thornborough's squadron to patrol the Bay of Biscay. This assignment was intended to keep him as much under the control of his superiors as possible. Happily, the Admiralty's intentions were frustrated by Thornborough who, knowing that he would have a half-share in all Cochrane's prizes, gave the *Pallas* considerable freedom. The frigate now boasted a special weapon, devised by her captain. This was an 18-oar galley, designed by Cochrane and built for him by the Deal boatbuilders at his own expense. When lowered for action, this craft had a formidable turn of speed and was, of course, not dependent on favourable winds.

The first nuisance-raids of the *Pallas* were among the islands of the Biscay coast between Les Sables d'Olonne and La Rochelle. The French fishing fleets were rounded up and boarded. Since the fishermen were poor and he had no quarrel with them, Cochrane allowed them to keep their boats but insisted on taking their catch so that it should not reach the hands, and stomachs, of England's enemies. However, he paid them the cost of the fish out of his own pocket.

Moving inshore, towards the port of Les Sables, he ordered out the galley and took a French merchantman loaded with casks of wine, which were gratefully received aboard the *Pallas*. By this time, the rumours of his activities had spread along the coast of the Vendée, so that at the first sight of the frigate and her galley, French merchant captains ran their ships on to the sandy beaches and abandoned them, to avoid being captured. Cochrane sent his men after them, carrying the war literally on to enemy soil. With two prize vessels already accompanying him, he noticed a brig anchored just off the harbour mouth of Les Sables. The boats of the *Pallas* were lowered and made towards the prize under the very eyes of the local inhabitants on the harbour mole. It was growing dark but the Sablais and their local militia ran for their muskets and opened fire on the boats of the *Pallas*. Cochrane gave an order from the quarterdeck and there was a long flicker of flame, as the first broadside thundered from the open ports. The shells burst widely in the town and the local musketeers, accepting the inevitable, ceased fire. Cochrane remained off the town all night, bringing the *Pallas* inshore the next morning to collect another brig which had been run on the sands near the mole. There was nothing for it but to send the boat crew ashore to bring her off. Once again the Sablais assembled but a single shot from the *Pallas*, booming across the surf, was enough to dissuade them from action. The men of the frigate landed and brought off their new prize while the citizens, whose armed republic was supposed to be the terror of Europe, watched with sheepish self-consciousness.[37]

The prizes of March 1806 were not in themselves of much consequence, but Cochrane's value in terms of propaganda was incalcul-

able. News of his raids was briefly and rarely reported in England
but the effect of them in France was significant. Paris might echo
to the triumphs of Ulm and Austerlitz, the battle honours of Wagram
and Jena might embellish the standards of Napoleon's legions, but
on the Biscay coast men wondered why it was, if France was the
conqueror of Europe, that their coastal trade was mercilessly harried
and that along the sandy beaches of the Vendée merchant captains
ran their vessels ashore indiscriminately at the sight of a solitary
frigate and her fast-moving galley.

Sooner or later the French Navy must intervene to protect commerce. Cochrane had no intention of avoiding such an encounter.
Indeed, it seemed to him entirely appropriate to crown months of
prize-taking by victory in a sea fight. On 29 March 1806, he delivered
to Admiral Thornborough some of the captured wine "of fine quality,
on its way to Havre for the Parisian market". Thornborough then
despatched the *Pallas* in pursuit of another French convoy. Having
captured one of its ships, Cochrane sailed into the mouth of the
Gironde, the long river estuary of Bordeaux. It was reported that
several French corvettes were stationed near the mouth of the
Gironde as a first line of defence for the great city against an attack
from the sea. The corvettes were smaller than the *Pallas* but three or
four of them ought to have been more than a match for her.

On the night of 5 April 1806, Cochrane dropped anchor off the
Cordouan lighthouse, several miles out to sea from the fortress of
Royan and Fort du Verdon, on either side of the river's mouth. He
was aided by a thick fog which helped to conceal the *Pallas*, while
the light of Cordouan acted as his guide. The frigate's boats, including Cochrane's patent galley, were lowered, requiring so many sailors
to man them that only forty out of the crew of 220 were left on board.
Cochrane was obliged to remain with the *Pallas* but the boats, under
the command of First Lieutenant John Haswell, dipped their oars
and cut the cold Biscay swell. Presently, they faded into the darkness
and the fog which shrouded the estuary several miles away.

At 3 a.m. on an uneventful night, anchored almost within the
river system of France, the men of the watch on the corvette *Tapageuse*, duty guard-ship in the mouth of the Gironde, were puzzled by
a gentle bumping alongside, a sudden scrambling of men, and the
appearance of armed British sailors and a detachment of marines in
scarlet and white. The *Tapageuse* was roused in an instant, men
clambering up from the lower deck to join the confused fight. Resistance was fierce but brief and those who were not quick enough to

jump and swim for the shore soon found themselves prisoners of
Lieutenant Haswell and his men. Two French corvettes, realising at
last what had happened, put out to rescue the *Tapageuse*. But the
prize crew had too great a start and, adding injury to insult, the men
of the *Pallas* were already working the guns of the corvette, the
broadsides flaring through the fog. The pursuers fell back and the
*Tapageuse* sailed in darkness and stealth under the guns of Royan
and gained the open sea.

By this time, a general alarm had been raised. It was to be some
time before the captured corvette could rendezvous with the *Pallas*,
and Cochrane's ship was, in all theory, defenceless so long as he had
no more than forty men on board. Indeed, as the sea began to lighten
in the early dawn it seemed that the one disaster which had always
threatened his plan was about to occur. Three sails appeared to
windward, bearing down on his undermanned ship. He signalled
them in the current Admiralty code, hoping that they might be
from Admiral Thornborough's squadron. The signals were unanswered and the ships, being to windward, closed rapidly on the frigate. They were French corvettes, none of them as large as the *Pallas*
but carrying forty or fifty guns between them, against her thirty-
two, and over three hundred men against Cochrane's forty. The
situation was actually worse than this, since though the *Pallas*
had thirty-two guns, there were no crews to man thirty of them at
all.

The *Pallas* was riding at anchor with sails furled. Cochrane ordered
all his men aloft with instructions to fasten the furled sails with rope
yarn and undo the ropes by which they were normally reefed. The
canvas thus remained furled by the extra ropes which had been
used. At a given signal, the men were to cut through the rope so that
the sails billowed out in a sudden cloud, a manoeuvre which would
require the entire crew if it had been carried out in the orthodox
manner. The captains of the French corvettes concluded that the
sudden spread of canvas indicated "a numerous and highly discip-
lined crew" on board the frigate. "The manoeuvre," Cochrane recorded, "succeeded to a marvel." The three corvettes, believing that
they were sailing into a trap, turned about and began to head along
the shore. The *Pallas* set off in pursuit, her two chase-guns in the
bows firing at the fleeing enemy. Had the French captains only known
it, the two chase-guns were the only ones for which Cochrane had
gun crews. The *Pallas* was otherwise defenceless.

The nearest of the corvettes, desperate to escape, ran ashore on the sandy coast, the captain and crew hastily abandoning their vessel. Cochrane allowed them to get clear and then crippled her with his chase-guns, ensuring that she would never float off with the tide. Running up the British ensign for the first time in the engagement, he then closed on the second corvette which also ran ashore, dismasting herself in the process, and was abandoned and destroyed. The third corvette sailed out of range while Cochrane was disposing of the second. Indeed, he had no more leisure to spend in the action, since he was shortly due to rendezvous with the *Tapageuse* and her prize crew off the Cordouan lighthouse. As he approached the lighthouse, he found himself quite by chance on a course to intercept the third corvette which had escaped out to sea and was now circling back in as she attempted to reach the Gironde. At the sight of the *Pallas*, the captain of the corvette ran his ship aground as well, allowing her to be destroyed as the others had been. Cochrane collected the *Tapageuse* and her captors, as well as an entire crew of French prisoners who were shortly transferred to Admiral Thornborough's ships. Before Cochrane's arrival off the mouth of the Gironde, the waterway to Bordeaux had been defended by six corvettes. But twelve hours later, three of these had been destroyed and one captured, while the defences of one of the great cities of France had been thrown into alarm and disarray.[38]

News of Cochrane's raids on the Biscay coast reached Napoleon, embroiled in his eastern campaign against Austria, Prussia, and the Czar. He recognised the man and the tactics, knowing of Cochrane from the *Gamo* incident and a number of other Mediterranean exploits. The great Consul listened to the catalogue of disasters, and then he bestowed that soubriquet which, like so many of its kind, was part insult and part grudging flattery. "Le loup des mers!"[39]

Sea wolf or not, Cochrane's reputation as a prize-taker reached new heights in Plymouth and Portsmouth. As he came ashore from the *Pallas* there was a new audacity and self-confidence in his dealings with friend and foe alike. He never needed a press gang again to fill the vacancies on his ship. It was enough to placard the dockyard walls with his simple message "WANTED. Stout, able-bodied men who can run a mile without stopping with a sackful of Spanish dollars on their backs."[40]

The Board of Admiralty and its civil servants were unimpressed by Cochrane's exploits in the Gironde. Alone among the prizes of the squadron, the *Tapageuse* was not bought for the navy and no prize money was allowed for her. There was, of course, the consolation of the captured merchantmen and their contents. Moreover, on the voyage home, the *Pallas* had attacked, grounded, rammed, and disabled a French frigate, with such vigour that Cochrane's ship itself had to be towed away by the *Kingfisher*. He also led his marines on to the Ile de Ré, drove off a hundred French militia, destroyed the signal station and blew up the artillery battery. Though Cochrane was no favourite of St Vincent's, the latter acknowledged Thornborough's despatches and added that the deeds of the *Pallas* "reflect very high honour on her captain, officers, and crew, and call for my warmest approbation". Apart from this, it was left to the press and the public, rather than to the Admiralty, to acknowledge the valour of Cochrane and his men.[41]

Reflecting the fame of the *Pallas*, matters seemed more promising in respect of Cochrane's political career. With the death of Pitt in January 1806, the "All-the-Talents" coalition of the Whigs with some Tory support was formed by Grenville. Soon the shining talent of Charles James Fox, was also extinguished. In October, there was a further general election. Cochrane returned to the scene of his previous defeat at Honiton.

If he felt intimidated by his opponent's triumph in the Honiton election of the previous year, his entry into the town in October 1806 certainly showed no sign of it. He drove into the main street in a smart carriage, known as a vis-à-vis, drawn by six fine horses. Behind him came a procession of carriages-and-four filled with officers and seamen of the *Pallas* who were once again the eager volunteers in his election campaign. Those citizens who had supported him before were ready to do so again, but his victory would depend on some of Cavendish Bradshaw's paid voters changing sides. His appearance and demeanour were such, however, that even these political realists did not yet dare to raise the question of a bribe with him.

When the polls opened, no man could predict the outcome. Many of the voters who were up for hire seemed strongly tempted to settle for Bradshaw's five guineas and give him their vote. On the other hand, they were tormented by the knowledge that they had lost ten guineas in the last election by doing so. Some of these civic heroes succumbed to greed and some yielded to discretion, remaining with Bradshaw. But when the final day of polling arrived and the result was announced, more than enough of them had taken a chance on Cochrane's generosity to make him the winner of the contest and Member of Parliament for Honiton. Among the jubilation of the

*Pallas*'s crew and the carnival of celebration in the streets of the little town, Cochrane was approached by the same smiling faces who had assured him in the last election that they always "votes for Mr Most". They had come for their ten guineas.

"Not one farthing!" said the tall uniformed post-captain disdainfully.

"But, my lord, you gave ten guineas a head to the minority at the last election, and the majority have been calculating on something handsome on the present occasion."

"No doubt," said Cochrane coolly. "The former gift was for their disinterested conduct in not taking the bribe of five pounds from the agents of my opponent. For me now to pay them would be a violation of my own previously expressed principles."

The smiling, hopeful faces assumed an air of affronted dignity. For a man who had just been elected to parliament to start talking about "principles" was sickening enough. But Cochrane had done the almost unheard of thing of getting himself elected without either bribery or an influential patron. The cost of rewarding his supporters on the first occasion was less than it would have cost him in bribes so that, financially and morally, he had outmanoeuvred his opponents. But, worst of all, he had triumphed at the expense of the voters in one of the most corrupt boroughs of England. The Honitonians already felt an uneasy suspicion that when the story spread, they would be a political laughing-stock. It might be many years before they could command the fat prices for their votes which they had enjoyed before the advent of Cochrane.[42]

The men of the borough took such small revenge as lay in their power. Of course Cochrane would never be returned for Honiton again but, for the time being, they were content to persuade him that the least he could do would be to give a dinner for those who had elected him. To this he agreed. When the dinner took place, the electors brought their wives, relations, and friends, who included those who had voted for Cavendish Bradshaw. The dinner was "converted into a public treat", the entire borough eating and drinking itself into a stupor at the victor's expense. When the evening was over, Cochrane was presented with a bill for £1200. He refused to pay it and the money was eventually extracted from him, some years later, after a good deal of unpleasant litigation. For the time being, he was content to shake the dust of Honiton off his feet and prepare for battle in the House of Commons.[43]

The Board of Admiralty and its civil servants learnt with dismay that Cochrane had succeeded in defeating the ministerial candidate at Honiton. Before they could recover themselves, he had set himself up in lodgings at Old Palace Yard, Westminster, and had opened the attack. A letter arrived for the attention of the Commissioners of the Admiralty on the subject of their refusal to promote the gallant Lieutenant Parker of the *Speedy* and Lieutenant Haswell, who had captured the *Tapageuse* in the Gironde. In Haswell's case, the Admiralty had denied him a right to prize money as well as promotion. The Secretary to the Admiralty board replied evasively, whereupon Cochrane delivered a sharp reminder. He informed the Secretary that if there were any more prevarication over the promotion of the two lieutenants, "it would be my duty to bring before the House of Commons a partiality so detrimental to the interests of the navy".[44]

Much as they might detest Cochrane, the men of the Admiralty were obliged to consider that he now entered the Commons as the hero of the Mediterranean and Biscay. It would be necessary to fight him sooner or later, but perhaps not over so small a matter as this. After five years of repeated refusal, their Lordships promoted Parker to the rank of commander and bestowed the same seniority on Haswell.

Cochrane made no formal complaint about the injustice done to himself and his crew after the latest cruise of the *Pallas*. Most of the prize money due to the frigate depended on the Bordeaux wine seized from *chasse-marées* in the spring of 1806. But before the wine could even be brought ashore at Plymouth, customs officers boarded the *Pallas* to assess the duty on the cargo. The price offered to Cochrane for the wine was actually less than the duty which the authorities proposed to charge on it. In vain, he offered the wine, which was finest claret, to the Victualling Board, in order that it might be served out to the men of the fleet in place of beer. The Admiralty declined his offer of the gift. Determined that he and his men would not surrender the value of the prize for which they had fought so hard, Cochrane ordered that the bungs should be knocked out of the casks and the wine emptied overboard into Plymouth harbour.

Seven pipes of the claret were spared, Cochrane arranging to pay duty on these and forward them to the cellars of his uncle, Basil Cochrane, late of the East India Company and now of Portman Square, in the fashionable residential area just north of Oxford Street. Following his election to Parliament, Cochrane drew on this supply for the dinners which he gave at his lodgings in Old Palace Yard.

One of his guests was a clean-shaven young man with dark, receding hair, full face, and cold appraising eyes. The deceptive softness of his gaze concealed the calculating and keen intelligence of John Wilson Croker. The election of 1806 had given the Whigs a majority in the House of Commons, and Croker, as a Tory, had little to hope for. His malice as a literary reviewer was such that he went down in the history of English poetry as the man who killed John Keats, while Macaulay vowed that he detested Croker more than "cold boiled mutton".

However, Croker showed an evident interest in naval affairs and Cochrane was only too glad to inform him of the abuses which bedevilled the efficient conduct of the war against France. Croker listened, sipped his wine, and remarked softly, "Superb claret." Cochrane continued to expound the problems of the war against France. Croker listened and then asked him if he would be so good as to let him have some of the excellent Bordeaux. Cochrane promised that he should have as much as he liked for no more than the cost of duty and bottling. Then the host returned eagerly to the discussion of naval affairs.

In the spring of 1807, George III demanded an assurance from the Whig leaders that they would not press the issue of Catholic emancipation. They refused to give the pledge and were duly dismissed. The Tories, under the Duke of Portland, came in and confirmed their position by winning yet another general election a few months later. Now that his party was in power, Croker kept clear of Cochrane's dinner table. Shortly afterwards, the two men met in Whitehall, Cochrane amiable and talkative, Croker smooth and reserved. Despite their party difference, Cochrane thought they had interests in common. Croker remained cool and evasive. Cochrane inquired when Croker proposed to collect the "superb claret" which awaited him. Croker turned his pale face and cold eyes on the young captain. "Why, really," he said, "I have no use for it, my friends having supplied me more liberally than I have occasion for!"[45]

The calculated insolence, with which Croker announced that Cochrane was henceforth not a friend of his, infuriated his companion. Cochrane had hardly time to congratulate him ironically on his new-found patrons and the quality of their wine when Croker turned on his heel and walked away, the hungry placeman whose enemies described his Irish origin as "of low birth" and the man himself as having "no principles". Chief among his new friends and patrons was the Wellesley family. It was his assiduous service to them which was to win him the appointment of First Secretary to the Admiralty in 1810, in succession to Wellington's brother. He was an implacable agent of official reprisals against Cochrane. Among those shadowy figures who made up the office of the Admiralty was another of Cochrane's acquaintances, the young Lord Palmerston. Palmerston had devoted himself consistently to politics and parliament since he and Cochrane studied under Dugald Stewart at Edinburgh. But unlike most of Stewart's pupils, Palmerston had embraced the Tory cause. He was rewarded in April 1807 when Portland appointed him a junior Lord of the Admiralty at the age of twenty-two.[46]

As for parliament itself, the House of Commons was not due to begin the business of the new government until after Christmas. Autumn sittings were still unpopular and, as late as 1820, on the famous occasion of the Queen's trial, Creevey reported the "rage" of the House of Lords at being compelled to attend in October. "It interferes with everything – pheasant shooting, Newmarket, &c., &c." But when the new year came, there was still to be no chance for Cochrane to make his mark in the House of Commons. Instead, there came the demand from George III that the Whig government should not attempt to restore civil rights to Catholics. Once he had dismissed them from office, in favour of the minority Tory party, there was no means of continuing parliamentary business effectively until yet another election had been held. Before it took place, the Admiralty tried to remove Cochrane from parliamentary politics by ordering him to sea again.[47]

The new command was the frigate *Imperieuse*, whose captain he was to be for three years. Carrying thirty-eight guns, she had been the Spanish warship *Medea* until captured by the Royal Navy in 1804. Larger and faster than the *Pallas*, she was 1046 tons, carrying three hundred men who included thirty-five Royal Marines. Most of the *Pallas*'s crew transferred to her, with one new arrival whose popular fame was to eclipse even that of Cochrane. He was a young midshipman, Frederick Marryat, who was to be the celebrated novelist Captain Marryat.

Marryat kept a private journal of life on the *Imperieuse*, confirming much that Cochrane independently recorded, and also assessing his commander's character. Cochrane ruled by the degree of discipline needed for the safety of his ship in war. He was not morally opposed to hanging or flogging. The log of the *Imperieuse* shows, for example, one sentence of thirty-six lashes for drunkenness carried out on 7

January 1809, and three of twelve lashes each for "negligence". However, these are to be compared with the homicidal military discipline of a thousand lashes against which Cobbett and others were campaigning. To his contemporaries, Cochrane's true humanity was in never sacrificing his men to his own glory. "I never knew any one so careful of the lives of his ship's company as Lord Cochrane," Marryat wrote, "or any one who calculated so closely the risks attending any expedition. Many of the most brilliant achievements were performed without the loss of a single life, so well did he calculate the chances; and one half the merit which he deserves for what he did accomplish has never been awarded him, merely because, in the official despatches there has not been a long list of killed and wounded to please the appetite of the English public."[48]

On occasion, Cochrane subordinated sentiment to seamanship to a degree which surprised the young Marryat. During a gale, one of the marines on the deck of the *Imperieuse* was swept overboard and carried out of reach of any rope which might be thrown. But the men on the deck of the frigate could see him, his head rising with each wave and they began instinctively to lower a boat. Before they could complete the lowering, Cochrane saw them and shouted from the quarterdeck, "Hold fast!" The men stopped and watched the marine being carried further and deeper into the storm. Cochrane walked forward from the quarterdeck, obviously distressed and muttering to himself, "Poor fellow!" The drowning man at last raised his hands and then disappeared under the waves. Marryat and some of the others were dismayed that Cochrane had called back the willing rescuers. It was the master's mate, the Hon. William Napier, cousin to the assorted and illustrious Napiers of Victoria's reign, who took Marryat aside and explained what had happened. Napier had considerable experience of ships' boats in various weather conditions. He knew, and Cochrane knew better, that to have lowered the boat in such a sea would have meant the loss of a score of lives instead of one. What they witnessed was one of the infinite human tragedies at sea, in the face of which men were almost powerless to aid one another.[49]

In the case of the *Imperieuse*, the Admiralty and its flag officers seemed determined to augment these tragedies as soon as possible. On 17 November 1806, the frigate was lying half-laden at Plymouth. Indeed, her rudder was being adjusted and was still not hung in position properly. However, Cochrane received an order via Admiral Young, the port commander, that he was to put to sea at once.

Protests against such impossibilities were unavailing. Work on the
rudder was quickly completed and the *Imperieuse* sailed with a
lighter carrying provisions lashed to one side, a second lighter carrying ordnance stores lashed to the other, and a third lighter, filled with
the ship's gunpowder, being towed astern. Worst of all, no delay had
been permitted in order that the guns should be made fast and the
quarterdeck carronades mounted on their slides. In the event of a
storm, the savage weight of the bronze cannon might have been sent
crashing from one side of the ship to the other.

Cochrane's attempt to delay the sailing of his ship in this condition
had been answered, in Marryat's account, by the admiral enforcing
the order by firing "gun after gun" as the signal that he must put to
sea at once. There was no reason for this, no emergency which required the *Imperieuse* to guard the Western Approaches within the
next few hours, the enforcement was merely a matter of satisfying
the Admiralty.

As soon as the frigate was out of sight of land, Cochrane gave the
order to heave to while the loading was completed and the guns
secured. The gunpowder was the last thing to be brought on board
and, as Cochrane remarked, if a French warship had approached at
this point, she could have taken the *Imperieuse* with little difficulty.
"We could not have fired a shot in return," he noted bitterly.[50]

Though the rigging was not properly set, the frigate was otherwise
now in a state to proceed. The weather closed in and the sea began to
rise under a freshening breeze. Then, with the rigging set and sails
shortened, the *Imperieuse* struggled towards the mouth of the Channel on her way to the Biscay hunting grounds. The cloud was thick
and it was impossible to judge her exact position from observation.
Of course, she must have drifted some distance while hove to, but the
compass was enough to take her clear of any danger.

The night of 19 November was "so dark that you could not dis-
tinguish any object, however close," Marryat recorded. Worse still,
the storm had risen to a full gale, the wind squealing and snapping
at rigging and canvas. Just before dawn, the ship's company were still
asleep on the lower deck when they were almost hurled from their
hammocks by a series of violent shocks and there was a loud grating
and rending sound. Courageous though they might be, there was a cry
of terror from the men, in the certain knowledge that the frigate had
struck rocks, far from help and in a murderous sea.

Midshipman Marryat was in his berth, deep in the ship's hull where
he and his companions shared the orlop deck with the closely-

packed hammocks of the crew. In his journal he noted down the
sights and sounds as the frigate hit the rocks.

> The cry of terror which ran through the lower decks; the grating
> of the keel as she was forced in; the violence of the shocks which
> convulsed the frame of the vessel; the hurrying up of the ship's
> company without their clothes; and then the enormous waves
> which again bore her up. . . . will never be effaced from my
> memory.[51]

As the half-dressed or naked men scrambled out on to the deck in
the light of the winter dawn, the largest wave of all drove into the
stern of the frigate and, as Marryat and the others felt, "carried her
clean over the reef". The grating of the timbers on rocks as she was
driven forward rang hideously above the storm, but at least she was
in deeper water and Cochrane at once ordered the lowering of the
anchors. The *Imperieuse* was now "surrounded by rocks, some of
them as high out of the water as her lower yards and close to her".
She was miles off course, trapped by the notorious rocks off Ushant.[52]

There was no leisure to investigate the error in navigation until
later. Cochrane ordered the ship's carpenter to survey the hull and
see what damage had been done. It soon appeared that the vessel
and her crew had been luckier than anyone dared to hope. The impact
of the rock had been taken by the false keel, which had been torn off
in the collision, but the hull itself was sound. The company of the
*Imperieuse* escaped death by the very narrowest of margins.

The immediate danger was past, since the frigate was now held in
deeper water by three anchors, but the only way out was through the
rocks by which she was surrounded. It was a painstaking business as
Cochrane took the frigate forward, yard by yard, the leadsman in the
bows singing out the depth by his line. Not until 3 p.m. that afternoon was the *Imperieuse* clear of the reefs.

Even though it had been impossible to determine the distance
which the frigate might have drifted while hove to, or to check
her position by observation, no captain would have risked steering a
course likely to bring him within the rocks of Ushant, the most
notorious and carefully-avoided hazard of its sort. How had it
happened? A careful examination revealed the answer. Iron round
the compass binnacle, which had taken the *Pallas* off course during
convoy duty, had nearly destroyed the *Imperieuse*. The compass had
not been accurate within 30 degrees and Cochrane was completely
deceived as to his position.[53]

He signalled the Admiralty, asking that he should be court-
martialled for hazarding his ship. He did not, of course, believe that
he had done any such thing but he longed for some court of inquiry
at which the conduct of the Admiralty itself, and Sir William Young
as their representative at Plymouth, could be brought under public
scrutiny. Young Frederick Marryat had already given his opinion
on the escape of the frigate. "How nearly were the lives of a fine
ship's company, and of Lord Cochrane and his officers, sacrificed in
this instance to the despotism." The Admiralty knew full well that
it could expect three hundred eager witnesses for the defence and
decided, on this occasion, to avoid all inquiry into Cochrane's
conduct.[54]

During the rest of the winter, the *Imperieuse* was assigned to the
blockading squadron in the Bay of Biscay, though once again being
allowed considerable independence of action. On 19 December,
Cochrane arrived off Les Sables d'Olonne and took two prizes in the
same day. He sailed south to the Gironde, and there took another
vessel in the river estuary on 31 December. During this cruise off the
western coast of France, Midshipman Marryat noted his impressions of
the ship's routine. There was no leisure for men whose eyes were fixed
upon the prizes and spoils of war. Raiding parties and crews to "cut
out" or board French ships were organised so frequently that "the
boats were hardly secured on the booms than they were cast loose
and out again". Cochrane moved his frigate rapidly from one point
to another, day or night, and his men learnt to make the best of
"the hasty sleep, snatched at all hours". Cochrane's "coolness and
courage" was an example to all on board, fortified by their sense of
superior fighting ability in consequence of the regular gunnery
practice, which gave a "beautiful precision" to the frigate's fire-
power. Marryat recalled frequent experiences of falling asleep exhausted in his cot after one encounter, only to wake with the guns
above him roaring out a broadside as Cochrane opened fire on yet
another French vessel or coastal fort. After so much cannonading,
the gun-deck of the *Imperieuse* seemed to reek perpetually with
smoke. Officers and men found "the powder so burnt into our faces
that years could not remove it". And, most vividly of all, Marryat
remembered the courage of Cochrane "inoculating the whole of the
ship's company". Writing long after, the great novelist confessed,
"when memory sweeps along those years of excitement even now,
my pulse beats more quickly with the reminiscence."[55]

Cochrane was already meditating plans which, he believed, might alter the entire course of the long war against Buonaparte, bringing victory to England with dramatic suddenness. But first the naval war must be carried ashore. In the new year of 1807, the *Imperieuse* was south of the Gironde, just off the Bassin d'Arcachon. This flat, wooded coast, with its long sandy beaches and dunes, concealed the narrow entrance to the almost landlocked anchorage of Arcachon. In that entrance, a convoy of French merchant vessels and a few escorting gun-boats had taken refuge from Cochrane's activities. Their position was well chosen. The shoals prevented the *Imperieuse* from coming in close, while the convoy itself rested securely under the guns of Fort Roquette, guarding the entrance to the Bassin d'Arcachon. Knowing that Cochrane might attack the convoy with his ship's boats, the French beached their vessels and moved the troops from Fort Roquette to stand guard over them at night.

Cochrane ordered his attack before daylight on 7 January, using cover of darkness to approach, since Fort Roquette was formidably armed on all sides, not merely on its seaward walls. The frigate's boats pulled slowly towards the low coastline of south-west France, where the convoy lay. The French troops on the beach were watching, well-prepared for an assault. But as they scanned the dark, calm sea, they saw nothing. Cochrane guessed that they would expect him to attack the convoy and had allowed them to post the infantry on the beach. Most of the garrison was there when he entirely out-manoeuvred them by launching his marines against the feebly-held battery of Fort Roquette itself. Such an attack would have been unthinkable if it had been fully garrisoned, but the troops guarding the convoy knew nothing until the pre-dawn sky behind them was suddenly rent with the flashes and explosions of Cochrane's attack. There was little the convoy party could do to reach their base, while the men of the *Imperieuse* systematically destroyed the four 36-pounders of Fort Roquette, as well as two field-guns and a 13-pound mortar. Then came a roaring explosion, flames streaking like rockets into the sky, as Cochrane's men blew up the powder magazine, sending up with it the gun platforms and carriages, the military stores, and reducing Fort Roquette to a ruin.

Worse still, the French troops on the exposed shore now had to retreat to a defensive position elsewhere. Cochrane's landing party fell upon the undefended French convoy, setting ablaze the seven merchant vessels and gun-boats. Only then did he give orders to withdraw, remarking that it was "prudent" to leave since, no doubt, "a general alarm had been excited along the coast". He regretted not having the leisure to warp the French vessels off the sand and take them as prizes. But the risk to his men would have been too great, and so the coasters had to be destroyed.[56]

With three French naval vessels and twelve merchant ships destroyed or captured, he returned to the main squadron, now cruising off Rochefort. Captain Keats, squadron commander, ordered him to provision and water two ships for a further six weeks, one of them, the *Atalante*, having already been on blockade for eight months without a break. As the *Atalante* was hauled alongside, Cochrane was appalled at her condition. The refusal of squadron commanders and the Admiralty to allow such ships to return to port had reduced her to a useless hulk. Eight months, he remarked, was enough "to ruin the health, break the energy, and weary the spirit of all employed in such a vessel".

There was worse yet. The commander of the *Atalante* and some of his officers came on board the *Imperieuse* to tell Cochrane of the desperate plight of their sloop. The foremast, the bowsprit, and the foreyard were all sprung. The *Atalante* was leaking so badly that she shipped twenty inches of water an hour and the pumps could hardly keep pace with it. In short, she was "wholly unfit to keep the sea". The next gale, said her commander, would see the end of her.

Cochrane confirmed these fears, all too easily, by his own inspection of the vessel. He reported the state of the *Atalante* at once to the squadron commander. But Captain Keats was unimpressed. From time to time, he had sent some of the junior officers from the flagship to inspect such hulks. These young lieutenants invariably reported back that the wallowing blockaders were fit for weeks or months of further duty before it was necessary to allow them to put into a port. Cochrane was invited to mind his own business and Keats sent the *Imperieuse* back to Plymouth to ensure that he did so. The frigate herself had not been in dock since the previous November, the mere loss of a false keel on the Ushant rocks being considered too trivial to take a ship out of service for proper inspection and repair.

At Plymouth, Cochrane went at once to the official dockyard builder and to Admiral Sutton, the officer commanding. They listened unmoved as he protested at the plight of the *Atalante* and her crew. When it was evident that he had made no impact upon them, Cochrane drew himself up and launched one of those melodramatic thunderbolts, which he was apt to resort to in such difficulties. "The first news we shall have from Rochefort, if there should happen to be a gale of wind, will be the loss of the *Atalante*," he announced.

Admiral Sutton was not won over by such stage rhetoric as this. The weather grew worse and then the storms passed. There was quiet satisfaction among Admiral Sutton and his entourage at being able to quote the words of the troublesome young Scot against him. And then came the signal, which the gales had delayed. H.M.S. *Atalante* had foundered in the heavy seas off the Biscay coast.[57]

It was the end of the *Atalante* but the beginning of a new crusade. The schooner *Felix*, also in Keats's squadron had gone down, taking her crew with her. There soon came into Cochrane's hands copies of letters written by the commander of the *Felix* to Keats, imploring him to take account of the state of the ship and the number of men sick, and to allow him to sail for England at once. The request was dismissed. The ship's surgeon wrote confidentially on 14 November 1806, "She sails worse and worse, and I think the chances are against our ever bringing her into an English port." On 14 January 1807, he added that "every endeavour" had been made by himself and the commander, Lieutenant Cameron, to get the *Felix* sent home, "but without success". Eight days later, the schooner and her exhausted crew went down in a Biscay squall.[58]

The financial arithmetic of ministerial dishonesty had been an uncertain political platform for Cochrane, in terms of general electoral appeal. But no man of sense would fail to respond to the dark, simple drama of the lost ships, the criminal indifference of a squadron commander, the callousness of Lord St Vincent commanding the Channel Fleet, and the open cynicism of the comfortable Admiralty placemen. While the *Imperieuse* was docked for repairs, he was given leave of absence to stand for parliament in the general election of May 1807, which followed the dismissal of the Whig government by the King and their replacement by the Tories under the Duke of Portland. "Naval reform" had given him a banner under which to fight. All he needed was a battleground.

There was no question of standing for Honiton again. Those voters who had been done out of a bribe on the last occasion were prepared to take an easy revenge upon him. The strategy which had served him in 1806 was now so well-known as to be a national joke, and there was not even the hope of repeating his Honiton success elsewhere. A young man with political ambitions would normally have surrendered his independence and gone to a political patron who, in effect, owned seats in parliament, constituencies where there were few electors, all of whom voted under their master's scrutiny. He might promise to act in the House of Commons as his patron dictated, or he might buy the seat. The patrician Radical, Sir Francis Burdett, had bought Boroughbridge in Yorkshire for six years for £4000 from the Duke of Newcastle's trustees in 1796. But since Cochrane had sworn to destroy such political corruption, he could hardly afford to enter the Commons by means of it.

Fortunately there was one constituency which, even before the Reform Bill of 1832, had moved far towards representative democracy. This was the City of Westminster, which had the incidental advantage of being the best-publicised electoral district in the country. It was a constituency in which male ratepayers were entitled to vote and where many of the residents were, in fact, ratepayers. Geographically, it extended from the City of London in the east to Kensington in the west, from Oxford Street in the north to the Thames in the south. Instead of the half dozen or few score electors upon whom the "rotten boroughs" depended, Westminster boasted some 10,000 voters. They were not entirely incorruptible, but it proved notoriously difficult to bribe all of them to the same end.

The Westminster electors were not always progressive or Radical in their views. One of the members had been Charles James Fox, until his death the year before. Sheridan had put himself forward as a successor at the by-election but the electors preferred Earl Percy, son of the Duke of Northumberland. Francis Place remembered with disgust the sight of the Duke distributing bread, cheese, and beer to the mob from the steps of his house near Charing Cross, in order to ensure his son's election. The beer, ladled out in the hats of coalheavers, led to a riot among the crowds and to the gutters running with the spilt brew.

At the general election of 1806, however, Westminster had returned Sheridan and Samuel Hood. By the spring of 1807, after so many elections in a few months, the mood of the constituency was hardly predictable. Yet Westminster was the one seat which offered Cochrane even a faint hope of re-election to the House of Commons. He did not propose to stand as a Radical but as an "independent" candidate, devoted to the cause of naval reform.

Sheridan was first among his opponents, an extinct volcano of rhetoric, now under a régime of three to six bottles of wine a day, fortified by brandy, which gave him the appearance of a worn-out debauchee and the constitution of a man with dropsy and an inflamed liver. He, least of anyone, wanted to face an election fight.

When the King dismissed the Whigs, Sheridan conceded that men banged their heads on brick walls, but George III was uniquely determined to collect the bricks to build the wall to bang his head against. Referring to Cochrane, Sheridan wrote to his son Tom, "I will have nothing to do with the Popery Lord." For all his reforming sympathies, Cochrane had a deep Protestant suspicion of the Catholic Church and was opposed to any extension of its political influence so long as it retained the practice of hearing confessions.[59]

The defeated Radical candidate at the last election, James Paull, a former merchant, ran again under the banner of "Liberty, Protection, Peace". Francis Place and the official Radical organisation disliked him, however, and withdrew their support. John Elliot, a brewer was the "ministerial" candidate.

When Cochrane joined the contest, the Radicals themselves were first to attack him. One of them, Henry Hunt, *alias* "Orator" Hunt, described the scepticism of the movement in the country and of its wealthy leader, Sir Francis Burdett. "So little faith had Sir F. Burdett and his friends in the sincerity of Cochrane's principles that they never drank his health, or even mentioned his name." Francis Place and the Radical electioneers of Westminster ignored him. William Godwin, father-in-law of Shelley and prophet of the new intellectual order, dismissed Cochrane with contempt. "He is the greatest fool I ever met with." By contrast, when James Paull addressed his supporters at a grand election dinner on 1 May 1807, he conceded that Cochrane was "a young man of understanding, and who had received a good education; but . . . he did not conceive him a fit representative for Westminster".[60]

Undeterred by this, Cochrane moved into the constituency. He lodged with his rogue uncle, Andrew Cochrane-Johnstone, in Harley Street, and set up his committee rooms in hotels and taverns in Covent Garden, Golden Square, Cockspur Street, and New Bond Street. His election dinners were held in Willis's Rooms, St James's, and other meetings of his supporters by the glimmering yellow oil light of upper rooms in Westminster taverns. At the St Alban's Tavern he was closely questioned as to why he had chosen to stand for Westminster, having already been member for Honiton. He replied disingenuously: "A man representing a rotten borough cannot feel himself of equal consequence in the House with one representing such a city as Westminster."[61]

It was a well-chosen reply. To ready applause from the guests at his election dinner at Willis's rooms, Cochrane repeated his pledge.

"Independence is the Ground on which I am determined to stand or fall." And while the echoes of applause died away, his supporters took up the refrain of the song which had been specially composed for the election fight.[62]

> All hail to the HERO – of ENGLAND the boast,
> The honor – the glory – the pride of our coast;
> Let the bells peal his name, and the cannons' loud roar,
> Sound the plaudits of COCHRANE, the friend of her shore.[63]

And then the reason for so much brotherly vindictiveness by the Radicals became clear. The seat at Westminster was not intended for Cochrane but for the leader of the movement, past revolutionary and future Tory, Sir Francis Burdett. Born to great wealth, which he increased enormously by marrying the daughter of Thomas Coutts the banker, Burdett boasted two estates, one at Ramsbury and another, complete with Palladian mansion, at Fonmarke. His town house, at 78 Piccadilly, was also a convenient base for the Westminster election. He had been member for Middlesex since 1802, spending many thousands of pounds to ensure his return. But now Burdett, like Cochrane, felt the lure of representing a "democratic" and famous seat.

As a matter of fact, the most offended man in Westminster was James Paull, the Radical candidate, since he had been assuring everyone that he had the support of Burdett. One morning he woke to see placards and banners in Burdett's colours, dark blue with yellow lettering, proclaiming, "Burdett and Independence!" and "Burdett and Purity of Election!" and even, "Sir Francis – a plumper!" The last was particularly wounding, since it urged voters to use only one of their two votes and withhold the second, which might well have gone to Paull. To plump for Burdett was, inevitably, to spoil the chances of all other candidates, most of all the Radical who might have got the second vote.[64]

Offended honour knew only one consolation. Paull confronted Burdett at Kingston, in Combe Wood, and shot him in the thigh, suffering a minor leg wound himself from Burdett. To his existing reputation, Burdett was able to add the kudos of the wounded hero. He appeared rarely and then with the injured leg propped on a stool as he reclined upon cushions. But his campaign was vigorously conducted by proxy and he was the greatest of all threats to Cochrane's election.

The hustings, at which the candidates presented themselves to the voters, were to take place in Covent Garden on 7 May. Prior to that, however, there was leisure for the assassination of character. On 4 May, the Radicals announced from the Crown and Anchor Tavern in the Strand that "the recent conduct of Mr Paull has been such as to induce us to *withdraw* from him our support". Since Place and his friends had never seriously contemplated giving him their support this was the sort of gratuitous smear which was considered an elementary precaution in electioneering. But Paull was too busy slandering Sheridan to care about Place. His placards, the work of "Dolly Bull", appeared on wall and pillar, ironically listing the virtues of Sheridan.[65]

Has he ever basely made his friend's credulity the picklock to his property?

Has he ever by the most profligate extravagancies reduced honest tradesmen to penury and despair?

Does he pass his nights in inebriety and his days in sloth?

Does he pay homage to the smiles of Princes whilst he defies the laws of his God?[66]

The ironic answer to all these questions was "No", thereby refurbishing the image of Sheridan as an incompetent politician, an inordinate drunkard, the habitué of the Royal Pavilion who now lived in dread of the bailiff and the debtors' prison. The next day, the same walls carried an answer, denouncing Paull as no better than "the beastly Drunkard – the base Seducer – the deliberate Murderer". As for Elliot, "supported by the minister and the Aristocracy", his opponents dismissed him as a joke. They dubbed him "Colonel Narcotic" and drew up an entirely bogus election address on his behalf, which was printed and distributed, showing him as feebleminded to the point of imbecility.[67]

Whatever Cochrane's faults, he appeared the epitome of dignified restraint by comparison with the poster war of Westminster's walls and pillars. His election dinner was characterised by "great mirth and good humour". He refused to ally himself with any faction or to pin the "Radical" label to himself. But he was adamant in his support for reform. "Victory! Cochrane! and Reform!" was the slogan of his placards. He might share the reforming zeal of the Radicals but he believed firmly that tyranny in France must be put down by England's military and naval resistance. His election song acquired a final verse, balancing these conflicting demands of war and peace.[68]

Thus while conquest and glory he spreads far and near,
And the sons of fair ALBION their COCHRANE revere:
While he hurls round the thunder and rides in the storm,
He is more than all this! He's the FRIEND of REFORM![69]

On 7 May, the morning of the hustings, he put a small advertisement in the columns of the *Morning Post*, announcing that he would
leave the British Coffee House in Cockspur Street at nine o'clock,
"when I shall be thankful to any Gentleman who will do me the
honour to accompany me to the Hustings".

The proceedings opened at ten o'clock, the High Bailiff reading the
royal proclamation for the election of two Members of Parliament for
the constituency. The officials and the candidates stood on the platform under a wooden roof, the whole structure resembling an open
barn. Beyond the surrounding rails, the thousands of electors were
packed into the square. After the election speeches formality
required that the High Bailiff should demand a show of hands and
would declare two candidates elected. But formality also required
that those who had not been elected would then object and a poll
would have to be held lasting for the next couple of weeks.

Burdett was not present but the first outburst of the hustings
came when Paull and his supporters howled down his proposers,
accusing them of "political apostasy and fraud" in withdrawing
their support from Paull. Cochrane was better received, despite
jeering from "Colonel Narcotic's" supporters in the crowd. In his
naval uniform, his face reddened and freckled by months of Mediterranean sun and Biscay storms, he made an impressive figure. With an
agility which he was more accustomed to show when boarding ships
like the *Gamo* or reefing those like the *Généreux*, he sprang on to the
dividing rail, holding his balance where all could see and hear him.
Characteristically, he went straight to the attack, dealing briskly
with those who suggested that a naval officer was an unfit representative for Westminster:

> Let those who say so give us a list of those who are actually
> unfit to represent you in Parliament – Such as Placemen,
> Pensioners, and Fops – such as those who drive and dash about
> in their curricles in Bond-Street – they are a damned deal
> more unfit to represent you than such a man as I am.

The crowd responded to his quarterdeck rhetoric, the tepid
applause soon drowned by a storm of cheering.

"Gentlemen," shouted Cochrane, "I would put a question to you. Do you think that a creature whose whole time almost is employed in making a noise at the head of his horses, and grinning to please the ladies; or, when he is displeased himself, breaking the heads of beasts by the hand of a brute – is such a man fit to represent you?" It was an apt portrait of ministerial men.

There was more cheering when Cochrane reminded his listeners that they, as electors, were liable to be prosecuted at law for bribery. Why not extend the law to apply also to those whom they elected and who, at the moment, practised parliamentary bribery on a massive scale with complete impunity?

By the time that Cochrane sat down, he had made a considerable impression by his homely oratory. If his posters and placards were more reticent than those of his opponents, the simple honesty and determined attack of his speech more than made up for this. When Elliot, the ministerial candidate, rose to speak, it was evident that Cochrane had stolen the limelight. Elliot spoke of his principles and policies, against a rising barrage of abuse, which ended, as the press remarked, in "uproar, and a manifest disinclination to hear any thing on these topics".[70]

The speeches being over, the High Bailiff called for a show of hands and declared Cochrane and Elliot elected. The other candidates then demanded a poll, which opened about an hour later. At the end of the first day, Cochrane was in the lead with 112 votes to 99 for Elliot and 78 for Burdett. It was already clear that Sheridan and Paull were out of the race.

Day after day, the speeches and the riots of the hustings continued, as the votes were cast. The Westminster election became a national attraction, never more celebrated than in Gilray's cartoon which now occupied pride of place in the Piccadilly print-sellers and in the portfolios which lay open upon the drawing-room tables of the politically sophisticated. *Election Candidates: or, The Republican Goose at the Top of the Pole*, showed the hustings complete with a greasy pole (or poll) to whose top the candidates struggled to climb. Burdett, the republican goose, was assisted by a pitchfork applied to his feathered rump by the Radical clergyman Horne Tooke. The goose's droppings fell copiously on the next scrabbling figure, "Sawney McCockran, flourishing the Cudgel of Naval Reform, lent to him by Cobbett". The defeated Sheridan appeared as "an Old Drury Lane Harlequin, trying in vain to make a spring to the Top of the Pole, his Broad Bottom always bringing him down again".

There was a particularly rowdy day at the hustings on 12 May when Cochrane was accused of "swearing publicly". He admitted that he had sworn once. "You swore *twice!*" roared the ministerial supporters in the crowd. "Well, it might be twice," said Cochrane impatiently. He could hardly credit that while electoral bribery and parliamentary corruption were matters of indifference, a candidate who said "damn" at the hustings had mortally injured the moral susceptibilities of the voters.

Among growing disturbance, Cochrane launched his main attack of the election on naval abuses. Then, as he began to talk about a certain "Noble Lord", the mob grew quiet and listened.

"What will those who hear me think," asked Cochrane, "of ships, wholly unfit for service, being purchased from Borough Proprietors, under the auspices of the Noble Person in question, for three times their value, merely to enable a man who has not a foot of land in the country, to raise himself into some consequence by purchasing in this manner an interest in rotten boroughs? Every one who hears me must understand to whom I allude."

"Lord Melville! Lord Melville!" shouted a wag.

"No," said Cochrane sternly, "it is not Lord Melville, but a Noble person who has command of the Channel Fleet."[71]

By the next morning, this denunciation of Lord St Vincent as the political jobber responsible for the fates of such ships as the *Atalante* and the *Felix* appeared in every major newspaper. Cochrane's friends read with dismay of the manner in which he seemed determined to destroy his naval career: his enemies in the Admiralty rejoiced to see him delivered yet more surely into their clutches.

As the hustings drew to a close, Francis Place and the official Radicals worked untiringly for Burdett, who stood in danger of losing the contest to Cochrane and Elliot. Eagerly they tried to persuade the voters that though Burdett might appear to be a Tory gentleman with an obsession for fox hunting, and though he had spent £100,000 to secure his earlier election for Middlesex, he was in fact the pure apostle of reform, if not of revolution. Their efforts were well directed. When the final result was announced, Burdett had polled 5134; Cochrane, 3708; Sheridan, 2645; Elliot, 2137, and Paull, 269. Burdett and Cochrane were thus the two new members for Westminster. Sheridan had done unexpectedly well in the later stages but, as Francis Place explained, there was a special reason for this. "Sheridan was so far behind that he had no chance of outpoling Cochrane and as he begged hard to be permitted to make as respectable a shew of numbers as he could, Lord Cochrane took his inspectors away, and Sheridan polled whom he pleased and the same man over and over again as many times as he pleased."[72]

In winning the Westminster election, Cochrane had triumphed in no more than a preliminary political skirmish. The procedures and tactics of the House of Commons were as treacherous in their way as the rocks of Ushant. Indeed, there already lay in wait for him humiliations and defeats so frequent as to make some of his colleagues wonder if, after all, Cochrane might not be the stupidest man in politics, as Godwin believed. The courage which he had shown in war and the breezy honesty of his mob oratory were neither of them assets in an assembly whose older members were jaded to the point of cynicism.

However, Parliament opened on 26 June and Cochrane at last took his place on the benches of the Commons. It was a smaller and more intimate arena than its reputation suggested. Its dimensions were those of a small chapel with narrow galleries above the opposing benches, the bare Georgian interior having as its focal point the three rounded windows behind the Speaker's chair. The galleries were low enough, as Creevey describes, for a noble visitor like the Duke of Clarence, later William IV, to lean óver and "halloo" into the debating chamber, in his amiable and simple manner, as though he were part of the proceedings. Beneath each gallery rose four tiers of benches, for government and opposition respectively, with a dozen feet of bare floorboards between the two parties. Far back under the galleries were the curtains, behind which elderly members were able to doze while still being available to vote if a division were called, and from behind which younger and more impatient members would interrupt proceedings with loud cock crows when they felt that their elders had allowed debate to dawdle on too late into the night.

The new Tory leader, the Duke of Portland, sat in the Lords, the government leader in the Commons being Spencer Perceval. Of the government ministers responsible for naval affairs, Lord Palmerston sat in the Commons, his Irish peerage being no disqualification, and John Wilson Croker also adorned the government benches. If Cochrane had any allies, they were the so-called "Mountain", a collection of the more liberal Whigs, the Radicals, and such men as himself. At Burdett's victory dinner after the election, Cochrane's health was still not drunk and all reference to him was avoided. Yet he and

Burdett became personal friends and it was clearly only a question of time before they entered into political alliance.

Cochrane wasted no time in opening his attack on the government. In the debate on the King's Speech he denounced the political corruption of Tories and Whigs alike. They hardly seemed to notice that they were being attacked. On 7 July, he introduced a long and complicated motion demanding an inquiry into sinecures and places enjoyed by members of the House of Commons. This was the blow by which he intended to rock the political establishment on its heels. Spencer Perceval said gently that it would be "invidious and improper to convey to the public an insinuation that members of parliament were influenced by considerations of private advantage". The motion was tastefully amended so that it would not give any such offence, nor serve any useful purpose, and was passed in its new form despite Cochrane's anger. "It is notorious," he burst out, "that commissions in the army and navy have been given for votes in this House!" But the old hands, who knew the rules intimately, silenced him with cries of "Order! Order!"[73]

Three days later, he returned to the attack again by introducing a motion for papers relating to the loss of the *Atalante* and the *Felix* to be made public. His opponents were Sir Samuel Hood, and Admirals Harvey and Markham, who began a baying chant of "Order! Order!" whenever he seemed likely to reveal anything discreditable to St Vincent or the Admiralty. At last they lured him into mentioning the lucky escape of the *Imperieuse* near Ushant, and howled him down with "Order! Order!" The Speaker, turning towards him, said calmly, "The Noble Lord must confine himself to the motion before the House."[74]

After the election triumph, the defeats and rebuffs of his experience in the Commons seemed a sour reward. The government mocked his crusading zeal and the Radicals began to regard him as a dangerous and foolish ally. If this was the best that "Sawney McCockran" of the election cartoons could do, his political career would be very brief indeed. However, since he might have damaging evidence about the Admiralty and its ways, and was certainly in a position to present it before the public, however ineptly, it seemed safer to evict him from parliament. He was ordered back to the *Imperieuse*, which was now ready to sail for the Mediterranean. If he went, he would be expected to resign his seat in the Commons. If he stayed, he must forfeit his naval career and the income upon which he depended.

But though he had made a poor impression in the House, the

electors of Westminster liked what they had read of him. His attempt to reform parliamentary corruption and naval abuses within the first week of his Commons' career had been ill-judged. But he had shown great courage, fearing no man and no party. Unlike some reformers he had not forgotten his promises to those who elected him. Hearing that he had been ordered to sea again, the electors of Westminster met and decided to give him "unlimited leave of absence". His zeal and honour had been no match for the intrigues of parliamentary procedure, but they had won him a seat in the Commons which he was to hold virtually unopposed for more than a decade and during the most awesome personal scandals.

# 4

# "Excessive Use of Powder and Shot"

THE calm azure waters of the Mediterranean between Sicily and Corsica combined with the routine drill of a frigate on active service to soothe uncomfortable recollection of Cochrane's parliamentary humiliation. The *Imperieuse* had sailed from Portsmouth on 12 September 1807, in charge of a convoy of thirty-eight merchant ships, many of them packed with red-coated infantry companies on their way to reinforce Gibraltar and the island base at Malta. Demands on his attention and patience left Cochrane little leisure to shudder at memories of the Tories jeering at his ineptitude across the floor of the narrow chamber of the Commons. A merchant convoy of such size, each ship offering half a regiment of troops as prize, was the classic nightmare of an escort captain. Through the squalls and the cold rain-flurries of the Atlantic autumn, the slow troopers wallowed and straggled, while the signal gun on the *Imperieuse* boomed out its impatient warnings.

By 31 October the last of the convoy had been brought safely to Valetta, and Cochrane sailed again to join the squadron of the Commander-in-Chief, Lord Collingwood, who was cruising off Palermo.

Everywhere the news was bad. With a few exceptions, notably Portugal and Gibraltar, the entire coastline of continental Europe was hostile. Even Portugal, it was said, would be compelled to close her ports to British ships. At sea, the Royal Navy was supreme, but that seemed to matter little to Napoleon and even less to some groups in England. The newspapers and journals which reached the Mediterranean from London or Edinburgh spoke increasingly of the need to end a war in which there could be no victory. "The game, we fear, is decidedly lost," announced the *Edinburgh Review* echoing soberly the theme of newspapers and peace movements alike. Public petitions for peace were organised in manufacturing areas like Manchester, Bolton, and Oldham, the petitions being presented to parliament with great publicity.[1]

It was impossible that England, with a population of 15,000,000 should attempt to match Napoleon's army of 500,000 as well as finding 120,000 men to protect her vital maritime links. How, then, could the war be continued? Suggestions were made for scattered guerrilla warfare or commando attacks under the protection of the Royal Navy. It was thought possible that a beach-head might be seized in Holland or in northern Spain, round Santander. Moira and Ponsonby favoured a landing to secure the passes of the Pyrenees and cut Spain off from France. All these things would be a nuisance to Napoleon but it was difficult to see how they would overthrow him. At best, they would improve England's negotiating position when the inevitable peace talks began. Characteristically, Cochrane believed that the war could be won and that the Royal Navy could do it. He dismissed the complex plans of his superiors and devised a simple strategy to bring about a collapse of Napoleonic power from Moscow to Lisbon, and the Arctic Circle to Naples, in a matter of months and with no more than minimal allied casualties. He had yet to show that such theories could be put into practice, but his chance was soon to come.[2]

Meanwhile, he cruised the waters between Sicily and Corsica, lulled by the routine of the *Imperieuse*. It was homely, by comparison with the hostility of his political experience. The rattle of buckets and holystone as the off-duty watch scrubbed the decks to blinding white-ness was accompanied by the more martial tread and shouted orders of the red-coated Royal Marines at drill. In the warmth of the Medi-terranean day there was repeated gunnery practice, the crews going through the routine of running out the 18-pounders, firing, swabbing, reloading, and firing again. There was target practice, too, firing at casks in the water, though Cochrane preferred to let his men spend their powder in earnest. And, of course, there were the routine duties of a ship's captain who was responsible for the welfare of his men. Stores had to be carefully and continually checked. "Cask of Pork, No. 1619," as it was officially designated, held a disagreeable consign-ment, 524 pounds of meat in a state of rapid decomposition. "Rotten and stinking occasioned by the weakness of the Cask," Cochrane noted.[3]

Lord Collingwood's squadron had left Sicilian waters to join the blockade against Toulon, leaving Cochrane to catch up with them.

On 14 November, nine days out from Malta, the *Imperieuse* sighted the sails of two ships, close under the cliffs of the western coast of Corsica. The one which drew Cochrane's attention was a three-masted merchantman, built for fast sailing. But the sides of the ship had been pierced to take guns and she was evidently a privateer. Cochrane guessed she might be from Genoa.

In a calm sea, the only practicable way of investigating was to lower the three boats of the *Imperieuse*, filled with Royal Marines and naval officers, including Midshipman Marryat, and to row across to the other ship. Two of Cochrane's officers, Napier and Fayrer were in command. As the three boats with their red-coated marines, pipe-clayed belts gleaming white in the sun, drew closer, there was a scurry of activity and the mysterious privateer hoisted out a Union Jack and draped it over the side. The leading boat of the *Imperieuse* stopped and hailed her, ordering the captain to identify his ship. He appeared at the rail and announced that she was the *King George*, a British, or rather Maltese, privateer. In that case, shouted Napier, she would have no objection to being inspected by the men of a British frigate.

The privateer captain, whose name was Pasquil Giliano, insisted that Napier and his marines were French, masquerading as British. If they attempted to board, his men would resist them. "I must board," shouted Napier. "You must take the consequences," Giliano retorted, and disappeared from sight.

Napier gave his order and there was an echoing cheer from the marines as the boat crews pulled with all speed for the sides of the privateer, avoiding the field of fire of the guns at her ports. They came alongside the *King George* without difficulty. Then, as if from nowhere, there was a fusilade of musket fire, the air filled with the hiss of bullets and the whistle of grapeshot. Marines and sailors fell, clutching their sudden wounds, blood darkening the scarlet uniforms. Fayrer's arm hung shattered and Napier had been brought down with blood streaming from behind his ear. Giliano's men had been concealed by the boarding nets hanging down the ship's sides and were firing at point-blank range upon the men in the boats.

Marryat and the survivors knew there could be no going back. Of the fifty-four men in the boat, they had already lost fifteen, but to pull away from the side of the privateer would be to expose themselves to the annihilating force of grape and musket fire. Swarming determinedly up the sides and on to the deck the remaining marines found themselves on a well-defended pirate ship. They did not yet know it, but the authorities in Malta had already offered a prize of £500 for the capture of Giliano and his vessel.

"A most desperate conflict ensued," Marryat recalled, "the decks were strewed with the dying and the dead." The pirates guessed what their fate might be if they were taken, while the boarding party had no hope of retreat. In the end, Giliano fell dead in the fight and some of his men surrendered. This gave the marines a sufficient advantage and, though one group of the pirates fought on, they were, as Marryat put it, "cut to pieces" by the bayonets and cutlasses of Cochrane's men.

Until the attack, Cochrane had no idea that he was attempting to board a notorious pirate, and he was badly shaken by the heavy losses which his men had sustained. Marryat observed him as the *King George* was taken back to Malta. "I never, at any time, saw Lord Cochrane so much dejected as he was for many days after this affair. He appreciated the value of his men – they had served him in the *Pallas*, and he could not spare one of them."

Worse still, as Cochrane informed Lord Collingwood, though the *King George* had at one time been allowed to sail under the British flag, the only subjects of the King were three Maltese boys, one Gibraltarian, and a naturalised Maltese, among the crew of fifty-two.

But that was not all. The Admiralty court at Malta ruled that, despite the reward offered for her capture, no prize money would be paid to Cochrane or his crew for bringing in the *King George*. Instead, he was presented with a bill for the legal costs of the hearing. Privately, he was informed that certain officials of the court had shares in the vessel and that their investment must not be forfeit. He vowed that when he had leisure he would give his full attention to the Admiralty court at Malta.[4]

However, Cochrane's prospects were not entirely unpromising. Lord Collingwood, who had served for long enough under Nelson to recognise initiative when he saw it, was impressed by his new subordinate. Talking of Cochrane and his kind, he remarked, "the activity and zeal in those gallant young men keep up my spirits and make me equal to bear the disagreeables that happen from the contentions of some other ships".[5]

For the moment there were "disagreeables" in store for Cochrane and the *Imperieuse*. Collingwood sent both captain and ship to take over command of the British blockade in the Adriatic from Captain Patrick Campbell. On arriving, Cochrane was astonished to find that Campbell was issuing passes freely to merchant ships and that the British blockade was virtually no blockade at all. Cochrane ignored the passes, seized the ships, and sent them off to Malta under prize crews. Campbell wrote privately to Collingwood, warning him against Cochrane, and added: "from his want of discretion he is unfit to be entrusted with a single ship, much less with the command of a squadron."[6]

Collingwood had no idea what was going on, being preoccupied with the blockade of Toulon. His personal acquaintance with Cochrane was still slight and he decided, from prudence, to replace him as commander of the Adriatic blockade squadron. The *Imperieuse* was redirected to waters with which Cochrane had long been familiar, the Spanish Mediterranean coast.

The spring of 1808 was the final season of Cochrane's buccaneering in the manner he had perfected since assuming command of the *Speedy* eight years before. He was thirty-three years old, fifteen of those years having been passed in the navy, and he had reached that point at which a commander had either to act a significant part in the total strategy of war, or else become an old man in a junior rank. His acts of patriotic piracy were remarkable enough in themselves but because he repeated them with such ease and predictability, the public reaction to them grew progressively milder.

None the less, in his final cruise of this sort, Cochrane took a score of prizes and acted out enough naval dramas to fill several novels of Captain Marryat's type. On 21 February, for instance, he sighted a large French merchantman at dawn. She was carrying munitions for the 100,000 French troops in Spain and her capture would be both personally and strategically profitable. She was lying, in apparent safety, under the Spanish shore batteries in the Bay of Almeria, which would have been enough to deter any captain, except one who typified the hero of so many boys' adventure stories. Cochrane hoisted the American flag and sailed in to the attack.

In what was almost a parody of heroic action, the *Imperieuse* closed on her prey with boats hoisted out in readiness. As she dropped anchor, the boarding parties of marines were rowed across to the French ship at full speed. Only at the last moment did the French and the Spanish see what was happening, and then smoke and flame broke from the shore artillery as it opened on the *Imperieuse*. The boarding party clambered on to the deck of the French ship through a storm of musket fire. Casualties were heavy and Lieutenant Edward Caulfield, who led the attack, fell dead as he reached the deck. But the second boatload of Cochrane's men overcame the French resistance, the cable was cut, and the sails set. While all this was going on, and

Cochrane was exchanging salvoes with the guns ashore, his men were also rowing through the smoke and the plumes of water thrown up by the shells to round up several smaller vessels which happened to be in the harbour.

No sooner had they done this than the wind dropped. The *Impérieuse* and her flock of prizes lay becalmed before the Spanish shore-batteries. In his journal, Midshipman Marryat recorded that the whole bay was "reverberating with the roar of cannon, the smooth water ploughed up in every quarter by the shot directed against the frigate and boats". From the quarterdeck, he watched the duel between the ranked mouths of the cannon ashore and their elusive target.

> The *Impérieuse* returned the fire, warping round and round with her springs, to silence the most galling. This continued for nearly an hour, by which time the captured vessels were under all sail, and then the *Impérieuse* hove up her anchor, and, with the English colours waving at her gaff, and still keeping up an undiminished fire, sailed slowly out the victor.[7]

During the hour of the duel, Cochrane had felt the first breath of wind, just enough to turn impending catastrophe into triumph.

He repeated escapades of this sort a score of times in the spring of 1808. Yet the truly sensational event of that period was one in which he had no direct part. The *Impérieuse* reached Gibraltar on 31 May, having had no contact with Spanish forces since 20 May, when the guns of Cape Palos fired on the passing frigate. But the day after Cochrane's appearance at Gibraltar, H.M.S. *Trident* and a merchant convoy arrived from England. The news they brought was the most portentous since 1793. On 2 May, in Madrid, and subsequently throughout much of Spain, the people had risen in a "War of Liberation" against Napoleon, determined to restore their captive king, Ferdinand VII. The patriotic movement was spreading like fire throughout the country. Already the native army, or guerrillas, were fighting the French. In England, there was talk of an expeditionary force to Spain. Before the month was over, Lord Castlereagh, as Secretary of State for War, had written a letter on the subject to the Chief Secretary for Ireland, Sir Arthur Wellesley.

To Cochrane, the news of revolution in Spain was a gift from the gods of war. There had never been the least doubt of his ability to disrupt enemy commerce or to harry a hostile coast. But now the war presented a quite different prospect, no less than one of the largest armies of France caught between the Spanish guerrillas ashore and the swift manoeuvring of frigates like the *Imperieuse* at sea. Geographically, the French position in eastern Spain was dependent largely on the coastal roads and the sea routes between Marseille and Catalonia. For the first time since Trafalgar, naval power might determine the outcome of the great land campaigns.

Napoleon's response to the defection of his Spanish ally was prompt and predictable. Ferdinand VII was summoned to Bayonne and there made a prisoner of the French. Napoleon's brother, Joseph Buonaparte, King of Naples, was proclaimed by the Emperor as King of Spain. Every insult that could have been contrived seemed to be offered to the patriotic feelings of the Spanish people. They had gained little by their alliance with France and had lost much. Now they were to be reduced to the state of a satellite power, under a foreign army of occupation and under the rule of a foreign puppet.

After a fortnight's refit at Gibraltar, the *Imperieuse* put to sea again on 18 June 1808, Cochrane having received "orders from Lord Collingwood to assist the Spaniards by every means in my power". Five days later, the frigate passed close to Almeria, where Cochrane had seized the French munition ship and her convoy four months previously. This time, he hoisted Spanish colours as well as English, acknowledging the enthusiasm of the townspeople who watched him pass. Two days later, he anchored off Cartagena, the scene of some of his "recent hostile visits". But this time, a party of senior Spanish officers came out in a boat to welcome the *Imperieuse*, and Cochrane was invited ashore by the Governor. He and his men received an enthusiastic welcome in the hot streets of the port, the crowds shouting for Cochrane, King George, and England. At every landfall along the Catalan coast, the same cheers and flag-waving greeted him in "one continued expression of good feeling".[8]

Of course, the French had not withdrawn from the area, indeed they were hastily reinforcing their positions against the attacks of Spanish troops, who were known as guerrillas even when uniformed and in regular formations. At Barcelona, Cochrane cruised just out of range of the shore-batteries, which none the less opened fire on the *Imperieuse*. By way of reply, he hoisted English and Spanish colours, with the French tricolour flying lower down in a position of defeat. Then, for good measure, he fired a derisive 21-gun salute to the enemy shore-batteries. This provoked a storm of salvoes, the plumes of spray rising just short of the frigate as she continued to cruise, tantalisingly, beyond their range. Cochrane went through his repertoire of insults, goading the French batteries into reply, as they used up the powder and shot which were soon to be in critically short supply.

During the exchanges, Cochrane attended to the most important matter of all. Standing on the frigate's quarterdeck, he surveyed the town and harbour of Barcelona carefully through his spy-glass. The streets were empty, except for the blue uniformed groups of infantry patrols and the white of the French cavalry. But the roof tops were crowded with the inhabitants who watched the skirmish and, conspicuously, did not cheer on the French gunners. It was common knowledge that the French under General Duhesme had entered Barcelona in February and were now an army of occupation. But even the 100,000 men whom Napoleon had sent to Spain were too few to police a country of such size. Cochrane concluded his survey, which confirmed that the French position in Catalonia depended on concentrations of troops in such towns and cities as Barcelona, supplied and reinforced from France by means of the coastal road. It was the challenge of which he had dreamed.

With a final salute, Cochrane turned the stern of the frigate to the French and sailed northward along the coast, towards the enemy frontier. Each time that the *Imperieuse* dropped anchor, the inhabitants of such towns as Blanco and Mataro came off in small boats with presents for the crew and complaints for Cochrane about the manner in which the French were helping themselves to the possessions, the girls, and even the lives of the Catalans on the pretext that some act of "resistance" had been committed. When the Spanish guerrilla army blew up a section of the vital coast road, the French commander compelled the local inhabitants to fill in the gap with their own furniture, agricultural implements, even their clothes. Once the work had been completed, Napoleon's grenadiers destroyed the buildings of the village. Cochrane, seeing the devastation from the *Imperieuse*, led his marines ashore at Mataro, blew up the road in a number of new places, and located the nearest French shore-battery. It was on the cliff outside the town. Using sailors as well as marines, he attacked from the rearward slope, where the battery was undefended, drove out the gunners, and before the main body of the French army could be summoned he ran the four brass 24-pounders over the cliff and re-embarked his men safely. To add insult to all this, he quietly put his men ashore on the following day to collect the brass artillery and ferry it out to the *Imperieuse*. On the next day, the frigate raced the French troops to Canette, which they had left in order to deal with Cochrane at Mataro. To his delight, there were more brass cannon, hardly defended, on the cliff top. It was easy enough to seize the position, carry hawsers from the frigate to the cliff, and "hop" the guns on board by use of capstan and tackles. Then, while the French army struggled back through the heat of the Catalan summer, Cochrane noted with satisfaction, "took a party of seamen and marines on shore, and broke down or blew up the road in six different places".[9]

All this was excellent for morale, both English and Spanish, but Cochrane had yet to show that it could have a decisive effect on the course of the war. His chance came three days later, on 29 July 1808, when the *Imperieuse* anchored off Mongat, ten miles on the French side of Barcelona. General Duhesme's army had left Barcelona some time before in order to besiege the Spanish at Gerona. The siege being over, he was now marching back to the garrison at Barcelona, Mongat being the only other French fortress on his route. The fort at Mongat was quite well defended and, though Duhesme had not yet reached the town with his main body of troops, his heavy artillery had already been formed into a park at a little distance on the Gerona side.

No sooner had the *Imperieuse* dropped anchor, at sunset, than the local guerrilla leaders came out in a boat and promised that they had eight hundred men ready and that, with Cochrane's assistance they could take the fortress of Mongat.

As Cochrane afterwards remarked, he would have done better for himself and his men if he had kept to the business of taking prizes, but there was something about sabotage and demolition which had evidently begun to grip his imagination. Waiting until it was properly dark, he went ashore with his more experienced marines and worked with silent efficiency. The advance guard of Duhesme's force, which now formed the garrison of the fortress, woke to the sound of two massive explosions lighting the night sky on either side of them. As the summer dawn broke, they saw, towards Barcelona, a formidable gap blown in the road, as well as piles of rock from above brought down to block it still more effectively. There could be no escape nor reinforcement in that direction. Worse still, on the Gerona side, the road had been blown up between the fort and Duhesme's artillery, which now stood forlorn and immobilised. Its present position was quite useless in any defence against Cochrane.

Cochrane put to sea for the rest of the day, anchoring off Mongat again the next morning. The French infantry had spent an unhappy day calculating their position. They were cut off from help, without their heavy guns, and surrounded by eight hundred guerrillas intent not only on victory but on vengeance. As the *Imperieuse* anchored and Cochrane went ashore in his gig to survey the position, the guerrillas stormed a French outpost on a hill top, and put to death the survivors who fell into their hands.

Cochrane ordered the *Imperieuse* to open fire with broadsides against the French position. It took only a couple of these before the defenders of Mongat signalled to the frigate their wish to surrender. The guerrillas stormed the slope with great cheering. But the French had no intention of surrendering to those who were intent on personal vengeance. They had only offered to surrender to Cochrane and now proceeded to open fire again to drive back the Spanish. At length Cochrane was led through the crackle of musketry to parley with the French commander, who insisted he would not surrender to the guerrillas. Cochrane gave him a stern lecture on the barbarity with which the French had behaved, deploring "the wanton devastation committed by a military power, pretending to high notions of civilisation".

Then the second battle of Mongat began, the struggle to get ninety-five French prisoners down to the beach and on to the frigate without allowing them to be lynched by the guerrillas. In a bizarre sequel, ragged men and women emerged from their hiding places to join the guerrillas in cheering Cochrane's marines, while the marines themselves used fists and musket butts to beat back those guerrillas who were trying to scale the parapet of the fort and get their hands on the French prisoners. The French commander had surrendered his sword to Cochrane and the entire garrison had laid down its arms. After a good deal of argument between Cochrane and the Spanish commander, it was agreed that there would be no lynching but that, as a recompense, the guerrillas should be allowed to loot the fortress. The prisoners were duly marched down to the boats followed by the abuse of the guerrillas and the jeering of the Spanish women. When the looting was over, Cochrane set a charge under the French ammunition and the fort of Mongat went skyward in a spectacular explosion. The display attracted H.M.S. *Cambrian* to the scene, and Cochrane transferred some of his prisoners to her.[10]

The first official news of what had happened was contained in Cochrane's despatch to Lord Collingwood, which announced the bewildering but very welcome intelligence that the major French fortress between Gerona and Barcelona "surrendered this morning to his Majesty's ship under my command". The implications were considerable. General Duhesme had lost the advance guard of his force, and the whole of his artillery which he had been obliged to abandon. The road through Mongat was impassable for regular troops and he arrived at Barcelona a month late, after an arduous journey through the interior, where his column was more easily a prey to guerrilla ambushes. Cochrane in no way underestimated the abilities of the Catalans in all this, paying tribute to their "patience and endurance under privation". From the British point of view, the damage done to General Duhesme's army and the whole French presence in Spain was out of all proportion to the effort expended, which amounted to the use of one frigate for two or three days. But as Cochrane sat in his stern cabin on the night of the action, writing his despatch to Lord Collingwood, the *Imperieuse* was already sailing towards the marine frontier of Spain and France.[11]

If every English coastal town from Dover to Torbay had been at the mercy of the French fleet, the signal stations burnt, the militia routed, and local commerce threatened, this would have been comparable to the effect of Cochrane on the French coast, from Marseille to the Pyrenees, in August 1808. Day after day, the log of the *Imperieuse* recorded the bare details. "7.00 boats ret$^d$ having destroyed the Telegraph, a battery of 2 Brass 24 pdrs & Burnt the Barracks." More specifically, Cochrane aimed at "diverting troops intended for Catalonia, by the necessity of remaining to guard their own seaboard". With evident satisfaction, he added, "It is wonderful what an amount of terrorism a small frigate is able to inspire on an enemy's coast."[12]

Apart from signal stations and customs houses, the marines from the *Imperieuse* were occupied in burning French merchant vessels, whose crews had beached them and fled at the sight of the frigate. Yet the signal stations were the principal target. As the French militia retreated before the muskets and bayonets of Cochrane's marines, they saw the red-coated "lobsters" fall indiscriminately on the building and its contents, setting fire to everything within reach. When the attack was over and the marines had embarked on the frigate again, the defenders crept back to search the debris. With relief they found half-burnt pages of official documents. Cochrane's uniformed ruffians had not known the value of such papers and had destroyed signal codes which would have been beyond price to the British commanders.

As a matter of fact, Cochrane and his men knew perfectly well what they were about. The half-burnt pages had been carefully left to reassure the French. All the vital details of the French semaphore system were first abstracted, allowing Cochrane to make a present to Lord Collingwood of the enemy's secret code. In consequence, a British frigate cruising within spy-glass range was able to pass on the movements of French naval vessels before they were known to their own commanders-in-chief.[13]

Cochrane's audacity and the superb ease with which he handled his frigate were repeatedly illustrated in these local attacks on the French coast. By 10 September, for instance, he had worked his way to Port Vendre near the Spanish frontier. His log shows that he was now joined by H.M.S. *Spartan* commanded by Captain Jahleel Brenton. A column of French infantry, with an advance guard of cavalry, was marching towards the village from Perpignan on its way to reinforce the garrisons in Spain. Even with the support of the *Spartan*, there was no hope of fighting the entire column as well as the shore-batteries by which Port Vendre was defended.

He assembled the ship's boys from the *Imperieuse* and the *Spartan* and, as though it were all a great practical joke, ordered them to dress in the scarlet uniforms of marines. They were then put into boats and rowed towards the Spanish side of the town, in full view of the advancing column. The white-uniformed squadrons of the French cavalry put spurs to their horses and charged through the quiet streets in a tumult of dust, in order to reach the place and repel the invaders before they could establish a defensive position ashore.

Cochrane watched them go, and then brought the *Imperieuse* in to bombard the town at close range. The French batteries on the cliffs were unable to depress their guns sufficiently to fire on the frigates without hitting their own men in the streets. For an hour the bombardment continued until the beach was masked under a pall of blue-grey gunsmoke in the warm stagnant air. Using this as a screen, Cochrane then put ashore his real marines, landing them in the chaos of half destroyed buildings and fires burning beyond control. The redcoats disappeared in the smoke and the débris, heading for the cliffs, and presently there came the first sounds of a French shore-battery being demolished.

The main body of the French infantry was still advancing towards the town but was too far off to intervene. The cavalry squadrons had reached the shore, where the other "marines" were expected to land, but found nothing except several small boats, filled with ships' boys in oversized uniforms, bobbing about offshore. As the horsemen collected their wits, the first sounds of demolition reached them from Port Vendre. They turned and began to gallop back. Captain Brenton and his officers on the quarterdeck of H.M.S. *Spartan* foresaw catastrophe. The cavalry would return in ample time to cut off the marines from the two frigates, turning audacity into folly.

But the officers of the *Spartan* were about to witness a superb example of what Brenton afterwards called the "ready seamanship . . . displayed by Lord Cochrane upon this occasion". The cavalry were out of sight during most of their return gallop, but there was one stretch of coast where they would appear at full length, their white uniforms picked out against the rock behind them. The two frigates were cruising offshore at three knots with no conceivable means of engaging cavalry. Then, as the horsemen appeared against the rock, the *Imperieuse* responded to a sudden order. The anchor splashed down and, to Brenton's disquiet, she began to swing at the anchor cable, almost across the bows of the *Spartan*. As she turned in this arc, her starboard side turned, briefly, parallel with the shore. With perfect judgement of range and precisely at the moment when the cavalry was at full stretch and the ship's side facing them, every gun roared out in a hoarse cannonade and a bank of rolling smoke. When the smoke cleared, those on the quarterdeck of the *Spartan* saw that the squadron of cavalry had virtually ceased to exist. A few dismounted figures were scrambling clear of the débris but, as a military formation, it had been totally destroyed by the terrifying accuracy of Cochrane's fire.

There was puzzlement afterwards as to how this precision of angle, range, and timing had been achieved. Brenton, who saw it all, admitted that no captain on any quarterdeck in the world would have been able to coordinate such an attack. But Brenton had also been able to see that Cochrane was not on his quarterdeck. He had directed the whole operation from the masthead, which most Royal Navy commanders regarded as a place climbed to only by common seamen or by junior officers as a punishment. The marines destroyed such French shipping as they could find in harbour and returned with three wounded. The damage to the ships was confined to torn rigging.[14]

The tactical value of such attacks was unquestioned, but their effect on French morale was of still greater consequence. The name of the *loup des mers* was only too well known to the inhabitants of the French Mediterranean coast and to their armies in Catalonia. Lord Brougham recalled a visit to the Tuileries after the war had ended. When he mentioned the name "Cochrane", there was "a general start and shudder" among the French leaders, an instinctive reaction of fear which was quite different to the chivalrous admiration bestowed upon such reputations as those of Nelson or Wellington.[15]

Lord Collingwood shared few of the reservations over Cochrane expressed by St Vincent or Keith. As the *Imperieuse* continued to harry the French coast during September 1808, Collingwood received news of the exploits on board his flagship, H.M.S. *Ocean*, which was cruising off Toulon. Writing to Wellesley Pole, Collingwood confirmed that Cochrane had not only pinned down French regiments which were otherwise intended for the Spanish war, he had actually obliged the French to withdraw 2000 troops from the garrison of Figuras in order to defend their own coasts from his attacks. "Nothing can exceed the zeal and activity with which his lordship pursues the enemy," wrote Collingwood. "The success which attends his enterprises clearly indicates with what skill and ability they are conducted." But as Cochrane's fame spread from official reports to more popular literature there was an even more important point to make, as Sir Walter Scott explained.

> Lord Cochrane, during the month of September 1808, with his single ship, kept the whole coast of Languedoc in alarm. . . . Yet with such consummate prudence were all Lord Cochrane's enterprises planned and executed, that not one of his men were either killed or hurt, except one, who was singed in blowing up a battery.[16]

Cochrane's care and concern for his men was one of his noblest characteristics, earning him personal loyalty and their confidence in his fighting abilities. He had also informed the French who became his prisoners in Catalonia that war was not an excuse for "extermination", and their conduct towards the Spanish population was all the more reprehensible as the action of a civilised nation.

Early in October, the *Imperieuse* returned to Gibraltar. The frigate had been able to undertake cruises of unusual length as a result of Cochrane's unorthodox manner of replenishing food and water. Water was the greatest problem to other captains. However, when the casks of the *Imperieuse* ran dry off Marseille, Cochrane set sail for the mouth of the Rhône at full speed, relying on his reputation to send the enemy running in all directions. He sailed up the river to the point where the fresh water was "pure", lowered the studding sails from the foretopmast over the side, having sewn them up as water bags, and pumped the water aboard from them by using the fire pump. He also attempted to round up a herd of cattle from the river bank but the animals set off inland at speed and, after a chase of three miles, the crew of the *Imperieuse* gave up the pursuit. Throughout this expedition, Cochrane treated the Rhône as though it were as much his territory as the Thames or the Medway might have been. His supreme control of the situation is ample confirmation of the reports of Collingwood and the eulogies of Scott.[17]

At the end of October, the *Imperieuse* sailed from Gibraltar again, carrying Cochrane towards his last Mediterranean exploit. It was to eclipse the *Gamo* incident and all the harrying of enemy coasts. More important, it was to convince at least some of the British commanders that such abilities and audacity must be employed at the highest level if the war was to be won.

Cochrane's orders from Lord Collingwood were to assist the Spanish guerrillas in any way which seemed practicable. At the same time, a French column of 6000 men with considerable Italian reinforcements was marching into Catalonia to decide the military issue with the Spaniards once for all. Anything that could be done to divert or impede the advance would be of the utmost value. The next town on the route of the approaching army was Rosas. The northern arm of Rosas Bay was Cape Creux, where the Pyrenees came down in a long grey spur to the Mediterranean.

The *Imperieuse* dropped anchor in the bay on 21 November. Cochrane himself was already in the town, having gone on ahead by gig when the *Imperieuse* was becalmed ten miles short of Rosas Bay. He judged this essential, since the town and citadel were coming under fire from the head of the approaching column. When he arrived, the Spanish commander was already preparing to withdraw in the face of superior numbers. Cochrane begged him to hold on until the arrival of the *Imperieuse* with her crew and her marines. As a token of his faith in this, he announced that he would remain to assist the defenders of Rosas until the frigate arrived.

His plan was, as usual, very simple. The town and its citadel could not hold out indefinitely against the French. Napoleon's gunners had perfected the technique of breaching such defences by firing repeatedly at the same area in the base of a wall, bringing down a section of the structure at the precise moment required, and allowing their infantry to pour through the gap before the defenders had time to shore it up.

But Cochrane, with his long experience of gunnery, had surveyed the cliffs above Rosas and noticed an old and rather dilapidated fortress, Fort Trinidad. It consisted of three towers, rising like three steps because of the sloping ground, the tallest of them 110 feet high. The only way in which it could be attacked by the French artillery was from still higher ground, but Cochrane guessed that their guns could not be depressed sufficiently to hit anything but the leading tower about 50 feet above its base. The shells would certainly blow a breach in the wall but at such a height it would take scaling ladders for the infantry, in their frontal attack, to reach the opening. To most commanders, Fort Trinidad had one over-riding disadvantage. It backed directly on to the edge of the cliff, making access, supply, and retreat equally hazardous. But to men whose lives were spent climbing masts and rigging, cliffs and ropes presented no problems. An army commander might not like fighting with the sea at his back, but at Cochrane's back there would be the *Imperieuse* with her 18-pounder guns.

It was a tenable position, and as long as his men could hold it, the French regiments would be halted. They could not risk leaving Fort Trinidad and an attacking force in their rear, even supposing that they could bypass the fortress and the town. It was just possible to imagine that Cochrane and his crew might throw back the enemy advance into Catalonia, a feat which would have been more appropriate to a force the size of Sir Arthur Wellesley's new army.

As soon as the *Imperieuse* arrived, Cochrane and his seamen took possession of Fort Trinidad. He stationed about fifty of them there and reinforced them with his thirty marines. They were few enough to fight against a column of thousands of Franco-Italian infantry and grenadiers accompanied by cavalry and artillery. As he expected, the French soon mounted their heavy guns on the height above, training them on the middle of the leading tower, which was their most promising target.

During the first few days, his men endured a bombardment which was far worse than anything they had known at sea. The thunderclap of the enemy 24-pounders, 300 yards away, was followed by the howl of shells, an earth-shaking impact, and an explosion which was almost drowned by the harsh roar of falling masonry. Worse still, at every detonation the granite blocks of the wall disintegrated into small, flying splinters, each of them sharp and lethal.

The interior of Fort Trinidad, even before the shelling began, resembled a scrap heap of military equipment. Midshipman Marryat, who acted as Cochrane's adjutant during the action, recalled, "Heaps of crumbling stones and rubbish, broken gun-carriages, and split guns." For days, and then weeks, the men of the *Imperieuse* made this their home. "We all pigged in together," said Marryat, "dirty straw and fleas for our beds; our food on the same scale of luxury." It had been hoped that boats from the frigate would maintain a supply of food, but the French had installed sharpshooters on every side, some of them dug in no more than 50 yards away, and there were days when the boats could not land. None the less, Cochrane insisted on having the hands piped to dinner, even when there was nothing but cold water to "dine" on. "Regularity", he observed was good for the character.

While all this was going on, Cochrane prepared for the inevitable French attack. There was no doubt that it would come by way of the breach which the gunners had made in the wall of the leading tower, and which proved to be 60 feet above its base. He evacuated all his men from this tower and concentrated the defence in the other two. But once again, as though it were an elaborate practical joke, he began to booby-trap the breach. He first knocked out an internal arch so that the attackers would find that the surface beyond the breach caved in under them. For good measure he used deal planks brought from the *Imperieuse* as a platform in the breach and then coated them with "cook's slush" or grease. No French infantryman would retain his footing for more than a few seconds on the slippery wooden surface before being precipitated 50 feet down into the "bug trap" as the English sailors christened the device.

Between the abandoned tower and the one behind it, where his sailors and marines were concentrated, he built a barricade, reinforced by sandbags which were filled during the hours of darkness and comparative inactivity. This redoubt within the fortress was also protected by top chains from the frigate to which large fish hooks had been securely fastened. As Cochrane enthusiastically pointed out, an enemy who tried to scramble over such a parapet would find himself impaled helplessly on the hooks and might be despatched at leisure.

Finally, Cochrane mined the breach, so that if the French succeeded in taking the outer wall and overcoming the obstacles, he could at least blow up the leading tower of Fort Trinidad and a good number of grenadiers before his little army was overwhelmed. He was joined by a few dozen guerrillas and some Irish mercenaries in Spanish pay, all of whom assisted in the preparations which he had undertaken. He won their allegiance not only by his almost boyish enthusiasm and energy for the great "game" with the French but also by his well-chosen dramatic gestures. On 25 November, some three hundred hits were scored on the massive walls of Fort Trinidad. In such a bombardment it was not surprising that the Spanish flag was brought down by one salvo and lay in the ditch before the fortress, directly in the path of the French artillery barrage and in the line of fire from their sharpshooters. With apparent unconcern, Cochrane walked out of Fort Trinidad and round to the front of the leading tower where the flag had fallen. He paid no more attention to the musket balls which whizzed about him than if they had been flies on a summer day. While the artillery salvoes hurtled overhead with the sound of the sky being rent apart, he stooped down, retrieved the Spanish flag and hoisted it triumphantly. Then, to the cheers of compatriots and allies, he walked slowly back. So far as the alliance with Spain was concerned it was an astute act of showmanship.

But the tall figure in the blue captain's uniform, complete with gold braid and cocked hat was unmistakable to the enemy. Later on, Cochrane noticed an ominous lull in the firing and went to investigate. This time, as he peered towards the French artillery, another shot boomed out across the cliffs, the sky rent again by the path of the shell, the flash and chaos of the explosion veiling the scene. When the smoke cleared, it was evident that Cochrane had been hit. His head was bowed and there was blood down his face and on his uniform. He stumbled back to the care of the ship's surgeon, Guthrie, who was acting as medical officer in Fort Trinidad. It was not the shell which had hit him but one of the flying splinters of granite from the tower wall. It had broken his nose and penetrated through the roof of his mouth.

Guthrie did his best to dress the wound and Cochrane, breathing through his mouth, resumed command of his little army. There was no leisure to convalesce, since the situation on either side of his fortress was deteriorating by the hour. After a week of bombardment the French had failed to dislodge him, but they had driven off the ship's boats which were approaching the cliff and so isolated him from the *Imperieuse*. Worse still, though the citadel of Rosas still held out, the French infantry had entered the town. The enemy was able to reinforce the siege of Fort Trinidad and on the ninth day he found five artillery batteries trained on his position from the high ground above him. On the same day, 29 November, he also heard that in Rosas itself the defenders of the citadel were cut off from all assistance.

Cochrane woke long before dawn on 30 November with a quite irrational conviction that the French had got into Fort Trinidad. This was clearly absurd, since as he lay there and listened, the entire building was silent. But the premonition was so strong that he could not sleep and in the end got up and went out to the rampart "half ashamed of having given way to such fancies". The rampart was defended by a single mortar. This had been carefully sited the day before so that its shells would land on the path which came over the height in the distance, down into the declivity and so to Fort Trinidad. It was the obvious choice of route for the French infantry when they attempted to storm the fortress.

Without any sufficient reason, Cochrane put a taper to the touch-hole and fired the mortar, the hiss of the shell was followed by an explosion on the distant path, the echoes dying away among the surrounding hills. But even before the last echo had died, Cochrane and his companions on the rampart ducked down as a volley of musketry "pattered like hail on the walls of the fort". The main French infantry column had advanced under cover of darkness and was within a few minutes of the point at which the storming of the fortress would begin.

Cochrane shouted, "To arms! They are coming!" and in a few moments the seamen, marines, and Spanish troops woke to the sound of the call, and scrambled for the places allotted them at the walls. Midshipman Marryat timed them and found that it took just three minutes for every man to be at his post. Looking out across the terrain between Fort Trinidad and the French positions he saw that the streak of fog which had filled the valley during the night, was now beginning to rise and the stars were fading in the first pale light of the day. Napoleon's grenadiers and infantry regiments were marching in strength against Cochrane's position. "The black column of the enemy was distinctly visible," Marryat recalled, "curling along the valley like a great centipede." But though it stretched so far back, the head of the "centipede" was already close to the foot of the leading tower with the breach in its wall. Since there was no further point in attempting a secret assault, the drums beat out the familiar "rum-dum, rum-dum, rumma-dum, rumma-dum, dum-dum," of Napoleon's legions marching to the attack. Ahead of the blue-coated infantry regiments strode the French grenadiers, their impressive height exaggerated still further by their tall black headgear. The first ranks advanced, firing as they came, towards the tower where the shells had brought down piles of granite to serve as a rough ramp upward to the breach. Other parties among the attackers were carrying scaling ladders with which they ran forward, attempting to position them and get the first wave of infantry through the breach and into Fort Trinidad before a defence could be organised.

Cochrane gave the order to fire. From slits and chinks in the walls his marines and seamen opened crackling volleys of musketry on the swarming mass of the French infantry which was already beginning to scale the breach. But a hundred men with muskets could never hold off an attacking force of thousands. Muskets took too long to reload, a whole minute in inexperienced hands, and were notoriously inaccurate except at close range. There was no hope that such weapons alone would turn back a major assault of this kind.

Cochrane had guessed what the French would expect. They would assume that the defence of Fort Trinidad was based on a vain hope of driving back the grenadiers and infantry before they could clamber into the breach. They would hardly suppose that his true defence was concentrated inside the fortress.

Within ten minutes of the attack being launched, forty of the grenadiers reached the opening midway up the leading tower. Once there, they either found that they could not keep their footing because of the boards well greased with "cook's slush" and were duly thrown 50 feet down, or else they clung precariously, unable to advance farther than the breach, since Cochrane had demolished everything below them on the interior side. It was then that the men of the *Imperieuse*, manning the position between the two towers were presented with the French soldiers in the breach, silhouetted like targets in a shooting gallery. Except for those who fell to their deaths in the "bug trap" there was no advance, and the pressure of others behind them made retreat impossible. In several minutes of confusion and horror, the volleys of British musketry scythed among them, cutting down rank after rank, until the breach was clear.

While his men within the fort kept up their fire on the breach, Cochrane saw that the piles of stones and ladders leading up to it were crowded with French infantry waiting to follow and having no idea what caused the hesitation. It was under all this that he had laid his mine and, accordingly, he now gave orders for the fuse to be lit. In a moment more Fort Trinidad was shaken by the greatest explosion of the siege. Midshipman Marryat, watching the French advance, wrote, "up they went in the air, and down they fell buried in the ruins. Groans, screams, confusion, French yells, British hurras, rent the sky!"

The first French attack had been broken, but a second mass of infantry was pressing forward to follow over the dead bodies of its comrades. Cochrane had expected this. From the top of the tower he had suspended carefully-contrived bombs, which could be released, with fuses lit, on to the enemy below. He had also gathered up there his stock of hand grenades and had ordered his men to reserve some of their ball and powder for this second attack. There was always the danger that the defenders might exhaust their ammunition if the French attack persisted but after the fate of the first assault the infantrymen who followed it were less than enthusiastic.

As they approached the tower wall, Cochrane's crew greeted them with a volley of musketry which brought down the leaders, including the French colonel who commanded the attack. Then, like fire from heaven, the bombs and hand grenades fell from the tower above. Leaderless and unnerved, the second wave of infantry began to fall back. Marryat saw the retreat turn into a rout. The surviving French officers drew their swords and ordered their men back into the attack, but it was to no avail. They simultaneously led the men on and shouted "Suivez-moi!" as they tried to control the demoralised troops. Marryat even saw them driving their swords through the backs of men who turned to run. But the formations scattered. Marryat thought the French infantrymen "had had fighting enough for one breakfast".

The crew of the *Imperieuse* and their companions had, as it proved, thrown back an attack by an advance guard of 1200 infantry. The main body of French troops on the surrounding hills entirely misjudged the situation and apparently assumed that those grenadiers who had disappeared into the breach had taken possession of Fort Trinidad and that the battle was won. Accordingly, they marched from every direction down towards the scene of the débâcle, drums playing and the early sunlight glinting on the Imperial Eagles. At their approach to the fortress, Cochrane gave the order for a concentrated volley of musket fire, which caught the columns in open country. They had no independent means of reaching the hole high up in the tower wall and were, in any case, expecting only to occupy a position which had already been captured by their advance guard. They halted and, as a second volley of musketry dropped a score of men in their leading ranks, the royal blue infantry fled ignominiously back to the cover of their position.

Cochrane was no less exhilarated than his men. If only for another day, he had stopped the advance of the French column into

Catalonia. Moreover, as he surveyed the wreckage and the bodies lying outside, he counted over fifty enemy dead to which had to be added the bodies of some who had been carried back in the retreat. His own losses amounted to three, two of them Spaniards and the other being one of his marines. He had surely proved, if proof were needed, that with half a dozen frigates he could not only disrupt the commerce, communications, and military movements of the enemy, he could also inflict losses on them which were out of all proportion to those suffered by his own men. The French column before him had lost fifty or a hundred of their most highly-trained attacking force and were no nearer to Catalonia now than they had been ten days before.

In the midst of the smoke and the carnage of that early morning engagement, however, there had been one incident which illustrated how many of the courtesies of war had survived into the more earnest age of hand grenades and mortars. When the rest of the attacking force had retreated, one French officer, refusing to withdraw until his men were safe, stood with his drawn sword upon the rubble. Cochrane, carrying an ordinary musket, came face to face with him and covered him with the weapon at once. But instead of lowering his sword in token of surrender, the Frenchman flourished it aloft and stood firmly "like a hero to receive the bullet". It was exactly the type of gesture to win Cochrane's admiration. "I never saw a braver or a prouder man," he remarked. Lowering his musket he added that such a man was not born to be shot like a dog and invited the Frenchman to take his leave and make his way back to his own lines. "He bowed as politely as though on parade, and retired just as leisurely."[18]


Instead of persuading him that he might now retire with honour from Fort Trinidad, Cochrane's success on 30 November increased his determination to hold the position for as long as possible. On 3 December, he actually assumed the offensive and led his men out in an attack on the French infantry, who had dug themselves in on the hillside. This was of less use tactically than in terms of morale. It was evidently the occasion on which he came back from the sortie in company with Midshipman Marryat. While ordering his men to run back for the cover of Fort Trinidad, Cochrane himself "walked leisurely along through a shower of musket-balls". Marryat, who also longed to run with the men, was obliged to walk beside Cochrane at the same "funeral pace". It was a fixed principle with Cochrane, he learnt, that he "never had run away from a Frenchman, and did not intend to begin".

As they walked on, Marryat tried to edge round so that Cochrane was between him and the French muskets. Cochrane noticed this, and as though it were a great joke, ordered Marryat back into position again. "Just drop astern, if you please, and do duty as a breastwork for me." If nothing else, it was the first lesson in supreme self-confidence.[19]

After so much jubilation there was a sour conclusion to the affair of Fort Trinidad. On the next day, 4 December, the French artillery in the town of Rosas succeeded in opening a breach in the citadel walls which the defenders could not close. The citadel duly surrendered. At the same time, there was a message from the *Imperieuse* that a gale was blowing up and that the frigate must put to sea. There could be no certainty when, or if, she would be able to bring further supplies or lend military support to her commander in his fortress. The situation was further complicated on 5 December by the withdrawal from battle and the surrender of the Spanish troops in Fort Trinidad. Accepting the inevitable, Cochrane arranged an evacuation of his men.

The *Fame* and the *Magnificent* anchored in Rosas Bay in response to signals from the *Imperieuse*, the three ships keeping up a steady bombardment of the French positions. Under cover of this, Cochrane withdrew his men from Fort Trinidad on the morning of 5 December and got them down to the beach by means of rope ladders. He also evacuated those other defenders who preferred to sail on the *Imperieuse* rather than to surrender to the French. The last two men to leave Fort Trinidad were Cochrane himself and the gunner of the *Imperieuse*. They set the charges, lit the fuses, and then followed the others down to the beach. One charge failed to go off but as the *Imperieuse* and the accompanying ships sailed out of Rosas Bay, the main tower of Fort Trinidad went skyward in an impressive display of the art of demolition.[20]

The reception awaiting Cochrane on his return from this cruise was varied. He had, predictably, become a hero of the Spanish war of liberation. The story of how he had rescued the Spanish flag from the ditch, under the fire of the French, was told as an illustration of his valour. "This gallant Englishman," said the *Gerona Gazette*, repeating the story, "has been entitled to the admiration and gratitude of this country from the first moment of its political resurrection." At home, the *Naval Gazette* reported the story enthusiastically, assuring its readers that with a mere "handful of men . . . Lord Cochrane made the most astonishing exertions".[21]

The enthusiasm of the Admiralty was, predictably, more muted. In reply to Collingwood's account of the action of Fort Trinidad and the prodigious damage done to the French for the loss of three men, they sent a reprimand to Cochrane for excessive use of powder and shot. They also showed evident dislike of his excessive use of the *Imperieuse*, which was apt to require more in repairs and maintenance than ships which kept out of harm's way. Cochrane observed bitterly that captains who avoided combat and brought ships home unblemished were rewarded with pensions of £1000 or £1500 a year by Admiralty placemen. He himself received nothing for thirty years and then, through the intervention of the Earl of Minto, was at length granted the ordinary good service pension.[22]

The "res angusta domi" of childhood, as well as the fierce sensitivity of his pride had left him acutely sensitive to financial injustice and the thought that he was being made a fool of by its agency. His action at Fort Trinidad had been at the expense of scouring the Mediterranean for prizes. It was not in the least inconsistent with the figure of the public hero that he should demand some practical reward for this sacrifice. His superiors might call on him to shed his blood or lay down his life for his country, but they must not expect to pick his pockets. It was a belief latent in the minds of most serving officers and their men, though in Cochrane's case the circumstances of his life caused him to hold it with a certain bizarre prominence. It would have been simple to condemn him as grasping and materialistic, but this would hardly explain the acts of generosity attributed to him throughout his life. Though he had need of money, as a post-captain, his care for it was essentially the manifestation of his sense of pride and justice.

However, his correspondence and despatches began to show another and more urgent preoccupation. He was convinced that he had the key to Britain's victory in the war against Napoleon and that the recent exploits of the *Imperieuse* showed that he had mastered its use. He had shown what could be done on the French coast and in eastern Spain. The same could be done on the Atlantic coast, with a few frigates and their marines assisting the Spanish to impede or block French military operations. Best of all, a small military force, supported by frigates, should be landed on the ill-defended French islands of the Bay of Biscay. From there, such operations might be

carried out against the west coast of mainland France as would make
it impossible for Napoleon to maintain an army in Portugal or in
Spain. By contrast, for Wellington to land in one of the remotest
parts of the Iberian peninsula, and to fight a long overland campaign
to reach the Pyrenees and enter France was a military absurdity. By
making it impossible for the French to supply or reinforce their
troops, and by putting them at the mercy of the guerrillas in consequence, the tide of war might be turned quickly and spectacularly.
As Cochrane later wrote, "neither the Peninsular War, nor its enormous cost to the nation, from 1809 onwards, would ever have been
heard of".[23]

This was no mere eccentricity on Cochrane's part. In England, the
*Naval Chronicle*, echoing the view of the *Morning Chronicle* and the
non-ministerial press, was an advocate of this new strategy.

> Seeing what Lord Cochrane *has* done with his single ship
> upon the French shores, we may easily conceive, what he would
> have achieved if he had been entrusted with a sufficient squadron
> of ships, and a few thousand military, hovering along the
> whole extent of the French coast, which it would take a con-
> siderable portion of the army of France to defend.[24]

After his eventful cruises of the summer and autumn of 1808,
Cochrane received orders to bring the *Imperieuse* back to England
early in 1809. He had asked for leave to return, in any case, so that he
might bring his plan for attacking the Biscay islands before the
Board of Admiralty. In bringing him home, their Lordships had
recognised their need of him, but it was not quite for the purpose he
supposed. When the *Imperieuse* dropped anchor off Plymouth,
Cochrane was greeted by news of impending naval disaster.

Its architect was Admiral Lord Gambier, an evangelist in a cocked
hat, who had been commanding the blockade of the French battlefleet at Brest. St Vincent described him privately as "a compound of
paper and packthread". The poet Thomas Hood, in his "Ode to
Admiral Gambier, G.C.B.", mocked his opposition to drink in all its
forms.

> OH! Admiral Gam—— I dare not mention *bier*,
> In such a temperate ear;
> Oh! Admiral Gam—— an Admiral of the Blue,
> Of course, to read the Navy List aright,
> For strictly shunning wine of either hue,
> You can't be Admiral of the Red or White.[25]

Gambier, round-faced, smooth-shaven and earnest, had been pre-occupied with the salvation of his crews. When high winds and a strong sea carried the blockade force from its position briefly, Rear-Admiral Willaumez seized the opportunity. In a matter of hours, the naval might of France was at sea, ready to fall upon the fat prey of England's West India convoys. The size of the threatened calamity, and the political influence of the West India merchants, allowed no leisure for the gratification of personal hatreds at that moment. There was only one man with the experience and resource to retrieve the situation. Through their clenched teeth, the ministry and its placemen admitted as much. At Plymouth, Cochrane found a letter awaiting him from Johnstone Hope, Second Lord of the Admiralty, describing the disaster. He had not even had time to step ashore before the semaphore of the flag officer commanding the Plymouth station began to telegraph the *Imperieuse* with the message which had been signalled urgently from London. Cochrane was to report immediately to Whitehall.

# 5

# In the Face of the Enemy

———

THE extent of the threatened naval reverse was clear at a glance. By 21 February, Gambier had been blown off station in a westerly gale. At dawn that day the French squadron of eight battleships and accompanying frigates slipped its moorings and, under the command of Rear-Admiral Willaumez, glided away from the Brest anchorage in a fresh north-east wind. By 9 a.m. the last of the ships had rounded the Vendrée rock and the entire squadron stood out to sea in line of battle. Willaumez carried regiments of troops and provisions for an Atlantic voyage. The first target might be the British convoys but the ultimate destination was the French West Indian base at Martinique.

H.M.S. *Revenge* sighted the French ships off the coast of southern Brittany within a few hours of their escape, but she soon lost them again. The next sighting was by Commodore Beresford, commanding H.M.S. *Theseus* and three other 74-gun ships. Beresford was blockading a smaller French group of three ships of the line plus frigates in the port of Lorient. It was on the following afternoon, as the winter light began to fail that he saw Willaumez's squadron and formed his four ships into line of battle with the *Theseus* at their head. By 6 p.m. he had lost contact with the enemy. During this diversion, three French ships of the line and their five frigates escaped from his own blockade.

Gambier and the Admiralty remained in comfortable ignorance of the eleven French battleships and their frigates now at large in the Bay of Biscay. They represented a powerful striking force which could remain supremely elusive. Royal Navy captains did not need to be reminded that it had taken Nelson over six months to bring Villeneuve to battle in 1805. Unlike Villeneuve, Willaumez had the advantage of starting in the vast spaces of the Atlantic.

So far as Gambier and the Channel Fleet were concerned, the French ships were nowhere to be found. Gambier detached a squadron of his own, in the hope that Willaumez was running for the Mediterranean. The squadron made a voyage to Madeira and back without a sight of the enemy.

On 23 February, H.M.S. *Caesar*, flying the flag of Rear-Admiral Stopford, passed an agreeable day taking on stores, including five live bullocks, brought out from England by the supply frigate *Emerald*. The *Caesar* was one of four ships keeping up a blockade on the few French warships in the port of Rochefort, almost at the midpoint of the Biscay coast. She was anchored at a discreet distance from the tip of the Ile de Ré, which sheltered the northern flank of the approach to Rochefort and La Rochelle, as the Ile d'Oléron sheltered the south. The outer anchorage was known as the Basque Roads. Further in, among the shoals and smaller islands of Aix and Madame were the so-called Aix Roads. These offered a natural anchorage and a good defensive position, which had become important to the French fleet and was therefore blockaded as a matter of routine.

At 10 p.m., having taken on stores, the guns of the *Caesar* were run out for some belated gunnery practice, followed by small-arms drill. During this, the sky to the north-west was suddenly lit by the flare of signal rockets fired by another blockader, H.M.S. *Amazon*. The *Caesar* got under way immediately and joined her ally, in time to discover that a large French fleet was heading for the Basque Roads and the anchorage of the Ile d'Aix. Willaumez, having mustered all the ships from Brest and Lorient was now preparing to add those at Rochefort to his fleet. Fully supplied and manned, the entire force might then sail for Martinique.

Stopford made no attempt to engage a group of such size, judging it more important to get word to the Channel Fleet. He sent the frigate *Naiad* to "proceed with all haste", bearing the news to Gambier and their Lordships of the Admiralty. There was hardly any need to add that an anchorage as extensive and irregular as the Basque Roads would be extremely difficult to blockade. If the French could give Gambier the slip at Brest, they could probably leave their anchorage in Aix Roads as soon as they wished. To attack them there would be extremely hazardous. Indeed, there were few Royal Navy captains who had been so foolhardy as to risk raiding that stretch of enemy coast. But the *Pallas* and the *Imperieuse* had given their commander considerable experience of it. So it was that Lord Mulgrave sent for Cochrane, as a matter of extreme urgency.[1]

The interview in the First Lord's room at the Admiralty was a bizarre one by any standard. From his ornate apartments, beyond whose windows the milkmaids tended the cattle which grazed St James's Park, Mulgrave was apt to rule his unseen ships as though they were part of his estates. He was no naval strategist, though he had been Colonel of the 31st Foot. In private he liked to think of himself as a patron of the arts, collecting Rembrandt and Titian, commissioning Wilkie to paint such genre pieces as "Rent Day" and "Sunday Morning", and having his portrait painted, with a certain inevitability, by Sir Thomas Lawrence. Mulgrave had not enjoyed a political career of much distinction. He had been a nondescript Secretary of State for Foreign Affairs from 1805 until 1806 and had gone out of office with the Tories. When they came back, Portland made him First Lord of the Admiralty in 1807. In appearance and behaviour he was, as Benjamin Haydon remarked, "high Tory and complete John Bull". During a period when the news of the war seemed to be invariably discouraging, he also had the undoubted gift of dismissing catastrophes as though they were mere inconveniences. The Walcheren disasters he spoke of as "adverse winds and unfavourable weather", in the tone of one whose garden party had been rained upon.[2]

It was impossible to imagine a man who had less in common with Cochrane. Yet Mulgrave greeted him with great frankness and a certain bonhomie. Their Lordships, he announced, were most concerned about the Basque Roads. They feared and expected that "the French fleet might slip out again". Blockade being a doubtful preventative, they had decided that the French ships should "forthwith be destroyed". No one, of course, had been able to suggest how this admirable strategy was to be implemented. Willaumez was in an excellent defensive position, and there were soldiers and guns on the Ile d'Aix. A man of enterprise and daring might, perhaps, risk an attack with fire-ships.

"However," said Mulgrave, "there is Lord Gambier's letter."

And he duly handed over to Cochrane the "most secret" despatch of 11 March, as though it had been the bill of fare in a hostelry. Cochrane read it. He was dismayed to find that Gambier had a pious objection to fire-ships and weapons of a similar nature on the ground that they were "a horrible mode of warfare". To use them in the Basque Roads, he added, would be "hazardous, if not desperate". All the same, their Lordships had set their hearts upon fire-ships as being the only devices which stood the least chance of success. One after another, the senior officers whom they approached had refused to have anything to do with the scheme. At last, swallowing their pride, they had sent for the one man who was ruthless enough, and mad enough, to attempt it. Cochrane was offered the command of the fire-ships and of the attack on the French fleet.[3]

As Mulgrave explained, the Admiralty Board and the ministers had worked out carefully the possible consequences.

"You see," he remarked breezily to Cochrane, "that Lord Gambier will not take upon himself the responsibility of attack, and the Admiralty is not disposed to bear the *onus* of failure by means of an attack by fire-ships, however desirous they may be that such attack should be made."[4]

Portland's government was already in difficulty over the French escape from Brest and the other Biscay ports. If the entire enemy fleet were now to break out of the Basque Roads and fall upon the West India trade, the ministry might well not survive. By attacking with fire-ships, however, the ministers stood to gain popularity if the assault succeeded. If it failed, they could wish for no better scapegoat than Cochrane.

It was, of course, open to Cochrane to refuse to have anything to do with the venture. He had hardly been back a week from a long and arduous tour of duty in the Mediterranean and he was, in truth, exhausted. But he knew quite well that if he declined absolutely, he would be marked as the "hero" whose courage failed when he was offered the command of a desperate venture in the hour of his country's need. He handed back Gambier's despatch to Mulgrave and dismissed the idea of conventional fire-ships.

"If any such attempt were made," he told the First Lord, "the result would in all probability be, that the fire-ships would be boarded by the numerous row-boats on guard – the crews murdered, – and the vessels turned in a harmless direction."

In that case, it seemed to Lord Mulgrave, there was nothing to be done. He was astonished when Cochrane, having dismissed the idea of an attack by fire-ships, added with hardly a pause: "But if together with the fire-ships, a plan were combined which I will propose for your Lordship's consideration, it would not be difficult to sink or scatter the guard-boats, and afterwards destroy the enemy's squadron."

Such was the urgency of the situation that Cochrane was required at once to set down his plan, which called for an initial assault by some of his own specially-constructed "explosion vessels". Mulgrave took it to another room where the Board of Admiralty had been sitting waiting to receive it. He returned after a short while and informed Cochrane that the plan had been unanimously approved.

"Will you undertake to put it in execution?"

Cochrane had already prepared his refusal. He was exhausted to the point of sickness by his Mediterranean duties. Moreover, as he made clear to Mulgrave, he could imagine the jealousy and vindictiveness of senior officers at the Basque Roads when they discovered that a junior captain had been put in charge of the attack on the French fleet. Mulgrave protested that most of these men had been given their chance and had refused it. But Cochrane remained firm and Mulgrave undertook to "reconsider the matter, and endeavour to find someone else to put it in execution".[5]

The next day, Cochrane was summoned to the First Lord's room at the Admiralty again. This time, all Mulgrave's joviality had gone.

"My Lord," he said coolly, "you must go. The Board cannot listen to further refusal or delay. Rejoin your frigate at once. I will make you all right with Lord Gambier."

At every objection to the attitude of his seniors, Mulgrave continued to soothe Cochrane's anxieties.

"Make yourself easy about the jealous feeling of senior officers," he repeated confidently, "I will so manage it with Lord Gambier that the *amour propre* of the fleet shall be satisfied."

Still under protest, Cochrane withdrew. As a matter of self protection he wrote the First Lord a letter, stating his reservations in obeying the Board's command. Almost at once he received a reply from Mulgrave, congratulating him on his patriotic spirit and then adding in a brisk and businesslike postscript, "I think the sooner you go to Plymouth the better."[6]

While the formalities of Admiralty etiquette were observed and Cochrane was manoeuvred into a position where he could no longer refuse the command, the situation in the Basque Roads was growing critical. It was not merely that the French fleet might break out before the fire-ships were prepared, but rather that Gambier was now beginning to have doubts as to whether an attack could be mounted. His despatch on 11 March spoke of the French shore defences as being no impediment, but by 26 March he was convinced that any warship coming close to the enemy fleet would be "raked by the hot shot" from the batteries which he had previously considered to be "no obstacle".[7]

The *Imperieuse* arrived in the Basque Roads, where Cochrane found that the captain of every other ship was his senior. He had with him a private letter from Wellesley-Pole, Wellington's brother and First Secretary to the Admiralty, to Lord Gambier. Circumspectly, Wellesley-Pole described Cochrane's command of the attack as "conducting" it "under your lordship's directions". Since Gambier and his ships were to be nine miles out to sea, his "direction" of the operation might seem problematical.[8]

When the *Imperieuse* anchored with the fleet and Cochrane went aboard the *Caledonia* to report to the commander-in-chief, he found that the British captains and admirals were already fighting one another with a belligerence beyond anything which they showed to the French. There was intense dislike of Gambier personally and jealousy of him professionally on the part of men like Admiral Sir Eliab Harvey, who was present on the flagship. Gambier was notorious for being better acquainted with a desk in Whitehall than with the quarterdeck of a ship of the line. During the first twenty-two years of his life as a Royal Navy officer he had contrived to spend seventeen of them ashore. On the other hand, he had commanded H.M.S. *Defence* at the Glorious First of June and had emerged with his ship scarred and smoke-blackened from the thick of the fight. Captain Pakenham of the *Invincible* had hailed him waggishly across the water, "I see you've been knocked about a good deal. Never mind, Jimmy, whom the Lord loveth he chasteneth!"

Though men like Harvey swore that Gambier owed his promotion to kinship with Pitt and the Barham family, it was the air of suffocating piety exuded by their leader which they found so intolerable. Even as a junior officer, Cochrane was irritated by Gambier's insistence on having dozens of evangelical tracts delivered to the *Imperieuse* with orders for their distribution and perusal by officers and men alike.

While Gambier regarded Harvey as a heathen beyond the power of salvation, Harvey dismissed his commander's piety as canting humbug. Eliab Harvey was a man of courage and temper. As captain of the "Fighting *Téméraire*" at Trafalgar, he and Nelson had borne the main onslaught of the enemy battleships. At one point, the *Téméraire* had a French ship of the line grappled on one side and a Spaniard on the other, both trying to take her. When the smoke cleared at length, it was the men of the *Téméraire*, led by Harvey, who had captured the other two ships. At the gaming tables, Harvey was as courageous as in battle, according to Horace Walpole. His account occurs in a letter of 6 February 1780, when Harvey was a mere midshipman, written at Strawberry Hill to his friend Sir Thomas Mann.

> Within this week there has been a cast at hazard at the Cocoa Tree, the difference of which amounted to an hundred and fourscore thousand pounds. Mr. O'Birne, an Irish-gamester, had won £100,000 of a young Mr. Harvey of Chigwell, just started from a midshipman into an estate by his elder brother's death. O'Birne said "You can never pay me." "I can," said the youth; "my estate will sell for the debt." "No," said O, "I *will* win ten thousand – you shall throw for the odd ninety." They did, and Harvey won.[9]

There was almost every reason for Harvey and Gambier to detest one another. While Cochrane was on board the *Caledonia*, discussing his plan of attack with Gambier, Harvey was shown in. He demanded that Gambier should now put him in charge of the operation, and he produced a list of officers and men who had volunteered to serve under him in that event. Blankly implacable, Gambier reminded him that the Board of Admiralty had chosen Cochrane.

"I do not care," Harvey announced. "If I am passed by, and Lord Cochrane or any other junior officer is appointed in preference, I will immediately strike my flag, and resign my commission."

"I should be very sorry to see you resort to such an extremity," Gambier replied, though his sorrow was generally doubted by those who knew him. Even Cochrane himself was astonished by the outburst from Harvey which followed this.

"I never saw a man so unfit for the command of the fleet," he began, and then went on to accuse Gambier of wasting time with roll calls or musters instead of getting on with the attack. "If Lord Nelson had been here, he would not have anchored in Basque Roads at all, but would have dashed at the enemy at once."

Having delivered this final barb, Harvey stormed out. Cochrane found him in Sir Henry Neale's day cabin a little while later, still denouncing Gambier to anyone who would listen. However, he assured Cochrane that he had no personal quarrel with him. It was Gambier and his air of self-important piety which were Harvey's aversion.

The feelings of all concerned had now been heated to an intensity which was to cause the court-martialling of two British admirals in the next few months. Harvey threw aside all restraint and according to Cochrane's evidence, said to the assembled witnesses in the day cabin:

> This is not the first time I have been lightly treated and that my services have not been attended to in the way they deserved, because I am no canting Methodist, no hypocrite, no psalm-singer, and do not cheat old women out of their estates by hypocrisy and canting.

After this outburst, Harvey went up to the quarterdeck of the flagship and, in front of the flag-captain, William Bedford, listed the insults he had received from Gambier, which were a proof of the commander-in-chief's "methodistical, jesuitical conduct, and of his vindictive disposition". Bedford prudently kept clear of the dispute but he was already qualified to be a witness at the subsequent court-martial. For good measure, Harvey added:

> Lord Gambier's conduct, since he took command of the fleet is deserving of reprobation. His employing officers in mustering the ships' companies instead of in gaining information about the soundings, shows him to be unequal to the command of the fleet. You know you are of the same opinion.

But Bedford, once again, refused to be drawn into the argument. The next news of Sir Eliab Harvey was that he was on his way back to England to face a court-martial "for grossly insubordinate language on board the *Caledonia*, in consequence of not having been appointed to command the fire-ships". For his outbursts against Gambier he was sentenced to be dismissed the service. However, there were misgivings before long. He was, after all, the same Sir Eliab Harvey who had commanded the *Téméraire* at Trafalgar. In the following year, in recognition of his "long and meritorious services", he was reinstated in his rank and seniority. But it was only an act of grace, since the Admiralty never employed him again.[10]

Returning to the *Imperieuse*, Cochrane was alarmed to discover that Gambier ordered the frequent musters of ships' companies principally in order to examine them as to whether they had learnt the contents of the tracts distributed to them. He read through several of these, the work of Wilberforce, Hannah More and their associates. He found the contents "silly and injudicious". More disturbingly, the fleet was now divided into two irreconcilable factions. First there were the supporters of the tracts, "officers appointed by Tory influence or favour of the Admiral". Then there were those who

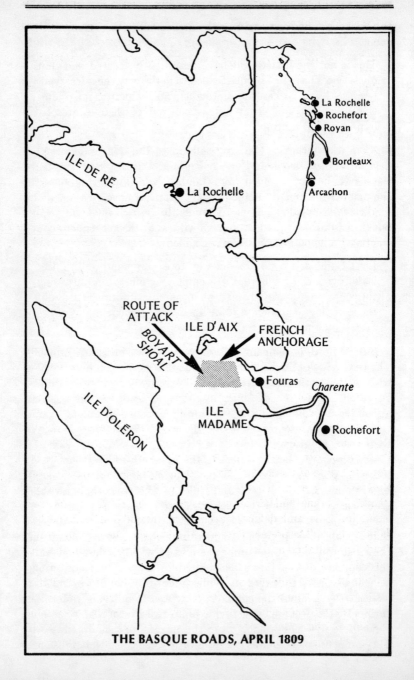

**THE BASQUE ROADS, APRIL 1809**

hated Gambier and his ostentatious piety. But because he was determinedly carrying out Admiralty instructions and allowing Cochrane to command the attack, this second group also disliked Cochrane himself quite as much as the first.[11]

While this diverting squabble was occupying the attention and energies of the Royal Navy, the French expeditionary force might well have made its escape. Fortunately for England, the French were busy with an unpleasant little dispute of their own. One of their captains, Jacques Bergeret, complained to the Minister of Marine that Willaumez had taken two days longer than was necessary to reach the Basque Roads. The Minister paid heed and replaced Willaumez by Vice-Admiral Allemand on 17 March.

Allemand anchored his fleet in two lines within the comparative safety of Aix Roads. The approach to the anchorage from the sea lay along the channel between the Ile d'Aix and the Boyart Shoal, a passage which was some two miles wide. Beyond it lay the mainland, the two arms of the Charente estuary. At low tide, some three miles of the Boyart Shoal were uncovered, as well as mud flats round the islands and the arms of the estuary. Allemand's ships were anchored inshore of the Aix-Boyart channel, just clear of the Palles Flat which was the extreme southern arm of the Charente estuary.

Even at low tide, the approach channel was still two miles wide and Cochrane knew that it was the inevitable route for an attacking force. There were soldiers and shore-batteries on the Ile d'Aix and, at a greater distance, on the Ile d'Oléron to the south and on the mainland. None of these would interfere with his plan.

He first sent back Lord Gambier's tracts, refusing to distribute them to his men. He included a few of them in a letter to his friend William Cobbett, merely in order that the world should see the deplorable "state of the fleet". He also sent a private despatch to Lord Mulgrave on 3 April. Though he had hardly arrived in the Basque Roads, Cochrane had already reconnoitred the Ile d'Aix and had found its walls and defences even more dilapidated than he had dared to hope. "At present the fort is quite open," he told Mulgrave, "and may be taken as soon as the French fleet is driven on shore or burned."

Cochrane repeatedly urged Mulgrave and the ministry to send a small force of troops so that the Biscay islands might be seized. French coastal trade and the main link between north and south on this side of the country would be at an end. The south would be starved of corn, the north of oil and wine. "No diversion which the whole force of Great Britain is capable of making in Portugal or Spain, would so much shake the French government as the capture of the islands on this coast. A few men would take Oléron."[12]

That Cochrane was right in supposing such an attack might tie down 100,000 French troops seems likely. That he had the capacity to lead an inventive and audacious attack had been proved. But perhaps the cavalier reference to Spain and Portugal was unfortunate. His despatch was bound to pass through the hands of the First Secretary at the Admiralty, William Wellesley-Pole, whose brother, in a few months more, was to be celebrated in verse by John Wilson Croker and in popular acclaim as Viscount Wellington of Talavera. All Cochrane's urging was greeted by a profound silence on the part of their Lordships.

Worse still, the days had passed and the fire-ships, which Mulgrave had promised, failed to arrive. Cochrane went to Gambier in desperation and demanded the use of some of the transports accompanying the fleet, which he proposed to transform into fire-ships and "explosion vessels" for the attack. Gambier agreed. Cochrane left the preparation of the fire-ships to the rest of the fleet and personally supervised the "explosion vessels".

Fire-ships were easily constructed. William Richardson was put to work on a brig from South Shields, which was anchored in the Basque Roads. He and his companions laid troughs of powder fore-and-aft on all the decks, crossing these with other troughs, and stacking wood and canvas between them. Tarred canvas was hung from the beams, and four large port-holes cut on each side of the deck, through which the draught would suck the fire with the effect of a furnace. The rigging was festooned with tarred ropes, the vessel was doused with resin and turpentine, and grappling chains fixed to it so that it would be more difficult for the French to dislodge it once it had drifted against any of their ships.[13]

Unlike the fire-ships, whose virtue was that they burnt long and slowly, the explosion vessels were designed to go up in a single devastating roar. Setting to work on a captured French coaster, Cochrane first had its decks and sides strengthened with logs and spars, to provide that resistance to the explosion which would in fact increase its destructive power. 1500 barrels of gunpowder were then packed into casks in the ship's hold. On each cask he placed a ten-inch shell and had the entire group of casks lashed together to resemble "a gigantic mortar". He packed 3000 hand grenades round this and laid a fuse to the stern of the vessel. The fuse would burn, he judged, for twelve to fifteen minutes, giving the volunteer crew of the explosion ship a chance to scramble into their little boat and row for safety.

Three explosion vessels were prepared as well as thirteen fire-ships. On 10 April the eight fire-ships promised by Lord Mulgrave arrived at last from England. Cochrane was to lead the attack in person but all those who went with him had to be volunteers. It was not only Gambier who regarded this as a horrible mode of warfare. In the French view, those who practised it and were captured must go before a firing squad.

It was later said that any British warships which had attempted to follow up the attack by these vessels would have been in great danger from the French batteries on the Ile d'Aix. Cochrane had reconnoitred the island and he knew better. The ineffectiveness of the French guns could hardly be more cogently demonstrated than by the willingness of men to act as crew on the explosion vessels. Gambier swore that the French were prepared to fire red-hot shot at any ship which foolishly approached Allemand's fleet by way of the Aix-Boyart channel. He and his supporters when asked why they had remained far out to sea swore that the risk of any approach involved unacceptable danger to themselves and their ships. If this were so it seems extraordinary that Cochrane and his men were prepared to go in with a ship whose hold contained 1500 barrels of gunpowder, a hundred or more ten-inch shells and some 3000 hand grenades. A single hit from one of the batteries on the Ile d'Aix would have ended the career of every man on board in the most spectacular fashion. However, it has also to be conceded that unacceptable danger was not a concept by which Cochrane was greatly preoccupied.

Once the fire-ships had arrived from England it was imperative to make the attack as soon as possible. It was not only that delay would give the French fleet a further opportunity of escape, the newly-arrived ships from England were being surveyed with interest from the mainland. It would only be a short time before Allemand and his captains identified these ships and their purpose.

However, the officers of the French fleet were uncomfortably aware of the weakness of their position, despite the fears which Gambier expressed for his own ships if he attempted a traditional attack. While he and the Admiralty hesitated, an officer of the French battle-ship *Océan* in Aix Roads wrote that an attack upon the Ile d'Aix would be "our destruction". Gambier and his supporters later pleaded that the strength of the island, its garrison and its batteries

was formidable. Only a madman of Cochrane's stamp would risk the
fleet against it. "Its garrison, it is true, is 2000 men strong," wrote the
officer of the *Océan* on 10 April, "but they are all conscripts who have
never seen any firing, and the island is strong only in that part which
protects the fleet on the N.E. side, or towards the coast of the Bay of
Rochelle. There are but a few guns placed at a distance from each
other and in bad condition." From a better vantage point than
Gambier ever enjoyed, he confirmed Cochrane's assurance to the
Admiralty that the fortress of Aix was "quite open".[14]

On 10 April, with the attacking force assembled and the weather
favourable, Cochrane went to see Gambier and asked that he should
be allowed to go in at once. To his astonishment, the admiral refused,
objecting that "the fire-ships might be boarded and the crews murdered" by the French. Impatiently, Cochrane pointed out that there
was a greater danger of this happening if the attack was delayed and
Allemand was given time to recognise the vessels for what they were.
Indeed, Gambier's objection would logically mean that no attack at
all could be made against the enemy.

"If you choose to rush on to self-destruction that is your own
affair," said Gambier haughtily, "but it is my duty to take care of the
lives of others, and I will not place the crews of the fire-ships in
palpable danger."[15]

Exasperated by this, Cochrane returned to the *Imperieuse*, which
was cruising off the Aix-Boyart passage. He was depressed but not
surprised to see that on the next morning Allemand had altered the
formation of his fleet, so that only the bows of half his ships, rather
than the sides of all of them, were offered as targets for attack.
While Gambier was protesting at Cochrane's impulsive folly in "rush-
ing on", Allemand had identified the fire-ships, as he reported in his
despatch of 12 April, and had taken precautionary measures. Ahead
of his battleships, his frigates awaited the attackers, behind a massive boom across the entrance of the anchorage.

On 11 April, the wind gathered strength and there was a high sea.
In these conditions, Gambier at length consented to the attack being
made. If he hoped that Cochrane himself would be deterred by the
squally conditions, he was due to be disappointed. The flood tide
that evening would be ideal for carrying the fire-ships and explosion
vessels in, while making it harder for the French guard-boats to row
out and forestall them. As Lord Gambier and his fleet put out to sea,
where they anchored some nine miles from the scene of the action,
Cochrane anchored the *Imperieuse*, with an explosion vessel in tow,

at the seaward end of the Boyart Shoal. With the frigates *Aigle*, *Unicorn*, and *Pallas*, and H.M.S. *Caesar* standing by to pick up the returning crews of the fire-ships, all was ready for the attack. The prize was a destructive blow against the power of France, equal perhaps to Trafalgar or the Nile.

As darkness fell on the early evening of 11 April, the volunteer captains of the fire-ships assembled on board the *Caledonia* for their final orders. They were to form the second wave of the attack, going in on the flood tide soon after 8 p.m. The initial assault on the French anchorage was to be made by the explosion vessels. No one had to inquire who would be in command of them. On the first vessel, far out in front of the rest, Cochrane himself would ride into battle at the flood tide, with a ton or two of assorted explosives under his feet.

At six in the evening, Allemand from the deck of the *Océan* sighted three frigates, four brigs, and three coasters coming to anchor at the far end of the Aix-Boyart channel. The weather was far from ideal for an attack but Admiral Allemand took no chances. He ordered out the ships' boats of the French fleet, fully armed, and instructed them to row for the great two-mile boom which enclosed the anchorage of Aix. This was his secret weapon. It was in the shape of a rather flat arrow-head, two miles in length and solidly constructed. On the surface it floated as a solid barrier of enormous spars lashed together and bound securely with heavy chains. But it was also anchored to the sea bed with such a weight of iron that it served almost as an impenetrable wall. No fire-ship, not even a ship of the line, would ever break through it.

The cutters and small boats were to take up their defensive position just within the sheltering arm of the boom, where it lay at the mainland end of the Aix-Boyart channel. An officer of the *Océan* watched them set out and saw that they had chosen almost the worst time of the tide for it. "Wind from the N.W. and blew very strong," he noted, "the sea high and the flood . . . beginning to make strong."[16]

Cochrane's men had a rather different problem. The flood tide was in their favour, carrying the explosion vessels and fire-ships in. But when they took to their little boats, they would have to row back at least three miles, against a tide which would be funnelling at full strength into the Aix-Boyart passage, before they could hope to be picked up by the waiting frigates or H.M.S. *Caesar*, which was about all that remained of Gambier's force.

On the *Imperieuse* there was a bustle of activity. Cochrane noticed that "it blew hard with a high sea", and then turned his attention to more important matters. Midshipman Marryat, waiting to go aboard the second explosion vessel, was encouraged to see that "the night was very dark, and it blew a strong breeze directly in upon the Isle d'Aix and the enemy's fleet". Like his companions, Marryat was prepared with a story of being from a sunken victualling vessel, if he were captured. It might mean the difference between a French prison and a firing squad.[17]

Cochrane went aboard the first explosion vessel, a converted coaster, accompanied by his brother, the Hon. Basil Cochrane, Lieutenant Bissel of the *Imperieuse*, and four seamen from his frigate who made up the volunteer crew. What Admiral Allemand saw as frigates, brigs, and coasters, was a mixture of the attack ships and the rescuers who would wait to pick up survivors. Beyond the *Imperieuse*, the dark outline of three rescue frigates rode at anchor. Farther out, the battleship *Caesar* acted as mother ship to the small boats of the fleet, which stood by to go in after the fire-ships and pick the crews out of the water.

The sloops *Redpole* and *Lyra* were anchored as far in as possible, each showing a light to mark the channel for the attackers. With the wind wailing in the rigging, and Lord Gambier waiting cautiously beyond the horizon, Cochrane cast off his explosion vessel and sailed into the attack. On the battleship *Caesar*, William Richardson and every man who could be spared waited in silent expectation on the crowded deck for the beginning of the great spectacle.

As Cochrane led the way, the second explosion vessel with Marryat aboard followed him. At the crucial moment, the two officers and three seamen who made up the crew had to scramble into a four-oared gig and, literally, row for their lives before the ship went up. It was not a comforting thought to Marryat, as the vessel passed between the lights of the two sloops, that the narrow shape of the little gig had earned it the sailors' nickname of "the coffin".

Leaving behind the two trim ship-rigged sloops with their guiding lights showing out to sea, Cochrane's explosion vessel drove hard towards the massive boom protecting the Aix anchorage. It was after eight o'clock and the darkness so intense that he could see nothing of Allemand's squadron which lay a mile or so ahead. But the tide and the wind were carrying the coaster forward, her hold packed with its mighty explosive charge. Judging the distance, Cochrane calculated that in another ten minutes or so she would be driven hard against the boom. He ordered his crew into the gig and remained alone on the explosion vessel. She was on course and moving with the breeze. He lit the fuse, scrambled down to join the others in the gig and ordered them to row for their lives away from the coaster. Straining against the flood-tide, they pulled for the open sea, but when they had drawn a hundred yards from the explosion ship it was realised they had left a dog on board, the mascot of the voyage. Cochrane turned the gig about again and headed back to the vessel whose fuse was already sputtering dangerously close to the powder in the hold. He jumped aboard, snatched the dog, leapt into the gig, and once more set his men to pulling for safety as the coaster drifted in towards the boom.[18]

A mile away, on the French flag-ship *Océan*, one of Allemand's officers came on deck at about half past eight. From the darkness of the Aix-Boyart channel he suddenly saw an apocalyptic flash and the world shook under him. The brilliance of rockets and shells ripped the night sky in every direction. He could think only of barges loaded with "shot, shells, and fire-rockets". To the English ships out to sea, the gigantic flash was followed by the sky glowing "red with the lurid glare arising from the simultaneous ignition of 1500 barrels of gunpowder". The French guard-boats which had reached the boom were now swamped or scattered by the detonation. Captain Proteau of the French frigate *Indienne*, one of the advance guard-ships, was close enough to see the great harbour boom ripped up from its sea-bed mooring, the heavy spars torn apart and hurled across the surface of the anchorage.[19]

Ten minutes later, while the burning wreckage of the first detonation drifted on the dark water, and the blue flares of the French defences rose into the sky to illuminate the scene, there was a second massive explosion, right against the remains of the boom. Captain Proteau and the frigate screen had been prepared for fire-ships, which could be boarded, or sunk, or at least fended off. But these new devices were something else, the work of a maniac who disregarded every convention of civilised warfare and apparently set as little value on his own life as on those of his enemies. The protecting boom was now shattered and the effect of the explosion vessels within the crowded anchorage would be annihilating.

At 9.30 p.m., while the guns from the Citadel of the Ile d'Aix maintained a fitful bombardment of the channel, the frigate H.M.S. *Mediator* crashed through the remains of the boom and the way to the anchorage lay open. Following her, came a flotilla of other vessels, dark and sinister at first then bursting into an outline of flame. The third explosion vessel was out of action, but the second wave of the attack, which was to be made by fire-ships, was now going in. On the *Indienne* and the *Océan* alike there was a horrified conviction that these were explosion vessels also. As they closed upon the anchorage, apprehension began to grow into panic.

While all this was going on, Cochrane and the occupants of a score of other "coffins" were rowing desperately against the flood-tide to get clear of the boom. When the first of the explosion vessels went up, he was still much closer to her than he had intended, partly because the fuse was so short and partly because he had gone back to rescue the dog. But it proved to be his salvation. As the roar of the explosion burst behind them, he and his oarsmen ducked down while the fragments of the blast sliced and whistled over their heads, rocketing into the sea beyond them with jets of dark water rising like fountains on every side. By an irony which he had no leisure to savour just then, Cochrane realised that if the gig had not been delayed, he and his crew would have been directly and fatally under the hail of shot and shell where it pitched into the sea.

And then, as the impact of the explosion reached the gig, "the sea was convulsed as by an earthquake". A huge wave, rising behind the gig, lifted them "like a cork", and then dropped them into a vast trough, "out of which, as it closed upon us with a rush of a whirlpool, none expected to emerge". But the boat's crew kept the little gig upright and afloat until the great swell had passed. After that, Cochrane noted, "nothing but a heavy rolling sea had to be encountered, all having again become silence and darkness". Neither the silence nor the darkness was destined to last for long. During the three-mile pull back to the *Imperieuse* the first fire-ships passed them, heading for Aix Roads. Since he could only go in with one wave of the attack, Cochrane had naturally chosen to lead the first and was unable to supervise the fire-ships personally. None the less, by the time that they reached the British frigates, he was able to look back and see that the first fire-ships were past the boom and among the French guard-ships. It was gratifying to see the disarray among the enemy and to see that, in the confusion, the French battleships were actually firing on their own frigates.[20]

The crew of the battleship *Caesar* had a grandstand view of the action as they waited for the ships' boats to return with the fire-ship crews they had picked up. "Shells and rockets were flying about in all directions," said Gunner Richardson, "and the blazing light all around gave us a good view of the enemy." Having turned night into day by his mortar shells and rockets, Cochrane regained the *Imperieuse*. There he received news of the fire-ship attack which demonstrated that the Royal Navy was as capable of folly and confusion as the French. Having gone with the explosion vessels he had left the fire-ships to others. The consequence was that only four out of the twenty had reached Aix Roads. The *Imperieuse* was anchored three miles from Allemand's fleet, and the captains of some fire-ships were igniting and abandoning them a mile and a half out to sea from the *Imperieuse*. Indeed, the frigate had the last explosion vessel in tow and the ship's company were horrified to see an abandoned fire-ship bearing down on them and their charge. The explosion vessel had to be hastily cut adrift and the frigate was hauled round by her cable, so that the fire-ship drifted harmlessly by and then grounded and burnt out on the Boyart Shoal.[21]

Gambier subsequently reproved Cochrane for having denounced some of the captains of the fire-ships. Certainly he swore to Captain George Wolfe of H.M.S. *L'Aigle* that Gambier's officers, left to their own devices, "had made such a bad business of it" that the attack was bungled. Wolfe was obliged to agree that his own frigate was "very nearly burnt by two that were badly managed". Apart from this, a man who had sailed 1500 barrels of gunpowder and detonated them 600 yards from the guns of the French fleet, according to Captain Proteau's own account, was entitled to a certain warmth of feeling over officers who prudently abandoned their attacking vessels four and half miles from the target.[22]

Most of the fire-ships drifted harmlessly aground to one side or other of the French fleet, but those which got through to the anchorage managed to compound the confusion and panic among Allemand's crews. At nine o'clock, one of the attackers looking like a splendid set-piece in a firework display, crashed into the 74-gun battleship *Régulus*, the heavy grappling chains hooking and holding her to her victim. The crew of the *Régulus* hacked through the anchor cables with desperate speed and tried to drift clear of the burning hulk. As the other fire-ships cruised menacingly into the anchorage, the frigate *Hortense* cut her cables too and opened fire on them. Worst of all, there were three fireships closing on Allemand's flagship, *Océan*. There was no time to lift the anchor. "We were obliged to cut this cable also," wrote one of her officers, "and steer so as to avoid Le Palles, the bank of rocks on which the *Jean Bart* was lost." Like so many well defended bases, Aix Roads offered little chance of manoeuvre, being surrounded by shoals and mud flats at very little depth, except towards the seaward channel and the mouth of the Charente.[23]

At 10 p.m. the *Océan* herself, manoeuvring desperately to avoid the fire-ships, ran aground. It was now apparent that those fire-ships which reached their targets did so because their crews remained with them all the way, in some cases being towed by the small boats which would rescue them subsequently. It was one of these which now made straight for the helpless flagship and grappled on to her stern. There was consternation on the *Océan*. Some of the French seamen played the fire pumps on their own decks to keep them wet, others tried to push the fire-ship off with spars, and a few used axes in an attempt to cut the grapplings. The rest of the French fleet tacked and drifted in the confined roads with predictable results. As the *Océan* struggled with the fire-ship, the battleship *Tonnerre* rammed her in the bows and, when she had parted from her, the flagship was rammed by the battleship *Patriote*. However, her crew succeeded in working free of the fire-ship which glided forward along her starboard side and drifted away. The *Océan* survived the ordeal of the night, though losing fifty of her crew through fire, shot, and collision. "In general," wrote one of her officers, "the whole of the fleet was very lucky on this dreadful night."[24]

On board the *Imperieuse*, Cochrane saw the matter differently. The fire-ship attack had failed in itself to destroy the French, but the falling tide was now on England's side. He knew the anchorage better than any other man in Gambier's fleet, at first-hand. By midnight, all the men who could be rescued had been brought back to the frigates or the *Caesar*. Cochrane remained on watch. At 3.30 a.m. the next morning, 12 April, he could see that most of the French ships were broadside on to the wind and tide. It was almost too good to believe but they appeared to be grounded helplessly, and the tide was falling. The fire-ships had not destroyed them but Cochrane's explosion vessels and his general plan had worked. Confusion and panic in the confined space would drive the French captains to run their ships aground as the only escape from fire and demolition charges.[25]

The tide fell further. French battleships on the Palles Shoal and elsewhere heeled over as the water fell away from them. Some presented nothing more warlike than the bottom of the hull towards the English frigates. The men of the *Caesar* saw the flagship *Océan* stranded with her stern up on a mud flat and her bows down in the water. Soon they saw the French crews begin to throw their guns overboard in order that the ships might float as soon as possible when the tide began to flood the anchorage again. Cochrane was jubilant. The next few hours would present the Royal Navy with an opportunity which even Trafalgar and the Nile could hardly have rivalled.

With the falling tide, the *Imperieuse* had anchored farther out, though to be within range of the French ships she would in any case have had to sail into the Aix-Boyart channel. Not doubting that Gambier would give his permission for an attack to begin, and that his lordship would follow with the rest of the fleet, Cochrane signalled the *Caledonia* at 5.48 a.m. "Half the fleet can destroy the enemy. Seven on shore." An answering pennant fluttered from the *Caledonia*'s mainmast. "Very good."

Cochrane waited. He was not authorised to take the small ships in alone, indeed his only command was of the attacking vessels of the night before. Even the *Imperieuse* had been captained by John Spurling during the action. He had no authority whatever over the other captains of the fleet, every one of whom seemed to be his senior. Impatiently, he awaited Gambier's instructions. Hearing nothing by 6.40 a.m., he signalled the *Caledonia* again. "Eleven on shore." To his own companions he pointed out the pride of the French fleet, "lying on their bilge, with their bottoms completely exposed to shot, and therefore beyond the possibility of resistance". At length an answering signal was run up the mainmast of the *Caledonia*. "Very good."[26]

Cochrane's agitation began to grow. There was a crucial moment for making the attack. As soon as the tide began to flow into the anchorage, the British ships must go in and rake the stranded French with their broadsides. They would have the flood tide and a favourable wind to take them in, and having destroyed the enemy, the ebb tide would be in their favour for withdrawal. But Gambier and his ships rode peacefully at anchor on the horizon, nine miles out from the Aix-Boyart channel. The tide had fallen almost as far as it would and the best moment for launching the attack was already passing. Cochrane surveyed the anchorage again and saw that, with the exception of two battleships, the *Foudroyant* and *Cassard*, 80 and 74 guns respectively, the entire French fleet was stranded on the mud flats and shoals in attitudes of most unmartial indignity. At 7.40, when the tide was already turning, he signalled Gambier, "Only two afloat." Surely a man did not have to be a born hero to find that temptation irresistible. The *Caledonia* replied with the familiar pennant. "Very good."

However little he admired Gambier, Cochrane was unable to believe that any man who had at his disposal eleven battleships, including the 120-gun *Caledonia*, seven frigates, and an assortment of sloops, brigs, and bomb vessels was afraid to take on two enemy battleships. There were guns on the Ile d'Aix, but to judge by their performance on the previous evening they were not likely to decide the issue of a battle. In terms of fire-power, the two French ships still afloat carried 154 guns. Gambier's force boasted 1270 guns, as well as the mortars in the two bomb-ketches. When the news of the Basque Roads affair reached England there was bewilderment that the men who had fought under Hood, or Nelson, or St Vincent, had been obliged to wait placidly while their commander replied to every signal with his predictable "Very good", and the tide was allowed to turn, literally, in favour of the French.

Realising that Gambier was not prepared to seize the advantage himself, Cochrane decided to ask for permission to attack alone. He signalled insistently to *Caledonia*, "The frigates alone can destroy the enemy." The signal was not even acknowledged, apparently because it was considered "impertinent". Cochrane's orders were to remain where he was until instructed to do otherwise. Worst of all, he had not the least idea of what was happening on the battleships or what Gambier intended. It was perfectly possible that the commander-in-chief was engaged in a muster of the crews to see whether they had imbibed the contents of the last bundle of evangelical tracts handed out to them. It was at nine twenty-five, with the tide filling the anchorage of Aix Roads that Cochrane signalled despairingly, "Enemy preparing to haul off." And in reply came the imperturbable "Very good."[27]

Cochrane, who watched the French heaving guns and stores overboard and even trying to haul their ships through the mud to meet the rising tide, swore that "the Commander-in-Chief would not permit such a catastrophe". Accordingly, the *Impérieuse* nosed in and anchored by the Boyart Shoal, ready to dash down the channel as soon as the order was given and lead the attack. The main French shore-batteries on the Ile d'Oléron were firing at them now but the splashes of the shells were far short of the frigate. The flash of cannon and the drifting smoke along the wooded shore of Oléron were three miles or so distant from the anchorage. Cochrane, surveying the batteries through his glass, saw that the French commanders were using mortars, which they loaded perilously to the muzzle in order to reach their distant target. The gun-crews were obliged to fire them by lighting fuses and then running for cover. Yet, as Cochrane remarked, "not a shell, even thus fired, reached our position".[28]

It was not only Cochrane who saw how easily the stranded enemy might be destroyed. On H.M.S. *Caesar*, Gunner Richardson heard from a French pilot that the Ile d'Aix had "as many guns as days in the year", trained on the two-mile passage between the island and the Boyart Shoal. It was a remarkably short year. When at length the *Caesar* was permitted to enter the channel, said Richardson, "we could not find above thirteen guns that could be directed against us in passing; and these we thought so little of that we did not return their fire." The truth, as the French accounts admitted, was that these guns were manned by conscripts with no experience of battle. For all that, thirteen guns on Aix and 154 on the two remaining French ships afloat deterred Lord Gambier with his 1270 cannon. It was hardly a shining example of the Nelson Touch.[29]

The French sailors were carrying stream anchors across the mud to the deeper water, with six cables running back to each ship. By winding in the cables, it was proposed to haul the ships across the mud to the point where they could float off. But before this happened, the officers on the *Océan* were dismayed, at 11 a.m., to see their remaining ships afloat, the *Cassard* and the *Foudroyant*, drift inshore with the tide and run aground on the shoal of Fouras, the northern tip of the Charente estuary.

Cochrane could hardly have asked for more. Then, at last, he saw that Gambier's fleet was coming in. They had left it late, very late, but something might still be done. On the quarterdeck of the *Imperieuse*, he waited in a state of growing agitation. And then the unthinkable happened. Three and a half miles short of their target, at a point where the opposing fleets were still just out of range of one another, Gambier's ships dropped anchor. "It was now evident," said Cochrane, "that *no attack was intended.*" Gambier, as he later learnt, was of the opinion that the object of the attack had been achieved and "there was no occasion to risk any part of the fleet".[30]

By noon, the French flagship *Océan*, a splendid three-decker, was afloat. Four more ships on the mud near her soon followed. At this point, Gambier made his gesture of defiance, sending in the bomb-ketch *Etna* with her 13-inch mortar. Because of her range, she was able to shell the French anchorage without coming under fire herself. But as the French ships floated, Cochrane saw them "making sail for the Charente", where they would find sanctuary in the mouth of the river beyond even the range of the mortar. The bomb-ketch was hardly more than a floating mortar battery, a squat unattractive little vessel with no foremast but a large triangular sail. Cochrane hailed her captain.

"What attack is going to be made on the enemy by the fleet?"

"I know nothing further than that I am ordered to bombard the ships ashore," replied Captain Godfrey stolidly.[31]

It was clear that there was to be no attack, but Cochrane was not done with Gambier yet. "I made up my mind, if possible, to force him into action by attacking the enemy with the *Imperieuse*." This was not so easy to do, since he had to contend with two opponents, the French and Gambier. If the *Imperieuse* was seen to be making sail for the anchorage, she would be ordered back at once by the *Caledonia*. The ruse which Cochrane adopted was entirely Nelsonian, though rather more perilous than putting a telescope to a blind eye. Without making sail, he ordered the anchor of the *Imperieuse* to be weighed and the frigate began to drift, slowly, almost unobtrusively into the Aix-Boyart channel, stern-foremost. Cochrane later defended himself on the grounds that if he had not done this, Gambier would have let the entire French fleet escape.[32]

"Better to risk the frigate, or even my commission," he said grimly, "than to suffer such a disgraceful termination."[33]

For half an hour, the frigate drifted past the guns of the Ile d'Aix, which opened up on her without effect. It was one-thirty, when she was past the point of recall, that Cochrane gave his order. The sails billowed out, and he bore down to engage the enemy. At the same time he made a signal to the *Caledonia*, inviting Gambier to show his courage. "Enemy superior to chasing ship, but inferior to fleet." Five minutes later he signalled more irritably, "In want of assistance." Unfortunately the signalling code also used the same flag for the message "In distress", and it was this news which the signal officer of the *Caledonia* conveyed to Gambier.[34]

Gambier looked towards Aix Roads, where the flashes of gunfire and the drifting smoke signalled more clearly than any pennant the action which had begun. The *Imperieuse* was among the French fleet but seemed singularly undistressed. The French battleship *Calcutta* originally an East Indiaman converted to take supplies, was exchanging broadsides with *Imperieuse*, much to the advantage of the latter. With his stern and bow guns Cochrane was simultaneously pouring shot into two more stranded battleships, the *Aquilon* and the *Ville de Varsovie*.

While Cochrane turned a blaze of fire on to the three great ships,

Gambier hesitated a moment longer. The ambiguous signal had its uses for Cochrane. The commander-in-chief would not come well out of any subsequent inquiry if he refused aid to a frigate in distress. On the other hand, if he complained that Cochrane had pretended to be in distress without cause, Cochrane could always claim that he had merely requested assistance in destroying the French fleet.

By now the *Imperieuse* was incurring casualties. Marryat saw the captain of the forecastle killed, his head taken off by a cannon shot, and reported Cochrane as saying:

"Poor fellow! Throw him overboard; there is no time for a coroner's inquest now."

Another casualty in the forecastle was a young seaman whose body was blown in two by a shot in the midriff, except for the connection of the spinal cord. Marryat and another midshipman, half blinded by the scattered flesh, were then confronted by an extraordinary phenomenon. The severed body sprang suddenly to its feet, "stared us horridly in the face, and fell down dead". The spine was still carrying the brain's messages to the lower limbs.[35]

By this time the boats of the *Imperieuse* were closing on the *Calcutta*, whose commander, Captain Lafon, led the evacuation by clambering ignominiously out of his stern cabin window and taking flight across the mud. For this, he was later court martialled and shot. At three twenty, the *Calcutta* surrendered and the crew of the *Imperieuse* cheered heartily as "assistance" arrived in the shape of five British frigates and the battleships *Valiant* and *Revenge*, each carrying seventy-four guns. Not realising what had happened, the *Revenge* opened fire on the *Calcutta*, now in the possession of Cochrane's men and had to be warned off. Gambier subsequently overlooked this and noted that the French ship had not been taken by Cochrane but by those who came to assist him.

The *Aquilon* and the *Ville de Varsovie*, also engaged by the *Imperieuse*, struck their colours at five-thirty. Half an hour later, the crew of the *Tonnerre* set fire to their ship and took to the boats. At 7 p.m. the *Tonnerre* blew up, and two hours later the burning hulk of the *Calcutta* exploded. Most of the French ships had taken refuge in the estuary of the Charente, in whose narrower channel under the batteries of Fort Fouras they were reasonably safe from attack.

The great chance had been missed but Cochrane's determination to force Gambier into action had, at least, achieved something. Indeed, the general opinion on the French flagship was that the day had been one of unmitigated defeat. "This day of the 12th was a very disastrous one: four of our ships were destroyed, many brave people lost their lives, and by the disgraceful means the enemy made use of to destroy our lines of defence." Plans for the expedition to Martinique, which Gambier would have done nothing to prevent, were in chaos as a result of the attack launched by the *Imperieuse*. The troops on the French ships had been put ashore and the operation abandoned.[36]

At 4 a.m. on the morning of 13 April, Cochrane saw that three lights had been hoisted by Gambier's squadron offshore. It was the signal for all those ships which had been sent to Cochrane's assistance to return to the fleet. Before they left, the crews set fire to the two captured battleships, *Aquilon* and *Ville de Varsovie*. Cochrane was greatly angered by this, since he had proposed to tow the two fine ships away and claim them as prizes.

As a last hope, he hailed the captain of the frigate *Indefatigable*, asking him if he would join the *Imperieuse* in a final attack to sink the French flagship, *Océan*. She was still within reach and could be destroyed, Cochrane suggested, by a frigate on either side of her.

"I will not," replied Captain Rodd piously, "we are going out to join the fleet."[37]

Unaccompanied by any vessels other than brigs and bomb-ketches, Cochrane expected that he too would be ordered to leave the Boyart Shoal and rejoin the fleet. He anticipated this by signalling Gambier on the *Caledonia*, "If permitted to remain can destroy the enemy." Some time after this he sighted a small boat from the fleet making for the *Imperieuse*. Gambier's written instructions to him were brought aboard.[38]

> My dear Lord,
>
> You have done your part so admirably that I will not suffer you to tarnish it by attempting impossibilities, which I think, as well as those captains who have come from you, any further effort to destroy those ships would be. You must, therefore, join as soon as you can, with the bombs, etc, as I wish for some information, which you allude to, before I close my despatches.
>
> Yours, my dear Lord, most sincerely,
> GAMBIER.

> PS. I have ordered three brigs and two rocket vessels to join you, with which, and the bomb, you may make an attempt on the ship that is aground on the Palles, or towards Ile Madame,

but I do not think you will succeed; and I am anxious that you should come to me, as I wish to send you to England as soon as possible. You must, therefore, come as soon as the tide turns.

The letter was carefully and indecisively phrased. Of Cochrane's support vessels, the bomb-ketch was about to split her mortar and the brigs would hardly be of much use in attacking battleships. The *Imperieuse* was the only ship which was likely to be of real effect in such an attack, and only then because her comparatively light armament was compensated for by the audacity and versatility with which she was commanded. It was the only hope and Cochrane accordingly replied to Gambier.

My Lord,
   I have just had the honour to receive your Lordship's letter. We *can* destroy the ships that are on shore, which I hope your Lordship will approve of.

I have the honour, &c.
COCHRANE.

The response to this was a recall signal hoisted in the shrouds of the *Caledonia* and, first thing on 14 April, a final message.

My dear Lord,
   It is necessary I should have some communication with you before I close my despatches to the Admiralty. I have, therefore, ordered Captain Wolfe to relieve you in the services you are engaged in. I wish you to join me as soon as possible, that you may convey Sir Harry Neale to England, who will be charged with my despatches, or you may return to carry on the service where you are. I expect two bombs to arrive every moment, they will be useful in it.

Yours, my dear Lord, most sincerely,
GAMBIER[39]

It was evident that Cochrane's command was at an end. He must either return to England or else resume his duties at Aix Roads under the command of a senior captain, Captain Wolfe, loyal to Gambier.

In the first place, however, he had to report to Gambier in the commander-in-chief's cabin on the flagship *Caledonia*. There was, he later admitted, "no evading Lord Gambier's letter this time without positive disobedience to orders". But when the two men confronted each other, it was Cochrane who assumed the offensive, charging Gambier with "the extraordinary hesitation which had been displayed in attacking ships helplessly on shore". His record of the interview vividly contrasts the character and disposition of the two men.

> I begged his lordship, by way of preventing the ill-feeling of the fleet from becoming detrimental to the honour of the service, to set me aside altogether and send in Admiral Stopford, with the frigates or other vessels, as with regard to him there could be no ill-feeling: further declaring my confidence that from Admiral Stopford's zeal for the service, he would, being backed by his officers, accomplish results more creditable than anything that had yet been done. I apologised for the freedom I used, stating that I took the liberty as a friend, for it would be impossible, as matters stood, to prevent a noise being made in England.

The flaw in this piece of reasoning was that Stopford had shown no great enthusiasm for going in. It was also an error of judgement for Cochrane to begin, at this stage, pretending to "friendship" for Gambier.

"My lord," he added, "you have before desired me to speak candidly to you, and I have now used that freedom."

So far as Gambier was concerned, the action at the Basque Roads was over, and Cochrane, like the others, would have to rest on his laurels. Indeed, the admiral's last words on the matter were ominous enough: "If you throw blame upon what has been done, it will appear like arrogantly claiming all the merit to yourself."

Since it was clear that Gambier proposed to remove him from the vicinity of the battle, Cochrane lodged a last but futile protest: "I have no wish to carry the despatches, or to go to London with Sir Harry Neale on the occasion. My object is alone that which has been entrusted to me by the Admiralty – to destroy the vessels of the enemy!"

Gambier, however, "cut the matter short". Before he left the *Caledonia*, Cochrane received his written orders. He was no longer allowed the option of returning to the Aix Roads, even under the supervision of Captain Wolfe. He was to sail with the *Imperieuse*, carrying Sir Harry Neale and the despatches to England. Nor was there to be any delay. The frigate was to leave the Basque Roads on the next morning.[40]

Having sailed from the scene of the action on 15 April, the *Imperieuse* dropped anchor in Spithead six days later. From the evidence of her shot-torn decks and the blackening of timber by smoke, it was evident that she had as usual been in the thick of the action, which at once roused interest in her. Then Sir Harry Neale and his escort galloped into Whitehall and delivered Lord Gambier's despatch to an expectant First Lord and nation.

"The Almighty's favour to his Majesty and the nation has been strongly marked," began Gambier piously, and then briskly got down to the main business of the French anchorage having been attacked and four of the capital ships destroyed. There was praise for the way in which Cochrane had led the final attack on the afternoon of 12 April "with his accustomed gallantry and spirit". Nor was that all. "I cannot speak in sufficient terms of admiration and applause of the vigorous and gallant attack made by Lord Cochrane upon the French line-of-battle ships," Gambier conceded.[41]

So far, all was well. Cochrane was received at every appearance by the familiar brazen strains of, "See, the conquering hero comes, sound the trumpet, beat the drums!" His admirers in Westminster had a new verse to their street ballad in which his fame was sung.

> Hark the news of *Basque Roads* all Europe astounds,
> Where fearless of death and each danger around;
> With volcanoes tremendous he routed the foe,
> And dealt from the *Imperieuse* the conquering blow![42]

On the other hand, his supporters had not forgotten their political attachments.

> The laurels of Fame, that encompass his head,
> Shall bloom when the triumphs of warfare are fled;
> For the friend of REFORM and of FREEDOM at home,
> More immortal shall make him in ages to come![43]

Among the cheers, the dinners of welcome and the addresses of congratulation, Cochrane was informed on 26 April that George III had made him a Knight Commander of the Bath.

Lord Gambier's despatch was then made public. Cochrane read it with dismay. He was not even mentioned as having led the most perilous attack of all to destroy the boom with his explosion vessels.

There was no more than a reference to "some vessels filled with powder and shells, as proposed by his Lordship, with a view to explosion", and no indication of their part in destroying the boom. Indeed, while omitting Cochrane's name, Gambier described the attack on the evening of 11 April as having been "led on in the most undaunted and determined manner by Captain Wooldridge, in the *Mediator* fire-ship". From his safe anchorage, nine miles away, Gambier was convinced that it was Wooldridge and the *Mediator* who broke the boom, despite the fact that the French captains like Proteau had seen it blown out of the water by Cochrane an hour earlier. The whole purpose of the boom, indeed, was that no ship should be able to break through it into the anchorage, and certainly not a mere frigate like the *Mediator*.[44]

Gambier, having abolished Cochrane's heroism on the first day, then went on to consider April 12. He reported a signal that seven of the French ships were aground, which Cochrane made at five-forty-eight, and swore that he "immediately" proceeded to destroy them! How was it that, over seven hours later, he was still a few miles short of the target, despite favourable wind and tide? He had decided that Cochrane's suggestion of an attack was "too hazardous", precisely because the wind and tide would have carried the British ships into the anchorage and thus, he regretted to say, would have risked them in confronting their enemy.[45]

Finally, he reminded the world, that though Cochrane had actually undertaken the attack at the Admiralty's insistence, there was no lack of senior officers who would have done it just as well. He mentioned Admiral Stopford and Sir Harry Neale, remarking that they had both been ready to lead the attack and that "the result of their efforts would have been highly creditable".[46]

The extraordinary manner in which Gambier omitted Cochrane's leadership of the initial attack, while paying handsome tribute to the way in which it would have been led by men who in fact took no part in it, was indicative of the public row that was being prepared. The Battle of the Basque Roads had not been a victory on the scale of Trafalgar or the Nile, but in its own time it was just as famous for other reasons. The action was re-fought in parliament, the press, and the courts for the next decade. The final exchanges of debate still echoed in the 1860s, in an age of iron-clads and steam power.

Cochrane was extremely annoyed by the despatch, though hardly surprised. For the time being he was prepared to let matters rest. But when Gambier returned to England at the beginning of May, Lord

Mulgrave told Cochrane in the course of discussion that, of course, a vote of thanks would be proposed to Gambier in the Commons, as it had been to other commanders after such great victories as Copenhagen, the Nile, and the Glorious First of June. Cochrane, as he later confessed, was appalled by the announcement. Without further thought, he informed Mulgrave of his intention:

> In my capacity as one of the members for Westminster, I will oppose the motion, on the ground that the commander-in-chief has not only done nothing to merit a vote of thanks, but has neglected to destroy the French fleet in Aix Roads, when it was clearly in his power to do so.[47]

It was now Mulgrave's turn to be appalled. For a vote of thanks to be opposed in this manner was an unheard of thing. Whatever the misgivings of parliament might be, accusations of this sort would make the Basque Roads a national scandal, undermining public confidence in the conduct of the war and giving comfort as well as amusement to the enemy. For a long while, Mulgrave solemnly warned Cochrane "not to persist in this determination". The warning was unheeded.

"Such a course," said Mulgrave pointedly, "will not only prove injurious to the Government but highly detrimental to yourself, by raising up against you a host of enemies."

Given the number of enemies already on the list, it seemed that there was little scope for adding to them. Cochrane remained unmoved. Seeing that the defiant captain would not yield to threats, Mulgrave, as the reasonable man of affairs, decided to take the only other course traditionally available. He must be bribed.

"The public is satisfied with what has been done," said the First Lord soothingly, "and they give you full credit for your share therein. You shall be included in the vote of thanks, so that the recognition of Lord Gambier's services can do you no harm!"

Mulgrave's obtuseness is evident from the manner in which, despite several interviews, he had still not appreciated the ferocious sensitivity of Cochrane's pride.

"Speaking as a member of the House of Commons," said Cochrane angrily, "I do not recognise Lord Gambier's services at all, for none have been rendered. As for any thanks to myself, I would rather be without them."

The First Lord, unable to credit this, insisted that Cochrane would be seen as attacking Gambier in his naval capacity.

"The public will not draw the distinction between your professional and parliamentary conduct," he said wearily.

"I regret the public want of discrimination," Cochrane replied acidly, "but that will not alter my determination."[48]

The interview ended. The Portland ministry was in an acutely embarrassing dilemma. They loathed Cochrane, personally and politically, quite as much as he detested them. But he held the initiative firmly. They had promised Gambier his vote of thanks but could not give it him in the face of the public scandal which Cochrane was prepared to raise. Men had opposed votes of thanks before, but for the leader of the attack to oppose one voted to his commanding admiral was unthinkable.

Under pressure from the government, Mulgrave tried again to make Cochrane see reason. He sent for him and "entreated" him to "reconsider" his conduct. Then he warned Cochrane that he had reported every word of the previous conversation to the government, "which was highly dissatisfied therewith". Unless the opposition to the vote of confidence were dropped, Cochrane could count upon feeling the "high displeasure" of those in power.

"The displeasure of the government," said Cochrane calmly, "will not for a moment influence my parliamentary conduct, for which I hold myself answerable to my constituents."

As on the previous occasion, Mulgrave turned quickly from threat to bribe, eagerly offering a solution to the difficulty which by his standards ought to be acceptable to a man of honour. If there was a good and agreeable reason for Cochrane to be absent from the Commons, then the question of opposing the vote of thanks would not arise. The government would get its vote and Cochrane's principles would not be compromised.

"If you are on service, you cannot be in your place in parliament," Mulgrave suggested knowingly. "Now, my lord, I will make you a proposal. I will put under your orders three frigates, with *carte blanche* to do whatever you please on the enemy's coasts in the Mediterranean. I will further get you permission to go to Sicily, and embark on board your squadron my own regiment, which is stationed there. You know how to make use of such advantages."

With studied patience, Cochrane thanked the First Lord for his offer, and then went on to point out the irremovable impediment, as though it were a difficulty so subtle that Mulgrave could not have been expected to see it for himself.

"Were I to accept this offer," said Cochrane slowly, "the country would regard my acquiescence as a bribe to hold my peace, whilst I could not regard it in any other light. Self-respect must, therefore, be my excuse for declining the proposal."

So far as any argument was concerned, that was the end of the matter. Even Mulgrave now accepted that Cochrane could not be threatened and would not be bribed. The ministry might take its revenge in due course, but there was no easy way out of the present difficulty.[49]

Cochrane's flawless skill in battle was matched, in the view of his Victorian successors, by two fundamental errors of judgement in public affairs: the feud with St Vincent and the campaign against Gambier after the Basque Roads. His own son acknowledged that "He made enemies where a cautious man might have made friends." J. W. Fortescue described Cochrane's "unfortunate readiness to convert the championship of a cause into a personal enmity. An honourable conflict against the Admiralty's corruption becomes a duel first with St Vincent and then with Croker." St Vincent was not a figure of great humanity but he shared Cochrane's antagonism to corruption and to such ineffectual commanders as Gambier. Had Cochrane been able to subdue his own pride, he might have made one important enemy the less. As it was, the public squabbling went on even after the First Lord had left the Admiralty and become commander of the Channel Fleet. On 14 April 1806, St Vincent wrote angrily to the First Sea Lord, Admiral Markham: "Did you ever read such a madly arrogant paragraph as that in Lord Cochrane's public letter, where he lugs in Lieutenant Parker for the avowed purpose of attacking me, his commander-in-chief?"[50]

However, in the case of the Gambier quarrel, Cochrane seemed more demonstrably in the right than he ever had been over St Vincent. William Beckford, author of the oriental extravaganza *Vathek*, writing in the new Gothick splendour of Fonthill Abbey, compared the scapegrace uncle and the valiant nephew:

What the devil is C. Johnstone up to? There's another person who will not come to a good end. But the Hero! The Hero is predestined to glory according to my scriptures; discreet, modest, silent – short in speech, long in thought – there is stuff in that man to become one day a cloak of ermine and gold.[51]

The press began to echo such sentiments in Cochrane's case. In the *Naval Chronicle*, he was referred to as "Our Hero". There was praise for his "true courage and greatness of mind" in the dangers he faced so that he might rescue French officers and seamen from the burning hulk of the *Ville de Varsovie*. The paper at first denied that there was any quarrel between Cochrane and Gambier over what it now termed Cochrane's "late brilliant exploit". But in case Gambier's supporters were preparing to denounce Cochrane's version of events publicly, the *Chronicle* issued a muted threat:

> It very forcibly struck us, that an extraordinary time *did* elapse from the appearance of Lord Cochrane's telegraphic communication "that seven of the enemy's ships were on shore, and might be destroyed", till the period when the requisite assistance was afforded.[52]

The same point was being made more generally in the press. On 25 April 1809, *The Times* expressed the obvious surprise of the public at finding that Gambier had not been prepared for the possibility of going to destroy the French ships, even before Cochrane signalled him. "Why, then, if seven might be destroyed, were there only four? Had Admiral Lord Gambier to unmoor at the time he received this intelligence? Did he not expect this might be the case? Or with what view was Lord Cochrane sent up to the Roads?"

Gambier kept silent until 30 May, when he wrote to Wellesley Pole, "I had flattered myself that I should have received some signification of an approbation of my conduct." He was irritated to hear that there were now "some doubts" about the reward he expected to be given.

> Feeling that even a doubt upon such a subject cannot be entertained consistently with my reputation as Commander in Chief, I request that you will be pleased to move the Lords Commissioners of the Admiralty to direct a Court Martial to be assembled as early as possible, for the purpose of enquiring into my conduct as Commander in Chief.[53]

With such ease was Cochrane outmanoeuvred in the quarrels of public life. A court-martial would enable Gambier and the Admiralty to fight on their own terms. If there was an acquittal, the vote of thanks would pass the Commons easily, no matter what Cochrane said or did. For the time being, Gambier also obliged the Admiralty by rewriting his Basque Roads despatch so that all reference to Cochrane's gallantry was now omitted from the official record.[54]

On 4 June, Wellesley Pole wrote to Gambier, informing him that the Lords of the Admiralty had acceded to his request and that a court-martial would be held upon "your conduct as Commander in Chief". The arrangements had been ordered "agreeably to your desire". The trial was eventually to open on 26 July and was to be held on the hulk H.M.S. *Gladiator*, moored in Portsmouth harbour.[55]

The court-martial of a naval commander-in-chief was bound to be a national sensation. It was said that Cochrane himself had brought it about and was the prosecutor, but it was entirely Gambier's doing. Indeed, as Cochrane later protested, he was regarded as responsible for the prosecution being brought, but was neither invited nor allowed to act as prosecutor. He was treated as any other witness might be and was not even allowed to be present in the court when testimony was being given by others.

The Admiralty chose as president of the court Sir Roger Curtis, Commander-in-Chief at Spithead and Portsmouth. It was hardly the most impartial decision. In 1790 there had been an unfortunate court-martial scandal when Curtis had taken part in a trial in an unauthorised and illegal capacity. But it was something more than unfortunate for the credibility of naval justice that one of Curtis's closest friends was Lord Gambier himself.[56]

On 26 July, when the court assembled, the tweeting whistles and the smart files of Royal Marines presenting arms as the members came aboard, the scene was one of official splendour. The seven admirals and four captains who made up the tribunal were rivalled in their display of royal blue and gold by the witnesses who thronged H.M.S. *Gladiator*. The court assembled as usual in the great stern cabin with its windows looking out across the sunlit anchorage of Spithead.

Curtis sat as president at the head of the long table, Gambier's sword lying on the green baize before him. The other members of the court filed in and took their places on either side. First was Sir William Young, Admiral of the Blue, the man who had nearly destroyed Cochrane, the *Imperieuse*, and her crew on the rocks of Ushant, and whom Cochrane had denounced in the House of Commons for his conduct

Young was followed by Sir John Duckworth, Vice-Admiral of the Red, whom Gunner Richardson and his comrades knew as "Old Tommy", with his Christmas Day hangings, his Boxing Day floggings, his tyranny to his subordinates and his sycophancy towards those from whom he had something to gain. By any normal standard of impartiality there was an even better reason for disqualifying Duckworth, since he had been – and still was – Gambier's loyal second-in-command.

Of the other four admirals, Sir John Sutton was another significant choice, having also crossed swords with Cochrane over a public and controversial matter. It was he who had refused to listen to Cochrane's plea for the crew of the *Atalante* and the state of their vessel, and who was in part responsible for the loss of the ship.

Moses Greetham, the judge advocate, took his place at the far end of the table from Curtis. At eleven o'clock the court was opened and Gambier was brought in under the escort of the Marshal of the Admiralty. The judge advocate then read out the charge as their Lordships had drawn it up.

> It appears to us that the said Admiral Lord Gambier, on the 12th day of the said month of April, the enemy's ships being then on shore, and the signal having been made that they could be destroyed, did, for a considerable time, neglect or delay taking effectual measures for destroying them.[57]

The witnesses for the prosecution were then called. There was no way in which the court could convincingly avoid calling Cochrane himself, but it excluded the evidence of two men whom it knew to be ready to support him. One was Francis Austen, later and better known as Admiral Sir Francis Austen, who told Cochrane that he blamed some of Gambier's subordinates as much as the admiral himself. The other was Frederick Maitland, who commanded the *Emerald* in Aix Roads and who supported Cochrane so publicly that he was sent on service to Ireland until the court-martial should be safely over.

There were other witnesses whose evidence, in part at least, was not to the court's nor to Gambier's liking, but these were on the whole dealt with firmly and efficiently by Curtis and Admiral Young. William James, observing their conduct, remarked that both the senior officers of the court "evinced a strong bias in favour of the accused". The treatment of Cochrane and other witnesses whose evidence was unfavourable to Gambier was far from impartial in James's view, resembling closely the most hostile kind of cross-examination which an opposing counsel might have undertaken. Junior captains or men like John Thompson, master's mate of H.M.S. *Beagle*, who were not prompt or helpful in their replies to the distinguished court, were subjected to withering irony in such terms as, "Have I been fortunate enough to express myself clearly to you?"[58]

As soon as the accuracy of various logs had been established by witnesses, Cochrane was called. It has to be admitted that in a court of law, even more obviously than in the House of Commons, he was not in his element. This was not the type of warfare in which he excelled. He was asked, for instance, if there had been any delay by Gambier in sending assistance when Cochrane signalled for it after taking the *Imperieuse* in alone. He conceded that there had not been.

"But had the attack been made in the morning," he insisted, "it is my opinion that seven sail of the enemy, including the three-decker, might have been destroyed with facility, by two sail of the line, assisted by the frigates and smaller vessels; and that after the hour of half past eleven . . . the frigates alone, assisted by the smaller vessels, might have destroyed the whole of the above-mentioned ships."

Sir Roger Curtis, as president, decided to blunt this particular attack on Gambier by taking over the questioning of Cochrane himself.

"What were the circumstances that induced your Lordship to believe that from half-past eleven o'clock to one o'clock the frigates alone were capable of destroying the enemy's ships?" he demanded. "If they could do it after eleven, why could they not do it before?"

Cochrane began a long and elaborate explanation of the way in which the French had run aground, providing a perfect target, and how he had been amazed to see Gambier sail to within a few miles and then drop anchor again. Sir Roger Curtis cut short the laboured reply.

"Really," he snapped, "I very humbly beg your pardon, but I do not see how this can be an answer!"

Cochrane tried to stand his ground in front of the assembled admirals.

"If, when it is written, it shall appear not to be an answer to the question, then I humbly submit it may be struck out."

It was his old adversary Admiral Young who squashed this line of argument.

"If the court is of opinion that their time is taken up with any thing which is not relevant, they may I apprehend stop it, when they see that."

"I apprehend that cannot be seen till the court see what it is I am about to say," retorted Cochrane angrily, and then went on to describe Gambier's failure to attack. "Twelve o'clock arrived, no signal was made to weigh anchor; half past twelve, still no signal."

Admiral Young cut him short again.

"This is really very improper!" he announced. "This has no sort of connection whatever with the question which is asked, and is only a series of observations to the disadvantage of the prisoner."

"I wish to speak the truth," thundered Cochrane, "the whole truth, and nothing but the truth!"

To the dismay of his friends and the delight of his adversaries, the interruptions and browbeating had thrown him badly off balance.

"This really has nothing at all to do with the question which is asked you," said Admiral Young coldly.

"If the question is put by a person *ignorant* of the whole proceedings, and which does not lead to get the truth and the whole truth, I hold that I am to give the whole truth!" insisted Cochrane.

Such an attack on the court might have caused a sensation in King's Bench but there was a shocked silence in the crowd of assembled officers as the tall, red-haired captain stood before the green baize of the table denouncing the senior admirals for their ignorance and their attempt to muzzle the truth. Cochrane, in his anger, almost spat out the word "ignorant" at Admiral Young. Lord Mulgrave's men had goaded their prey to the point where his destruction might be accomplished. In a moment he was protesting, "In three words more I shall finish what I have to say."

But Admiral Stanhope had other views.

"Would it not be better, at once, to clear the court. . . . ?"

"I really should wish the court to be cleared upon it," added Admiral Sutton.

The president accordingly cleared the court. When it opened again, he first reprimanded Cochrane for "the very digressive manner in which you answered, or were proceeding to answer the question put". In future, he was directed to give "a short and decisive answer to the question put to you".

Then there was the offending word "ignorant".

"Considering all the circumstances together," said Curtis, "it was, in no small degree, indecorous to the court, to make use of such an expression."

Cochrane was questioned and cross-questioned by the admirals of the court for much of the first day, virtually the whole of the second, and part of the third. Aggression, boldness, determination, the qualities which served him well with his crew or at the hustings were his undoing in the court-martial with its nicely-defined rules of argument. He began to appear very much as the fool Godwin took him for. Towards the end of the second day they drove him to exasperation yet again, and he burst out angrily:

> I have felt that if I had answered yes or no to all the questions which have been put to me, I ought to be hung; and that if a court-martial was held upon *me*, and only the answers yes or no appeared to those questions, I should be hung for them!

"I believe nobody has desired your Lordship to answer merely yes or no," said the judge advocate drily. Nor had they, despite the numerous interruptions of Cochrane's answers. It was characteristic of him that the more passionate his feelings in debate the worse he countered the opposing arguments.[59]

It seemed likely that his conduct under prolonged examination by the court would tell against him when the proceedings were published by Gambier's supporters. But so far as the issue of the trial was concerned, the documentary evidence was surely irrefutable. Cochrane had the most reliable charts of all, from the *Neptune Français*, showing the area of the Aix Roads, the Aix-Boyart channel and the soundings. They were based on the work of the best French hydrographers, who had every reason to know the waters better than anyone else, and he had proved their practical accuracy by using them for the attacks made by the *Pallas* and the *Imperieuse*. Naturally, Cochrane produced his copy of the French chart to substantiate his claim that the attack on the French fleet was possible at any state of the tide.

"This chart is not evidence before the court," said the judge advocate quickly, "because his Lordship cannot prove it accurate."[60]

Proof of accuracy was strictly insisted on by the court. It would require Cochrane to produce the French hydrographer who had drawn the chart, perhaps even the men who had taken the soundings. The fact that England was then at war with France did not excuse the necessity of parading the experts in question on board the *Gladiator* at Portsmouth to be examined as to the accuracy of their work. Failing that, the charts were to be dismissed.

Instead, the Admiralty produced charts of its own, one set drawn by Thomas Stokes, master of the *Caledonia*, and another by Edward Fairfax, master of the fleet. Both men had drawn up their charts under Gambier's orders during the Basque Roads affair, and both were in court to testify to their accuracy. These, then, were the charts accepted by Sir Roger Curtis and the members of the court.

Being a mere witness, rather than Gambier's prosecutor, Cochrane had no right to see these new Admiralty charts. They were based on the work of Stokes and Fairfax but he was refused access to them by the Admiralty for fifty-one years. In very different circumstances, when he was an old and dying man, his reputation long since vindicated, he was permitted to see them. Yet even at the court-martial, the more bizarre details of the Admiralty "charts", which the court took as proved beyond question, had begun to emerge.

It was said, in support of their accuracy, that Stokes and Fairfax agreed upon the depth of the Aix Roads and the approach channel. As Cochrane remarked, it would have been surprising if they had differed, since much of Stokes's chart relied on figures which he admitted had been supplied by Fairfax. "It cannot be expected," said Stokes defensively, "that from the opportunities I had of sounding in this place, I could accurately point out the distance between the sands." He had, however, pieced out his distant observations with information from an unspecified "French manuscript". It was not available for inspection but Stokes swore that he took it to be correct. Fairfax claimed to have taken soundings of his own, but he was unable to say that he had been much further in than the Boyart Shoal.[61]

On the basis of the resulting charts, which were not available for scrutiny or challenge, the Admiralty had now reduced the navigable width of the Aix-Boyart channel from two miles to one. According to this, the danger of British ships running aground under the guns of Aix was immensely increased. How wise, it seemed, Lord Gambier had been to ignore Cochrane's suggestion of hazarding his entire fleet in the narrow and treacherous waterway.

But there was a far more original and extraordinary feature on the charts. Once again, it was one upon which both Stokes and Fairfax agreed. Close to the landward end of the Boyart Shoal and the Palles mud flats were hidden rocks, not shown on any French chart, barring the way to the anchorage except at high tide. How it was possible for Stokes or Fairfax to "reconnoitre" the anchorage of Aix itself was not explained, nor did they claim specifically to have done so. But where the French charts showed a good depth of 30 feet of water even at low tide, the new Admiralty charts revealed the unsuspected hazard of rocks no more than 12 to 16 feet below the waves. Only a madman would have tried to sail a battleship like the *Caledonia* in 12 feet of water.[62]

Exactly how the two Admiralty hydrographers discovered these rocks was not explained. Stokes referred vaguely to "my own observations" without specifying how he or Fairfax could observe rocks 12 feet under water from a minimum distance of three miles, while their French counterparts sounding directly over the place had never found them. Of course, the charts were not available for closer inspection. Perhaps Stokes and Fairfax had made an understandable error in their general and distant survey. Perhaps, in Cochrane's view, the rocks had been fabricated to save Gambier. Cochrane had believed that he could fight the Admiralty and win, as though it were merely a matter of seizing the *Gamo* from Spain or defending Fort Trinidad against France. Through many bitter years he was to find that the extent of his miscalculation was beyond anything that even he would have credited.

In practical terms, the "dangers" of the Aix-Boyart channel and the mysterious rocks had been refuted by Cochrane and those who had twice attacked the anchorage of Allemand's fleet. If the guns of Aix threatened certain destruction would any man have sailed past them in a ship loaded to capacity with explosive? How was it that these same guns, which threatened such destruction on 12 April, had not been able to stop a single ship the day before?

But since Cochrane was permitted only to answer questions, not to ask them, these issues were never debated. When he strayed from the short and direct answer to carefully phrased questions, the judge advocate, or the president, or Admiral Young, would order him back to the point.

The majority of the witnesses, when asked if Gambier had done everything that might reasonably be expected of him, said that he had. They were his captains and subordinates for whom there was nothing to be gained by slandering their commander-in-chief. Moreover, they had heard of the evidence of Stokes and Fairfax. The Aix-Boyart channel was no more than a mile wide, beset with shoals on every side, and there was the mysterious group of rocks between the British fleet and the French anchorage, a hidden peril lying no more than a dozen feet or so below the surface. When asked if Gambier had done all that his duty required, most of them were content to agree that he had. In any case, they felt no great affection for Cochrane who had, in a sense, been promoted to lead the attack in preference to them. If they were going to risk their careers and

reputations at the court-martial it would not be merely in order
to vindicate him.

One of the captains who seemed likely to support Cochrane was
George Seymour of H.M.S. *Pallas*, who was to become an admiral and
Knight Commander of the Bath in the years ahead. Gambier called
him to give evidence but as soon as his unwillingness to co-operate
became clear, Gambier said swiftly, "I have no further questions to
propose to Captain Seymour."[63]

Seymour, like Cochrane, protested that his oath obliged him to tell
the whole truth and, despite exchanges and interruptions, he went on
to confirm that Gambier might safely have attacked at 11 a.m. on the
morning of 12 April when virtually the entire French fleet was
aground. But Gambier had waited at anchor for three hours more,
only sending in an attacking force after Cochrane had gone in alone
with the *Imperieuse*.

Another future admiral, Captain Pulteney Malcolm of H.M.S.
*Donegal*, gave evidence that the delay actually increased the risk to
the British ships, since the French fleet was righted and set afloat
during that time. Finally, he was asked whether, when the French
fleet was afloat once more, he would have shown prudence and hesitation or risked an attack with his ships. "The risk was then
small," said Malcolm, "and, of course, I would have sent them in
instantly."[64]

Captain Broughton of H.M.S. *Illustrious* was a third officer who,
independently of any attachment to Cochrane, swore that Gambier
could have sent in the fleet, in response to the signals from the
*Imperieuse*, two or three hours earlier. But Broughton had an even
more interesting piece of information. As soon as the attack was
over, he had taken soundings in the very place where Fairfax and
Stokes had discovered their now famous "rocks". There were no
rocks. At this injudicious revelation, the president halted that line
of questioning abruptly. Broughton's evidence on other matters was
equally compromising. From the safe distance of the *Caledonia* once
more, Stokes had calculated that any attack via the Aix-Boyart
channel would have been "at half range of shell and point blank
shot". Captain Broughton, reconnoitring the channel, not only
found that some of the fortifications on the island had no guns in
them, but that even those which fired could not reach him.[65]

Despite the evidence of Broughton and others who had been in the
forefront of the action, the general opinion of Gambier's officers was
unequivocally that he had done all that might be expected of him.

Gambier's defence was, repeatedly, that to have attacked the French fleet on 12 April, in the manner suggested by Cochrane, would have involved danger and "risk" to the ships of the Royal Navy. To Cochrane, this sort of talk was preposterous. Of course warships incurred risk and danger, that was their purpose. Had Nelson, or Hood, or St Vincent ever pleaded that it was too dangerous or risky to attack the enemy?

Day after day, the battle of the Basque Roads was re-fought at the green baize table on H.M.S. *Gladiator*. On the morning of 4 August, Gambier announced that his defence was concluded, and the officers of the tribunal remained alone in the great cabin, considering their verdict. At one o'clock, the court was opened again and the spectators admitted. The judge advocate took the sheet of paper on which the findings had been written and read out the verdict:

> The charge has not been proved against the said Admiral the Right Honourable Lord Gambier . . . his Lordship's conduct on that occasion, as well as his general conduct and proceedings as Commander-in-Chief of the Channel Fleet . . . was marked by zeal, judgment, ability, and an anxious attention to the welfare of His Majesty's service . . . the said Admiral the Right Honourable Lord Gambier is hereby most honourably acquitted.

"Hand me up my Lord Gambier's sword," said Sir Roger Curtis, acting his part as president. He returned it to Gambier, expressing his "peculiar pleasure" in carrying out this official duty. "Having so far obeyed the command of the court," he added, "I beg you will permit me in my individual capacity, to express to you the high gratification I have upon this occasion."[66]

Now that justice had apparently been done, Gambier was the subject of many more congratulatory messages. "My dear friend," wrote Wilberforce to him, actually undertaking such secular correspondence on a Sunday, "surely even on this day it cannot be improper for me to mix my congratulations with yours on the happy tidings which, on my return from Church, have just now reached me – congratulations animated with a grateful sense of the Goodness of Him who has established your righteous cause."[67]

While Wilberforce spoke boldly of Gambier as this "true specimen of Christian heroism", Morton Pitt went further in denouncing the Order of the Bath as a degraded award since the authorities had bestowed it on Cochrane. Gambier must refuse to defile himself by wearing it even if it were offered him. "My dear Jim," wrote Morton

Pitt, "If they could undo what they have foolishly done, and with-draw that ribbon from Lord Cochrane's unworthy shoulder, it might be deemed a decoration or an honour; but to accept it now would be assenting to a stigma being put upon you, for such it must be thought. The Order of the Bath is degraded for a time."[68]

Hannah More also rejoiced with an almost evangelical fervour at Gambier's acquittal. But, behind everything, she saw the plotting of revolution, as she complained to Lord Barham:

> What a tempestuous world do we live in! Yet terrible as Buonaparte is in every point of view, I do not fear him so much as those domestic mischiefs – Burdett, Cochrane, Wardle, and Cobbett. I hope, however, that the mortification Cochrane, &c., have lately experienced in their base and impotent endeavours to pull down reputations which they found unassailable, will keep them down a little.[69]

Not all the opinions were on Gambier's side. There was one, ad-dressed by a French prisoner to his captor, which merited at least some respect. "The French admiral was an *imbécile*," he admitted, "but yours was just as bad. I assure you that, if Cochrane had been supported, he would have taken every one of the ships. They ought not to have been alarmed by your *brûlots*, but fear deprived them of their senses, and they no longer knew how to act in their own defence."[70]

The opinion was, of course, that of Napoleon during his long exile on St Helena.

There remained only the vote of thanks. The parliamentary session of 1809 was over by the time of Gambier's acquittal, so that the vote was postponed until the opening of the next session in January 1810. Cochrane tried to forestall the ministers by demanding in the Com-mons that the minutes of the court-martial should be produced be-fore the House. This would have enabled him to debate their contents, as well as the conduct of the trial and the way in which evidence had, allegedly, been manufactured or suppressed. Cochrane promised to prove that the charts of Stokes and Fairfax must be false. Moreover, since Gambier himself had at no time been closer than seven miles to the guns of the French fleet – let alone within range of them – on what conceivable argument was he entitled to a vote of thanks?

The ministry had had six months to prepare for this onslaught and, once again, they deflected Cochrane's attack with the greatest ease.

First of all, they amended Cochrane's motion so that it asked for the "sentence" of the court-martial, instead of the minutes of the proceedings, to be produced before the House. The amendment, which was carried easily, had the effect of reminding the world that Gambier had been acquitted, without detailing any of the evidence or argument leading up to that verdict. Whatever disquiet there might have been in the press, the ministry was master in its own house.

There was, of course, the added consideration that whatever Gambier had done, or not done, the government needed the vote more than he did himself. Despite the misgivings of the more liberal Whigs and the Radicals, their numbers were, as Cochrane admitted, "nothing compared to the organised masses in power, or eager to place themselves in power". When the members of the Commons had passed through the lobbies, 161 had approved the vote of thanks and only 39 had opposed it.[71]

Something of Cochrane's tarnished reputation as a naval hero survived, and he still claimed the loyal support of many Radicals. But to the majority of his contemporaries he had suffered a considerable humiliation at the hands of the Admiralty and of those whose power he had sworn to curb. In reality, his plight was worse than he knew. His career as a Royal Navy captain was over. Morton Pitt's vision of the Order of the Bath and his other honours being stripped from him was prophetic, as the high adventure of the *Gamo* and Fort Trinidad was darkened by the public drama of disgrace. The most extraordinary events of his life lay ahead, deeds performed where all the world could see, in countries which were mere names to most of his compatriots. But for the immediate future, the many enemies he had made in the government and the Admiralty were triumphant over him. For several years, at least, the courage required of him was of a higher order than any he had so far shown.

# 6

# "Announce Lord Cochrane's Degradation"

---

THE displeasure of the Admiralty and the ministers over Cochrane's behaviour was quickly and clearly shown. In the very month of Gambier's court-martial, the first troops and ships of the so-called Walcheren expedition crossed the Channel. Their object was the destruction of French ships in the Scheldt, and the seizure of three arsenals and dockyards: Flushing, Antwerp, and Terneuse. Under the Earl of Chatham and Sir Richard Strachan, a total of 40,000 troops, 35 sail of the line, 5 smaller ships, 18 frigates and 200 attendant craft was to be employed.

Cochrane first urged the Admiralty to undertake an invasion of the Biscay islands instead. In default of this, he argued in favour of an attack on the Scheldt, using the same weapons as at the Basque Roads, rather than the cumbersome invasion fleet with its 40,000 troops. Their Lordships were not interested. Off the Kentish coast, the great armada rode at anchor. A more impressive display than the fine ships with their cheering men would have been hard to imagine. True, the Earl of Chatham, as Master General of the Ordnance, was not much qualified by experience to command such a force, but the court and the ministry had favoured him.

With his plans rejected, Cochrane was prepared merely to serve as captain of the *Imperieuse*, since the frigate was to form part of the expedition. To his dismay, he was informed that he had been superseded in his command. There was no further employment for him in the Royal Navy. During the bitter months which followed the court-martial he was left to draw his own conclusions as to his future prospects. At Walcheren, the expeditionary force, badly led and appallingly provisioned, lost half its men in the fever-infested islands of the Scheldt estuary. The nation mocked its leaders.

> Great Chatham with his sabre drawn,
> Stood waiting for Sir Richard Strachan;
> Sir Richard, longing to be at 'em,
> Stood waiting for the Earl of Chatham.

In three months, 11,000 men were prostrate with dysentery. There was one hospital ship and no proper medicine. The water was so foul that every drop had to be shipped from England. Medical authorities knew the islands as breeding grounds of fever, but no one consulted these authorities before the expedition sailed. As for the military initiative, its advantage of surprise had been lost by anchoring the great armada off the Kent coast as conspicuously as though for a royal review. In consequence, Flushing was taken in the first attack, and then nothing more was accomplished. After months of sickness and misery, the English invalids disembarked at the Kent ports again, bringing the "Walcheren sickness" with them. Cochrane reflected that a French fleet, inferior in strength to that of the Aix Roads, had evaded a force infinitely more powerful. The Portland government fell, scapegoat for the humiliations of the Scheldt. The reputation of the navy fared worse than that of the army, as Byron later described it in the fourth stanza of *Don Juan*, discussing "heroes".

> Nelson was once Britannia's god of war,
>    And still should be so, but the tide is turn'd;
> There's no more to be said of Trafalgar,
>    'Tis with our hero quietly inurn'd;
> Because the army's grown more popular,
>    At which the naval people are concern'd;
> Besides, the prince is all for the land service,
> Forgetting Duncan, Nelson, Howe, and Jervis.

The faces of the new ministry were familiar enough, its leader, Spencer Perceval, having been Cochrane's opponent while Chancellor of the Exchequer. Cochrane turned to his own affairs, withdrawing to Portman Square to perfect his secret war plans at his uncle Basil's house. He soon crossed swords with the Hon. Charles Yorke, the new First Lord of the Admiralty. When it was known that Cochrane proposed to attack the new ministry in the Commons, Yorke informed him that he could have his command of the *Imperieuse* again, if he sailed that week. Cochrane reacted indignantly, and Yorke thereupon dismissed him observing that, "It is neither my duty nor my inclination to enter into controversy with you." In any case, scientific

warfare occupied Cochrane's time. In March 1812, he revealed to the
Prince Regent his array of secret weapons and well-laid plans. While
Napoleon remained undisputed master of most of Europe and
Wellington struggled onward through the Peninsula at stupefying
cost, Cochrane saw total victory within his grasp. To the Prince
Regent in his fairy palace beside the sea at Brighton, he offered
triumph over France in a matter of weeks at the cost of virtually no
British casualties. He was not drifting into the deceptions of lunacy
but had, at last, turned his father's example as a scientific innovator
to practical use. As the taste of the civilised world turned from the
minuet to the quadrille, Cochrane had conceived the principles and
demonstrated the techniques of poison gas and saturation bombardment.[1]

His scheme appeared, at first glance, so preposterous that he made no
attempt to convince the Admiralty or the ministry to begin with. All
too easily, they would have found means to dismiss him as a fool as
well as a villain. Instead, he drew up a "Plan for the Destruction of
the Naval Power of France", and addressed it to the Prince Regent
directly on 2 March 1812. It was simply argued but carefully detailed,
including diagrams of the weapons and their methods of use. Against
such forms of warfare there could be no resistance and little form of
defence. The world would wake one morning to find the British army,
with naval support, in control of the entire coast of France. A military
blow would thus be delivered which would infallibly cripple the
power of Napoleon to continue the war. His surrender might be
expected within a few weeks as the British overran France itself.

The proposal needed to be carefully and tactfully introduced, if
Cochrane were not to be disregarded as a madman. He justified it to
the Prince with massive understatement.

> On the first blush of the proposition, it might, by some persons
> be considered as speculative and visionary, and even Your
> Royal Highness may probably regard it as extravagant and
> improbable; but, I confidently trust, there will be no difficulty
> in removing such impression from Your Royal Highness's
> mind, as the plan calculated to sustain it, is of the simplest kind
> and founded on the known principle that, the expansion of
> ignited powder is in the line of least resistance.[2]

The first part of Cochrane's secret plan was to replace the conventional bombardment of enemy ports by a close-range attack of

such intensity that every ship in the harbour or anchorage would be destroyed or crippled. Indeed, as he promised the Regent, he could "destroy them in the strongest lines of defensive anchorage". Conventional bombardment of dockyards was a long-range attack of doubtful accuracy. Mortars had the best range, but their short squat barrels were anchored at an angle of 45 degrees. Even their range could only be adjusted by using a stronger or weaker charge to fire them. For the Royal Navy to sail in at close quarters was not only dangerous but involved a technical problem which was not always easy to overcome. The closer the battleships came to the harbour, the more effectively the harbour mole or walls screened their targets from them. Cochrane asked only for the use of three old hulks in order to conquer this difficulty and saturate the harbour at Flushing with a devastating storm of 6000 shells, raining down on the helpless French fleet within a matter of minutes. He would "in an instant overwhelm Flushing . . . dismount the cannon, and destroy the Ships to which they may afford protection".[3]

Flushing was, of course, only the first of many targets. Within a matter of days, Toulon, Brest, and the great anchorages of France would be a graveyard of burnt and half-submerged ships.

How were the attacks to be carried out? In an illustrated appendix to his plan, Cochrane revealed the design of his "Temporary Mortars or Explosion Ships". The old hulks would first have their sides reinforced and braced by extra timbers. The bottom of the hull would be filled in with old cannon and iron embedded in clay. These precautions would ensure that the force of any explosion went upward and not through the bottom or sides of the vessel. Above the clay there must be a layer of gunpowder the length and width of the ship. Above that there would be a thinner layer of junk wadding, and finally the ranks of shells and carcases. This huge mortar would then be packed round on either side by old mooring chains and cables.[4]

The explosion ships would be guided to their targets during the hours of darkness and anchored at a convenient distance from the mole or outer fortification. These barriers, which made close bombardment so difficult for conventional ships, were no impediment to Cochrane's "temporary mortars", since their whole purpose was to lift shells up and over the defences. As he explained to the Prince Regent, "The Explosion Vessels would be invisible in the darkness of the night, until the Shells and Carcases, rising in the air, and spreading as they fly, should scatter devastation on all around."[5]

It was true that the mortar was fixed in one position and could not itself be adjusted. But Cochrane had found a remedy for this by means of shifting the ballast of the vessel so that it could be made to list further towards its target, thus angling the mortar to do the most damage. He had perfected this "so as to give the largest Carcases and Shells a sufficient, but not more than a sufficient momentum to plunge through the Decks of large Ships, and lodge in the holds of those of a smaller Class".[6]

To forestall his critics, Cochrane also revealed that he had undertaken a "confidential trial" in the previous year with the aid of Sir John Stuart. He had converted a wine pipe into a mortar, using only three pounds of powder for each shell. In the resulting explosion, it had bombarded an area 230 yards across with 8-inch shells. By a logical extension, three old hulks, of which there was no shortage in English yards, would saturate an area half a mile square with 6000 missiles. The attack would be swift, devastating, and decisive in its psychological effect on the enemy. Because of the intensity which Cochrane envisaged, it might well have been the Regency equivalent of a nuclear weapon.

Yet that was only the beginning of the plan. The destruction of the French fleet and coastal fortifications would swing the balance of the war in England's favour, but it was a mere preparation for the decisive blow. The next appendix to Cochrane's proposals showed the construction and mode of operation of "Sulphur Ships", or, as he called them more familiarly, "Stink Vessels".

His inherited enthusiasm for chemistry had led Cochrane to experiment in the manufacture of a gas which might be used for military purposes. The most promising was a mixture of vapour given off by burning charcoal and sulphur. The effect of the gas was, as Cochrane politely put it, to destroy "every animal function". Had the Spanish been possessed of such a weapon before 1808, he demonstrated how they might have taken the fortress of Gibraltar without firing a shot. "Had Lord Nelson understood the principles now submitted to Your Royal Highness, he could have destroyed the Danish Fleet without the loss of a man."[7]

The hulks which were to be used for the gas attacks, or to release "volumes of noxious effluvia", as Cochrane termed it, were intended for use against Flushing and Cherbourg, in the first instance. "If conducted at a proper time to a fit situation," said Cochrane, "their effect is inevitable." Once again, a bed of clay was to be laid at the bottom of the ship, with the charcoal on an upper deck so that air would circulate between the two layers and aid the coal in burning steadily but not too fast. Above the charcoal, the sulphur compound was laid. With the wind blowing inshore, the sulphur ships would be driven broadside-on against the mole or wall, and the gas or vapour would roll inland like a thick yellow fog. As it engulfed the dockyard and defences, perhaps already shattered by saturation bombardment, the enemy would be faced with the choice of suffocation or precipitate retreat. As the gas moved inland, carrying all before it, the wind would clear the air around the burnt-out stink vessels. The British troops might then occupy the fortifications at their leisure.[8]

It was never suggested that Cochrane's plans were in the least preposterous. Indeed, the secret committees appointed to consider them in the nineteenth century feared only that they might fall into the hands of other nations. As late as 1895, his Victorian biographer, J. W. Fortescue, wrote:

> Wherein this plan consisted it is impossible to say, for its secret is still buried in the archives of the War Office; but it is generally supposed to have had its root in some new and appalling explosive.[9]

The details of the "secret weapons" were not divulged until the end of the nineteenth century, when the papers were deposited in the British Museum, and Cochrane's offer to Palmerston of even more elaborate devices was outlined in the posthumous publication of the latter's correspondence in the *Panmure Papers* in 1908. Cochrane kept his original promise to the Prince Regent never to divulge the plans of the weapons "except for the honour and advantage of my own country".[10]

To Cochrane, in 1812, the possibilities of the new weapons seemed awesome. Wellington had reached Badajoz, but he was two years and hundreds of miles from the French frontier. Napoleon, driving the Russian armies back to Borodino and thence to Moscow, held the initiative. But what if the secret weapons were used? The French would wake one morning to find their Channel ports in the hands of the Royal Navy, their fleet sunk, and the invading English army already on the road from Normandy to Paris. The power of Napoleon would be destroyed at its root.

The lessons of the Western Front in 1914–1918 may make such optimism seem naïve. No one who has read such accounts as Robert Graves's *Goodbye To All That* needs to be reminded how effectively the British gas-companies devastated their own front line as the wind briefly but capriciously changed direction. The risk of failure, even of disaster, in 1812 was considerable, yet the gamble might have been justified. Cochrane had already proved his ability to command an attack with conventional weapons. With his secret devices and a much smaller number of men than had been squandered in the Walcheren affair, he might well have done decisive damage to the defences and morale of France.[11]

Shock, rather than admiration, was the reaction of some of the Regent's advisers on examining the ingenious proposals, as men who remembered the elegance and propriety with which many of the European battles of the eighteenth century had been fought. At Fontenoy in 1745, for instance, as the red and blue ranks of the two armies faced one another with the decorum of a ceremonial parade, silent and still before the opening of the battle, it was said that a group of French officers had crossed to the English lines and said gallantly, "Messieurs les Anglais, fire first!"

Apart from all these considerations, Cochrane had not chosen the most propitious time to put forward his plans. With the final collapse of the old King's mind, the Prince of Wales had entered upon his Regency in high spirits. He had not, as had been hoped, dismissed Spencer Perceval and the Tories in favour of the Whigs but life at Carlton House and Brighton sparkled for him as much as ever. Nothing more belligerent than a fishing-smack appeared on the glittering waters of the Channel beyond the Royal Pavilion. On the shaded promenades, among the lawns and trees of the Steine, rouged dandies with their high collars and low hat brims, their female companions or "flashers" hanging on their arms, rivalled the splendour of military fashion. Thomas Creevey surveyed the officers of the Prince of Wales's Hussars at the Pavilion and thought them, "very ornamental monkeys in their red breeches with gold fringe and yellow boots".[12]

The Prince himself, "uncommonly well, tho' very fat", appeared in full Field Marshal's uniform at the evening receptions, but his interest in the war was minimal. "Portugal and Lord Wellington begin to be out of fashion," Creevey remarked, as he watched the Regent slapping his fat thighs to keep the band in time. He not only slapped, he sang lustily until midnight, when there was a pause for iced champagne punch, lemonade, and sandwiches. "Better heard from the next room in my opinion," said John Wilson Croker, of the musical entertainment.[13]

Such was the society upon which Cochrane launched his secret plans. At Carlton House or the Pavilion the principal doubt was less likely to be over the feasibility of the plans than over the comparative claims of Cochrane and Napoleon to be the greatest enemy of mankind. Given the merciless choice between such weapons and the long ordeal of the Peninsula, it was Cochrane's suggestion which was regarded as outrageous by the standards of civilised warfare.

None the less, a secret committee was set up to investigate the proposals. The Regent's brother, the Duke of York, presided over it, its members including two naval commanders, Lord Keith and Lord Exmouth, as well as Sir William Congreve, inventor of the Congreve rocket. At first there was some encouragement for Cochrane. The Duke of York was in favour of the principle of attacking French ports. Congreve, "after some days' consideration, gave a favourable opinion as to the practicability of using Explosion and Sulphur vessels". When Admiral Keats was approached by the new Lord Melville, the second of his line to act as First Lord of the Admiralty, he was cautious over Cochrane's scientific warfare but added, "I should feel inclined at least to give it some trial." Lord Keith, as a member of the committee, spoke with less enthusiasm. "Of the combustible weapons I am not so well able to judge," he concluded. "Considerable nautical and military science must be combined."[14]

The general opinion seemed to favour Cochrane's proposals, though with some caution. Wellington, as it later proved, was opposed to them on the ground that "two might play" at such a game. Cochrane pointed out that the one who played first was going to win. At the Admiralty itself, Lord Melville seemed at first cautiously inclined to favour the plans. And then, as the spring of 1812 turned to summer, and summer to autumn, there was a long silence. Melville might be sympathetic, but Melville's voice was not the only one at the Admiralty, let alone among Spencer Perceval's ministry.[15]

In August, it was suggested to Cochrane that he might be given the command of a frigate to raid the Spanish coast. After all that he had done, he found the idea preposterous. It would not, he wrote angrily to Melville, "produce material change in the affairs of Europe". And then he began to inquire eagerly of the First Lord as to what decision had been made about his secret plans. "Five months have elapsed without anything being undertaken, or His Majesty's Ministers having pointed out a single obstacle or difficulty," he wrote. "I have waited day after day with increasing anxiety."[16]

But during those five months the swarm of enemies promised him by Mulgrave over the Gambier affair, and other affairs before that, had done their work. Melville's enthusiasm had cooled and his interest had turned elsewhere. The permanent officials, the senior commanders, the holders of places and sinecures had one opinion of Cochrane for the most part and they were not slow to let the First Lord know it. He was, said St Vincent, untruthful and not to be trusted out of sight. Lord Keith thought him crackbrained. Gambier detested him and Mulgrave despised him. Croker and Wellesley Pole were well-trained in their aversion to him. Even William Windham joined the chorus of calumny by announcing that Cochrane's "firmness of character" would make him "a bad antagonist to a French general".[17]

By the end of 1812, the position was clear. It had been decided that the limit of official recognition would be to give him command of a frigate. But since he had not shown himself a grateful recipient of such preferment, he was to be given nothing at all, and his secret war plans were to be dismissed from the official mind.

Perhaps Cochrane was to blame, in one respect. Throughout his negotiations with Melville, he had made it clear that he was going to fight the most bitter war against the iniquities of the prize-money system. He came close to refusing the command of a vessel, even without the offer being made, when he wrote to the First Lord, "Whilst the present system of distribution exists, I have determined not to accept a shilling of prize money."[18]

As soon as the old grievance of prize money was mentioned, the officials of the Admiralty had a further reason for deciding to dispense with Cochrane's services, whatever the consequences to the war or the nation. While completing his secret plans he had been at the centre of a scandal which had revealed corruption on the most bizarre scale in the administration of the system.

The experimental firing of shells from the wine pipe, as a "temporary mortar", had been carried out in the Mediterranean. Cochrane, as an unemployed naval officer, had sailed there in his little yacht, the *Julie*, one of the armada of ships he had seized from the French at various times. Apart from his interest in the experimental firing of the mortar, he now had the leisure to do battle with the most corrupt of all the Admiralty courts, at Malta. In Cochrane's own case, the court at Malta announced that not a penny was due to him for all the prizes the *Imperieuse* had taken in the Mediterranean. Instead, he was in debt to the court for the cost of the legal proceedings. Leaving the

*Julie* at Gibraltar, he embarked on a brig-of-war for Malta, determined to make the court's practices public knowledge.

The farce of the Admiralty system was quickly revealed. A ship
captured from the enemy as a prize was first under the jurisdiction of
the marshal of the court. The marshal would then place it under the
jurisdiction of the proctor. These two officials were entitled to charge
for attending one another, instructing one another, and administering
oaths to one another. All these charges were paid out of the prize
money which would otherwise have gone to the officers and crew who
had taken the enemy ship in battle.

The great discovery of Cochrane's visit to Malta was that one man,
Mr Jackson, held both posts and both salaries of marshal and proctor.
He was busily and legally amassing a fortune by fees for visiting himself to ask himself to sign monitions and other legal documents, and
for agreeing with himself to do it. He was also paying himself for
negotiating fees with himself, and indeed for administering the oath
to himself. Still more extraordinary was the fact that the monitions
which he asked himself to draw up were also addressed to himself. As
Cochrane pointed out, Jackson was entitled to consult with himself as
often as he felt necessary and to charge the victims of the court several
pounds for doing so. The legal convolutions involved in one monition
or simple standard document were charged for at about £5 or rather
more than £50 by modern values. In the rare event that any prize
money was actually payable once Jackson had finished with it, he
also took a standard five per cent commission upon it.[19]

Cochrane walked into the Admiralty court one day, while the court
was not sitting, and demanded to see the official table of fees. The
judge advocate, who was in his office, denied that any such table
existed, although an Act of Parliament required it to be displayed.
Cochrane explored the building, even entering the judge's robing
room, without finding a copy. Before leaving, he decided to make use
of the judicial lavatory. "And there," he recalled, "wafered up behind
the door of the Judge's retiring-chamber, was the Admiralty Court
table of fees!"

He prepared to leave the law court and, as he passed the judge
advocate, Cochrane was "in the act of folding up the paper, previously
to putting it in my pocket". The judge advocate tried to prevent him
leaving the building by standing in his path. According to Cochrane
his own reply to this was reasonable enough. "I have no cause of
quarrel with or complaint towards you. Guarding the judge's water-
closet forms no part of your duties as judge advocate."

It is a matter of record that in general war or personal confronta-
tion men were apt to be deterred by Cochrane's height and build.
The judge advocate stood aside and Cochrane at once took the table
of fees to a friend who was sailing for Sicily, and entrusted it to him.
If there was consternation among the judge and court officials at the
irretrievable loss of the paper, it was not to be wondered at. As
Cochrane gleefully remarked, the table would, "when laid before the
House of Commons in connexion with the fees actually charged . . .
infallibly betray the practices of the Maltese Court".

Mr Jackson duly attempted to arrest Cochrane for an "insult" to
the court. Cochrane replied that the court had not been sitting, and
that Jackson's tenure of the office of proctor made his action as
marshal illegal. If, as marshal, he tried to carry out the arrest, said
Cochrane, "I will treat you as one without authority of any kind, so
that you must take the consequences, which may be more serious to
yourself personally than you imagine."

Jackson withdrew, to be replaced by another willing arrester. But
this one too was the illegal holder of an office, the deputy auctioneer
of the court at Malta, and Cochrane met him with the same threat.
The man followed him all over the island, however, until an official
of unimpeachable legality arrived and the arrest was peacefully
carried out.

The deputy marshal informed Cochrane that he would be on parole
and might live at a nearby inn.

"I will do nothing of the kind," said the prisoner firmly, "if you
take me anywhere it must be to the town gaol."

The deputy marshal agreed and asked Cochrane to accompany him
there. The reply was unpromising.

"No. I will be no party to an illegal imprisonment of myself. If you
want me to go to gaol, you must carry me by force, for assuredly I
will not walk."

This farce was played out before a growing audience of delighted
Royal Navy officers, including Cochrane's friends. But there was no
alternative for the deputy marshal. Cochrane was taken to prison in
a coach with a file of armed soldiers as escort. On arrival there he
announced that he would eat nothing.

"I have been placed here on an illegal warrant, and will not pay for
so much as a crust. So that if I am starved to death, the Admiralty
Court will have to answer for it."

It was no secret to the court that Cochrane was member for Westminster, as well as a naval hero, and that he had put into safekeeping

the damning evidence against his captors. Even a hunger strike, let alone his death, might bring ruin upon the ingenious Mr Jackson and his colleagues.

Cochrane relented, agreeing to eat on condition that food and drink were supplied from a hotel of his choice, for himself and his guests, and that it was all paid for by the court. This was acceded to and, night after night, the officers of the fleet were wined and dined in Cochrane's prison room at the expense of the Admiralty court.

After two weeks of this, he was brought before the judge. With feigned innocence, he maintained that he could hardly have taken a table of fees if, as the judge advocate had said, no such table existed. And if, as the Act of Parliament laid down, the table had to be publicly displayed, it would surely not have been kept on the door of the judge's lavatory. Ignoring this, the judge offered to release him on bail. Cochrane refused and was escorted back to prison.

But the friends who visited him urged that some action must be taken. There was a mood of increasing resentment among the seamen in Malta and a real possibility that they would storm the prison to set Cochrane free. The only solution was for him to escape. A file and a rope were solemnly smuggled in so that he could work on the bars of his third-floor room in preparation for the chosen night. He held his dinner party as usual. "The gaoler was purposely made very tipsy," he recalled, "to which he was nothing loth." At midnight, he lowered his possessions to his servant who was waiting below, removed the bars, looping the rope round one which he had left intact. It was easy enough to climb down from the window and draw the looped rope after him. The gig of H.M.S. *Eagle* was waiting to take him to sea, where he boarded an English packet. He arrived in Gibraltar, sold the *Julie*, which he had left there on his way to Malta, and returned to England.

His denunciation of the Admiralty court to the House of Commons was one of his few parliamentary triumphs, the members rocking with laughter at the story of his imprisonment and escape. As an illustration of the costs deducted by Mr Jackson for talking to himself in a single case, Cochrane unrolled the bill of charges along the floor of the Commons. It stretched from the speaker's table at one end of the House to the bar at the other.[20]

If he pursued the wretched sinecurists of the Admiralty court with less tenacity than was customary in him, after his return to England, there was a good reason for it. In his deeds of valour, in the comic opera plot of his Maltese escapade, and in almost every aspect of his life, Cochrane was the child of that period in which he lived, and which was so responsive to the "romantic" in art and behaviour. On his return from Malta he lived with his uncle, Basil Cochrane, in Portman Square. It was then that he first set eyes on a sixteen-year-old schoolgirl, the beautiful orphan daughter of a Spanish dancer and an English father. Katherine Barnes, though less than half his age, was everything he could have wished. And to make her still more appealing, the match was forbidden. The most proficient novelist of Sensibility could have devised no more touching a story.

At the time of their first meeting, Kitty Barnes displayed the soft features and wide eyes of her age. Her skin was fair but her hair almost black, worn in the clustering corkscrew ringlets which were then fashionable. As she grew out of her teens, her portraits show her developing a finer and more delicate appearance. This delicacy was certainly not an indication of physical frailty. She followed Cochrane in his exile, crossed the Andes, and faced disgrace, as well as danger, at his side. In dealing with the entrenched ministerial hostility to him, she fought Cochrane's battles as diligently and enthusiastically as he had ever done himself. "Without a particle of romance in my composition," he later wrote, "my life has been one of the most romantic on record, and the circumstances of my marriage are not the least so."[21]

Kitty Barnes lived under the guardianship of John Simpson, of Portland Place. So far as the marriage market was concerned, she had few assets apart from her appearance and natural abilities. To Cochrane, her material circumstances were not important. Within a few weeks of meeting her he had proposed marriage and had been accepted. In view of his ward's reduced circumstances, John Simpson probably felt that a future Earl of Dundonald was not a bad bargain.

It was at this point that Basil Cochrane heard a rumour as to his nephew's interest in Kitty Barnes. Uncle Basil had amassed a considerable fortune from his activities in India and was looked upon by the other members of his family as the one likely source of a substantial legacy. In his turn, Basil Cochrane enjoyed the sense of power this gave him, hinting or specifying certain actions or forms of behaviour which he would require from them as his beneficiaries. In his nephew's case, he now revealed that he had arranged a marriage for him.

There was something essentially absurd in a man of thirty-seven returning home after nearly twenty years of warfare to discover that a marriage was being arranged for him, as though he were an incompetent adolescent. But that was by no means the worst of it. Uncle Basil had chosen as the prospective bride the daughter of an Admiralty court official, who had made "a very large fortune" by swindling the officers and men of the Royal Navy in a manner with which Cochrane was only too familiar. He had no intention of allowing his uncle or anyone else to dictate to him his choice in marriage. In any case, a well-publicised marriage to the daughter of such a man would make him the laughing stock of his naval comrades, his enemies, and his constituents. He told his uncle as much.

"Please yourself," said Basil Cochrane snappishly, "nevertheless, my fortune and the money of the wife I have chosen for you, would go far towards reinstating future Earls of Dundonald in their ancient position as regards wealth."

The argument continued until the point at which Cochrane finally and absolutely refused the bride whom his uncle had chosen for him.

"No," he announced, "I would rather not. It is a thing for money only, and I abhor the idea of marrying for money. I cannot and I will not."[22]

It was then that Uncle Basil began to make plans for getting married himself, a clear indication that his nephew had forfeited some or all of the proposed inheritance. Cochrane went to Kitty and urged her to elope with him. At first she refused, shocked by so extreme a measure and alarmed at the probable ruin of her reputation. But Cochrane persisted, and in the end the sixteen-year-old girl agreed. They would ride to Scotland and there conclude a "runaway" marriage. The truth was that Kitty Barnes, for all her demure appearance, was a formidable young woman and never more so than in her attachment to Cochrane. Exactly half a century later she was to proclaim publicly the depth of her feeling for him. "Such a God of a Man! A Man who could have ruled the World upon the Sea!" she called him:

The Hero of a Hundred Fights! I have followed the Fortunes of that great Man. I have stood upon the Battle Deck. I have seen the Men fall. I have raised them. I have fired a Gun to save the Life of a Man for the Honour of my Husband, and would do it again. He was a Glory to the Nation in which he was born, and there is not a Member of the Family of Dundonald that need not be proud of belonging to such a noble Man as he was.[23]

The spirit of this proclamation, latent in a girl of sixteen, perhaps made it inevitable that Kitty should at last have given way to her importunate hero. They left London in a carriage on the evening of 6 August 1812, with Cochrane's servant Richard Carter riding outside and Kitty's maid, Anne Moxham, accompanying her mistress. They drove northward with hardly a rest, using two horses or four to pull the carriage according to the availability at the stables on the way. After travelling day and night, with Kitty "very worn", Cochrane suddenly said, "Well, thank God, we are all right." They were in Scotland.

Turning to the exhausted girl and using his pet name for her, he added, "It is all right, Mouse, we are all right now. Moxham, mind you get a comfortable room for Lady Cochrane at the Queensberry Arms. We shall soon be there."

They had passed Gretna Green and were driving towards Annan, with Cochrane in high spirits, snapping his fingers with delight.

"Mouse," he said, "we are over the Border. Here we are over the Border now and nothing but God can separate us. You are mine now, and you are mine for ever."

They went through the form of civil marriage at the Queensberry Arms at Annan on the evening of 8 August, the two servants acting as witnesses. As soon as the papers had been signed, Cochrane began to dance a sailor's hornpipe round the room, saying, "Now you are mine, Mouse, mine for ever."

"I do not know," said Kitty doubtfully, "I have had no parson or church. Is this the way you marry in Scotland?"

"Oh yes," said Cochrane happily, "you are mine, sure enough; you cannot get away."

It was hardly the most prepossessing start to married life. Cochrane had to return to London almost at once, since he was supposed to attend his uncle's own wedding in a few more days. Kitty, exhausted by the journey, was left to follow with the servants in due course. Once Cochrane had gone, she discovered that the Queensberry Arms was a far from agreeable lodging. There were no baths, no soft water for washing, and the woman who kept it was "a cross old thing". She soon followed Cochrane back to London.[24]

For the time being, the marriage remained a secret from his family and the couple lived apart. There was later to be considerable family argument over the first ceremony and Kitty and Cochrane were remarried in an Anglican church, at the request of her guardian, in 1818. They were married a third time, according to the forms of the

Church of Scotland, in 1825. At the 1818 wedding, the liturgy required them to be referred to as "spinster" and "bachelor". This, as well as the secrecy surrounding their first marriage, gave rise to the supposition that the eldest son, Thomas Barnes Cochrane, born in 1814, might be illegitimate. Inevitably, this proved a fruitful source of dissension as to which of Cochrane's sons was entitled to succeed him. The matter was decided in favour of Thomas when the first marriage was proved before a House of Lords committee in 1863.

Basil Cochrane soon discovered the truth of the relationship between his nephew and Kitty Barnes. He not only disinherited the rebellious young man but accused him of siding with the government over the matter of the money which Basil Cochrane believed was owing to him from the Victualling Board of the Admiralty. During Cochrane's courtship of Kitty, the Tory Prime Minister, Spencer Perceval, had been shot dead in the chamber of the House of Commons by John Bellingham, an insurance broker with a lunatic determination to avenge the financial "injustices" he had suffered at the hands of the government. Basil Cochrane sought an interview with Perceval's successor, Lord Liverpool, and took the opportunity to denounce his nephew. A similar denunciation was later made to the Prime Minister on behalf of Cochrane's father the old Earl of Dundonald. Cochrane remained indifferent to all this, showing no regret over his uncle's estate, which he had lost by his marriage. "I had a rich equivalent in the acquisition of a wife whom no amount of wealth could have purchased."[25]

While Cochrane the romantic hero appeared to triumph in war and love, the more sombre drama of his political downfall had already begun. It was his misfortune that, with rare exceptions, he performed poorly in the House of Commons and so rashly outside it that some of the Radicals themselves were prepared to disown him. Of course, he showed his habitual courage and an earnest integrity yet he was an easy prey to his political enemies. It was an essential feature of his conduct that he believed in politics as a war to be fought, but his associates had already had enough of this when Cochrane announced his intention of blowing up part of Piccadilly in defence of Sir Francis Burdett.

The origin of this plan was the House of Commons committee in February 1810 which was to look into the disaster of the Walcheren expedition. In order to restrict the details of incompetence on the part of the military authorities, the ministry decided that the proceedings

would be secret and that no member of the public would be allowed
to hear them. This provoked anger among the Radicals of Westminster, whose debating society, "The British Forum", placarded the
walls of the city with a denunciation of the Commons' action as an
"outrage upon the public feeling".[26]

On 19 February, the attention of the House was drawn to this
affront by the Hon. Charles Yorke, and the Bill of Rights of 1689 was
invoked to commit the author of the placard, John Gale Jones, to
Newgate for daring to infringe the privileges of parliament by his
criticism. Jones was still in prison several weeks later. Burdett rose in
the House on 12 March, denouncing the imprisonment as an abuse of
power, and demanded his release. His motion was defeated by 139
votes.

Frustrated by the ministerial power in the House itself, Burdett
took up his pen and denounced the imprisonment still more strongly
in *Cobbett's Weekly Political Register* of 24 March 1810. He described
the unreformed Commons scathingly as "a part of our fellow subjects,
collected together by means which it is not necessary for me to
describe". He accused them of arbitrary government, under the pretext of "parliamentary privilege", which rivalled the authoritarian
régimes of the Tudors and Stuarts.

Three days later, Thomas Lethbridge, the member for Somerset,
laid the article before the Commons and complained of a breach of
privilege. On 5 April, a debate on this matter took place, lasting all
night, and at seven thirty the next morning, the Commons voted by
189 to 152 for the committal of Burdett to the Tower of London.
Within an hour, Charles Abbot, the Speaker of the House, had signed
the warrant. Half an hour after that, the serjeant-at-arms, Francis
Colman, arrived at 78, Piccadilly to arrest the culprit. But Burdett
was not there. He had been at Wimbledon during the debate and
returned to his house in Piccadilly after Colman's visit. He agreed to
see Colman the next day, but made it quite clear that he had no
intention of submitting to arrest.

By 7 April, there was considerable danger of a riot in the streets of
London. The serjeant-at-arms insisted to Burdett, "I shall be
obliged, sir, to resort to force, as it is my duty to execute the warrant."
Burdett replied that the warrant was illegal and that he would never
submit, except to "overwhelming force". Already a mob of Radical
sympathisers had gathered in the street outside and it was clear that
a regiment of troops would be needed to carry out the arrest. Other
sympathisers blocked the approaches to the Tower on land and even,

by the use of small boats, on the river itself. The crowd in Piccadilly obliged all passers-by to shout, "Burdett for ever!" and when the Earl of Westmorland, going past them, refused to chant the words at their command, they pelted him with mud and garbage.[27]

By night, the growing swarm of spectators outside number 78 spilled from Piccadilly into the squares on either side. In Berkeley Square they found the house of the unfortunate Thomas Lethbridge, who had raised Burdett's breach of privilege. Even though he had let it to someone else, every window was smashed. The assault on Lord Castlereagh's house was equally vigorous, Castlereagh hastily slipping out in his greatcoat and trying to disguise himself as one of the attackers. The houses of Lord Chatham, Spencer Perceval, Charles Yorke, and other ministerial figures had their windows broken, frames torn out, shutters wrenched off, even the chandeliers, glass, and furniture in the rooms themselves destroyed. By the light of the flaring torches or links which the rioters carried, the same scenes were enacted in St James's Square, Albemarle Street, and along Piccadilly. From such combustible indignation, the long-feared spectre of revolution might rise. There were troops at hand, but it was by no means certain that the regiments in question, the Life Guards, the Foot Guards, and the 15th Light Dragoons, could be relied upon. Francis Place was assured "that the Foot Guards and the 15th Light Dragoons were much more disposed to fight the Life Guards than they were disposed to obey an order to attack the people".[28]

Improbable though such a drama might seem, the ministry and the authorities grew more apprehensive by the hour. The guns at the Tower of London were mounted and made ready for action, while the ditches around it were flooded as a defensive barrier. Piccadilly itself was the scene of a cavalry charge by the Life Guards, who temporarily scattered the crowd up a number of side streets. But the sympathisers reassembled. Indeed, they collected long ladders and boarding from a nearby building site, provoked the cavalry to charge again, and suddenly ran out a shoulder-high obstruction across Piccadilly. As the horses shied away, the rioters bombarded the Life Guards with missiles and mud.

During all this, Cochrane was inside the house with Burdett, Francis Place, and the Radical leaders, organising the defence. Unfortunately, he took his task far more literally than they did. This was war, albeit the enemy was the serjeant-at-arms of the House of Commons rather than Napoleon. He arrived on 8 April with a large barrel and set to work, announcing that he had contrived "an effectual mode of defence against any force that could be used". Francis Place, Henry Hunt, and the other Radical leaders soon realised with dismay that the barrel contained gunpowder. As though he had been defending Fort Trinidad again, Cochrane was mining the front of 78 Piccadilly. When the time came, he would be able to blow up an entire regiment of attackers, taking the front of Burdett's house and a considerable portion of Piccadilly with them.[29]

Accustomed by long practice to a deft military solution of such problems, there is no indication that Cochrane had thought of the political or criminal consequences. It seems not to have crossed his mind either that Sir Francis Burdett's commitment to the Radical cause might stop short of having his elegant and fashionable town house reduced to rubble. For all concerned, the act was the one thing needed to turn riot into revolution, and to increase the penalty for failure from a short period under arrest to public execution. However, the plan certainly brought the defenders of 78 Piccadilly to a sense of the real alternatives facing them: surrender or bloodshed.

As the appearance of the gunpowder concentrated the minds of the Radical leaders on this prospect, they convened a Piccadilly "council of war". Francis Place, more thoroughly alarmed than most by Cochrane's hot-headedness, asked the one relevant question. "It will be easy enough to clear the hall of constables and soldiers, to drive them into the street or to destroy them, but are you prepared to take the next step and to go on?" They were not. The use of gunpowder was rejected and Cochrane withdrew to the tranquillity of Portman Square.[30]

When he returned next day, Burdett had gone. During the early morning, the sheriff and a party of soldiers had crept into the basement area at the rear of the house, broken in through a servant's window, and surprised Burdett in his drawing room. With improbable aptness, he was engaged in teaching his son to translate Magna Carta. Still protesting that the warrant was illegal, he was arrested, the crowd outside having no idea that anything of the kind had happened. He was bundled into a coach and driven away before his supporters could help him. Escorted by cavalry, he reached the Tower by a circuitous route. There he remained a prisoner until 21 June, when parliament was prorogued and his confinement automatically came to an end.[31]

Cochrane dutifully played his part in the resulting meetings and addresses of protest. Yet it was in the Commons that he scored a rare and notable political success in a well-prepared speech on the abuses of sinecures and the failure of England's rulers to reward the merits and valour of the nation's servants.

On 11 May, John Wilson Croker proposed a vote for the ordinances of the navy. It was at this time that Samuel Bamford, one of the early Radicals, was admitted to the Strangers Gallery of the House as the guest of Cochrane and Burdett. For the benefit of England's unenfranchised masses he recorded the scene.

> I found myself in a small gallery, from whence I looked on a dimly lighted place below. At the head of the room, or rather den, for such it appeared to me, sat a person in a full loose robe of, I think, scarlet and white. Above his head were the royal arms, richly gilded; at his feet several men in robes and wigs were writing at a large table, on which lamps were burning, which cast a softened light on a rich ornament like a ponderous sceptre of silver and gold, or what appeared to be so.[32]

Some of the members were sombrely dressed, others wore military uniforms. There was Canning, "with his smooth, bare, and capacious forehead", and Castlereagh, "with his handsome but immovable features". On the opposition benches sat Brougham, Cochrane, and Burdett, "his head carried back and held high as in defiance". When Cochrane rose to deliver his attack on the abuses of patronage, it was a formidable ordeal. Indeed, if his speeches were sometimes less than impressive, it was not merely the failure of inspiration but the sheer impossibility of making himself heard against the mighty expression of ministerial disapproval. Bamford described the way in which Cochrane and the little band of Radicals struggled for audience, while the government supporters ignored them.

> Some of the members stood leaning against pillars with their hats cocked awry; some were whispering by half dozens; others were lolling upon their seats; some with arms a-kimbo were eye-glassing across the house; some were stiffened immovably by starch, or pride, or both; one was speaking, or appeared to be so, by the motion of his arms, which he shook in token of defiance, when his voice was drowned by a howl as wild and remorseless as that from a kennel of hounds at feeding time. Now he points menacing to the ministerial benches – now he appeals to some members on this side – then to the speaker; all in vain. At times he is heard in the pauses of that wild hubbub, but again he is

borne down by the yell which awakes on all sides around him. Some talked aloud; some whinnied in mock laughter, coming, like that of the damned, from bitter hearts. Some called "order, order", some "question, question", some beat time with the heel of their boots; some snorted into their napkins; and one old gentleman in the side gallery actually coughed himself from a mock cough into a real one and could not stop until he was almost black in the face.[33]

Against hostility of this kind, Cochrane rose to make his speech. The lounging ministerial members on the opposite benches listened a moment and withheld their jeering. In part, this was because of the gruesome nature of what Cochrane was describing. He was listing the tariff for lost arms and legs, detailing the pensions awarded to naval officers who had suffered such injuries in battle. The going rate for a leg was £40, and for both legs £80. Arms were rated at anything from £45 to £91 each. A senior officer like Sir Samuel Hood might receive as much as £500 for his injuries, but he was still nowhere near the top of the Admiralty pension list. That eminence was reserved, perhaps predictably, for a civil servant and political appointee who was not required to go to sea nor to expose himself to risk of injury: the Secretary of the Admiralty. "He," said Cochrane, "retired, in full health, on a pension of 1 500*l.* per annum."

That was only the beginning. Lord Arden's sinecure, paid to him for supporting the government of the day, exceeded by £274 "all that is paid to the wounded officers of the whole British navy, and to the wives and children of those dead or killed in action". The amount of Lord Camden's sinecure was only £1000 less than every pension paid to every retired officer of the Royal Navy from admiral down to lieutenant. Every disablement pension paid to the navy's wounded heroes was, in total, almost £4000 less than the sum paid to the Admiralty commissioners, their wives and their clerks.

For once, the House listened to Cochrane's denunciation of naval abuses. During his term of unemployment by the Admiralty he had found the time to compile his figures with care and to garb them with images of comparison which blazoned them before parliament and the public. Even his ministerial listeners shouted with laughter when he turned to his next victims.

I find upon examination that the Wellesleys receive from the public 34,729*l.*, a sum equal to 426 pairs of lieutenants' legs, calculated at the rate of allowance of Lieutenant Chambers's legs. Calculating for the pension of Captain Johnstone's arm, viz., 45*l*.. . . .[34]

The occupants of the opposite benches rolled and guffawed. Ministeral men they might be, but some of them had no great love for the Wellesleys, certainly not for Wellington himself. The absurdity of Cochrane's comparison appealed greatly to those who had never favoured sending the future Duke to the Peninsula in the first place, and who regarded his treaty with the French at Cintra as hardly short of treason. It was Wellesley-Pole who rose to deal with Cochrane. He made no attempt to deny the payment of a sinecure pension to the family, though he insisted it was paid to the head of the family, to console him for his delicate state of health and the large number of mouths he had to feed. It was not with anger but with studied menace that he delivered his last warning to Cochrane.

> Let me advise him that adherence to the pursuits of his profession, of which he is so great an ornament, will tend more to his own honour and to the advantage of his country than a perseverance in the conduct which he has of late adopted, conduct which can only lead him into error, and make him the dupe of those who use the authority of his name to advance their own mischievous purposes.[35]

Cochrane saw only in this a promise that "if I would quit Sir Francis Burdett, sell my constituents, and come over to the ministerial side, the Government would – despite the affair of Lord Gambier – put me in the way of advancement". That was only half the truth. Such statements and warnings also carried their implication of the chastisement which awaited those who perversely rebelled against established order. Cochrane had shown himself wilful and incorrigible. He was ripe for retribution.[36]

On 21 February 1814, some eighteen months after Cochrane's marriage to Kitty Barnes, there occurred one of the most extraordinary incidents in the history of the nineteenth century. By this time, Napoleon's army had fallen back into eastern France. Its strength was depleted but it was not yet routed. Indeed, there were constant rumours of counter-attack and victory by the French against Blücher and Schwartzenberg. On 14 February, the English newspaper the *Courier* reported that there were rejoicings in Boulogne and Calais for a great French triumph on the battlefields of Champagne. By 17 February there was news of a Napoleonic victory at Château-Thierry, in which the French had taken 6000 prisoners and thirty guns. On 18 February, the *Courier* reported Napoleon's attack at Montmirail. His campaign, though perhaps a desperate last defence had, in the words of *The Times*, "been attended with immediate success".[37]

Such was the situation on Saturday 19 February, with close fought battles reported from the eastern approaches to Paris and rumours of the Cossacks or the Prussians no more than fifteen or twenty miles from the city itself. But the victory which had eluded Napoleon after Moscow now seemed to be eluding the allies in France.

Early on the morning of Monday 21 February, a group of men in the parlour of the Packet Boat public house at Dover were suddenly aware of loud, insistent knocking at the door of the Ship Inn opposite. The landlord of the Packet Boat went out and found an officer in the red uniform of the general staff and grey coat, and assisted him in rousing the boots of the Ship. He gave his name as Lieutenant-Colonel Du Bourg, aide-de-camp to Lord Cathcart, who was British ambassador to Russia. Du Bourg said only that he had just been landed on the beach by a French ship and that he must have writing materials at once, as well as a horse and rider to carry an urgent message to the port admiral at Deal.

By 1 a.m. he had written his momentous despatch to Admiral Foley.

> I have the honour to acquaint you, that the *L'Aigle* from Calais, Pierre Duquin, Master, has this moment landed me near Dover, to proceed to the capital with despatches of the happiest nature. I have pledged my honour that no harm shall come to the crew of the *L'Aigle*; even with a flag of truce they immediately stood for sea. Should they be taken, I have to entreat you immediately to liberate them; my anxiety will not allow me to say more for your gratification than that the Allies obtained a final victory; that Bonaparte was overtaken by a party of Sacken's Cossacks, who immediately slayed him, and divided his body between them. General Platoff saved Paris from being reduced to ashes; the allied sovereigns are there, and the white cockade is universal; an immediate peace is certain.[38]

Admiral Foley, roused from his bed to read this despatch, sought some kind of confirmation from the bearer, who could only add that he had been instructed to bring the message from Dover and that Colonel Du Bourg had already left for London in a chaise-and-four, paying his way with gold Napoleons. There was nothing more that the admiral could do until dawn, when it would be possible to telegraph John Wilson Croker at the Admiralty by means of the semaphore system. Foley was not prepared to take the message at face-value, though there was nothing inherently unlikely about it. Napoleon had, as a matter of fact, very nearly been killed on 29 January when the patrol he was with was attacked by a group of Cossacks, one of whom had only been brought down within a yard or so of the Emperor himself. Moreover, it was generally expected that, barring some major reversal of military fortune, there would be an allied victory before long and that Paris would be occupied.

But when dawn came, Dover was shrouded in fog. There was no hope of using semaphore to telegraph to London, news from Calais. Foley sent a messenger after Du Bourg, who was by then approaching the city. The rumours spread along the way. There had been a great battle in which the French were utterly defeated and Napoleon was killed soon afterwards. Du Bourg had been present as Lord Cathcart's aide-de-camp and had been ordered by the Czar himself to bring the news to England.

On the outskirts of London, Colonel Du Bourg paid off the post-chaise and transferred to a hackney carriage, ordering it to drive him to Grosvenor Square. At this point, his work was apparently done.

Presently the news of Napoleon's death and the final allied victory was sweeping through London, and not least through the Stock Exchange. Apart from Bank Stock, East India Stock, and such government securities as 3 per cent Consols and 4 per cent Reduced, there was one dominant commodity on the Exchange, known as Omnium. It was made up of Consols and Reduced, and was well-known for the volatility with which its price might rise or fall. Moreover, it was much used for time bargains, by those who would not actually buy the stock but merely the title on it, hoping to clear a profit before payment was due without having to find the money to buy the stock outright. Buying "on margin" was the term later given to it.

Omnium stood nowhere near 100 per cent of its value on the Exchange. On Saturday 19 February, it had closed at 26¾, opening at 26½ on Monday 21 February. Du Bourg had arrived in London at 9 a.m. and the Stock Exchange opened for business an hour later. As the rumours became more detailed, prices of all stock began to climb, none more so than that of Omnium. By noon, it had moved up from 26½ to 30¼, to the manifest delight of those who had bought at 19⅛ only a fortnight earlier. But when it was discovered that not even the Lord Mayor had received confirmation of the rumours from any authority, the price of Omnium faltered.

The doubters were soon laughed to scorn. Over London Bridge, down Lombard Street, along Cheapside, and over Blackfriars Bridge came another post-chaise and four. By a happy chance, it passed right through the heart of the most sensitive and speculative area in the city. More to the point, the horses were decorated with laurels and the three occupants of the chaise were French officers, though now they wore the white cockade of the restored House of Bourbon in their hats. In case there was still any broker who remained unconvinced, the officers tossed papers out of the chaise, inscribed with "Vive le Roi! Vivent les Bourbons!" Omnium regained its momentum and surged forward to 32. Those who sold at the end of the morning realised a profit of more than 20 per cent in three hours. Those who had held it for a fortnight found themselves almost 70 per cent better off. As for men who dealt in the shadowy regions of options and time bargains, their profits were potentially enormous.

Even before the end of the day, however, there was little doubt over the "Stock Exchange Hoax", as the fraud was termed. It was soon discovered that Napoleon was still alive and undefeated. Omnium sank rapidly back to $26\frac{1}{2}$, the despair of all those who had not had the good sense to sell at 32.

While the great financial drama of 21 February was taking place, Cochrane was occupied over very different matters. Since 1812, England had been involved in war with the United States, brought about by British insistence on applying blockade measures to neutral countries trading with France. The Americans retaliated, and the Perceval government in London seemed inclined to compromise. But the assassination of Perceval and the general dilatoriness of his ministerial colleagues frustrated the decisive action which might have avoided war. At sea, it was discovered that the English frigates were no match for the Americans. This was hardly surprising, since the Americans built their frigates to a different design, more nearly resembling a British 50-gun ship. When this simple truth was at length appreciated by the Admiralty, there was a rush to reinforce the Royal Navy on the far side of the Atlantic. Cochrane was even offered temporary command of H.M.S. *Tonnant*, then fitting out at Chatham. The commander of the *Tonnant* was, in fact, his uncle, Alexander, who had already sailed on another ship. But Cochrane was to be allowed to take the *Tonnant* across the Atlantic and, with luck, to see active service of some kind after five years of enforced retirement.

At the time of the Stock Exchange fraud, Cochrane had a week's leisure remaining before he was to join the *Tonnant* for her Atlantic voyage. He was much preoccupied with a new type of lamp which he had designed and which was being made for him near Snow Hill. On the morning of 21 February, he left his house in Green Street, off Park Lane, and went to have breakfast with another uncle, Andrew Cochrane-Johnstone, in Cumberland Street. Cochrane-Johnstone was now busily engaged in Stock Exchange speculations and had acquired a partner in the business, Richard Gathorne Butt, a former pay clerk at Portsmouth dockyard. Cochrane himself had invested his prize money in Omnium. He held a nominal £139,000 valued at 28¼ per cent and had given instructions to his broker that it was to be sold as soon as the price increased by 1 per cent. His profit would then be about £2000 on an investment of some £36,000.

After breakfast on 21 February, he left Cumberland Street with his uncle and Butt, the three of them travelling by coach together. At Snow Hill, Cochrane got out of the coach and went to attend to the business of his new lamp, while the other two drove on to the Stock Exchange. There the first tremors of the sensational rumour brought by Du Bourg were already having their effect.

Cochrane had been at the factory in Cock Lane for about three quarters of an hour when his footman Thomas Dewman arrived from Green Street with an urgent message. The signature was illegible but it had been written by an army officer who had arrived at Green Street soon after Cochrane's departure and insisted on seeing him about a matter of great importance. Cochrane's first thought was that something had happened to his brother William, who was serving with Wellington in Spain. He left Cock Lane and returned to Green Street at once.

The officer who awaited him was not from Spain. His name was Random de Berenger, a soldier of fortune whom he had met at one of his uncle Basil Cochrane's dinner parties in the previous month. He had asked Cochrane to let him join the *Tonnant* in order to command the sharpshooters on board. Cochrane explained that the *Tonnant* was in no state to receive any more officers then but that he might join her later at Portsmouth. Berenger made no secret of his desperate financial plight. He was confined to the King's Bench prison for debt, though allowed out of it so far as the rules permitted.[39]

On the morning of 21 February he repeated his request to be taken on board the *Tonnant*. Cochrane explained that he could join her at Portsmouth. Berenger seemed desperate for some form of immediate military employment, so Cochrane advised him to approach friends who had already assisted him, including Lord Yarmouth.

Berenger's rather surprising answer was to say that he could not go to Lord Yarmouth in the clothes he was wearing, which included a grey greatcoat and what soon appeared to be a sharpshooter's green uniform underneath. He asked Cochrane to lend him a civilian hat and great coat. There was another reason for this, as Berenger explained. He was one of the debtors who enjoyed the privilege of being allowed out of the King's Bench prison but if he was seen coming and going in uniform, the warden or his servants would suspect that he was planning to abscond and the privilege would be withdrawn. It was an entirely reasonable supposition.

Cochrane fetched a hat and coat, while Berenger wrapped up his own in a towel. It was logical to suppose that Cochrane's compliance with the request was as much out of a desire to get rid of this visitor and return to his own affairs as out of any great concern for Berenger.

At that point, the whole affair might have ended. It was entirely true that Cochrane was one of those who made money out of Omnium that day. He had bought at 28¼ with orders to his broker that the stock should be sold on a 1 per cent rise. In fact, it was sold that morning at 29½. An astute speculator would have done rather better by selling at 32. In Cochrane's case, all his money was in Omnium, remaining there until the eventual 1 per cent rise took place, at which point he would collect a modest 3 or 4 per cent return on his outlay.

On the discovery of the great Stock Exchange fraud there was consternation and outrage in the city and the press. It was *The Times* which led the demands for discovery and retribution.

> Great exertions will, no doubt, be made by the frequenters of the Stock Exchange to detect the criminal. . . . If his person should be recognised he will probably be willing to save himself from the whipping-post by consigning his employers to the pillory, an exaltation which they richly merit.[40]

The Stock Exchange had at once set up a committee to examine witnesses and investigate the transactions carried out on 21 February. By no means all the evidence was reliable. Fearn, the broker employed by Cochrane-Johnstone and Butt, swore that Cochrane himself was

at the Exchange at 10 a.m. on 21 February. Since there were innumerable witnesses to account for his presence elsewhere during the
entire morning, this evidence was later withdrawn. Then, on 4 March,
the investigators asked all brokers who had done business on 21
February for Cochrane, Cochrane-Johnstone, Butt, and three other
men, Holloway, Sandom, and M'Rae, to "favour the Committee with
an interview". The last three men, who had gambled hard and unsuccessfully on the Exchange, were identified as the "French officers"
who drove through the city at mid-day on 21 February. Cochrane-
Johnstone and Butt had sold Omnium totalling £410,000 and
£224,000 respectively, and Consols to a value of £100,000 and
£168,000. They had not owned such amounts, having bought on
credit to resell at a 20 per cent gain before settling day.[41]

Cochrane was not yet finally implicated. To clear his name, he
swore an affidavit, detailing his movements on 21 February, admit-
ting that Berenger visited him in the green sharpshooter's uniform,
and that Cochrane lent him the coat and hat asked for. English law
did not allow a defendant to give evidence at his trial. so the preliminary affidavit was Cochrane's only means of self-justification,
and his one chance to swear that he had had no reason to suppose
Berenger was involved in any crime.[42]

On 8 April, Berenger was arrested at Leith under the Aliens Act.
His patron, Lord Yarmouth, had already been warned off by a private
letter from the Prince Regent. "The Bow Street officers are now after
him," wrote the Prince, referring to Cochrane and the others as "the
scoundrels with whom he is connected." Yarmouth should beware of
what these men "might from pique, resentment & disappointment
induce him or persuade him to invent against you". Papers in
Berenger's possession connected him with Cochrane-Johnstone and
Butt. He held bank notes which originated from Cochrane. Soon he
was identified as "Du Bourg", a truth he later confessed in order to
incriminate Cochrane. Why had Cochrane described Berenger's uniform as green, unless to conceal that he recognised the red staff coat
as part of a fraud, which he none the less aided? On 23 March, a
bundle was raised from the Thames river bed. It held a red uniform,
such as "Du Bourg" had worn, cut into pieces.[43]

There was no longer any question of Cochrane being allowed to sail
with the *Tonnant*. On 27 April 1814, he was indicted by the Grand
Jury of the city of London, at the Old Bailey, as one of the ringleaders of the most ingenious swindle of the age.

Whatever malpractices were subsequently proved or alleged against his enemies, it has to be admitted that Cochrane was a difficult man to defend in such circumstances. He had no doubt that his innocence would be clear to the eyes of any jury, and so he left the conduct of his defence entirely to his solicitors and counsel, not even electing to appear at the trial nor to attend the consultation with his advocate.[44]

There was some justification for his optimism. After all, it was his voluntary affidavit which revealed that Berenger had visited him on the morning of 21 February and that Cochrane had lent him a hat and greatcoat to disguise his uniform. Was it likely that a man who was party to a deep-laid fraud would come forward and offer the prosecution the very evidence which they needed to build their case? Again, if Cochrane had been a party to the conspiracy, why had he not altered his instructions to his brokers in order to profit by it? As it was, he had merely left them with the standing arrangement whereby they were to sell his Omnium stock when it moved up 1 per cent. That might have happened anyway in a week or two, without the fraud or hoax.

It was true that Berenger was found to have bank notes in his possession which were traced back to Cochrane-Johnstone, Butt, and Cochrane himself. These were alleged to be payment to Berenger for his part in the conspiracy. Yet Cochrane's notes had not gone directly to Berenger, having been paid first to Butt in order to discharge a loan. There was independent evidence from the bank to this effect.

On the other hand, Lord Mulgrave had promised him a host of enemies, and there was every indication that the promise had been fulfilled. As soon as the Stock Exchange committee voiced its suspicions, John Wilson Croker wrote to Cochrane on behalf of the Admiralty demanding a further explanation of his conduct. On 22 March, Cochrane sent an outline of his defence, including affidavits from his servants who confirmed that Berenger had been wearing the green uniform of the sharpshooters and not the staff officers' red uniform when he visited Cochrane. Their Lordships were not prepared to comment on this evidence, except insofar as they informed Cochrane that he had now been superseded in his command of the *Tonnant*. One of the key witnesses for the defence on the matter of the green uniform was Isaac Davis who was just leaving Cochrane's employment to join the navy. His affidavit was enclosed in the letter to the Admiralty on 22 March. However, when an attempt was made to recall him for the trial in June, it was discovered that the navy had despatched him to Gibraltar on H.M.S. *Eurotas* on 1 May.[45]

Cochrane had already had occasion to retain Richard Gurney as counsel for other purposes. Though Gurney later denied it, Cochrane described visiting him and confiding the whole matter of the pending Stock Exchange trial and the nature of the defence to him. Gurney had not, of course, been briefed for the defence at that point but he was clearly a possible choice.

Long before the trial took place, there were two developments which Cochrane and his friends found ominous. The Stock Exchange entrusted the prosecution, rather unusually, to an Admiralty solicitor, Germain Lavie. Not only was he an Admiralty solicitor, he had been deeply involved in the Gambier court-martial and was responsible for the production in that case of the strange charts with their mysterious "rocks" and "shoals". Cochrane denounced the "collusion between a high official at the Admiralty and the Committee of the Stock Exchange". But there was an equally disagreeable surprise in store for him when he discovered that the prosecution at the trial was to be led by no other than his former counsel, Richard Gurney.

Strictly speaking, there was nothing illegal in all this, and if Cochrane had given an early advantage to his enemies this was in part the measure of his own inability to fight on equal terms in courts and debates. The other arrangements for his trial were just as unpromising but, once again, there was nothing in them over which he could reasonably quarrel.

The trial judge was Lord Chief Justice Ellenborough, defender of Warren Hastings as Edward Law. Son of a bishop, his dry and precise Cumberland intonation reflected an attachment to the formalities of his profession. To the Radicals, he was the violator of the spirit of the constitution who in 1806 had been Chief Justice and political cabinet minister simultaneously. He was no longer in the cabinet at the time of Cochrane's trial, but the memory remained bitter.

Ellenborough's impartiality was doubted when he presided over the trials of such Radical publishers as Leigh Hunt and his brother John. In March 1812, the *Morning Post* had published a grotesque eulogy on the Prince Regent, announcing:

You are the *Glory of the People* – You are the *Protector of the Arts* – You are the *Maecenas of the Age*. Wherever you appear, *you conquer all hearts*, wipe away tears, excite *desire and love*,

and win *beauty* towards you – You breathe *eloquence* – You
inspire the Graces – You are an *Adonis in loveliness!*

In the *Examiner* on 22 March 1812 Leigh Hunt reminded his
readers of the truth behind this ludicrous sycophancy.

> What person, unacquainted with the true state of the case
> would imagine in reading these astounding eulogies, that this
> "Glory of the People", was the subject of millions of shrugs and
> reproaches! ... that this "Conqueror of Hearts" was the dis-
> appointer of hopes! – that this "Exciter of desire" (bravo!
> Messieurs of the *Post*) – this "*Adonis* in loveliness", was a cor-
> pulent man of fifty!

For good measure, Leigh Hunt added that the Regent was, in truth,
"a violator of his word, a libertine over head and ears in debt and
disgrace, a despiser of domestic ties, the companion of gamblers and
demireps, a man who has just closed half a century without one single
claim on the gratitude of his country, or the respect of posterity". The
Hunts were prosecuted for a seditious libel, though they saw more
signs of guilt in Ellenborough's behaviour.

> He knew that we were acquainted with his visits to Carlton
> house and Brighton (sympathies not eminently decent in a
> judge) and with the good things which he had obtained for his
> kinsmen; and we could not help preferring our feelings at the
> moment to those which induced him to keep his eyes fixed on
> his papers.[46]

As the Hunts went to gaol for two years, Tom Moore imagined the
Prince drinking Ellenborough's health among his cronies.

> A compliment too to his Lordship the Judge
> For his speech to the Jury – and zounds! who would grudge
> Turtle soup, though it came to five guineas a bowl
> To reward such a loyal and complaisant soul?
> We were all in high gig – Roman Punch and Tokay
> Travelled round, till our heads travell'd just the same way,
> And we cared not for Juries or Libels – no – damme! nor
> Ev'n for the threats of last Sunday's *Examiner*![47]

Such was the reputation of Ellenborough among the Radicals, a
creature of the ministry and tool of the sinecurists and placemen.

However undeserved it may have been, Cochrane felt every reason for looking on him as a natural enemy.

In such prosecutions, and indeed in the prosecutions of authors and publishers too, the crown had the right to demand a special jury. This was anathema to Cochrane and the Radicals as being the very antithesis of democratic justice. The panel from which the jury was chosen consisted of forty-eight city merchants selected by the Sheriff of London. The lists were revised in 1817 but, until 1816, the same men were trying case after case. Two hundred and seventy-four of them tried a hundred cases that year. Forty of them were summoned twenty times during the year, and fifty of them more than ten times. Whether, as Cochrane contended, the juries were packed by the authorities and the chosen members inevitably biased against the accused is a matter of speculation. At the very least, they were carefully selected.

Cochrane was defended by Serjeant William Best, who consulted with lawyers for the other defendants and agreed on a joint defence rather than separate trials. In retrospect, this was much to Cochrane's disadvantage. Though he would never admit so publicly, he must now have realised that Cochrane-Johnstone was one of the prime movers of the fraud, as indeed appeared by his uncle's later action. It was suggested subsequently that Cochrane, to some extent, sacrificed his own interest in the hope of shielding his uncle, a suggestion which he never refuted. However, the joint defence was a bad strategy.

The day before the trial began, Cochrane also noticed a mistake in the brief. One of his three servants, Mary Turpin, was credited with saying that Berenger's uniform at the time of the visit had been red whereas what she had actually said was that it was green, as appeared in her affidavit.

The trial opened in King's Bench, at Westminster, on 8 June 1814. King's Bench was nothing like the gladiatorial arena of the stereotyped criminal court and, indeed, it had much more the air of a court of appeal. The mediaeval hall with its high windows and carved figures in their niches was crowded with lawyers in wigs and gowns rather than by eager members of the public. Ellenborough sat at one end, his bench no more than a high desk, at which he perched like a clerk in a counting house. Below and in front of him, the wigged clerks with quills and parchments clustered at their table, a tall case of law reports to one side of them. On either side of the well of the court rose high boxes, one for the jurors and one for the witness giving evidence. Beyond that, several semi-circular rows of seats accommodated the watching counsel, some having a part to play in the case and the rest learning by example. A barrister who examined a witness or addressed the jurors did so from the well of the court, judge, witness, jurors, and watching counsel rising high above him on every side. Behind Ellenborough, a tapestry of the lion and the unicorn blazoned the royal coat of arms the width of the courtroom wall, with velvet hangings on either side. To that extent, the sense of theatricality was not entirely absent.

The other oddity of King's Bench trials was that the defendants were not necessarily required to be present. In this case, Cochrane chose not to appear. If convicted, he would be called upon to appear for judgement in a day or two. That was time enough to stand before his accusers. In this practice the English law appeared lax and easy-going, bloody and vindictive though it might be in other respects. Cochrane-Johnstone had already considered the possibility that a man might be convicted but whether or not he could be found for judgement was a quite different matter.

At 9 a.m., Gurney rose and opened the case for the prosecution. It was soon apparent that the accusations against Cochrane rested on three points. He had benefited financially from the rises in the value of Omnium. He had admitted giving Berenger a partial change of clothing but, according to the prosecution, he had lied over the colour of the uniform in order to suggest that he had no reason to suspect Berenger of anything unusual. Bank notes, or their proceeds, which had originally been in his possession were found on Berenger, and were presumably part of the sum paid to him by the chief conspirators for acting his part in the fraud. It hardly seemed that any of these bases of accusation would stand close examination. Cochrane had only benefited from the rise in Omnium by his standing instruction to sell on a 1 per cent rise and if a conspirator he had signally failed to exploit the fraud. As for the colour of Berenger's uniform, he was supported by his servants and, later, by other men who were not personally known to him. Apart from anything else, Berenger had travelled across London in a hackney coach with the blinds drawn. He had ample time to change and, though he might have started the journey in red, he could well have been wearing green by the time that he reached Cochrane's lodgings. As to the notes found in Berenger's possession, John Bilson of the Bank of England, and other bank witnesses, gave evidence that they must have passed through other hands, those of Butt and Cochrane-Johnstone, before reaching Berenger. Indeed, they had begun in Cochrane's hands as notes of

large denomination and had ended as one-pound notes with Berenger.
Serjeant Best, for Cochrane, had no trouble in disposing of this part
of the prosecution.[48]

> Gentlemen, I am sure, therefore, that if I have made myself
> understood upon this part of the case I have completely released
> Lord Cochrane from the effect of this evidence, for though the
> two large notes were once in his hands, those notes were never
> in the hands of De Berenger. The notes found on him were the
> small notes given in exchange for them at the Bank and these
> were given to Mr Butt, and not Lord Cochrane.[49]

The prosecution case was reduced to the fact that Cochrane was a
relative of Cochrane-Johnstone, that he had borrowed money from
Butt, that he had gained from the sale of Omnium, and that he had
lied over the colour of Berenger's uniform. In order to convict him in
respect of this last point, Gurney produced as a witness William
Crane, the driver of the hackney coach which had brought Berenger
to Cochrane's house. He swore that Berenger had worn the red uniform of a staff officer and had still been wearing it when he entered
the house. If this were true, Cochrane must have seen it as an impos-
ture at once and would certainly have been guilty of aiding a deception if he helped Berenger to carry it through by providing a change
of clothes.

Crane's evidence was of such importance that Cochrane and his
lawyers were remiss in not finding out a little more about him. As
lately as 25 May, The Times reported him as having been banned from
driving a hackney coach for three months because of his ill-treatment
of the horses and his abusiveness towards a man who reproved him
for it. He was twenty years old at the time of Cochrane's trial and was
already a figure of some notoriety. When the evidence he gave was
published, seven independent witnesses came forward, dismayed at
what they read, and swore affidavits before the Lord Mayor. They
were too late to give evidence at the trial and, in any case, the judi-
ciary and the House of Commons ignored them. Two of them, a
butcher and a fishmonger, saw Berenger enter Crane's coach. His
greatcoat was open and, even at this point, they saw clearly that he
was wearing the green sharpshooter's uniform. It had been argued
that, since there was some red on the collar of it, a sharpshooter's
uniform might be mistaken for a red one if the greatcoat was but-
toned and only the jacket collar appeared. But this hardly excused
Crane if the coat was open.

In any case, the five other affidavits were even more instructive. Charles King, a stable-keeper in Westminster Bridge Road, was told by Crane's father that his son was "going after the money" offered as a reward by the Stock Exchange. Two more witnesses swore that Crane told them he was going to take his oath that it was Cochrane whom he had driven as "Du Bourg". He would say that he knew Cochrane from having driven him a score of times to the Opera and other amusements. But Cochrane had only been to the Opera once in his life, as Crane was warned, and the story was abandoned. But Crane was not so easily to be defeated and had determined on whatever story would pay him best. This proved to be that Berenger, in a red uniform, was the man he had taken to Cochrane's house. As Crane remarked bluntly to separate witnesses, who swore the truth of it before the Lord Mayor, "I will swear black is white, or anything else, if I am well paid for it." Someone had evidently paid him well and, whatever the reason, official favours continued. In 1826, he was sentenced to seven years transportation for robbery, but after three years he was mysteriously pardoned and set free.[50]

The prosecution case was long and involved, lasting from 9 a.m. until 10 p.m. Serjeant Best, Cochrane's counsel, had now been in court for thirteen or fourteen hours that day and, like his colleagues, he was more than ready for an adjournment. To his dismay, he was told by Ellenborough to proceed at once with his defence. When there were protests at the unfairness of this to Cochrane and the other defendants, Ellenborough merely said, "There are several gentlemen attending as witnesses who, I find, cannot without the greatest public inconvenience, attend tomorrow." As a matter of record, it was the convenience of Lord Melville and Lord Yarmouth which took precedence over the presentation of the defence.[51]

Best rose and addressed the jury on behalf of Cochrane, Cochrane-Johnstone, and Butt, repeatedly demonstrating the feebleness of the case against Cochrane himself. He was still speaking after midnight. It was shortly before 1 a.m. when Ellenborough called on James Alan Park to address the court on behalf of Berenger, and to bring forward an alibi according to which the defendant was supposed to have spent the night of 20–21 February in bed in the King's Bench prison. An hour later, Serjeant Pell rose to speak on behalf of the three lesser defendants, concluding his address at 3 a.m. Only then did Ellenborough adjourn, announcing to the weary occupants of the smoky, candle-lit courtroom that he would sit again at 10 a.m.

By the next morning, the defence was in something of a dilemma.

If no defence witnesses were called, then it was defence counsel who had the last word to the jury. But if defence evidence was produced, it was the prosecutor who had the final right of reply. Best had decided that evidence must be called, but having made his choice it was arguable that he exploited it badly. Lord Melville and others were called to prove that it was Cochrane's uncle Alexander who was Berenger's patron and that Cochrane's only connection was in offering to ferry Berenger across the Atlantic from Portsmouth in the *Tonnant*. But the main point at issue was still whether Berenger had arrived at Cochrane's house in the red uniform of a staff officer or in his own green uniform of the sharpshooters.

Of those who could support Cochrane's claim, Isaac Davis had been despatched to Gibraltar on H.M.S. *Eurotas*, though Cochrane had informed the Admiralty three months before that he was a witness in the matter. The defence lawyers had wrongly copied Mary Turpin's evidence and presumably expected that, if called, she would swear the uniform was red. Thomas Dewman, the only servant called, was not even asked about the colour of Berenger's uniform. Worse still, Serjeant Best suggested to the jury that Cochrane had perhaps made a mistake over the matter of the uniform and, being accustomed to see Berenger in green, had thought the uniform was green when he came to make his affidavit, whereas it might have been red.[52]

Whether it was exhaustion or confusion occasioned by the protracted sitting, or merely an error of judgement, Best and his colleagues had given away a vital part of Cochrane's case. For Cochrane-Johnstone and Butt there could be little defence.

As the second and last day of the trial dragged on, Henry Colthurst, clerk to Cochrane's solicitors, hurried from the court to Green Street, where Cochrane was waiting. He delivered a message from Henry Brougham, who was in court, warning him urgently to expect the worst. Cochrane was dismayed, and asked whether Mary Turpin and others had not been called on the matter of the green uniform in order to vindicate him. He was told that his suggestion "was submitted to Counsel and not approved of by them". Referring to his solicitor, Cochrane said, "Mr Parkinson has put his foot in his case . . . he has botched his case . . . it is cruel in him."

But there was nothing to be done, the case for the defence was closed and Ellenborough was summing up.

"Mr P. should have done as I instructed him," said Cochrane helplessly. "I am to be the only sufferer, if convicted."[53]

Not only was Ellenborough summing up for a conviction of the defendants, Cochrane included, but he was doing it with relish. Referring to Berenger's visit to Cochrane and the subsequent discovery of the uniform in the Thames, Ellenborough announced, "You have before had the animal hunted home, and now you have his skin." The *State Trials* account calls Ellenborough's style, on this occasion, "a lofty tone of scorn and irony, and contempt, never suggesting a doubt".[54]

On the subject of Cochrane's truthfulness, Ellenborough accepted the evidence of William Crane. For a hundred years afterwards, there were those who complained that the Lord Chief Justice was a scrupulous judge, much maligned, who had given the defendants every benefit of the doubt. In the report of the trial, published some while after the case, Ellenborough is made to say that *if* Berenger arrived in his red aide-de-camp's uniform with decorations, and *if* Cochrane saw it and did nothing, he would be party to the deception. But, according to *The Times* report of 10 July 1814, taken in the courtroom, Ellenborough's language was far more direct. Berenger had worn the red uniform, Cochrane had lied on oath, and was almost inevitably one of the conspirators.[55]

De Berenger stripped himself at Lord Cochrane's. He pulled off his scarlet uniform there, and if the circumstance of its not being green did not excite Lord Cochrane's suspicion, what did he think of the star and medal? It became him, on discovering these, as an officer and a gentleman, to communicate his suspicions of these circumstances. Did he not ask De Berenger where he had been in this masquerade dress? It was for the jury to say whether Lord Cochrane did not know where he had been. This was not the dress of a sharpshooter, but of a mountebank. He came before Lord Cochrane fully blazoned in the costume of his crime.

Those who read the press reports were in many cases uneasy over Ellenborough's summing-up. Then, a month later, appeared the report of the trial, in which he spoke in far more reasonable and judicious terms. It was this report which was unhesitatingly accepted by the Admiralty and the ministry, the Attorney-General praising it in the Commons as an account which would "do away the effect of those imperfect statements which misled the public mind".[56]

So far as the special jurors were concerned, the effect of Ellenborough's summing-up was never in doubt. It was just after 8.30 p.m. when they brought in a verdict of guilty on Cochrane and all other defendants. In the case of lower criminal courts sentence would have been pronounced at once, but in King's Bench a separate sitting was required for that. In the days before this happened, Cochrane-Johnstone absconded from justice, Butt set to work on some spirited libels on Ellenborough, and Cochrane now began to repair some of the damage resulting from his own casualness. On 5 July, he faced the motion for his expulsion from the House of Commons. He attacked Ellenborough in language so bitter that Hansard's printers filled the report with asterisks, fearing prosecution for libel. Denouncing the Lord Chief Justice, however, Cochrane swore, "I solemnly assure this House, my constituents, and my country, that I would rather stand in my own name in the pillory every day of my life, under such a sentence, than I would sit upon the bench in his name, and with his real character for one single hour." The speech was much criticised for such improprieties, but the historian Sir Archibald Alison, having heard Cochrane on this occasion, "never entertained a doubt of his innocence".[57]

One of the minor conspirators, M'Rae, informed the Commons that Cochrane had no part whatever in the fraud. M'Rae had told the Stock Exchange investigators this before the trial. Their answer was to indict him as well. Since defendants could not give evidence in a trial, they thereby silenced him in the matter. The Commons chose to ignore this, as they ignored the post-trial affidavits in proof of Cochrane's innocence and the truth about such prosecution witnesses as William Crane. The ministry won the expulsion vote by 140 votes to 44, a result which was surprising only in the size of the minority. Here, as elsewhere, was the evidence that many contemporaries felt strongly that justice had not been done.

The Admiralty lost no time in dismissing Cochrane from the Royal Navy. Most important of all, however, had been his motion in King's Bench, on 14 June before Lord Ellenborough, for a new trial. He publicly admitted his mistake in agreeing to a joint defence with Cochrane-Johnstone and Butt. "Well had it been for me if I had made this distinction sooner." Since the evidence of witnesses not brought forward at the trial might now establish his innocence beyond question, Cochrane applied for a new trial. To his dismay Ellenborough refused this, on the grounds that all defendants must be present before he considered granting a new trial. Since M'Rae and Cochrane-Johnstone had fled abroad, the condition was impossible to fulfil, as

Ellenborough could see. On 20 June, Cochrane and the other defendants who had not absconded appeared for sentence. In his own defence, Cochrane offered the first affidavits sworn after the trial. Ellenborough refused them, saying that such evidence was only admissible at trial. By Ellenborough's own rule, however, a new trial was the very thing which Cochrane was denied, through no fault of his own. The snare of the law now held him fast.[58]

The court then proceeded to deal with the defendants who had appeared for sentence. All of them, including Cochrane, were sentenced to imprisonment for twelve months. Cochrane and Butt were also fined £1000 and the others £500. Cochrane, Butt, and Berenger were to be put in the pillory opposite the Royal Exchange for an hour. The indignity of the pillory, the culprit with his head and hands through its holes, helpless before the derision and missiles of the mob, might seem something of an anachronism in the early nineteenth century, but it had survived none the less.

Ellenborough felt that the pillory could well be the means of reducing the reputation of the hero of the Basque Roads, the *Gamo*, and Fort Trinidad to more agreeable proportions. Napoleon in exile on Elba thought otherwise: "Such a man should not be made to suffer so degrading a punishment." The government too had its doubts. Without wishing to save Cochrane humiliation, they knew that public feeling over the trial was increasingly sympathetic to him. There might well be a riot outside the Royal Exchange, a possibility made more likely by Burdett's announcement that if Cochrane were put in the pillory he, and no doubt others, would stand beside him. It was announced that the sentence of the pillory on the three offenders was to be remitted.[59]

What remained by way of disgrace was quite sufficient. Sir Thomas Byam Martin and other senior officers dined with the Prince Regent at the old Government House on the Parade at Portsmouth soon after the trial. When the meal was over and the officers were still seated around him, the Prince began to express "his indignation at the conduct of Lord Cochrane, and went on to state in strong and impressive terms, his determination to order his degradation". The Prince promised to give his personal command for Cochrane's name to be struck out of the list of the navy.

"I will never permit a service, hitherto of unblemished honour, to be disgraced by the continuance of Lord Cochrane as a member of it," said the Regent hotly. "I shall also strip him of the Order of the Bath."[60]

This had been anticipated by Cochrane's friends, including Mary Russell Mitford and her father. Miss Mitford's correspondence on the topic also revealed the extent of Cochrane's private grief in the days following the trial.

> Did papa tell you that he had seen poor, poor Lord Cochrane, that victim to his uncle's villainy, almost every day? He wept like a child to papa. And they say that the last dreadful degradation, the hacking off the spurs of knighthood, is actually meant to be put in force upon him.[61]

From the King's Bench prison, where he was now confined, Cochrane learnt that the Prince's instructions had been carried out, and that his honours had been stripped from him. He was not present to witness the bizarre midnight ritual of his own dishonouring. His banner, as Knight Commander of the Bath, was taken down from its place in King Henry VII's Chapel at Westminster. Banner and insignia were ceremonially kicked out of the chapel and down the steps. A nameless man stood proxy for him while the spurs of knighthood were hacked from the boot-heels with a butcher's cleaver. For years he had challenged, insulted, and attempted to undermine the established order. Now that order would break him.[62]

Two sources of strength remained to him. Kitty, at eighteen years old, was already prepared to fight his battles to the end. Secondly, there were his constituents. After his Commons expulsion, a writ was moved for a by-election at Westminster. On 11 July 1814, a mass meeting of 5000 constituents resolved unanimously that Cochrane was innocent of fraud and was a fit and proper person to represent them. Indeed, the support for him was evident beyond the Radicals themselves. When Sheridan was urged to grasp the opportunity of election, his reply was uncompromising. He would fight any other opponent but, "I absolutely decline to put in Nomination in opposition to Lord Cochrane." At the hustings, on 16 July 1814, Cochrane was proposed and elected by a roar of acclamation.[63]

Even those who were not necessarily convinced of his innocence began to have doubts as to the wisdom of a government treating Cochrane with quite such vindictive relish. Lord Ebrington was one of those who deplored the proposal to put him in the pillory. "If I am guilty," Cochrane replied, "I richly merit the whole of the sentence which has been passed upon me. If innocent, one penalty cannot be inflicted with more justice than another."[64]

Cochrane was accommodated in two rooms of the King's Bench State House, as that part of the prison was known. If this sounds like a generous allowance, it has to be remembered that he was obliged to pay for his board and lodging in gaol. Wardens of such prisons had customarily bought their jobs as an investment, recouping the outlay with interest by charging the prisoners for rooms, food, and in some cases water. In 1729 the Warden of the Fleet and the Keeper of the Marshalsea were tried for murdering their prisoners when the inmates could not afford to pay their demands.[65]

The King's Bench had improved since then but a man was still expected to pay his way. It was intimated to Cochrane that if he would put up the money, and petition humbly, he might even be allowed to walk for half a mile round the buildings. He refused to ask for anything. Instead, he spent his time perfecting his new oil-lamp, which soon began to replace the cruder type used for lighting the Westminster streets, but was replaced itself by gas before it could make him much money. He began a pamphlet war against Ellenborough and those who had convicted him, while outside the prison his supporters continued to show their feelings for him. Addresses of sympathy and belief in his innocence reached him from Westminster, Culross and Paisley.

No less remarkable was the reaction of the Princess Charlotte, daughter of the Prince Regent and his estranged wife, the Princess Caroline. The day before Cochrane's re-election for Westminster, the young Princess escaped from her father's custody and sought refuge in her mother's house in Connaught Place. The Regent's brothers and the law officers of the crown followed her and tried to persuade her to return. Before long, there were two mobs in the street outside, one shouting support for Charlotte and the other for Cochrane in the Westminster election. It was the Duke of Sussex who showed the young Princess the scene and warned her of the public unrest which threatened. There would be "a popular outbreak, which it was to be feared would end in bloodshed, and perhaps in the destruction of Carlton House itself". The Princess relented tearfully, observing of Cochrane and the ministers, "Poor Lord Cochrane! I heard that he had been very ill used by them. Should it ever be in my power, I will undo the wrong." Had the Princess lived, it would certainly have been in her power, since she would have succeeded her father and become Queen in her own right in 1830.[66]

For Cochrane himself, there appeared no course but to endure imprisonment. Yet as time went by, he became convinced that his detention in the King's Bench was not only unjust, it was illegal. He was a Member of Parliament and, as such, not amenable to imprisonment for the offence of which he had been convicted. Technically he was wrong. He had been expelled from parliament after his conviction. The fact that he had been re-elected subsequently did not invalidate the sentence on him. As the months of captivity passed, however, he planned his escape from prison and by 6 March 1815 he had made everything ready for it.

Because the rooms in which he was confined were so high, there were no bars at the windows. There hardly seemed any necessity, since even if a man could negotiate the sheer drop, he would still be within the prison walls. Indeed, the high outer wall, topped with spikes, rose up opposite the windows of the rooms. It stood higher than the windows but not more than a dozen feet away. Cochrane's servant had managed to smuggle him in some small lengths of rope, hardly thicker than stout cord, and with this he proposed to make his escape.

He waited until after midnight and until he judged that the watchman would be on his rounds in one of the most distant parts of the prison. Then he coiled the rope and climbed out of the window, scaling upward to the roof of the State House building. From there he could look down on to the top of the outer wall in the darkness. To one who was so accustomed to ropes and climbing, it was not too difficult, even by night, to throw a running noose over the spikes which topped the outer wall. Far more dangerous was the journey, hand over hand, hanging from the thin rope between the State House roof and the wall, with the dark and lethal drop below him. But the rope held, Cochrane reached the outer wall and spent an uncomfortable moment or two perched on the iron spikes while he paid out another length of rope down the outside of the wall and made it fast at the top. He began his descent, but he was still 20 feet above the ground when the thin rope snapped in his hands and he fell heavily on his back, knocking himself unconscious. He lay there, first unconscious and then stunned, for a considerable time. Though there were no bones broken, he was badly bruised and sprained, managing only to crawl to the house of a former servant of the family before daybreak.[67]

From London, he made his way to Holly Hill, a house he had taken in Hampshire, and wrote to the Speaker of the Commons that he proposed shortly to exercise his right as a member to assume his place on the opposition benches. Meanwhile a rash of official posters began to appear all over Westminster.

Escaped from the King's Bench Prison, on Monday the 6th day of March, instant, Lord Cochrane. He is about five feet eleven inches in height, thin and narrow chested, with sandy hair and full eyes, red whiskers and eyebrows. Whoever will apprehend and secure Lord Cochrane in any of His Majesty's gaols in the kingdom shall have a reward of three hundred guineas from William Jones, Marshal of the King's Bench.[68]

Like most literary productions of its kind, the "wanted" notice was curiously inaccurate. Cochrane was six feet two inches tall and impressively broad. He was reported to have been sighted in London, Hastings, Jersey, and France. He was also said to have gone mad and hidden himself somewhere in the prison. In fact, he appeared in the House of Commons on 21 March, dressed in his usual grey pantaloons and frogged greatcoat, and duly took his place on the benches.

He demanded the right to speak, but was told that he could not do so until he had taken the oath as a new member, and that he could not take the oath until the writ for the election had been fetched from the Crown Office in Chancery Lane.

Shortly before four o'clock in the afternoon, it was not the writ but a Bow Street runner and tipstaves who entered the House. The runner tapped Cochrane on the shoulder and invited him to return to the King's Bench prison. Cochrane turned on him angrily, demanding by what right he presumed to arrest a member of the Commons in the palace of Westminster itself.

"My Lord," said the runner, "my authority is the public proclamation of the Marshal of the King's Bench Prison, offering a reward for your apprehension."

"I neither acknowledge, nor will yield to, any such authority," Cochrane announced grandly. "I am here to resume my seat as one of the representatives of the City of Westminster, and any who dares to touch me will do so at their peril."

Two of the tipstaves seized his arm but, evidently using his height and strength, Cochrane shook them off and repeated his warning. When the runner reiterated that he had "better go quietly", Cochrane assured him he had no intention of going at all. The other members of the House were then treated to the unusual sight of a spirited brawl as tipstaves and constables fell upon Cochrane and at length hoisted him, struggling, on to their shoulders to carry him horizontally from the House as though they had been pall-bearers. The Bow Street runner was convinced that Cochrane might have a gun hidden in his clothing, so he was first taken to a committee room and searched. He had no gun, but there was another "weapon" in his pocket in the form of a box of snuff. When asked why he carried it, Cochrane said sourly, "If I had thought of that before, you should have had it in your eyes!"

Accordingly he was credited by the ministry with carrying substances to blind and disfigure those who crossed his path, the snuff soon being reported as a bottle of vitriol.[69]

For the next three weeks, Cochrane was confined in the so-called Strong Room of the King's Bench, a windowless and unfurnished cell of the sort which had been the death of one of the victims of the 1729 murder trials. It was subterranean and the dampness of its bare walls was in no way palliated by either heating or ventilation. After twenty-six days of confinement he was examined by a doctor who reported that Cochrane was experiencing severe chest pains. "His pulse is low, his hands cold, and he has many symptoms of a person about to have typhus or putrid fever. These symptoms are, in my opinion, produced by the stagnant air of the Strong Room."[70]

Cochrane was removed from the Strong Room, though still closely guarded. Apart from other considerations, he was hardly in any condition to attempt another escape so that the practical advantage of keeping him in the windowless cell was minimal. On 20 June 1815, as the first news of Waterloo and of England's final deliverance from Napoleon spread through London, the term of imprisonment expired. Cochrane would be freed on payment of his fine of £1000. As a token of his innocence he at first refused to pay. But after a fortnight's defiance, the advice of his friends prevailed and he handed his note for the amount to the Marshal of the King's Bench. The note, which still remains in the possession of the Bank of England, bore a remarkable endorsement.

> My health having suffered by long and close confinement, and my oppressors being resolved to deprive me of property or life, I submit to robbery to protect myself from murder, in the hope that I shall live to bring the delinquents to justice.[71]

As a matter of fact, the authorities had not finished with him. He was in due course tried at Surrey Assizes, at Guildford, for escaping from prison in March 1815. The trial was considerably delayed and took place on 17 August 1816. Accompanied by Burdett and other Westminster Radicals, Cochrane drove into Guildford in a post-chaise at

8 a.m. He found the court crowded with spectators of every class. So far as the law was concerned, the defence, which he presented himself, was no defence. He used the occasion to denounce the "crimes" of the Marshal of the King's Bench and accused him of doing nothing whatever to earn the £3590 a year which the state paid him. In his address to the jury, Cochrane swore, "The Marshal himself has repeatedly been accessory to more glaring violations of the sentence of the Court than that for which he now prosecutes me." The Marshal had taken bribes from prisoners for allowing them out of the gaol, while ill-treating those who would not acquiesce. But such a man, "instead of being punished for his violence and brutality, imprudently calls upon a Jury of his country to heap fresh oppressions on the head of his persecuted victim". It was spirited stuff, though hardly relevant to the charge. The jury returned the inevitable verdict, though with a qualification. "We take the liberty of saying, the punishment he has already received is quite adequate to the offence of which he was guilty." There was applause in the court at this but the jurors received no thanks from Cochrane. He rose angrily in his place and reiterated his now familiar words: "I want justice, not mercy!"

As it happened, the jury's recommendation was ignored and a fine of £100 was imposed. Cochrane flatly refused to pay it and was taken into custody. Almost at once, the electors of Westminster held a meeting and organised a subscription to raise the money. This was quickly accomplished and, despite himself, Cochrane was free once more.[72]

His popularity among his constituents and his Scottish friends, who had long maintained his innocence, was never greater. While he fought his own battle, Cochrane remembered his obligations to them as well, though the two interests often coincided. On the very evening of his release from the King's Bench, 3 July 1815, Cochrane took his seat in the House of Commons, which was debating an additional pension of £6000 a year to be given to the Prince Regent's brother, the Duke of Cumberland, on his marriage to Princess Frederica, daughter of the Duke of Mecklenburg-Strelitz. Of all the Regent's brothers, Cumberland was regarded as the most loathsome. According to Creevey, he had fathered a child, "Captain Garth", on his own sister, the Princess Sophia. He was also rumoured to have murdered his valet, and said to have indecently assaulted the wife of the Lord Chancellor. However unjust such accusations may have been, they reflect the estimate of many of his contemporaries. It was the birth of the Princess Victoria which was to save England from having Cumberland as King in 1837.

Lord Castlereagh had urged the Commons that the extra £6000 was a well-merited addition to the £20,000 income which the Duke already enjoyed. The bill had passed its first reading by a majority of seventeen, and its second reading by twelve votes. At the third and final reading, the thought of voting the extra money to Cumberland was too much for several of the ministry's supporters to stomach. There was to be a tied vote, but still the Speaker's casting vote would have to go in favour of the bill and that would see it through. It was at this point that Cochrane, in the familiar grey pantaloons and frogged greatcoat, appeared and demanded to be sworn in as member for Westminster. To the dismay of Castlereagh, it was now in Cochrane's power to decide the outcome, which he proceeded to do, voting with the Radicals and Whigs to deny Cumberland his marriage allowance.[73]

This spirited return to politics was greeted with anger by the ministry and delight by the opposition. But Cochrane had a more elaborate plan in mind, which he worked out during the parliamentary recess with the aid of Cobbett. His chance came on 5 March 1816 when he moved in the Commons the impeachment of Lord Chief Justice Ellenborough on charges of "partiality, misrepresentation, injustice, and oppression". He had already published an open *Letter to Lord Ellenborough*, condemning his conduct of the Stock Exchange trial. Now the protests took the form of a parliamentary accusation.

Cochrane, seconded by Burdett, had not the smallest hope of bringing the impeachment about. For all that, the defence of Ellenborough by the Solicitor-General and his colleagues was of the feeblest. They spoke of the necessity of maintaining "public confidence in the purity of the administration of justice", and the desirability that "the course of that administration may continue the admiration of the world". The alternative, as the Solicitor-General explained, was unthinkable. "The public opinion of the excellence of our laws will be inevitably weakened – and to weaken public opinion is to weaken justice herself."

Burdett, rising in Cochrane's defence, remarked that, "Such language would operate against the investigation of any charges whatever against any judge." But when the vote was taken, eighty-nine members of the House voted against the investigation and impeachment. Only Cochrane and Burdett were in favour. Cochrane himself was undismayed, and indeed hardly surprised, but he had won an important point.

> It gives me great satisfaction to think that the vote which has been come to has been come to without any of my charges being disproved. Whatever may be done with them now, they will find their way to posterity, and posterity will form a different judgment concerning them than that which has been adopted by this House.[74]

He was to be vindicated, at least insofar as Victorian jurists, including Lord Campbell in his *Lives of the Chief Justices*, deplored Ellenborough's conduct.

> The trial coming on before Lord Ellenborough, the noble and learned Judge, being himself persuaded of the guilt of all the defendants, used his best endeavours that they should all be convicted. . . . The following day, in summing up, prompted no doubt by the conclusion of his own mind, he laid special emphasis on every circumstance which might raise a suspicion against Lord Cochrane, and elaborately explained away whatever at first sight appeared favourable to the gallant officer. In consequence the Jury found a verdict of GUILTY against all the defendants.[75]

Nor was this the opinion of a dangerous Radical. Campbell had been first Attorney-General in the Tory cabinet and then Lord Chief Justice in his turn. As for Ellenborough's refusal to grant a new trial on the grounds of the affidavits sworn by new witnesses after the first verdict, Campbell thought it "palpably contrary to the first principles of justice".[76]

Leaving to posterity the ultimate judgement in his case, Cochrane involved himself in the Radical campaigns of 1816–1818. By the summer of 1816, the royal family and the supporters of the ministry were giving their support to movements which might stem the tide of revolution or reform by acts of philanthropy. The economic recession which had followed the peace of 1815 offered ample scope for such work. An Association for the Relief of the Manufacturing and Labouring Poor was set up with the Duke of York and the Duke of Kent among its leaders, one of its active members being William Wilberforce.

To some of the Radicals such organisations as this were merely attempts to buy off the reformers. To others, including Cochrane, they seemed even more despicable, since the money to do the buying had been filched from the pockets of the people in the first place. When the Association for the Relief of the Manufacturing and Labouring Poor held its major meeting of 1816, at the City of London Tavern on 29 July, Cochrane was present.

By any standard, it was a distinguished assembly. The Duke of York took the chair, flanked by his brothers, the Duke of Kent and the Duke of Cambridge. The three royal patrons were supported by the Archbishop of Canterbury, the Bishop of London, the Chancellor of the Exchequer and a host of public figures. After some carefully turned sentiments on the need to show liberality to the starving, the Duke of Kent moved the motion:

> That the transition from a state of extensive warfare to a system of peace has occasioned a stagnation of employment and a revulsion of trade, deeply affecting the situation of many parts of the community, and producing many instances of great local distress.

The motion was seconded, and then Cochrane rose at once to speak, among what the reports of the meeting described as equal factions of cheers and hisses. He denounced the way in which the coming of peace was cited as an excuse for the plight of the poor. Two-thirds of the money raised by the government was taken up by interest on the national debt, and too much of the rest of it went into the pockets of placemen. Cochrane turned to the Duke of Rutland, who was one of the organisers of the meeting.

> I came here with the expectation of seeing the Duke of Rutland in the chair; and with some hopes as he takes the lead on this occasion, that it is his intention to surrender that sinecure of £9000 a year which he is now in the habit of putting in his pocket. I still trust that all who are present and are also holders of sinecures have it in their intention to sacrifice them to their liberality and their justice; and that they do not come here to aid the distresses of their country by paying half-a-crown per cent. out of the hundreds which they take from it. If they do not, all I can say is, that to me their pretended charity is little better than a fraud.

There was uproar during much of his speech, but Cochrane moved an amendment to the motion, proclaiming the national debt and vast government expenditure as the real causes of distress. The Duke of Kent hastily removed all reference to the war from his original motion, and Cochrane withdrew the amendment. What remained was a rather fatuous declaration that the country was in a bad way.

It was the Duke of Cambridge who followed his brother with a motion calling upon the "generosity" of those who had money and urging them as individuals "to afford the means of relief to their fellow-subjects". The Duke of Rutland proposed that the Association should start collecting money, and the Earl of Manvers promised that anyone who gave one hundred pounds or more would be elected to the committee. The Bishop of London moved a vote of thanks to the Duke of York, but before it could be passed Cochrane stepped forward again. He denounced the proposed subscription as an inadequate measure, laudable though the intention behind it might be. The true source of aid was in the hands of "the placemen, the sinecurists, and the fundholders, who must give up at least half of their ill-gotten gains". He demanded that another motion be put, placing the primary responsibility in the matter upon "the Chancellor of the Exchequer and his majesty's ministers".

There followed "violent uproar and confusion", the Bishop trying to move the vote of thanks against shouts of "Put Lord Cochrane's motion first!" and "Chair! Chair!" The Archbishop appealed to the meeting to let the vote of thanks be passed. When someone objected that if it were passed, the Duke of York would leave and the meeting would close without discussing Cochrane's motion, the Duke of Kent announced that there was "no intention to get rid of the noble lord's motion by any side wind". The vote of thanks was passed.

The Duke of York immediately rose, bowed to the meeting, and withdrew, leaving his brother to face the commotion and the cries of "Shame! Shame! A trick! A trick!" The Duke of Kent appeared genuinely bewildered.

"I hope that, as liberal Englishmen, you will consider my situation and who I am," he called out, "and that after my illustrious relatives have retired from the meeting you will not insist upon my taking the chair."

He hurried away after the Duke of York and the meeting broke up.[77]

Cochrane had at least unmasked the fraud practised by some of the advocates of philanthropy. It was not in acts of private charity but by a new policy in public finance that some of the country's ills might be cured. The sight of a man who received thousands of pounds in sinecure payments buying his way on to the committee of a charity by returning one hundred pounds of it was, at the best, ludicrous.

As a reformer, it was Cochrane who had become the principal parliamentary spokesman for those who demanded universal suffrage and annual parliaments as the surest guarantee of democracy. Samuel Bamford was one of the reformers who brought their petition to him in 1817. The political crisis had deepened during the previous year and on the morning of Bamford's arrival, the Prince Regent had been jeered and hissed on his way to open parliament, a stone or possibly a bullet shattering the window of the royal carriage.

At Cochrane's lodgings in Palace Yard, Bamford and his companions were served with wine by Kitty, "a slight and elegant young lady, dressed in white and very interesting". Bamford was impressed by the homeliness and the hospitality of their reception, compared with the more formal and less generous treatment offered by Burdett. Cochrane was carried shoulder-high, in an armchair, through the gathering columns of Radical supporters, to the door of Westminster Hall. The great scroll of the petition went with him. At forty-two years old, the impression which he then conveyed to Bamford was still predominantly that of a youthful man.

> He was a tall young man; cordial and unaffected in his manner. He stooped a little, and had somewhat of a sailor's gait in walking; his face was rather oval; fair naturally, but now tanned and sun-freckled. His hair was sandy, his whiskers rather small and of a deeper colour; and the expression of his countenance was calm and self-possessed.[78]

While Cochrane tried to present the petitions of the reformers to the House, the crowd outside was addressed by Henry Hunt. In the Commons, Cochrane brought forward two petitions, one from 20,000 citizens of Bristol and its neighbourhood, the other from Yorkshire. The petitioners complained of national poverty and unemployment, protesting that it was futile to attempt relief by giving soup to the starving while so much of the nation's wealth was eaten up by sinecure payments. Cochrane summarised their views vigorously.

> The petitioners have a full and immovable conviction – a conviction which they believe to be universal throughout the kingdom – that the House does not, in any constitutional or rational sense, represent the nation; that, when the people have ceased to be represented, the Constitution is subverted; that taxation without representation is a state of slavery.

This provoked ministerial protest that the petitions were an insulting libel on the House of Commons. They were rejected by 135 votes to 48. On 5 February, he presented another petition signed by 24,000 Londoners, which suffered the same rejection. Cochrane angrily denounced the alternative remedies of charitable donations to the poor, recommended by the ministers. Lord Castlereagh, "the bell-wether of the House of Commons", and thirteen other men had drawn £309,861 from the country's revenue during the previous year. They had handed back exactly £1505 for "sinecure soup", as their charity was now called.[79]

The government responded to such attacks by suspending the Habeas Corpus Act and beginning a resolute campaign against the opposition press. During the following year, eighteen major prosecutions for seditious libel were brought in King's Bench. It may be a tribute to Cochrane's denunciations of Lord Ellenborough that there were acquittals in fourteen cases, as a result of Ellenborough's failure to control the irrepressible William Hone, who defended himself in the three most crucial trials.

The political choice for the reformers lay between open revolution and a broad alliance of those opposed to the ministry. Cochrane favoured the latter, since revolution might merely replace a corrupt parliament by a military despotism, whether revolutionary or ministerial. As the Whig party and the reformers moved more closely together, Cochrane wrote:

> I have resolved to steer another political course, seeing that the only means of avoiding military despotism from the country is to unite the people and the Whigs, so far as they can be induced to co-operate, which they must do if they wish to preserve the remainder of the Constitution.

But while English politics moved first to crisis and then to resolution, he was also preoccupied with several concerns of his own.[80]

Cochrane was now plagued by the legacies of disputes which had all but faded from the public mind. The matter of prize money for the Basque Roads affair had still not been settled after eight years. Gambier insisted that it should be divided among the entire fleet, while Cochrane argued that only the men of the ships who had actually attacked the French ought to have a share in it. He felt so strongly over this that he addressed his case to the Prince Regent and the Privy Council, complaining that the Admiralty court had accepted evidence from men who were nine miles away from the things which they purported to describe. Moreover, there had been a long wrangle in court as to whether Cochrane, who was regarded as having committed perjury by denying his part in the Stock Exchange fraud, was competent to give evidence in any court of law. The action was adjourned from term to term until the point at which he was no longer able to be present to continue with it. He put his case into print, addressing it to the Royal Navy and the public, and contented himself with that.[81]

In other respects, the law functioned with remorseless efficiency where he was concerned. After his election for Honiton in 1806, he had been persuaded to give a banquet for his supporters which had, in the event, been turned into a public treat. Discovering the trick too late, he had then refused to pay the bill for £1200 which the evening's celebrations had incurred. The matter had never been decided and his creditors were still demanding payment ten years later. By the spring of 1817, they succeeded in getting a court order for his house at Holly Hill, in Hampshire. Cochrane decided to fight to the end. "I still hold out," he wrote, as the sheriff of Hampshire and twenty-five constables laid siege to the house, "though the castle has several times been threatened in great force. . . . Explosion-bags are set in the lower embrasures, and all the garrison is under arms." This letter was probably intercepted by the officers of the law, since they treated the defences of Holly Hill with great respect thereafter. The explosion-bags contained only powdered charcoal, but they had heard of Cochrane's defence of Fort Trinidad, and his monstrous proposal for the defence of 78 Piccadilly, and did not regard martyrdom as part of their profession.[82]

After a month or more, one of the officers managed to slip through an open window and catch Cochrane sitting peaceably at breakfast. The siege was over and the ancient bill was paid under considerable protest. During the latter half of 1817, Cochrane began to sell his house and his possessions, collecting all that remained of his wealth and preparing to embark on the most unlikely adventure of all.

Though he was heir to the Earldom of Dundonald, it was little more than a title. His father, who disowned Cochrane to Lord Liverpool, the Prime Minister, was living on an allowance from Basil Cochrane, the only member of the family whose fortune had borne up well. But scandal and distress gathered about the figure of the old Earl, when he married for the third time in 1819, having been a widower for eleven years.

Basil Cochrane had paid his brother an allowance on condition that he lived in lodgings in Shouldham Street, near the Edgware Road, and submitted accounts of all his expenditure. The careful East India merchant had no intention of subsidising either scientific eccentricity or the bottle. When the Earl remarried, and went with his new wife, Anna Maria, to the splendours of Parsons Green, Basil Cochrane cut off their income. He disliked the new Countess, disapproved of marital extravagance, and insisted that unless they separated and the Earl went back to his lodging house, not a penny more would be forthcoming. Lady Dundonald wrote to Lord Melville and the Prince Regent on her husband's behalf, begging a pension for him, assuring the ministry that he had never "interfered in politics, nor is he answerable for Lord Cochrane's conduct, which his father has ever highly disapproved of & condemned". Her letters to Basil Cochrane mingled imprecation and threat with a judicious sense of style. "Oh, Sir! let me conjure you as you hope for Mercy hereafter to take pity on your unfortunate brother and not enforce our separation," she began. But in case Basil was not unduly concerned with the hereafter, she promised that if the present financial crisis lasted much longer, "the whole of the truth & the cause of my separation from my husband must come before the Public, which I do not think will redound to *your advantage*".[83]

The third Lady Dundonald restored some degree of harmony between the brothers in almost the only way open to her, by dying of a bilious fever soon after. The old Earl, living on donations from his family and from the Royal Literary Fund became an easy joke for pamphleteers. The author of the *Life of the Late Thomas Coutts*, recalled how the great banker had married a domestic servant Elizabeth Starky, known to the youthful Dundonald. The pamphlet described vividly how the young lord and Betty Starky had romped about the wash-tub, sousing one another in the suds and rolling about the floor. The Earl replied angrily in a pamphlet written for him, whose only effect was to promote a second edition of the original canard. The story was denied, the respectability and character of Elizabeth Starky upheld, and the old Earl's dignity defended. "If he is less affluent than Noblemen of the same rank, yet his fortune has not been spent in dissipation; but on the contrary, has been devoted with a long life to the purposes of science."[84]

The 9th Earl afterwards withdrew to France, beyond the reach of creditors, living in a Paris lodging with his mistress. He was almost eighty years old by this time but his querulous energy was still not exhausted. If he had chosen exile, that was at least one thing which he now had in common with his heir.

On 2 June 1818, Cochrane rose to address the House of Commons. He was seconding Burdett's motion in favour of parliamentary reform, and in doing so reminded them of Pitt's warning that if the House did not reform itself, it would be reformed from outside, "with a vengeance". With delight or dismay, according to taste, the members then heard him describe his speech as "probably the last time I shall ever have the honour of addressing the House on any subject". His sentiments on reform were predictable, but the reason which took him from the Commons at last was far more dramatic.[85]

Cochrane had been approached by Don José Alvarez, the Chilean representative in London. Throughout South America, the great territories of Chile, Peru, and Brazil, had risen against the colonial government of Portugal and Spain. In many areas it had been easy enough for the revolutionary armies to seize tracts of land, but the struggle had been frustrated by the Spanish and Portuguese fleets. These still held control of the seas, and they were able to maintain substantial garrisons ashore. Cochrane's supreme ability as a sailor, coupled with his devotion to the cause of liberty in his own country, had impressed the leaders of Chile. Alvarez offered him no less than the command of the naval forces which must be used to win the final liberation of South America. He briefly considered the offer and then undertook a role more improbable than any he had yet played, that of a mercenary admiral.

But Cochrane had a plan that was more bizarre than anything offered him. He knew that when South America was truly independent it would need a man of genius to shape the great new republic of the southern hemisphere. He had no doubt that there was such a man who was then languishing in "humiliating exile in a lone and barren island". Kitty recalled her husband's anger and contempt for "the disgraceful conduct" of Castlereagh and his minions in leaving a colossus of the modern world to rot in captivity. To rescue Napoleon from St Helena and place him on the throne of South America was the coup which Cochrane had in mind. He was "determined at all hazards to outwit the English Government, whose Ministers were full of suspicion against him, believing that he had a plot in view for the rescue of the Royal Exile".[86]

It is now a matter of historical record that, before Waterloo, Napoleon discussed his future with his commanders and confessed a private ambition to leave France to her own devices and devote himself to creating a great Latin American republic in the south, to rival the United States in the north.

At the beginning of August 1818, Cochrane, with Kitty and his two sons, Thomas born in 1814 and the five-month-old William, slipped away from the little port of Rye in an open fishing smack, bound for Boulogne and the South American war.

# 7
# The Devil's Admiral

—

THE wars of independence in Latin America had been in progress since 1794, in one form or another. Francisco Miranda, the Venezuelan leader, had been encouraged in his rebellion by Pitt and, more directly, by Cochrane's own uncle Alexander while in command of the West Indies squadron. When Miranda was defeated in 1812 and taken to Spain as a prisoner, leadership of the struggle passed to Simon Bolivar. By 1815 a powerful Spanish army under General Morillo had been despatched to meet the threat of Bolivar and his insurgents. At first, the Spaniards had been successful, driving the rebels from the mainland and forcing Bolivar to seek refuge in Jamaica. But within a year Bolivar returned, crossing from Trinidad to the northern coast of South America and leading his army in triumph through the surrounding territories. Under his command, the independent republics of Colombia and Bolivia had been established.

The essential problem of the South American wars had been repeatedly illustrated. The Spanish army could not police the hinterland of the great continent effectively and, to that extent, was at the mercy of the insurgents who could choose their time and place to strike. But the Spanish navy held command of the sea and was well able to supply and support the major coastal garrisons at such places as Callao or Valdivia. So long as these bases of power remained, total independence would be difficult to achieve.

On the Pacific coast, Chile and Peru illustrated this dilemma with more than usual vividness. Since both countries were shaped as long coastal belts, the Spanish garrisons were maintained by sea and the battlefleet was able to move more quickly and effectively than any army which relied upon the uncertain roads. The Spanish held Peru easily by virtue of a large garrison at Lima, reinforced through their naval base of Callao a few miles away. Only in Chile had there been a convincing attempt to win independence west of the Andes.

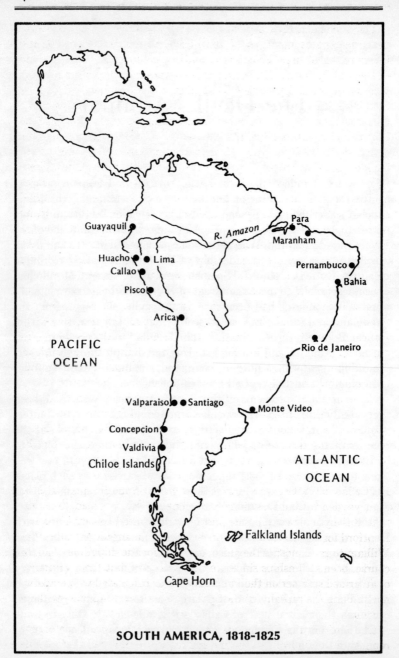

SOUTH AMERICA, 1818-1825

The movement for self-government was the work of those of European descent as much as of the native South Americans. It had begun in this form in Chile in 1810 and had come under the leadership of General Bernardo O'Higgins, whose Irish father had been Spanish viceroy of Peru. By 1814 O'Higgins and his army were beset by Spaniards on the one hand and the rivalry of other patriots, the Carreras brothers, on the other. During that autumn the Carreras brothers, by withholding their support, allowed O'Higgins to be defeated by the Spaniards. He and the survivors of the defeat fell back on the town of Rancagua near the foothills of the Andes. There followed a memorable two days' battle, in which the powerful Spanish army fought, house by house, to take the town until the little band of survivors, O'Higgins himself wounded, made their last stand in an open square. When this resistance was about to collapse, O'Higgins formed up all who were still alive into a phalanx to charge the Spanish, cut a way through, and reach the open country. He and his men escaped and, acting as escort to a refugee column of women, children, and old men, crossed the Andes to the comparative safety of Mendoza, some 200 miles inland from Valparaiso.

The dramatic, and indeed cinematic, quality of the defence of Rancagua caught the imagination of Europe to Chile's advantage. In 1817, O'Higgins and José de San Martin defeated the Spanish at Chacabuco Pass, thirty miles from Santiago and entered the capital. O'Higgins was named as director of the new republic. However, the freedom of Chile would be only a brief illusion so long as the Spanish fleet and the Spanish garrisons remained. Hence the departure of José Alvarez for London to raise money and seek assistance. After being enthusiastically received by Burdett and other sympathisers, he had sought out Cochrane and offered him the great command.

By August 1818, Cochrane and Kitty were at Boulogne, prepared for their voyage to Valparaiso, via St Helena. It was intended to undertake this by a steamship, the *Rising Star*, which was being built at Deptford for the Chilean navy. Cochrane had arranged for his brother William to raise most of the £20,000 needed for the ship. There had, of course, been steamships since the *Comet* of 1812, but the appearance of an armed steamer on the Pacific coast was calculated to spread dismay among the captains of the Spanish fleet, if she could be got there quickly.

But work on the *Rising Star* progressed too slowly. At the urgent request of the Chileans, Cochrane and his wife embarked at Boulogne on 15 August on a conventional sailing ship, the *Rose*. The first part of the voyage, as Kitty recalled, was undertaken "with the intention of making for St Helena, begging for an interview, and ascertaining His Majesty's wishes as regarded placing him on the throne of South America". The Chilean deputies on board the *Rose* had made no objection to this route. But while the sailing ship cruised through the South Atlantic she was overtaken by news that the Spanish army had recovered from its setback and was preparing to strike from Valdivia in the south against Santiago. There was to be no diversion to St Helena, the captain was under orders to make for Valparaiso with all speed. Cochrane could hardly object to this, since his Napoleonic dream was unlikely to be fulfilled if Spanish control over Chile was totally re-established. He postponed the greater plan, but did not abandon it.

The wild coastline of Tierra del Fuego, the penguin colonies on the rocks and the albatrosses floating over the ship, offered a novel distraction for Cochrane as the *Rose* struggled to round Cape Horn against a stiff westerly. The rain drove hard against the lumbering merchantman, and the snow flurries obscured even the bleak rocks of the cape. After three days, the wind changed and the *Rose* rounded the Horn. The snow and ice gave way to a gentle coolness, sea and hills almost suggesting to the passengers the Highlands of Scotland. At length, on 28 November, they landed in the mild cloudy climate of Valparaiso.

At this stage in its development, Valparaiso consisted of a semi-circle of principal buildings, following the curve of the bay, built on a narrow strip of land between the sea and the foot of the precipitous hills enclosing the town. With its road to the nearby capital of Santiago, it was the most important and most cosmopolitan of the Chilean ports. There was a large English colony, including merchants, mercenaries, and Royal Navy officers from several ships of the Pacific squadron. H.M.S. *Andromache* and H.M.S. *Blossom* soon organised rival cricket teams and found a sufficiently large stretch of level ground for their pitch, on a promontory jutting out into the Pacific. A cricket club was founded, its members accepting with equanimity that their ground was also used from time to time as a race course. The club met twice a week for dinner in a marquee. While boasting no talents as a cricketer, Cochrane was accepted in Chilean society readily. Among the Royal Navy officers, he was on the whole admired by junior ranks and, rather predictably, suspected by their seniors.[1]

Picnics and outings, grand balls or receptions, held at Santiago or

Valparaiso, made this an agreeable landfall. John Miller, brother of Major William Miller, mercenary commander of the Chilean marines, recalled, "The two presiding *belles* were Lady Cochrane and Mrs Commodore Blanco, both young, fascinating, and highly gifted." Englishmen were much taken with the beauty of mulatto girls, their dark abundant hair falling to their shoulders "adorned with jessamine and other flowers". On warm Pacific evenings the girls filled their hair with jessamine buds, "which in the course of an hour will open, and present the appearance of a bushy powdered wig".[2]

Dinners and receptions were held in honour of the Cochranes by the Governor of Valparaiso and others. Cochrane returned the compliment on St Andrew's Day, at a banquet over which he presided in the full costume of a Scottish chief, as William Miller recalled.

> Extraordinary good cheer was followed by toasts drank with uncommon enthusiasm in extraordinary good wine. No one escaped its enlivening influence. St Andrew was voted the patron saint of champaign, and many curious adventures of that night have furnished the subject of some still remembered anecdotes.[3]

Having established amicable relations so easily, Cochrane turned to the business of war. The Chilean commander, Blanco Encalada, had resigned his supremacy in favour of Cochrane, who was now appointed "Vice-Admiral of Chile, and Commander-in-Chief of the Naval Forces of the Republic". Those forces consisted of seven ships, either captured from the Spanish or bought from England. The flagship, pertinently named the *O'Higgins*, was a 50-gun vessel taken from the Spaniards. The *San Martin* and the *Lautaro* were old East India ships with 56 and 44 guns respectively. There were four smaller ships, boasting between 14 and 20 guns each, the *Galvarino*, the *Chacabuco*, the *Aracauno*, and the *Puyrredon*. The *Galvarino* had formerly been H.M.S. *Hecate*, an 18-gun sloop. She had been bought out of the navy by two captains, Guise and Spry, who had sailed her to Valparaiso and sold her to the Chileans. These two officers, bent on advancement through Chilean employment, were to be Cochrane's worst enemies in the whole war. Their simple and unambiguous slogan was "two commodores and no Cochrane". Their general sentiments were soon shared by Captain Worcester, a United States captain also serving in the Chilean navy.[4]

Against Cochrane's force, the Spaniards had fourteen ships and twenty-eight gun-boats. The most formidable of these were the heavily armed, purpose-built frigates, particularly the 44-gun *Esmeralda*. In any normal circumstances they should have been more than a match for Cochrane but this was not the sort of consideration by which he was discouraged.

He decided to start making trouble for the Spanish by sailing north to the adjoining coast of Peru, a territory more securely under their control than Chile had ever been. His destination was the naval stronghold of Callao, the key to the nearby capital of Lima. He took his four largest ships, the *O'Higgins, San Martin, Lautaro*, and *Chacabuco*. Many members of the crews were European or American mercenaries but there was also a leavening of Chilean conscripts, including men like José de San Martin, who had been a chieftain of banditti and was marched on board directly from the condemned cell. He shared both the name and the disposition of the commander of the Chilean army.

Far more alarming was an incident involving Tom Cochrane, his father's five-year-old son and heir. Having taken leave of her husband, Kitty had just been ferried ashore when the final gun boomed out from the *O'Higgins* to summon all hands for sailing. To her consternation, she saw an excited mob of citizens escorting the last members of the crew to the beach, with little Thomas Cochrane riding shoulder-high and calling shrilly, "Viva la patria!" Before she could reach them, the members of the crew and the child were in a rowing boat, heading for the ship, which was already getting under way. There was no alternative for Cochrane but to take the child on the voyage, the sailors cutting him out a set of clothes and dressing him as an infant midshipman.[5]

The attack on Callao was not in itself of much significance. Cochrane had discovered that the two most powerful Spanish frigates, the *Esmeralda* and the *Venganza*, were in the anchorage and he had intended to board and capture them. The *O'Higgins* and the *Lautaro* were to sail in, flying United States colours, and seize the frigates before the deception was discovered. Unfortunately, Callao and its approaches were swathed in fog, which made the attack impossible. Cochrane had to be content with capturing a Spanish gunboat and her crew. Then the fog lifted and revealed the *O'Higgins* and the *Lautaro*, becalmed under the powerful batteries of Callao.

The *Lautaro* contrived to drift clear, leaving Cochrane on the *O'Higgins* to face the combined power of 160 guns in the shore-batteries and 350 more on the Spanish ships which were anchored in a crescent across the bay. During this action, his first thought was for his son, whom he locked into his stern cabin as a precaution. But the five-year-old had no intention of missing such an adventure and found a means of escape by climbing out of the quarter gallery window as the salvoes from Callao howled over the ship. To his father's dismay he appeared on the quarter-deck in the middle of the action. Cochrane had no time to attend to him and the child at once made himself useful by handing powder to the gunners for the quarter-deck guns. It was during this that a Spanish cannon ball hissed across the deck and took off the head of a marine standing close by. Cochrane was sure his son had been hit and stood "spell-bound with agony". But though the dead man's brains had been scattered in his face, the boy ran safely to his father, announcing, "I am not hurt, papa; the shot did not touch me. Jack says, the ball is not made that can kill mamma's boy."

Cochrane gave orders for his son to be carried below but after wails of protest and violent struggles the attempt was abandoned. The *O'Higgins* came through the ordeal undamaged except for the rigging. Cochrane put to sea, landed on the offshore island of San Lorenzo, took the Spanish occupants prisoner and freed thirty-seven Chilean soldiers who had been kept there in chains for eight years. "The joy of the poor fellows at their deliverance, after all hope had fled, can scarcely be conceived," he reported.[6]

He now began a blockade of Callao, though offering to return the Spanish prisoners to their commander if the liberated Chileans were permitted to rejoin their families. While these negotiations continued, under flag of truce, the Spanish viceroy of Peru, Don Joaquim de la Pezuela, reproached him, as a British nobleman, with having joined a rebel navy. "A British nobleman is a free man," replied Cochrane sternly, "and therefore has a right to adopt any country which is endeavouring to re-establish the rights of aggrieved humanity." He added that the Duke de San Carlos, Spanish ambassador in London, had approached him on behalf of Ferdinand VII and had offered him an admiral's command in the Spanish navy. He had refused it, and had joined the Chileans instead. As the news spread among the crews at Callao and they learnt who their adversary was, memories of the *Speedy* and the Mediterranean war of 1801–1808 were revived. Cochrane learnt that he had a new nickname among them, not intended as flattery but which pleased him well: El Diablo. More than two hundred years before, Sir Francis Drake had raided Callao and earned the title of El Dracone. After Cochrane's death, his son Thomas wrote, "Drake the Dragon and Cochrane the Devil were kinsmen in noble hatred, and noble punishment, of Spanish wrong-doing."[7]

It was June 1819 before he returned to Valparaiso, the six months' cruise having been spent in raiding Spanish supply depots ashore, seizing currency intended to pay the Spanish troops, and intercepting ships at sea. At Huacho, the Spanish garrison hardly fired a shot before retreating and leaving supplies behind them. Cochrane's reputation had spread down the coast and he found, increasingly, that his enemies rarely bothered to contest the issue. His marines landed at Patavilca and seized 70,000 dollars belonging to the Spanish treasury. Five days later they boarded the brig *Gazelle* and took 60,000 more. On 16 June, the *O'Higgins* dropped anchor off Valparaiso and Cochrane went ashore to a hero's welcome.

The ships were refitted after their long cruise. It was not until September that Cochrane paid a return visit to Callao. Since his first attack, the Spanish had built a substantial boom across the harbour, sturdy enough to require an explosion ship to dislodge it. Cochrane contented himself with attacking the port by using rockets and a fire-ship, then he turned his attention to a more formidable enterprise.

Just as Callao was the great Spanish base to the north of Valparaiso, so Valdivia was the military stronghold to the south. Englishmen who saw it were apt to regard it as the equivalent of the rock of Gibraltar in terms of the Pacific coast of South America. It was also much closer to Valparaiso than Callao happened to be. If the infant republic of O'Higgins was to be crushed, the blow was more likely to be aimed at Santiago by a Spanish army using Valdivia as its base.

There was an equally urgent reason for attempting a spectacular coup against Spain. Though the Chilean republic had bought an American-built corvette, the 28-gun *Independencia*, following Cochrane's arrival, little or nothing was being spent on the armament of the navy. Cochrane had offered to surrender all his prize money to pay for the cost of rockets for attacking Spanish-held ports. The offer was refused and money was saved on their manufacture by making the Spanish prisoners undertake it. The consequence, as Cochrane found before Callao, was that many rockets were utterly ineffective. In almost every respect, the navy of the new republic was ill-equipped. A dramatic victory over the Spanish at sea might persuade O'Higgins and San Martin of the unrealised power which the little fleet put at their disposal.

The chances of a successful attack on Valdivia were diminished when the Chilean government declined to supply Cochrane with troops for an assault. It might have been possible, of course, to have attacked the base using only the crew of the *O'Higgins*, since Cochrane intended to make the attempt with the flagship alone, but it was hard to find trained men.

The crews for the most part consisted of *cholos*, or native peasants, whom it was difficult to shape into good seamen, though they fought gallantly when well led. The officers were nearly all English or North American, this being a redeeming feature, but very few of them possessed the tact to bring up the men to anything like a seaman-like standard.[8]

Despite this, Cochrane sailed in the *O'Higgins*, taking with him Major William Miller, the fellow mercenary who was commander of the Chilean marines. With his habitual coolness, Cochrane hoisted Spanish colours at the mast of the *O'Higgins*, dropped anchor off Valdivia on 18 January 1820, and signalled for a pilot. The trick succeeded because, as Cochrane knew, by reports from the Atlantic coast, where the ships had touched, Valdivia awaited two battleships and a new frigate from Spain. He also heard that one of the battleships had proved unseaworthy and was still on the Atlantic coast. The other battleship had foundered off Cape Horn, and the new frigate was sheltering in the Guayaquil river to escape his own squadron. It was that frigate, the *Prueba*, which the *O'Higgins* successfully impersonated. The Spanish commander sent out a boat with a pilot, an officer, and four soldiers, all of whom were made prisoner as soon as they stepped on deck. They were then persuaded, as Cochrane put it, that it was "conducive to their interests to supply all the information demanded". The pilot took the *O'Higgins* into the navigation channels of Valdivia, enabling Cochrane to map the approaches to the harbour and the position of all the forts.

The Spaniards on shore were puzzled to see what they took to be the *Prueba* turn and head for the horizon once more. Cochrane had now discovered from his prisoners that another ship was expected soon, the 18-gun sloop *Potrillo* with 20,000 dollars on board, that being the pay of the Valdivia garrison. Three days later, the sloop was hailed by a friendly warship under Spanish colours. When the captain at last realised that he had been boarded by the *O'Higgins*, it was too late to offer any resistance. Without firing a shot, Cochrane captured the sloop, 20,000 dollars, and a set of extremely valuable despatches detailing Spanish plans and troop movements.[9]

It was now clear that in southern Chile the Spaniards had enlisted the most savage of the Indian tribes on their side to attack and destroy settlements within the area loyal to the new republic. Accordingly, Cochrane sailed farther south still, to Concepcion, where he repeated his request for troops to attack Valdivia. Governor Freire listened and then agreed to lend him 250 men. If Valdivia could be taken and its province subdued, the Indian threat might largely be removed.

The attacking force sailed again on 25 January, the *O'Higgins* now accompanied by the schooner *Montezuma* with troops on board and the brig *Intrepido*. But the entire expedition almost ended in disaster on the night of 29 January, when the *O'Higgins* was some forty miles out to sea and not within sight of either the brig or the schooner. Cochrane had retired to his cabin and was sleeping, having left the lieutenant of the watch in charge of the flagship. Presently the lieutenant also decided to turn in, taking advantage of Cochrane's absence to hand over his duties to a midshipman.

Though the ship was far out to sea, there were numerous reefs and half-submerged shoals, which had made Cochrane leave orders with the lieutenant to call him at once if a breeze sprang up. But either the orders were not passed on to the midshipman or else he neglected them. The wind gathered strength and a sudden squall blew the ship's prow round. As the midshipman gave his commands, in an effort to bring her back on course, there was a jarring thud deep below the keel and the *O'Higgins* bucked and grated on a sharp ledge of rock.

The story of the *Pallas* off Ushant seemed likely to be repeated, though this time there was no hope of the sea lifting the ship clear. Instead, the surges were hammering her against the rock on which she was lodged. It was now in the small hours of a hazy morning and, unlike the men of the *Pallas*, the first thought of the crew of the *O'Higgins* was to take to the boats.

Cochrane arrived on deck, "half-dressed" according to his secretary W. B. Stevenson, and found that the ship was aground on a reef, which boasted a few trees, and that "the jib-boom was entangled among the branches". More ominous, the surface of the ocean was littered with fragments of the false keel and of the ship's "sheathing". First, Cochrane warned the ship's company that the boats would hold only a quarter of them, and that they were too far from land to attempt such a voyage in any case. If they reached the nearest shore, they would find nothing but "torture and inevitable death at the hands of the Indians". There had been stories enough of this at Concepcion and his warning had a sobering effect.

He ordered a kedge anchor to be carried out astern and securely lodged. By using the hawser it was then possible to heave the *O'Higgins* clear. However, she was leaking badly with three feet of water in the hold already, though the depth was not increasing as rapidly as might have been feared. For another thirty-six hours the flagship continued on course, the men at the pumps working to keep the flood in check. But the ship's carpenter was an unskilled member of the crew who had no idea of how to maintain the pumps. While the seamen seized buckets to bail out the ship, the depth increased to five feet and then seven, flooding the powder magazine. The carpenter and most of the Chilean crew had been peasants or agricultural labourers, to whom the mechanics of a ship's pumps remained a complete mystery. The European and American officers were more familiar with the pumps as such, but the technicalities of such devices had always been considered below the dignity of a gentleman to investigate.

It was left to Cochrane, as admiral, to prove the worth of the apprenticeship he had served to Jack Larmour on the *Thetis*, almost thirty years before. While his men formed a chain to use the buckets for baling he now stripped off his coat and went below to use such "skill in carpentry" as he possessed. It was uncomfortably evident that unless the pumps could be put back into working order, the *O'Higgins* and her crew were doomed. At its present rate, the sea would overwhelm the ship in a few hours. He worked until midnight and succeeded in repairing the pumps sufficiently for use. The men who had been bailing turned their energies to pumping. The level of water in the hold steadied, and then began to fall.

It was not surprising that the drama of the pumps decided many of those on the *O'Higgins* against making an attack on Valdivia. In the first place, the assault was one which no one but Cochrane would have contemplated. But the flow of water into the *O'Higgins* was likely to increase and the likelihood was that the ship would founder before the battle was over. Cochrane himself was undeterred, as he explained to Major Miller: "Well, Major, Valdivia we must take. Sooner than put back, it would be better that we all went to the bottom."

The dramatic simplicity of his decision was greeted by misgivings. Yet he knew that in terms both of strategy and of Chilean morale a spectacular victory was badly needed. The apparent impossibility of what he was about to do was the guarantee of success. It was the familiar argument which he employed throughout his career.

> Cool calculation would make it appear that the attempt to take Valdivia is madness. This is one reason why the Spaniards will hardly believe us in earnest, even when we commence. And you will see that a bold onset, and a little perseverance afterwards, will give a complete triumph.

With the schooner and the brig in attendance, he set sail for the Spanish base.[10]

The stronghold of Valdivia consisted of a well-defended and almost landlocked anchorage, guarded by forts on high ground to either side. As Major Miller and his marines discovered, these forts not only covered the entrance to the great natural basin but were able to enfilade every part of the harbour. Within that harbour basin there was also the fortified island of Manzanera, the centrepiece of an anchorage some four miles long and two miles broad. Deep within the shelter of the anchorage was a smaller bay and two estuaries, that of the Valdivia river leading to the town of Valdivia itself which was fourteen miles upstream.

The only entrance to the great natural harbour was about 1200 yards across, overlooked by Fort Niebla on the eastern height and Fort Amargos on the west. Any ship which attempted to force an entrance would be at the mercy of their artillery and, even beyond that, the harbour was an ideal trap in which the intruder would be helpless before the surrounding guns and troops. To make matters worse, from the attacker's viewpoint, the strong sea and the surf on the coast outside the harbour would make a landing at any other point difficult.

However, Cochrane studied the possibility of a landing outside the harbour itself. The one feasible place was the Aguada del Ingles, a small bay about a mile to the west of the harbour entrance. It was not an easy landing but an attack might be made at slack water. The compensating disadvantage was that it was guarded by the first of the forts on the western side, Fort Ingles. Since it was out of the question to attack through the harbour mouth, Cochrane decided to land at the Aguada del Ingles, storm Fort Ingles, and then advance by taking every fort on the western side of the harbour in succession, except possibly for the strongpoint of Corral Castle which might withstand a siege.

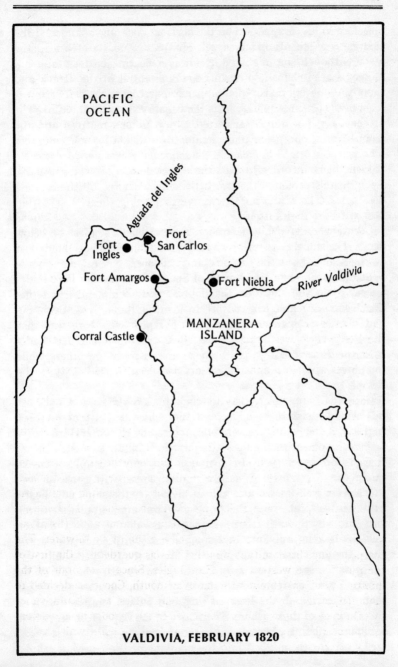

PACIFIC
OCEAN

Aguada del Ingles

Fort
San Carlos

Fort
Ingles

Fort Amargos

Fort Niebla

River Valdivia

MANZANERA
ISLAND

Corral Castle

**VALDIVIA, FEBRUARY 1820**

Before Valdivia appeared on the horizon, Cochrane abandoned the *O'Higgins* as an attacking vessel. She was in no state to lead the assault, though she might be useful as a floating battery later on. Moreover, the element of surprise was essential in the attack and there was too big a risk of the Spaniards recognising the *O'Higgins* from her recent masquerading as the frigate *Prueba*. Still out of sight of the base, Cochrane transferred Major Miller's marines and the troops from Concepcion under Major Beauchef, a French volunteer officer, to the brig *Intrepido* and the schooner *Montezuma*. He accompanied them, in order to lead the attack himself. On 3 February, flying Spanish colours, the two little ships anchored off the Aguada del Ingles. There was no alternative to putting themselves within range of Fort Ingles itself.

Cochrane ordered all his troops and marines out of sight below decks. The ships' boats in which they would land had been made fast at the seaward side of the brig and schooner, concealed from the Spaniards ashore. A detachment of Spanish troops from Fort Ingles appeared on the shore at the double, their commander ordering the *Montezuma* and her consort to identify themselves. Cochrane had chosen a Spanish-born officer to reply. His story was that the two vessels were part of the squadron which had left Cadiz with the *Prueba*. They had been separated from the others while rounding Cape Horn and their boats had been washed away in the storms.

Cochrane's aim was to play for time, until darkness and a slacker tide would assist the landing and the subsequent attack on Fort Ingles. But the Spaniards were unconvinced by the Cape Horn story. Cochrane's officer then added a request for a pilot. It was the usual thing to do under such circumstances but only a couple of weeks earlier the *O'Higgins* had made a similar request with consequences which were well-known at Valdivia. Those on the ships now heard with some apprehension the firing of alarm guns from the nearer forts and saw Spanish troops moving at the double from the other bastions to reinforce Fort Ingles. At 4 p.m., without further argument, the guns of Fort Ingles opened fire on the two little ships.

The action seemed precipitate, until Cochrane saw what had gone wrong. By an extremely bad stroke of fortune, one of the ship's boats, concealed on the seaward side, had broken loose and drifted into the view of those ashore. The falsity of the Cape Horn story had been embarrassingly revealed. Almost at once, two of the first shots from Fort Ingles smashed into the planking of the *Intrepido*'s hull, killing two of the soldiers on the lower deck. There was no chance of retreat and, therefore, no alternative to attacking at once.

Cochrane clambered down into the little gig, in which he was to bob about offshore, directing the landing. Major Miller and his forty-four marines were packed into one of the two remaining launches, and the seamen began to row them ashore as the vanguard of the assault. A further complication for Cochrane's men was that when the *O'Higgins* was holed on the rock, the water had reached the powder magazine, soaking much of the contents. As a result, it was the bayonet rather than the bullet which would decide the assault on Valdivia.

As the first of the launches pulled towards the beach, the Spanish troops of the advance party opened fire. Miller counted seventy-five of them defending the landing place. A heavy swell was still running and, to make matters worse, the sailors found their oars encumbered with masses of floating seaweed. In the opening volleys of musket fire, four or five of the marines were hit. More important still, the Spanish fire was directed at the boat itself. Miller was alarmed to see that his launch was being "perforated with musket balls, and the water rushed in through the holes". Two of the sailors refused to row any closer but when one of them was felled by a marine with a musket butt, the rest took up their oars again. The storm of bullets swept over the lowered heads of Cochrane's men, one musket ball passing through Miller's hat and another hitting the quartermaster of the *O'Higgins* who was acting as coxswain of the launch.

As the craft approached the shore, Miller ordered his men to use some of their precious ammunition against the Spanish defenders, who now found themselves in exposed positions at close range. Once the marines had landed, Miller led them in an immediate bayonet charge up the beach, routing the defenders and giving Cochrane's main force a precarious hold. The 250 Chilean troops were ferried ashore and, as soon as it was dark, Cochrane directed the attack on the first strongpoint, Fort Ingles.

As so often, his plan combined military skill and pantomime farce. The first half of his men advanced through the darkness towards Fort Ingles, firing in the air, cheering, and generally leaving the Spanish in no doubt as to their intentions. A second group, under Ensign Vidal, worked silently round to the inland flank of the forts uprooting part of a pallisade to make a rough bridge across the defensive ditch. These men moved with hardly a sound, any slight noise being drowned by their comrades in front of the fort. Moving softly over the rampart, they formed up among a group of trees and then opened a withering fire on the defenders of the fort from the rear. In the darkness and confusion, the Spanish commander did not wait to contest the issue as the attackers emitted wild Indian yells and charged forward. The garrison of Fort Ingles fled, running into the three hundred Spanish troops drawn up behind the fort and urging them into retreat as well. The Chileans followed hard, bayoneting their enemies, the pursuit being so close that when the gates of Fort Carlos were opened to receive the fugitives, the Chileans poured in after them. Fort Carlos was also abandoned, its garrison joining the general flight, the same bloodstained farce being repeated at Fort Amargos which commanded the western side of the great harbour entrance.

Before dawn, the defenders of the forts on the western side of the harbour had retreated into the Corral Castle, where they might have held out for some time. But morale was not good. They had lost about a hundred men dead and another hundred as prisoners in the rout. Colonel Hoyos, the commander of the castle had taken to the bottle, incoherent with rage and humiliation. Moreover, the castle was ideally placed for an evacuation by water across the harbour and even up the river to the town of Valdivia. A further incentive to this was that Cochrane's troops had captured the Spanish artillery on the height of Fort Chorocomayo and would almost certainly start bombarding the castle as soon as it was daylight. Those who could escape did so, and the remainder of the garrison, including Colonel Hoyos, surrendered to Major Miller. The entire operation had cost Cochrane seven dead and nineteen wounded.

The next day, the *Intrepido* and the *Montezuma* braved the fire of the eastern forts and entered harbour. Cochrane ordered two hundred of his men to embark for an attack across the harbour on the forts still remaining in Spanish hands. At the same time, the *O'Higgins*, by now leaking very badly, appeared off the harbour mouth. This was the final blow to the defence of the eastern half, since there was no equivalent strongpoint to Corral Castle on that side. Assuming that the *O'Higgins* brought fresh reinforcements, the commanders of the eastern forts abandoned them, withdrawing up the river to Valdivia itself. As a matter of fact, the *O'Higgins* brought no reinforcements at all. The ship herself was going down steadily and Cochrane ordered her to be beached at once until repairs could be carried out. None the less, he had calculated that the sight of a 50-gun warship would break the last resolve of the Spaniards, and in this he had been right.

On 6 February, he embarked his men on the *Montezuma* and the *Intrepido* to follow up his victory by a river attack on Valdivia itself. The *Intrepido* ran aground in the channel and had to be abandoned but it hardly mattered. Before he could reach the town, Cochrane was greeted by a party of men under a flag of truce. The Spanish army and the governor of the town had laid hands on whatever they could carry and had fled. The great military base in the southern half of the continent, the one remaining stronghold within Chile itself from which the Spanish might have launched their great counter-offensive, had been taken at a cost of twenty-six casualties.

The booty which fell into the hands of the Chileans at Valdivia was considerable. Cochrane counted fifty tons of gunpowder, 10,000 cannon shot, 170,000 musket cartridges, 128 pieces of artillery, a "large quantity" of small arms, and the ship *Dolores* which was sold at Valparaiso for 20,000 dollars. It was loot, or prize money, of the most promising proportions.[11]

On 27 February, Cochrane returned to Valparaiso. The Ministry of Marine had assumed that the attack on Valdivia would be defeated and, as a matter of face saving, they had carefully prepared charges of insubordination against him for having sailed there without proper authority. As news of the victory, and of a passing attack on the Spanish fort at Chiloe, spread through Valparaiso and Santiago, the government hastily withdrew its charges and publicly congratulated Cochrane on his "admirably arranged plan" and its "most daring and valorous execution".[12]

But the matter of prize money was no less productive of ill-feeling in Chile than it had been in England. Cochrane and his men received "nothing but promises". But in this case there was a remedy, which he exploited by retaining everything he had seized at Valdivia despite threats of prosecution for illegal detention of national property. Cochrane answered this, on 14 May, by offering O'Higgins his resignation as commander of the Chilean navy. This produced consternation and further promises of payment for the squadron. Cochrane himself was awarded 67,000 dollars and an estate at Rio Clara in the south of the country. He refused the estate, bought a hacienda of his own at Herradura, about eight miles from Valparaiso, and withdrew his resignation. When he offered to pay for the construction of a naval base for the Chilean navy at this place, he was warned not to start on the project in any way. The authorities were not prepared to pay anything towards it and, as he discovered, they showed their displeasure by holding back much of the prize money.

On 16 July, Cochrane offered his resignation again, supported two days later by twenty-three of the Chilean navy's European and American officers. By now, Cochrane's two English rivals, the captains Guise and Spry, were in open rebellion against him. Indeed, he had put Guise under arrest for direct disobedience to orders and was awaiting the arrangements for a court-martial which he hoped would secure the offender's removal from the service.

The Minister of Marine, José Zentano, wrote to Cochrane and begged him not to resign at this point. Cochrane's resignation would "involve the future operations of the arms of liberty in the New World in certain ruin; and ultimately replace in Chili, your adopted home, that tyranny which your Lordship abhors, and to the annihilation of which your heroism has so greatly contributed."

Cochrane cared little for Zentano, but he also received private letters from San Martin and O'Higgins, "begging me to continue in command of the naval forces and assuring me that there should be no further cause for complaint".[13]

From Cochrane's own point of view, there were strong enough reasons for remaining in his command. Setting aside his indignation over the question of prize money, he believed strongly in the Chilean cause. Personally, he had a great admiration for O'Higgins, whom he exempted from any part in the niggardly treatment of the naval squadron. Most important of all, there was nowhere else in the world, at the time, where he could exercise his supreme gifts as a naval commander. The purchase of the hacienda had been a gesture of commitment to the Chilean cause and to his continuing part in it. As Sir James Mackintosh informed the House of Commons, Cochrane now stood before the eyes of the world.

> Lord Cochrane is such a miracle of nautical skill and courage; his cause of banishment from his country is so lamentable – his adventures have been so romantic – and his achievements so splendid, that no Englishman can read them without pride, that such things have been done by his countryman; and without solemn concern that such talents and genius should be lost to the land that gave them birth.[14]

For Cochrane, there was a final and immediate reason which made his departure from Chile unlikely. The capture of Valdivia had removed the greatest threat to the young republic so far as the south was concerned. To the north, however, the Spanish still held the long coastal strip of Peru, by virtue of the garrison at Lima and the access to it by means of the neighbouring port of Callao. It was at Callao that the most powerful ships of the Spanish squadron were concentrated and Zentano was right when he warned Cochrane that this base was enough for the Spanish to reverse the whole course of the revolution in Chile itself.

In Santiago and in Valparaiso, preparations went ahead for the decisive battle of the war. It was proposed that the entire weight of the Chilean army and navy should be thrown against Lima and Callao under the joint command of General San Martin ashore and Cochrane at sea. The army would be carried as far as possible by sea, and then the double attack would commence. To placate the foreign seamen and their officers, San Martin signed a public promise that all arrears of pay would be made good on "my entry into Lima", a pledge also signed by Cochrane as witness.[15]

On 21 August 1820, the squadron with 4200 troops on board put to sea from Valparaiso, among the cheers of the inhabitants lining the shore. There had already been a less obtrusive departure. Believing the climax of the war was at hand, Cochrane had despatched a confidential messenger, Lieutenant-Colonel Charles, to a very different destination. Charles had served under Sir Robert Wilson in Egypt, and had made the acquaintance of several participants in that campaign. At Cochrane's instigation, he was about to renew one of those acquaintanceships by setting out on a long and momentous voyage to St Helena. But the dream of a great Napoleonic Empire in South America was never to be realised. By the time that Colonel Charles reached St Helena, the health of the exiled Emperor had begun its long and irreversible decline. His deterioration had already gone so far that there was nothing for Colonel Charles to do but to return to Valparaiso.[16]

The problems of Cochrane's attack on Lima began early. San Martin, as commander-in-chief of the army, informed him that the troops would go ashore at Truxillo, a considerable distance from their objective. Cochrane was disconcerted by this, believing that the landing should have been swift and close to the targets, enabling rapid and simultaneous attacks to be made on Lima by land and Callao by sea. He saw no point in invading an area where, as he put it, "the army could have gained no advantage, nor, indeed, have found anything to do, except to remain there safe from any attack by the Spaniards".[17]

It was the beginning of a long, final quarrel between the two commanders. San Martin might be an experienced leader in the struggle against Spain, but by Cochrane's standards he exhibited caution to a degree which approached cowardice.

In the event, San Martin revised his plan and went ashore with his army at Pisco, which was closer to the objectives, although still some one hundred and fifty miles short. He remained there for seven weeks, to Cochrane's fury, even declining to attack Pisco itself, which was defended by no more than three hundred Spanish troops. Then at length on 28 October, San Martin re-embarked his army on the transports for the last stage of the voyage to Callao. He was prompted by news that the province of Guayaquil, hearing that an army of liberation was on the way, had declared itself independent without further ado. However, when the squadron reached Callao, San Martin thought better of putting his army ashore there, and insisted on being taken back to Ancon, thirty miles to the north.

Irritated beyond endurance by San Martin's conduct of the attack, Cochrane returned with the *O'Higgins*, the *Independencia*, and the *Lautaro* to the waters off Callao. For San Martin's benefit, he announced that he was going to blockade the port so that Lima would not be reinforced by sea. What he had in mind was something more dramatic, a plan which he had no intention of confiding to San Martin. The latter was settling down peacefully at Ancon, a port which the Spanish hardly bothered to defend, since, as Major Miller observed, it consisted only of "a few fishermen's huts, half buried in the drifted sand".[18]

On 3 November, Cochrane began his close reconnaissance of the harbour of Callao, using the *O'Higgins* for the purpose. In one sortie, he outmanoeuvred the defences by sailing between the island of San Lorenzo and the mainland, through the Boqueron passage. The citizens of Callao crowded the shore to watch, knowing that the channel was suitable only for vessels of less than fifty tons. The Spanish gunboats waited to close on the wreck of the 50-gun warship. Cochrane's secretary, W. B. Stevenson noted the "utter astonishment" of the spectators as Cochrane brought his flagship through the narrow rocky channel with as little concern as if he had been handling a rowing boat. It was a show of seamanship designed to undermine the morale of the enemy. But it was more than that. He was now certain that neither the *Venganza* nor the *Prueba* were anywhere near. Callao was defended by shore-batteries, a floating boom, and most important of all, by the *Esmeralda*. The 44-gun frigate was the fastest and most powerful Spanish warship on the Pacific coast. Her destruction would be a decisive factor in loosening the grip of the enemy on the garrison towns. But if she could be captured intact, and incorporated into the Chilean navy, the advantage would swing so far in favour of Cochrane and his men that Spanish power in Chile and Peru might never be re-established.[19]

Like the attack on Valdivia, the only positive advantage which the Chileans enjoyed was that no one would believe them foolish enough to attempt to "cut out" the *Esmeralda*. So far as the Spanish possessed a "pocket battleship", she was one, well able to give a good account of herself in an exchange with any of Cochrane's ships. Apart from this, she lay securely at anchor in Callao harbour, protected by three hundred pieces of artillery in the shore-batteries, by a strong harbour-boom with chain moorings, by twenty-seven gunboats and several armed block-ships.

On 5 November, during the afternoon, Cochrane announced to the crews of his ships that he was about to strike "a mortal blow" at Spanish sea power in the Pacific. There was a surfeit of volunteers, perhaps impelled by his promise that, "The value of all the vessels captured in Callao will be yours." He chose 160 seamen and 80 marines, preparing to make the attack that night.

The men embarked in fourteen small boats which had been lowered and assembled alongside the *O'Higgins*. Cochrane himself went in the leading boat. All his other ships were out of sight and even the flag-ship had been anchored far enough out to sea to put the Spanish defenders off their guard. When the action should begin, he judged that it might be very confused and close-fought. Each man was therefore issued with a pistol and a cutlass, most suitable for hand-to-hand fighting, while the entire attacking force was dressed in white with blue bands on their left arms to identify friend and foe.

Like so many actions of its kind, the cutting out of the *Esmeralda* was over almost before the defenders realised that it was in earnest. Cochrane, timing it, noted that it lasted no more than quarter of an hour from start to finish. But before the action began, there was a long preliminary from about 10 p.m. to midnight, during which the loaded boats pulled silently across the dark water to a small gap in the harbour boom. The little craft were grouped into two divisions, under Cochrane's overall command, the first under his flag-captain, Captain Crosbie, the second under his most vehement critic, Captain Guise of the *Lautaro*.

As the flotilla glided past the boom, Cochrane in the bows of the first boat, a sharp challenge rang across the dark surface of the anchorage and the unwelcome silhouette of a Spanish gun-boat appeared ahead of them. Instead of answering, Cochrane ordered his oarsmen to bring him alongside the boat, a course which evidently impressed the Spanish commander as being that of submission. As they came alongside, Cochrane rose to his feet and addressed the commander.

"Silence or death!" he said softly. "Another word and I'll put you every one to the sword!"

By the time that the commander could think of a response, he found his launch surrounded by fourteen boatloads of armed men and the initiative had passed from him. Cochrane with the leading boats was already making for the *Esmeralda*.

There were two neutral warships anchored off Callao, both destined to play an innocent part in Cochrane's plan. The first was the United States frigate *Macedonian*, the second was the Royal Navy frigate *Hyperion*. The sentry at the gangway of the *Macedonian* hailed Cochrane's boats as they passed but, as W. B. Stevenson saw, the man was "immediately hushed" by the American officer of the watch. As Stevenson's boat passed the *Macedonian*, "many of her officers hung over the bulwarks, cheered us in whispers, wishing us success, and wishing also that they themselves could join us". There were no cheers and no good wishes from H.M.S. *Hyperion*. Indeed, her sentries continued to hail Cochrane's boats with all the power of their lungs, as though determined to alert the Spanish defenders.

Despite this, Cochrane's boat reached the side of the *Esmeralda*, still undetected by the watch. While he led the boarding party on one side of the ship, his rival Captain Guise led a second attack on the opposite side. But though the guards on the *Esmeralda* had noticed nothing as yet, they were fully alerted by the sound of Cochrane and his men boarding the ship by the main-chains. Cochrane raised himself to the level of the deck only to be met by a blow from the sentry's musket-butt. Losing his hold, he fell heavily into the boat below, driving the thole-pin, on which the oar rested, into his back near the spine. It was an injury which was to cause him considerable pain for years to come.

At the moment, however, he pulled himself up and began to climb the side of the *Esmeralda* once more. This time, he contrived to level his pistol and shoot down the sentry before the man could use his unwieldy musket again. The sentry on the far side of the boat turned and fired, Cochrane returning the fire at once with his pistol and killing the man outright. Then he broke the silence by turning to the boat-crew behind him and shouting, "Up, my lads! She's ours!"

As it proved, this was an extremely optimistic view of the situation. The Spanish crew had been sleeping at their guns, ready to defend the *Esmeralda* at a moment's notice. Even with Cochrane's seamen and marines, swarming on to the deck at every point, the defence was by no means overwhelmed. The Spanish commander withdrew his men to the forecastle, from which they swept the deck of the frigate with musket fire. Cochrane and Guise, struggling through the battle from opposite sides of the ship, met in the middle of the deck and, briefly forgetting their dislike of one another, exchanged congratulations. Hardly had this happened when a shot from the defenders of the forecastle hit Cochrane in the thigh. The bullet had evidently gone through the fleshy part and he contented himself with binding a handkerchief round his leg. Limping to the quarter-deck, he stood on one leg, perched on a gun, and laid the injured leg on the hammock netting. From this point of vantage, he directed the attack on the forecastle.

On board the *Esmeralda*, the fight was going in his favour, but its outcome might well be decided by the powerful batteries ashore, or even by the Spanish gun-boats. As the Spaniards in the forecastle were pressed harder, the first signs of a rout appeared, several of their sailors diving into the harbour and swimming for safety. The sound of pistol and musket fire dwindled and died, as Captain Coig the Spanish commander surrendered to Cochrane. But almost at once, one of the gun-boats sailed in astern of the *Esmeralda* and sent a shot up through the quarter-deck, wounding Coig himself.

With his customary foresight, Cochrane had ordered several men of his party to make for the rigging of the *Esmeralda* as soon as they boarded her, and to prepare for sailing. He now hailed the foretop and the maintop, and discovered that all was in order. "No British man-of-war's crew could have excelled this minute attention to orders," he wrote of his Chilean seamen.

Having seized the *Esmeralda*, for the loss of eleven men killed and thirty wounded, Cochrane now faced the hazardous business of sailing her out of Callao under the three hundred guns of the shore-batteries and the assorted artillery of the block-ships. Varying estimates of the time taken to capture the frigate from the moment of boarding put it at between fifteen and seventeen minutes. None the less, it was ample time for the guns of Callao to open up in a general bombardment of the darkened harbour. Rather oddly, Cochrane was paying little attention to the guns. He was studying the outline of the British and American frigates, which were now prudently making for the safety of San Lorenzo and the open sea.

In all the confusion, Cochrane knew there was one certainty. The Spanish would not want to provoke an international incident by sinking an American or British frigate. There must be some pre-arranged signal which the *Macedonian* and the *Hyperion* were to give in the event of a night attack. He gave orders that lights identical to those of the other two ships were to be hoisted by the *Esmeralda*. As soon as this was done, the shells from the shore-batteries, which had been pitching about the captured frigate, ceased. There was a puzzled but welcome silence.

When hostilities recommenced they were between Cochrane and Captain Guise, who had taken over as commander of the Chileans because of Cochrane's immobility. It had been Cochrane's intention to set the sails of the *Esmeralda* but not to cut the anchor cables until an attempt had been made to capture the Spanish brig *Maypu* and to attack and cut adrift every other ship within reach. At the best, he hoped that every vessel in the harbour of Callao "might either have been captured or burned". But Guise had ordered the cables to be cut at once, obliging the *Esmeralda* to put to sea forthwith, followed by two captured gun-boats. Cochrane confronted him angrily, but Guise replied that the frigate could not have remained because, "the English had broken into her spirit-room and were getting drunk, whilst the Chilenos were disorganized by plundering".

Impartial observers recognised only the superb audacity with which Cochrane had seized the *Esmeralda* under the guns of Callao and sailed her safely to join his squadron. Captain Basil Hall of H.M.S. *Conway*, serving in the Pacific, made amends for the hostility of the *Hyperion* by announcing the extent of Cochrane's victory. The *Esmeralda* had been lying "under the guns of the castle, within a semi-circle of fourteen gun-boats, and a boom of spars chained together". But, more important, the events of that night deprived the Spanish of their last advantage on the Pacific coast.

> The loss was a death-blow to the Spanish naval force in that quarter of the world; for, although there were still two Spanish frigates and some smaller vessels in the Pacific, they never afterwards ventured to shew themselves, but left Lord Cochrane undisputed master of the coast.

The cutting out of the *Esmeralda*, remote though it was from English preoccupations, became one of the legends of Cochrane's life. Only H.M.S. *Hyperion* maintained a studied neutrality, tinged with a certain personal hostility towards Cochrane. When one of the *Hyperion's* midshipmen so far forgot himself as to cheer on the attacking force during the fight on the *Esmeralda's* deck, Captain Searle of the English frigate threatened to have him put under arrest if there was any further unseemly enthusiasm of this kind. As a matter of prudence, Searle's threat may have been well-judged. The defenders of Callao could not believe that the *Esmeralda* had been captured without the connivance of one or both of the neutral frigates. On the morning after the incident, the market-boat of the *Macedonian* went ashore as usual for provisions. As soon as it landed, a furious mob fell upon the boat crew and lynched them forthwith.[20]

San Martin wrote to Cochrane himself and to the Minister of Marine, praising the capture of the *Esmeralda*. But San Martin was careful not to allow credit for the liberation of Peru to be given to anyone but himself. "This glory was reserved for the Liberating Army," he insisted. While San Martin remained idle, Cochrane intensified his blockade, until the Spaniards at Callao sensed that their stronghold had become their prison. Within a month of the *Esmeralda* incident, 650 Spanish troops followed by forty of their officers, deserted to the Chilean cause. Three months later, San Martin had still done nothing to effect the capture of Lima. Cochrane volunteered to make the attack himself, in March 1821, with half of the troops at San Martin's disposal. The offer was rejected by San Martin, whose purpose in avoiding battle now seemed to Cochrane to suggest a careful preservation of his army for the internal power struggle which must follow independence.[21]

> It now became evident to me that the army had been kept inert for the purpose of preserving it entire to further the ambitious views of the General, and that, with the whole force now at Lima, the inhabitants were completely at the mercy of their pretended liberator, but in reality their conqueror.[22]

Having persuaded San Martin to give him 600 troops, out of 4200, Cochrane embarked on coastal raids between Callao and Arica. Isolated by land and sea, Lima surrendered after three months of this harassment, on 6 July. Peruvian independence was declared on 28 July.

In addition to his other preoccupations, Cochrane also had to contend with a bitter dispute over the captured *Esmeralda* which had been put under the command of the troublesome Captain Guise. When the ship was incorporated into the Chilean fleet, her name was changed to the *Valdivia*, to commemorate the victory of the previous year. Unfortunately, Valdivia itself was the name of one of the Spanish conquerors of Chile, which led the officers to protest to Captain Guise in a strongly worded petition over the renaming of their ship. San Martin had been principally responsible for the choice of name but Cochrane was the target of their criticism. They had had no part in the victory at Valdivia and saw no reason why their ship should commemorate Cochrane's glory.

Cochrane ordered a court-martial on the rebellious officers of the new *Valdivia*, who were convicted and dismissed the service. As he was preparing to attack Callao, Cochrane sent orders to Guise to take part in the assault. Guise, indignant at the dismissal of his officers, replied by resigning his command. He was followed by Captain Spry, who resigned the captaincy of the *Galvarino* in sympathy. Cochrane court-martialled Spry, who was convicted and dismissed from his command. Both Guise and Spry went indignantly to San Martin and complained of Cochrane. San Martin consoled Spry by making him his naval adjutant. He sent Guise to the *O'Higgins* to patch up an agreement with Cochrane, but after several argumentative interviews nothing was accomplished. Guise sat out the rest of the campaign at San Martin's headquarters. The lesson drawn from the incident, by all but Cochrane's most determined admirers, was that he showed himself less adept as a general commander than as the piratical captain of a single vessel. Guise and Spry were not the easiest of men to deal with but nor, in many respects, was Cochrane himself.[23]

During the aftermath of the courts-martial, before the fall of Lima, the British frigate H.M.S. *Andromache* dropped anchor off Callao. On board her was Kitty, who had come to see Cochrane before leaving South America for England. In its own way, her life had been quite eventful during their separation. She had been busy at Valparaiso "where she diligently employed herself in promoting objects essential to the welfare of the squadron". Later she had gone to live in a country house at Quillota. She also survived two attempts at assassination.[24]

The first of these occurred at Quillota, where a Spanish agent, assuming that Kitty would know of any secret plans made by her husband, broke into the house and made his way to her room. He confronted her with "instant death if she would not divulge the secret orders". Apparently, the only document of the least significance was a paper lying on the table in the room. She snatched this up at once and there followed a determined struggle with the intruder for posses- sion of it. The man was armed with a stiletto but though he managed to use it once, she suffered only a single superficial cut before the noise attracted the servants and the man was overpowered. The republican régime condemned him to death "without the last offices of the Catholic religion".[25]

On the night preceding the execution, she was woken by a loud wailing outside her window. This dirge had been set up by the wife of the condemned man who sought "her Ladyship's intercession" to allow her husband confession and absolution before his death. Kitty, personally, was prepared to forgive the man entirely and on the next morning she found herself in the bizarre situation of pleading for the life of her would-be murderer, while the Chilean authorities remained in favour of despatching him. After some argument they agreed reluctantly that the death sentence should be commuted to one of perpetual banishment.[26]

The seriousness of the second attempt on her life might be doubted, certainly so far as any political motive was concerned. In October 1820, after Cochrane and San Martin had left for the campaign in Peru, she undertook a journey across the Andes to Mendoza, carrying confidential despatches with her. Even in October, some of the passes were already blocked by snow. On 12 October, she and her atten- dants arrived at the Ponte del Inca, 15,000 feet up, to find that further progress was impossible until the snow was cleared. She remained at a *casucha*, built as an emergency shelter, where the only bed was a length of dried bullock's hide. Cochrane spoke proudly of her as having endured "a degree of suffering which few ladies would be willing to encounter". It was while riding up a narrow path with a vertiginous drop on one side, just beyond the *casucha*, that Kitty was confronted by a soldier of the Spanish force who "disputed the path with her" in such a manner as to suggest that he was about to throw her over the edge. Happily, there was a Chilean soldier with the party, Pedro Flores, who galloped forward and struck the attacker "a vio- lent blow across the face", which drove him into headlong retreat. Cochrane swore it had been "another premeditated attempt on Lady Cochrane's life", but there is at least some doubt of that.[27]

When Kitty arrived off Callao, Lima had still not fallen, though the

Spanish troops had deposed the Viceroy of Peru, Pezuela, and replaced him with one of their own generals. Pezuela asked San Martin
for a passport, so that he might return to Europe. He was refused.
But Kitty took up the cause of the Vicereine, Donna Angela, and
arranged a passage for her on board H.M.S. *Andromache*. Captain
Sheriff of the *Andromache*, founder of the Valparaiso Cricket Club,
invited Cochrane on board to meet the wife of his late adversary.
Donna Angela was won over by him, announcing that, "His lordship
was a polite *rational* being, and not the *ferocious brute* she had been
taught to consider him." This forthright judgement, as Cochrane
observed, "caused no small merriment" among the other guests of
the *Andromache*.[28]

William Miller, now promoted to Lieutenant-Colonel, was impressed by the reaction of the Chilean troops to Kitty's beauty
and spirited behaviour. He was inspecting his men in the town
square of Huacho when Kitty arrived, having come ashore from the
*O'Higgins*.

> The sudden appearance of youth and beauty, on a fiery horse,
> managed with skill and elegance, absolutely electrified the men,
> who had never before seen an English lady: *que hermosa! que
> graciosa! que linda! que guapa! que airosa! es un angel del cielo!*
> were exclamations that escaped from one end of the line to the
> other.

Miller, with a happy inspiration, turned to his men and said
grandly, "This is our *generala*."

> Her ladyship turned her sparkling eyes towards the line, and
> bowed graciously. The troops could no longer confine their
> expressions of admiration to half-suppressed interjections; loud
> *vivas* burst from officers as well as men. Lady Cochrane smiled
> her acknowledgements and cantered off the ground with the
> grace of a fairy [29]

While Cochrane was blockading Callao, Kitty had taken her son on
an excursion into the interior, choosing an area which was supposedly
clear of the Spanish. During a visit to the Marchioness de la Pracer at
Quilca, she was warned that the Spaniards were making for the town
with the object of seizing her and the child as hostages. The party left
at once, Kitty on horseback and the child in a litter. By the following
day they had come to a swollen river whose only bridge was a cane

rope construction, four strips of hide with sticks fastened across forming the footway and two more strips of hide acting as handrails. There was no question of taking horses across, indeed even an in-expert foot passenger would start the bridge vibrating so alarmingly that it was impossible to remain upright. But then the bugles of the pursuers were heard. Kitty snatched up the child and tried to cross the bridge. By the time that she reached the centre, the ramshackle structure was swaying too violently for her to keep a footing. She lay down, clutching the child to her, while the decking rippled and swung above the swirling water. It was the same Pedro Flores, to whom she owed her safety at the Ponte del Inca, who urged her to lie quite still and, when the bridge was motionless once more, came forward on his hands and knees, distributing his weight as widely as possible because the ropes were only intended to bear the weight of one person at a time, and helped Kitty and the child across.[30]

Having learnt the lesson of cane-rope bridges, Kitty came safely down to the coast and joined the *O'Higgins* once more. Cochrane had just received intelligence that a ship loaded with the contents of the treasury at Callao was about to attempt an escape. The fastest boat of the Spanish squadron had been chosen and Cochrane knew that, if once she got clear, there would be no chance of overtaking her. Even with Kitty on board he had no alternative but to sail under the guns of Callao and cripple the proposed "treasure vessel".

As the drums beat to quarters and the *O'Higgins* sailed in, Kitty remained on deck. She was standing close to one of the ship's guns, which evidently made the gunner hesitate as to whether he ought to fire the piece so close to a delicate looking young lady. Conversation was impossible in the din of battle, but Kitty decided the matter by seizing the man's arm and directing the burning match to fire the gun. As the explosion deafened her and the iron cannon recoiled, rolling back on its wooden truck, the emotional effort took its toll and she fainted with becoming femininity. But the gesture of firing the gun grew into a legend. When she appeared at the end of the action, the men in the rigging as well as those on the deck sang their national anthem in her honour.[31]

It was Kitty's last experience of the Chilean war. She returned to England, to the society of other young women for whom the limits of emotional excitement were generally represented by the quadrille or the vicarious ordeals of Amy Robsart in the newly published *Kenilworth*.

For Cochrane and Kitty, the triumph of Valdiva and the cutting out of the *Esmeralda* were seen in the perspective of the news which reached them at Lima as it surrendered to the Chilean force. Ever since the failure of Colonel Charles's mission, they had been prepared for it, but its announcement put an end forever to their brave dream of a grand, renascent South America. On 5 May 1821, in his island exile at St Helena, the scourge of Europe whose conquests extended from Biscay to Moscow, from the Baltic to the Nile, had died at the age of fifty-two.

With Napoleon, much of Cochrane's remaining enthusiasm for the Chilean war died too. Victory over Spain was virtually achieved. Victory over San Martin and the men of political ambition was another struggle in which there could hardly be any part for him. After Callao and Lima, little remained but the duty of seeing his squadron properly paid for its services.

He entered Lima on 17 July, and was received as a hero by the citizens. Yet he was about to make the discovery, which he could well have predicted by this time, that men who lead "wars of liberation" frequently harbour schemes no less tyrannical than those whom they propose to overthrow. So it was with San Martin. His army seized Lima, ignoring the Spanish forts at Callao and the fugitive Spanish army which fled inland, looting and murdering as it went. Instead of continuing the fight, San Martin announced that, with his troops to enforce the claim, he had now assumed power as supreme ruler of an independent Peru.

Cochrane regarded this as an act of treachery to Chile and to O'Higgins, as well as a betrayal of the Peruvian struggle for true independence. San Martin responded by ordering him to hand over the Chilean squadron to the new "government". Cochrane refused. On 4 August, there was a fierce argument in the royal palace at Lima, San Martin insisting that he would "buy" the squadron for the amount of pay owing to the officers and men. If this offer was refused, they would remain unpaid. The argument continued until San Martin turned to Cochrane and his secretary, rubbing his hands agitatedly, and said, "I am Protector of Peru."

"Then," said Cochrane, "it now becomes me as the senior officer of Chile, and consequently the representative of the nation, to request the fulfilment of all the promises made to Chile, and the squadron, but first, and principally, the squadron."

San Martin came forward and snapped his fingers in Cochrane's face.

"Chile! Chile! I will never pay a single real to Chile! And as to the squadron you may take it where you please, and go when you choose: a couple of schooners are quite enough for me."

Then, more agitated still, San Martin paced up and down the room, turned and caught Cochrane's hand, saying, "Forget, my lord, what is past!"

"I will when I can," Cochrane replied coldly. He turned to go but San Martin caught him at the top of the staircase, eagerly suggesting that Cochrane had everything to gain from renouncing Chile and that he would be given a supreme command under the new "government" of Peru. Cochrane noted that "a proposition so dishonourable was declined". He left the palace with San Martin's voice ringing petulantly down the staircase.

"I will neither give the seamen their arrears of pay nor the gratuity I have promised."[32]

If San Martin mistook Cochrane's allegiance to honour as a weakness of character in the hard world of practical politics, he was soon to discover the extent of his error. Hostile but ineffective letters passed between the royal palace ashore and the O'Higgins, anchored off Callao. Cochrane still regarded himself as responsible to the Chilean government for his squadron but San Martin's refusal to pay its wages had brought most of the ships' companies to the point of mutiny or desertion. Happily, Cochrane discovered that San Martin's yacht, the Sacramento, accompanied by a merchant vessel, had prepared to sail from Callao to Ancon. On board was the fortune, or rather loot, which the "liberator" had acquired in the course of his campaign. The seas were now safe for such official cargoes, thanks to Cochrane's presence.

The men of the squadron watched angrily as the two ships sailed north to Ancon, well clear of the war zone and of any marauding parties of Spaniards. A suggestion was murmured among the crews. "My own views coincided with theirs," Cochrane wrote as the O'Higgins and her consorts set sail and left Callao in the wake of San Martin's treasure.

To a commander who had survived the Gamo and the Basque Roads, not to mention Valdivia and the Esmeralda, it was an absurdly simple exercise to overtake the Sacramento and her companion, board them at Ancon, and remove everything that could not be proved to belong to individual owners. The Sacramento represented a "yacht-load of silver", as well as seven sacks of uncoined gold. Cochrane issued a proclamation, inviting the owners of looted property to retrieve it. Of the rest, he gave 40,000 dollars to the commissary of the army and retained 285,000 dollars as one year's pay for the squadron. There was one exception, however, since he refused to take any of the money for himself.

San Martin was both furious and powerless to do anything about the outrage. Trying to turn the event to his own advantage, he first authorised Cochrane to "employ the money" as he thought proper, since he could hardly prevent this, and then sent "Peruvian" officers to take over the ships, on the grounds that Peru had paid the wages. Unable to enforce this change of command, though supported by Captain Spry, and growing nervous over the repercussions of his Peruvian independence, San Martin ordered Cochrane to return to Valparaiso. Cochrane ignored the command and instead sailed north to Mexico, in search of the two remaining Spanish frigates, the *Venganza* and the *Prueba*, which were reported to have escaped to a Spanish-held port there. On 29 January 1822, he anchored off Acapulco without sighting them, but three days later an incoming merchant vessel reported the two frigates as being far to the south. Having not the least doubt that his ship would be more than a match for them, Cochrane put about and went in search of them. His discovery of the two frigates was an anti-climax. They were both sheltering in the Guayaquil river, to avoid being attacked by the *O'Higgins* or her consorts. But shortly before Cochrane's arrival, the Spanish commander had recognised the hopelessness of trying to carry on the fight and had negotiated a surrender with the representatives of San Martin.[33]

Personally, Cochrane was angry that San Martin should have forestalled his capture of the *Venganza* and the *Prueba* in this manner. As a commander, he was bitter over the way in which his squadron had been cheated by San Martin and his cronies. But he was, more than anything, alarmed by the sight of Spanish tyranny being replaced by an equally abhorrent form of oppression, masquerading as an army of "liberation". If San Martin could consolidate his position in Lima, he would be well placed to strike against Chile itself and to overthrow the young republic of O'Higgins in the cause of his own dictatorial ambitions.

Accordingly, Cochrane returned to Valparaiso, anchoring off the port on 3 June 1822. He was granted the inevitable hero's welcome and medals were struck in his honour. In exchange, he brought only dire warnings of San Martin's betrayal of the cause. Happily, San

Martin was now opposed by the remaining Spanish troops in Peru and by growing popular opposition in Lima. His army proved inadequate to deal with both and, though Simon Bolivar assisted him in a campaign against the Spanish, San Martin was obliged to abdicate and withdraw to Chile as a matter of personal security. On his arrival in Santiago, Cochrane demanded that he should be court-martialled and offered to give evidence at any such trial. The offer was refused and he was forbidden to publish any correspondence he had entered into on the subject of San Martin, for fear of the bad impression it might make on the British cabinet, with whom Chilean representatives were then in negotiation.

By this time, even the reputation of O'Higgins had suffered as a consequence of the corruption among his subordinates. In November, Cochrane managed to secure payment of the arrears due to the men of his squadron, while in the same month the town of Valparaiso was almost destroyed by an earthquake. Most of the ship's companies had no wish to serve longer, the major port had gone, and there seemed little more left for the Chilean navy to do. Indeed, Cochrane judged that from the financial neglect of the navy, only the newest ship, the *Independencia* was still seaworthy.

In December 1822, he received a private despatch from Ramon Freire, the governor of Concepcion, for whose integrity he had a great admiration. Freire denounced the "corrupted administration" which ruled the country, and which had brought Chile to "a state of greater degradation" than it had known under the power of Spain. He invited Cochrane to assist him in staging a coup d'état against the O'Higgins régime. Though Cochrane sympathised with Freire's attitude, notably in his disgust at the power enjoyed by San Martin, he felt it wrong that a foreigner should take a leading part in a domestic struggle of this kind. Early in 1823, the coup d'état was successful, O'Higgins was sent into exile, in the wake of San Martin who had already fled across the Andes on his way to find asylum in Europe. But Cochrane played no part in the affairs of the new régime. At the end of 1822, he had received the first invitation from the Imperial Court at Rio de Janeiro to assume the command of the Brazilian navy in the struggle for independence from Portugal. He found it infinitely preferable to the weeks and months of haggling which now characterised his command of the Chilean fleet.[34]

On 18 January 1823, having resigned his command in Chile, Cochrane set sail with some of his officers who were to accompany him in the new adventure, setting out for the return journey round

Cape Horn in a chartered brig. Now that it was no longer needed against the Spanish, the steamer *Rising Star* had arrived safely in Valparaiso from London. Cochrane greatly regretted that he was not allowed to take it with him in lieu of the money he was owed by the Chilean government.

His Chilean debts were to sour his relationship with the new republic for the rest of his life. Whatever the accurate figures may have been, Cochrane's mood was not improved when he discovered that San Martin had been awarded 500,000 dollars and a pension of 20,000 dollars. 120,000 dollars was awarded to Cochrane for the capture of the *Esmeralda* but he swore that the bill for this, on the Peruvian government, was dishonoured at once. He was awarded 67,000 dollars after the capture of Valdivia, but the sum was never paid. He claimed that his situation was even worse than that, since he was later sued by owners of neutral vessels which he had seized during the blockade. He was obliged to sell his house in Regent's Park, which he had bought after the war, and the "cost" of his service to Chile was, by his own reckoning, £25,000. In 1845, the Chilean government awarded him £6000 in settlement of such sums as might still be outstanding. They had first deducted from his claim the costs and damages cited by neutral victims of his blockade. It was useless for Cochrane to protest that these "victims" had been trading under false papers and were thus liable to seizure. Nor were the Chileans impressed by his allegations that they were cheating him in order to appease the British business community at Valparaiso. So, as he complained to the world, he had lost £25,000 and gained £6000. His service to the cause of Chilean independence had been absolutely unrewarded. Indeed, it had "cost me £19,000 out of my own pocket!"[35]

But whatever his quarrels with the governments of the newly independent states, Cochrane's sympathy with their people was never in doubt. Before he left the Pacific for the last time, he addressed the people in terms which warned them against tyrants of every description, and he called them "Chilenos – My Fellow Countrymen!"

You know that independence is purchased at the point of the bayonet. Know also that liberty is founded on good faith, and on the laws of honour, and that those who infringe upon these, are your only enemies, amongst whom you will never find

COCHRANE.[36]

# 8

# Under Two Flags

By the beginning of 1823, the extent of Brazil's independence from Portugal was questionable. The origin of separate government lay in Napoleon's invasion of Portugal in 1808, when the future John VI had decided to take refuge in his great South American colony. In consequence, Brazil began to enjoy a degree of political freedom which was more commonly associated with a European imperial state than with any of its colonial possessions. By the removal of restrictions on trade and by the participation of Brazilians in government, the ties with Portugal were gradually loosened.

At the time of his departure for South America, Dom John had been regent of Portugal and had left behind a council of regency to govern the country in his absence. In 1816, while still in Rio de Janeiro, he succeeded to the throne of Portugal in his own right. Despite this, he remained in South America for a further five years, creating his son Dom Pedro regent of Brazil when he returned at length to Lisbon.

In both countries, the political future seemed unpromising. Portugal had been the scene of insurrection by reformers, whose movement was put down by the council of regency with British military assistance. Brazil was no less divided between supporters of independence and the adherents of the "Portuguese faction" who opposed it. As in Lisbon, so in Rio de Janeiro there were men who feared the loss of economic and political power which independence would bring. More to the point, the northern provinces of Brazil, including the major territories of Bahia, Maranham, and Parà, remained firmly in the hands of Portuguese troops supported by a Portuguese fleet.

So long as John VI ruled in Rio de Janeiro he could, in theory, command the allegiance of all factions and all forces. But with his return to Lisbon, there was every sign that the Cortes of Portugal would attempt to reduce Brazil to her former colonial status. On 1 December 1822, while Cochrane waited in idleness and with increasing

frustration off Valparaiso, Dom Pedro had yielded to popular pressure. Discarding his allegiance to his father, he put himself at the
head of the independence movement and was proclaimed Emperor of
Brazil.

In Brazil, as in Chile, it was easy enough to establish an autono-
mous region, in this case in the south and round Rio de Janeiro. But
the same problem of a hostile imperial army, supported and supplied
by its European fleet, stood between the new state and its final freedom. In the north of Brazil it was not merely a few fortified points,
like Valdivia or Callao, which held out against the new rulers. The
greater part of these provinces remained subject to colonial government so long as the Portuguese fleet controlled the sea routes. And so
long as that remained the case, Dom Pedro's southern empire and his
court at Rio de Janeiro would remain under the shadow of a Portuguese invasion.

If the struggle were to be decided in favour of the new Brazilian
empire, victory at sea was imperative. The Brazilian chargé d'affaires
in London was instructed to recruit officers and seamen to serve as
mercenaries in the new imperial navy. As admiral, there could only
be one choice. As early as November 1822, Cochrane received his first
invitation from Antonio Correa, Brazilian consul at Buenos Aires,
who was deputed to make the approach. While he hesitated and
balanced the claims of Brazil against certain other calls on his
allegiance, he received a more urgent appeal from Correa.

Venez, milord, l'honneur vous invite – la gloire vous appelle.
Venez – donner à nos armes navales cet ordre merveilleux et
discipline incomparable de puissante Albion.[1]

Antonio Correa was a confidant of Dom Pedro and evidently wrote
at his master's dictation. Cochrane, however, replied coolly at first,
since his immediate plans had been directed to serving a cause which
appealed more strongly to him than that of Brazil.

The war in the Pacific having been happily terminated by the
total destruction of the Spanish naval force, I am, of course,
free for the crusade of liberty in any other quarter of the
globe.
    I confess, however, that I had not hitherto directed my atten-
tion to the Brazils; considering that the struggle for the liberties
of Greece – the most oppressed of modern states – afforded the
fairest opportunity for enterprise and exertion.[2]

The freedom of Greece, the vision of democracy and the glory of the Hellenic dream, appealed to the imagination of liberal England. With the outbreak of open rebellion against Turkish rule in 1821, Burdett, Hobhouse, and Byron were among the most famous who warmed to the crusade for liberating from Turkish slavery the land of Plato and Demosthenes. To Cochrane, the challenge was simple and irresistible. None the less, he promised Antonio Correa that, since he would be rounding the Horn anyway, he would meet him on neutral ground, in Buenos Aires. Geographically, at least, Brazil was on the way from Valparaiso to Athens. But his promise was coupled with a warning. He knew little about the new government of Dom Pedro, and he had no intention of supporting it unconditionally. He would hold himself free to decline the command, "should the Government . . . differ so widely in its nature from those which I have been in the habit of supporting, as to render the proposed situation repugnant to my principles".[3]

No such difference appeared. The Brazilian government not only resembled others in its democratic aspirations but also in its reluctance to pay Cochrane and his men for services rendered, at least on the scale which the mercenary admiral judged proper. Undeterred by his experience of this in Chile, he arrived in Rio de Janeiro on 13 March 1823 and accepted the command of the Imperial fleet. He had been promised the same pay as in the service of Chile, 8000 dollars a year. When there was some doubt raised over this, he informed the Minister of Marine that "without condescending to chaffer on such a subject", he would seek redress from the Prime Minister and the Emperor himself. The Minister of Marine begged him to do no such thing, and the difficulty vanished, for the time being.[4]

Dom Pedro himself escorted his new admiral on a tour of inspection of the fleet. There were eight ships, though two of them were not in a state to put to sea for the time being and two others were only suitable as fire-ships. Of the remaining four, the *Maria de Gloria* was a smart looking clipper which on closer inspection proved to have been built of unseasoned timber and was "little calculated to do substantial service". But two ships, the 74-gun *Pedro Primiero* and the frigate *Piranga*, were well-built and quite sufficient for Cochrane's purposes. Ships like the *Maria de Gloria* were manned by "the refuse of the merchant service", even the *Piranga* and the *Pedro Primiero*, his flagship, had too many untrained recruits. Against him, the Portuguese had a battleship, five frigates, five corvettes, a brig, and a schooner with some 2000 miles of friendly coastline on which they might depend. But much of Cochrane's naval life had been spent in showing just how much he could do with a pair of reliable ships in a situation of this kind.[5]

Some 600 miles north of Rio de Janeiro, the first of the areas under Portuguese control was the sea port and province of Bahia. Cochrane put to sea on 3 April, the *Pedro Primiero* having 160 English and American seamen in her crew. He was less than enthusiastic about some of the other members who now appeared to be the "vagabondage" of Rio de Janeiro, nor was there any way of predicting the behaviour in battle of his 130 black marines, "just emancipated from slavery".[6]

The first encounter with the Portuguese battle squadron was a humiliation which might have become a disaster for him. The *Pedro Primiero* sailed into action, breaking through the Portuguese line and cutting off the four rearmost ships from the rest. Cochrane signalled the three ships of his squadron, the *Piranga*, the *Maria de Gloria*, and the *Liberal*, to join him in attacking and capturing the four separated ships. To his great anger, not one of them obeyed the order, keeping carefully clear of the skirmish. By now, the *Pedro Primiero* was engaging the enemy alone but Cochrane soon realised that something was badly amiss. The salvoes from his gun-deck were ill-directed and far fewer than they should have been. One of his English officers, Captain Grenfell, went below and discovered two Portuguese members of the crew withholding powder from the gunners and warning off the powder-boys from running their errands. Grenfell dragged the two miscreants on deck but by then the situation was hopeless. The *Pedro Primiero* might have fought alone against the enemy fleet with the sort of crew Cochrane had commanded on the *Speedy* or the *Imperieuse* but under the present circumstances he was compelled to break off the action.[7]

On 5 May, while still at sea, Cochrane wrote a long letter of complaint to the Prime Minister, Andrada, warning him that little would be accomplished with the fleet in its present state. Later in the same month, having been left to his own devices by the Brazilian government, he informed the Minister of Marine that he was stripping all the other ships of his squadron of most of their European and American officers and seamen in order to transfer them to the *Pedro Primiero*. Though the rest of his little fleet would still be in attendance, the flagship alone was to be relied upon when he sailed into battle against the Portuguese.[8]

By the beginning of June, Cochrane was ready for the attack upon Bahia itself. He prepared his two fire-ships ostentatiously and was gratified to hear that news of the preparation had caused "consternation" among the Portuguese authorities. Their admiral, Cochrane was told, was "in nightly expectation of a repetition of the scene in Basque Roads". During the first week of June, the Portuguese went through the motions of threatening an attack on Cochrane and his fire-ships before he could move against the port of Bahia itself. On the night of 12 June, Cochrane decided to make a close reconnaissance of Bahia with the *Pedro Primiero*, while the Portuguese commanders and officials were at a public ball. He also intended to destroy such ships as came within his reach in the deep bay and estuary which formed the anchorage.

The night that was chosen was particularly dark and the *Pedro Primiero* sailed between the outer vessels, mapping the position of the Portuguese fleet. When challenged, Cochrane replied that she was an English merchant ship. To the discomfort of all on board, however, the wind then dropped and the sails went slack. Their ship was suddenly becalmed, nine miles from the open sea, under the guns of the shore-batteries and of the enemy fleet. The attack which Cochrane had planned was out of the question. He could do nothing but let the flagship drift out with the ebb tide, keeping her off the shoals on either side of the channel by using the stream-anchor to drag her towards deep water.

But the reconnaissance had been invaluable for the fire-ship attack and for its effect on the Portuguese. When it was discovered that the mysterious ship, threading its way through the anchored vessels, had been the *Pedro Primiero*, the admiral at Bahia insisted on evacuation. If Cochrane could enter the harbour again, with fire-ships or explosion vessels, the result in the confined anchorage would be a catastrophe for the Portuguese campaign in Brazil. Apart from this, Cochrane's blockade had virtually cut off all supplies by sea. At the end of June, General Ignacio Madeira issued a proclamation to the inhabitants, informing them that he and his men would evacuate Bahia, proceeding with the fleet to the northern province and city of Maranham. Room would be found on the transports for Portuguese families who wished to accompany them.[9]

Nothing short of panic would have persuaded Madeira to put to sea, where the *Pedro Primiero* waited like a cat for so many mice. Cochrane played on the panic by sending letters to the Bahia junta, warning them, "for the sake of humanity" to surrender rather than attempt the escape. The letters referred to the heart-rending prospect of the "destruction of passengers" on the transports, "for in the obscurity of night it is impossible to discriminate ships in which they may be embarked". The reference to night attacks effectively revived the horror of fire-ships and explosion vessels, far out at sea and beyond hope of rescue.

On 2 July, demoralised even before it began, the evacuation fleet put to sea, the Portuguese battle squadron followed by armed transports with the troops on board and merchant vessels carrying the families. It was a huge and unwieldy armada of thirteen warships and between sixty and seventy transports. Cochrane's main disadvantage was that even if he captured all the transports he would not have the men to form prize crews. His remedy for this, in the case of troopships, was to order that the masts were to be cut away by boarding parties so that the vessels would have no means of escape from the waters off Bahia. Other transports were to have their water casks broken open, leaving them no alternative but to sail back to Bahia.

No sooner was the great armada clear of port than Cochrane fell upon it. One after another, the transports at the rear of the fleet were boarded. Main and mizen masts were cut down, which left the captains no option but to sail before the wind. The wind, as Cochrane had calculated, would take them inevitably back to Bahia, which was soon to be in Brazilian hands. Once the first day's batch of transports had been rounded up, the squadron set off in pursuit of the Portuguese again, easily overtaking them.

Cochrane spent 3 July attacking the warships with the *Pedro Primiero*, while the rest of his squadron picked off the troopships and merchantmen, one by one. Cochrane's object was to goad the Portuguese battleships and frigates into turning on the *Pedro Primiero* and attempting to hem her in. Then with a virtuoso display of seamanship, he would outmanoeuvre and outdistance them, drawing them into a futile pursuit. By sunset, the straggling line of troopships was getting thinner as the regiments of the Portuguese army were despatched to captivity with hardly a shot fired. On the next day, the *Gran Parà* and other transports were seized, this action alone resulting in the capture of a division of several thousand troops. With Maranham still 1000 miles to the north, Madeira had already lost half his army. In confirmation of the news, Cochrane sent the colours of the captured regiments to the Minister of Marine at Rio de Janeiro.

As the pursuit moved northward towards the equator, the weather became hazy and, for a time, all contact with the Portuguese was lost. Cochrane found them again and took the *Pedro Primiero* in to resume the attack on the battle squadron. At 3 a.m. on 16 July, in the course of a night attack, the mainsail of the flagship split in two and the action was broken off. It was as well for Cochrane that the accident occurred during darkness, since the sight of the *Pedro Primiero* temporarily disabled would have been irresistible for the Portuguese fleet.[10]

Since the flagship was now alone, Cochrane gave up the chase and the necessary repairs were carried out. The Portuguese ships, to the relief of their commanders, were left to make their way sedately to Maranham. If they believed that this was a respite shown them, they were about to fall victims to one of Cochrane's more ingenious deceptions. Whatever the ordeal of the convoy from Bahia, they counted at least on finding safety in Maranham, the securest of their bases. It cannot have crossed their minds that this particular haven would be one of the least safe landfalls of the entire continent by the time that they reached it.

With the *Pedro Primiero* under full sail once more, Cochrane skirted round the Portuguese ships, keeping well out of sight. His enemy moved at the speed of their slowest ships, while his own warship made straight for the river and port of Maranham. From the despatches he had seized on board the captured troopships, he had a good idea of what the commandant and junta of Maranham were expecting. They knew of the dramatic evacuation of Bahia and were awaiting the reinforcements which the Bahia garrison represented.

Hoisting Portuguese colours, the *Pedro Primiero* entered the Maranham river on 26 July. Don Agostinho Antonia de Faria, commandant of the town, had no reason to doubt that this was the first of his reinforcements. He sent out a brig with despatches and congratulations. The captain of the brig stepped on to the deck of the flagship and was astonished to find himself surrounded by European and American seamen in the service of the rebel Emperor. Generously, Cochrane offered to release him at once provided that he carried a sealed message to the commandant and the junta. The captain agreed and the messages which Cochrane had accordingly prepared were delivered at once.

The commandant was aghast to learn that the armada approaching Maranham was not Portuguese at all. The Portuguese convoy had been overtaken and destroyed, Cochrane sent him the proof of it. The *Pedro Primiero* was the first and fastest ship of a great Brazilian invading force. The transports of that force were filled with troops of the most bloodthirsty kind.

> I am anxious not to let loose the Imperial troops of Bahia upon Maranham, exasperated as they are at the injuries and cruelties exercised towards themselves and their countrymen, as well as by the plunder of the people and churches of Bahia.

Though there was not a soldier on board, Cochrane gave the commandant to understand that the *Pedro Primiero* was crammed below decks with an advance guard of wild-eyed fanatics, eager to storm ashore at the first provocation and take a bloody revenge upon the Portuguese and their sympathisers. Once the mythical Brazilian invading force arrived, Cochrane would be powerless to prevent scenes of the most horrifying vengeance. Now was the time when the commandant and his men might take advantage of the magnanimity with which he offered them terms of capitulation.

Even if the trick failed, it was well worth trying. Yet Cochrane must have been pleasantly astonished by the speed with which Antonia de Faria grasped at the offer of surrender by negotiation. Bahia had fallen, the evacuation fleet had been savaged, and the *Pedro Primiero*'s presence was apparent proof of Brazilian power. On 27 July, the local junta, accompanied by the bishop, filed aboard the flagship to swear allegiance to the new Emperor. Captain Grenfell took the marines ashore to relieve the Portuguese of their fortifications, to haul down the colours, and to raise the new flag of Brazil.

The hoax was not quite over. Though Maranham and its defences were now in his hands, Cochrane was uneasy as to the reaction of the Portuguese troops, far outnumbering his own men, when their country's battle squadron and transports appeared on the horizon. As a final gesture of magnanimity, he therefore allowed all his captives to board merchant vessels and sail home to freedom in Portugal. Somewhere far out to sea, and oblivious of one another's presence, the two halves of the Portuguese army passed one another, going in opposite directions.

When the battered survivors of the Portuguese evacuation fleet found Maranham firmly in Cochrane's hands, they turned away. But by adding the northern province of Parà to the spoils, Cochrane also denied them refuge there. Parà, bordering Maranham, contained the first 500 miles or so of the Amazon river inland from the sea. But the settlements of this vast territory covered only a coastal strip. Cochrane sent Captain Grenfell with the captured brig *Maranham* to practise the same deception which had just been successful in his case. Though the junta at Parà held out a little longer, they had news of the fall of Bahia and Maranham, and had not the least doubt that Parà must be the objective of any expeditionary force which was on foot. By 12 August, Grenfell was able to report that Parà had followed Maranham in acknowledging the sovereignty of the Emperor.[11]

Despite his misgivings over the seaworthiness of some of his ships and the loyalty of their crews, it had taken Cochrane just three months since his arrival at Rio de Janeiro to win for Brazil the great territories of the northern provinces. He returned to the capital, and to the usual triumphal reception, followed by the no less usual haggling over his pay. He was created First Admiral of the Brazils and Marquess of Maranham. He received the thanks of the Emperor, the ministry, and the assembly. More important still, when he reached Rio de Janeiro on 9 November, he found Kitty waiting for him. She had left England, assuming that he would still be at Valparaiso, but when her ship had called at the Brazilian capital she learnt for the first time that he was now in the service of the Emperor.

In Cochrane's case, after the spectacular events of the first three months, the remainder of that service was hardly congenial. On his return from Maranham, he quickly discovered that he had made enemies of the so-called "Portuguese" faction in Brazilian society. During his absence, that faction had brought about the dismissal of the Andrada government, the dissolution of the legislative assembly, and had almost reduced the capital to a state of martial law. Cochrane made matters worse for himself by advising the Emperor to adopt "the English constitution, in its most perfect practical form", and to find posts abroad for "those Portuguese individuals of whom the Brazilians are jealous". Not surprisingly, the individuals and their supporters resented this interference in their lives by a liberal-minded foreigner with only a few months' experience of the country. Their resentment took a practical form when the prickly question of prizes and prize money had, yet again, to be decided.[12]

Cochrane had "requested an order for the speedy adjudication of the prize property surrendered at Maranham", and he estimated the flagship's share of this at £121,463. The value of enemy property seized by the entire squadron he put at two million dollars. But the Portuguese faction held sway in the Admiralty court, so that the Tribunal of Prizes, commenting on Cochrane's claim, blandly announced that it was "not aware that hostilities existed between Brazil and Portugal".[13]

More to the point, every effort was made by Portuguese sympathisers in Brazil to avoid having their own property condemned as the spoils of war. In a situation where allegiances were uncertain and sympathies divided, Cochrane was extraordinarily naïve in believing that his claim was likely to be conceded. In the end, the squadron was awarded about one-fifth of the total amount, which led him to complain bitterly over the manner in which he had been cheated by the ministers of the new empire. Even more outrageous, in Cochrane's view, was the treatment of Captain Grenfell who had negotiated the surrender of Parà. One of the prizes at the port was a newly-launched frigate, which was hastily christened the *Imperatrice* and sailed by Grenfell to the capital. On arrival it was boarded and searched, all the prizes which had been promised to Grenfell by the Emperor were seized for the treasury, and he himself was put on trial for not carrying out the government's orders properly at Parà. Though Grenfell was acquitted and released, Cochrane's disillusionment with Brazil had grown apace.[14]

Sometimes the attempts made against him were sinister and sometimes farcical, but his unfailing supporter throughout most of these vicissitudes was the Emperor himself. By the beginning of June 1824, however, it was farce which characterised the proceedings most vividly.

Late in the evening of 3 June, Cochrane received a visit from Madame Bonpland, the wife of a French naturalist. She warned him that his house was surrounded by troops and that, under cover of a royal review next morning, the ministry had ordered the *Pedro Primiero* to be boarded and searched. Cochrane still held in trust for the squadron some 40,000 dollars, which he refused to surrender to the government. This and other treasure, which the ministers insisted had been hidden on the ship, were to be taken while he was detained ashore by virtue of his part in the review.

Thanking Madame Bonpland for the warning, he climbed over the garden fence, made his way to the stables without being seen by the surrounding soldiers, and chose a good horse. Then he rode at once for the Emperor's country palace at San Christoval. By the time of his arrival, Pedro had retired for the night. Cochrane confronted his gentleman-in-waiting and demanded admittance.

"But his Majesty has retired to bed long ago," said the courtier.

"No matter," Cochrane insisted loudly, "in bed, or not in bed, I demand to see him, in virtue of my privilege of access to him at all times. And if you refuse to concede permission – look to the consequences."

The noise and the threat of a scene brought Pedro himself "in a dishabille". Cochrane informed him of the ministerial plan but offered to allow the ship to be boarded by Pedro's own trusted advisers. If any of his "anti-Brazilian Administration" tried to do so, "they would certainly be regarded as pirates, and treated as such".

The Emperor swore that he had in no way authorised the search, assuring Cochrane of his complete trust in him. They discussed how to prevent the "outrage" to Cochrane's flag. At length they agreed that the Emperor must be taken ill next day and unable to review his forces. Cochrane's ship would be manned and safe. The ministers would attend their sick Emperor. Indeed Cochrane himself would be obliged to go through the farce of calling at the palace to inquire after the health of a man he knew to be well.[15]

While this bedroom comedy of avarice and suspicion was acted out at Rio de Janeiro, the news from the vast empire to the north reflected the incompetent and partisan nature of the new ministry. A republican rebellion had broken out more than a thousand miles away in Pernambuco. A second province, Maranham itself, was in the convulsions of civil war, fought between rival groups who all claimed to be loyal to the new Emperor but none the less found good cause for fighting each other.

It was a matter of the greatest urgency to get the squadron to sea and to embark the 1200 troops who were waiting to go with it. But the men of the squadron, feeling cheated of their pay and prizes, had left the ships and showed no intention of returning. The Brazilian government accepted their defeat to the extent of providing Cochrane with 200,000 dollars of the money owing to the ships' companies. The lure was sufficient to get them back on board. Cochrane paid his men, and the squadron with three troopships sailed on 2 August. He had been offered a further personal inducement by the Emperor and the ministry. He was to receive his pay as First Admiral of Brazil for as long as he chose to serve. When he retired, he would receive half-pay for the rest of his life. Should he die before Kitty, which was probable in view of the difference in their ages, she would inherit the income for life.[16]

On the orders of the government, Cochrane put the troops ashore about eighty miles short of Pernambuco. With his warships he sailed north and anchored off the city itself on 18 August. In principle,

Cochrane was not entirely hostile to the republican rebellion, which he thought had been inspired by a number of Americans who were resident in the city. The rebels insisted that, sooner or later, Dom Pedro would come to terms with his father and Brazilian independence would vanish. They wanted all the northern provinces to unite in a "Confederation of the Equator", based on the example of the United States.

At the same time, Portuguese ships were now using Pernambuco openly. Cochrane made no attempt to interfere with them. The "Portuguese faction" now enjoyed a majority of nine to four in the Tribunal of Prizes, and had decreed that so far from rewarding any interference with Portuguese shipping, they would make the appellant liable for damages. Ignoring the Portuguese, Cochrane began to negotiate with Manoel de Carvalho, the "President" of the new régime. He pointed out that division and anarchy in Brazil would destroy independence, and offered to mediate between the rebels and the Emperor. Carvalho replied by inviting Cochrane to change sides and join the republican cause. Cochrane refused, remarking that "it did not follow that, because the Brazilian ministers were unjust and hostile to me, I should accept a bribe from a traitor to follow his example".

When the rebel leaders refused his offer of safe conduct following surrender, Cochrane warned them that he must first blockade and then bombard their city. There were already rumours of clippers having been ordered by Carvalho from the United States, and steamships from England, so there was little time to be lost. Fortunately for the inhabitants, the waters off Pernambuco were too shallow for any ship other than the schooner *Leopoldina* to carry out the bombardment. A mortar was duly put on board her and fired. After several shells had been sent on their way it was evident that the explosions shook the schooner so badly that she was likely to go to the bottom before doing much damage to Pernambuco. Cochrane called off the attack. But the effect of the large shells exploding among them evidently turned the citizens against the rebel régime. At least, the force of 1200 loyal troops advancing from their disembarkation point farther down the coast took the city with little difficulty. Carvalho himself, after a last defence in one of the suburbs, escaped on board a fishing raft and was rescued by a British corvette, H.M.S. *Tweed*.[17]

It was 9 November when Cochrane and his squadron arrived at Maranham. The situation represented anarchy rather than any political rebellion. Miguel Bruce, the President, aided by an army of negro troops, was fighting the former military leaders. Cochrane quickly saw that "Bruce was unfit to be trusted with authority at all" but Bruce's opponents were fighting one another as well as their President. There were, said Cochrane, "two or three family parties fighting each other under the Imperial flag". According to the protests of the French and British consuls, it was Bruce's negro army, officered by newly emancipated slaves, who were responsible for most of the murder and brutality. Cochrane rounded them up and confined them on hulks in the harbour, under the guns of his fleet. He carried out a purge of the more notoriously corrupt officials and celebrated Christmas Day by deposing Bruce himself and replacing him by Manuel Lobo. Cochrane insisted that he had merely "suspended" Bruce, but the practical effect was to stir up a rebellion among those who believed their President had been overthrown.

For six months, anchored almost on the equator, Cochrane struggled with the petty but bloody politics of Maranham. He reported the situation to the government in Rio de Janeiro but received little acknowledgement. He argued the issue of prize money and pay with Brazilian authorities, both national and provincial. He got nowhere with it. Despite his loyalty to the Emperor, the empire at large had forgotten him. As though this were not enough, the pestilential climate had undermined his own health, as well as that of his officers and men. Having had his fill of Maranham and its intrigues, Cochrane left one ship to guard the port, sent the *Pedro Primiero* to Rio de Janeiro, and shifted his flag into the *Piranga*. On 1 January 1825, he had written privately to the Emperor, asking for leave to resign his command. "I have now accomplished all that can be expected from me," he concluded wearily. But his request had not been acknowledged. With his crew of mercenaries he sailed northward and eastward, in search of cooler waters. The frigate put to sea on 18 May and crossed the equator three days later. The winds carried them eastward, with little complaint on the part of the men. By 11 June they were off the Azores, which by any stretch of the imagination was an odd location for a Brazilian warship.

Cochrane claimed that he intended to sail from the Azores to Rio de Janeiro once his men had recuperated from their equatorial experiences. But strong gales caught the *Piranga*, her maintopmast was sprung, the main and maintopsail yards were unserviceable. The rigging was rotten and the provisions stank. On 25 June, the *Piranga* anchored in Spithead.[18]

For much of the remainder of his life, Cochrane was to be involved in financial quarrels with the Brazilian government, the question depending upon whether he had deserted the cause by bringing the *Piranga* to England. In his own view, he had had no choice in the matter. The frigate was not in any state to cross the Atlantic again, nor was she provisioned for such a voyage. To have put into a Portuguese port was out of the question and, under the circumstances, Spithead seemed a reasonable landfall. Cochrane protested that he was the one who had most to lose from it, since the Tory government had by now passed the Foreign Enlistment Act to make his activities on behalf of other governments a criminal offence. At the same time, it is not hard to see why the Brazilians were dismayed to discover that their flagship had left Maranham and was now riding at anchor off Portsmouth.

If Cochrane's career as a Latin American admiral was effectively at an end, he none the less returned from his six and a half years' exile with his reputation further enhanced among European liberals. Despite the petty quarrels of the day, the Brazilians themselves were destined to christen him "the South American Lafayette". Most important of all, at fifty years old he was still possessed of the enthusiasm and energy with which he had been accustomed to fight other men's battles as well as his own. He was, in every sense, an imposing figure, a certain middle-aged stoutness filling out his considerable height.

In the capture of Valdivia, the cutting out of the *Esmeralda*, and the winning of the northern provinces for the new Brazilian empire, Cochrane's admirers detected the same audacity and resolution which had made the *Gamo* and Fort Trinidad legends of the Napoleonic wars. Now he was no longer a lone crusader against the complacency and nepotism of British political life generally and of the Admiralty in particular. He had emerged on the world stage as the champion in arms of liberty and national independence, the warrior of a new century and a new political philosophy. The enemies who had snared him secretly a decade earlier would now be obliged to fight him openly, where the world could judge them, and this they seemed disinclined to do. The Royal Navy prudently fired a salute as the *Piranga* sailed into Spithead. When Cochrane went ashore, he was cheered and applauded by the Portsmouth crowds, as soon as they realised the identity of the stout naval gentleman. In the House of Commons, his ministerial enemies and their successors heard with deep apprehension the first demands that the injustice done him should be brought to light.

I will ask, what native of this country can help wishing that such a man were again amongst us? I hope I shall be excused for saying thus much; but I cannot avoid fervently wishing that such advice may be given to the Crown by his Majesty's constitutional advisers as will induce his Majesty graciously to restore Lord Cochrane to the country which he so warmly loves, and to that noble service to the glory of which, I am convinced he willingly would sacrifice every earthly consideration.[19]

The appeal of Sir James Mackintosh fell on unsympathetic ears. Lord Ellenborough was now dead, so for that matter was St Vincent, while Gambier was seventy years old and in decline. But George IV, who as Prince Regent had ordered Cochrane's "degradation" was still on the throne, and Lord Liverpool was still his Prime Minister. John Wilson Croker remained ensconced at the Admiralty until 1830, while the Duke of Wellington sat in the cabinet as Master-General of the Ordnance. Not only was he an opponent of Cochrane's principles, he had fought hard against recognising the new South American republics.

But the popular feeling for Cochrane was shown repeatedly and sometimes effusively, as when he and Kitty went to the theatre in Edinburgh on the evening of 3 October. Sir Walter Scott, who was also present, described how a reference to South America was included in the performance, whereupon the entire audience rose and turned to the couple with spontaneous and prolonged applause. Kitty, who had endured the perils of the Andes with comparative equanimity, was overcome by the occasion and at length burst into tears. But Scott commemorated the enthusiasm of the audience in a poem which he addressed to her, and in part of which he described the ovation.

> Even now, as through the air the plaudits rung,
>     I marked the smiles that in her features came;
> She caught the word that fell from every tongue,
>     And her eye brightened at her Cochrane's name;
>     And brighter yet became her bright eyes' blaze;
>     It was his country, and she felt the praise.[20]

In Scotland, Cochrane stood as a hero in his own right, but Kitty, by virtue of her striking beauty, contributed a further dimension to the heroic quality. She was, as Scott remarked, easily recognisable, as distinctive in appearance as the tall figure of her husband.

> I knew thee, lady, by that glorious eye,
> By that pure brow and those dark locks of thine.[21]

Beyond the enlightened and literate middle class, who saw in Cochrane the hero of Byronic campaigns and of revolutionary romance, his appeal to ordinary men and women was much simpler. With few exceptions, the victorious leaders of the country in the Napoleonic struggle had become the instruments of authoritarian government in the years of peace. The heroes of Waterloo were soon the villains of Peterloo. But the reformers saw clearly that they were oppressed by the same men as Cochrane and that the freedoms for which he had fought were those they coveted. Among his former colleagues, it was Sir Francis Burdett who publicly pronounced Cochrane the future "Liberator of Greece".[22]

The title was something of an embarrassment so long as he was, at least nominally, First Admiral of Brazil, and so long as there were no weapons available to him for doing battle on behalf of Greek freedom. For the time being, during the remainder of 1825 and the early months of 1826, Cochrane was involved in a protracted quarrel with the Brazilian envoy in London over the *Piranga* and his conduct in command of her. The upshot was that he was suspended from the office of First Admiral, later dismissed, and later still reinstated, at least so far as his pension was concerned. There was no absolute inconsistency between his bringing the *Piranga* to England for repairs and his intention to continue in Brazilian service. But there was virtually nothing left for him to do in Brazil, except haggle over prize money owing to him and damages for which he was liable in seizing vessels improperly. While he insisted that he had given no cause for dismissal, it would have taken an act of extreme credulity to suppose that he intended to return to Brazil at this stage. Having been dismissed from Brazilian service, on the grounds that he had abandoned his post, Cochrane speedily drew a bill on the imperial government for his pay up to the date of dismissal. On 10 February 1826 the bill was drawn and refused. With that, the South American adventure was at an end.

The immediate cause of annoyance to the Brazilian government was the rumour that shortly after arriving in England with the *Piranga*, Cochrane had accepted command of the Greek navy in the war of independence against Turkey. On 21 August 1825, while the *Piranga* was still at Portsmouth, Cochrane received a letter from the Chevalier

Gameiro, Brazilian envoy in London, demanding to know whether newspaper reports that he had accepted such an offer were true. Cochrane replied deftly that he had been approached by the Greek Committee in London but that it would be impossible for him to accept the invitation while in the service of Brazil. It was in no way improper for him to be approached, and he reminded Gameiro that the Brazilians had offered him a command while he was still in the service of Chile. He had neither accepted nor rejected the Greek proposal. Gameiro suspected, with every justification, that Cochrane was about to leave Brazilian service. While they exchanged letters, a formal invitation was on its way to Cochrane from Prince Alexander Mavrocordatos, secretary to the Greek National Assembly. With the authority of the rebel government, he asked Cochrane to take command of the navy in the war against the Turks.

Despite his evasive reply to Gameiro, Cochrane had virtually accepted the invitation of the Greek Committee in London as early as 16 August. While explaining that he was still in the service of Brazil, he agreed in general terms to accept the command as soon as he was free. It was evident that such freedom would not be long delayed. He was urged to consent by the leaders of the Committee, including Burdett, John Cam Hobhouse, the friend of Byron; Joseph Hume, the Scots radical leader; Edward Ellice, and John Bowring.

The enthusiasm for Greek freedom owed much to England's cultural and educational allegiance to Athenian democracy, but particularly to the idealism expressed in the poetry of Shelley and the example of Byron. In 1822, Shelley had published *Hellas*, dedicated to Mavrocordatos himself and portraying Greek women as slaves of the Turks. Byron, having died of fever at Missolonghi before he could take part in its defence against the Turks, had none the less served the cause of revolution by raising the first Greek loan of £300,000 in London, early in 1824. In the famous "Isles of Greece" verses in the third canto of *Don Juan* he had also provided English Philhellenes with a battle hymn more memorable than the windy neo-classicism of Shelley's drama.

> The mountains look on Marathon,
>     And Marathon looks on the sea:
> And musing there an hour alone,
>     I dream'd that Greece might still be free;
> For, standing on the Persian's grave,
> I could not deem myself a slave.

With an arguable lack of scruple, Cochrane transferred his allegiance from the Brazilian empire to the Greek rebellion. He had sufficient experience of new régimes to anticipate that the lyric purity of revolutionary hopes would not be reflected in practice. But while he finally extricated himself from his command of the *Piranga* and the rest of the Emperor's fleet, he turned his attention to the strategy and equipment which would be needed to bring victory to Greece.

Until 1821 there had been no generally organised attempt by the Greeks to free themselves from Turkish occupation. But if they looked to Russia or even to England for their freedom, they were deluding themselves, in Shelley's view.

> Russia desires to possess, not to liberate Greece; and is contented to see the Turks, its natural enemies, and the Greeks, its intended slaves, enfeeble each other until one or both fall into its net. The wise and generous policy of England would have consisted in establishing the independence of Greece, and in maintaining it both against Russia and the Turk; – but when was the oppressor generous or just?[23]

Writing in November 1821, Shelley had seen only the earliest developments in the Greek struggle and, indeed, in British policy with the advent of Canning as Foreign Secretary. He sensed the nervousness of European governments at the prospect of the Greek rebellion spreading a new revolutionary contagion, endangering "those ringleaders of the privileged gangs of murderers, called Sovereigns". Certainly, Russia disowned her protégé, Prince Alexander Hypsilantes, who led the initial uprising in March 1821.

The rebels fared badly in the northern mainland provinces but gained control of the Peloponnese. Both sides fought with bloody determination and vindictive fury. At Tripolitza, the Greeks slaughtered 8000 Turks; men, women and children. The Turks replied by the more famous massacre of Chios in April 1822. Some 25,000 of the island's inhabitants were put to death, apart from the numerous women who were taken as slaves. The incident was grandly commemorated in Delacroix's famous canvas of 1824 and stirred the indignation of European liberals still further.

In 1823 and 1824, the revolution degenerated into an obscure struggle. The independence of Greece had been proclaimed at the beginning of 1822, though large areas had been left to the Turks and, in any case, there was civil war between the contending Greek leaders.

During this period, however, the Greek navy, led by Miaoulis, had done much to prevent the Turkish ships from ravaging the islands and coastal towns. Sultan Mahmoud, carefully preparing his counter-attack, had called on the aid of Mohammed Ali, Pasha of Egypt. The Arab army, led by Ibrahim Pasha, invaded the Peloponnese. One after another, the Greek strongholds fell. By the time that Mavro-cordatos made his appeal to Cochrane, the rebellion was in danger of collapsing. Many of the islands remained loyal to the cause but on the mainland Missolonghi, in the west, was besieged by Ibrahim's army and Athens, in the east, was under threat.

The main hope for Greek independence seemed to lie with its sym-pathisers in Europe as a whole. As Cochrane accepted the command of the navy, Sir Richard Church was approached to lead the army. As a British army captain he had seen considerable Mediterranean ser-vice during the Napoleonic wars and then entered the Neapolitan army. More important still, the growth of Philhellenism throughout Europe and the United States was reflected in the enlightened policy of Canning as Foreign Secretary. In place of mere suspicion of revolu-tion, he had instigated a policy guaranteeing an agreed recognition of the right of Greece to independence on the part of England, France, and Russia. His object was to restore peace between the Greeks and Turks without involving England in war or allowing Russia to inter-vene militarily. To this end, he had despatched his cousin, Stratford Canning, as British ambassador in Constantinople, with instructions to undertake negotiations.

Cochrane's first concern was to equip a fleet which would win a deci-sive victory over the Turks and their Egyptian allies, cutting off Ibrahim's supply route to Alexandria. In 1825, a second Greek loan of £200,000 had been raised in London, of which £150,000 had been set aside for new warships. Cochrane decided on six steamships to be built in England and two frigates to be built in the United States. Though it would have been more convenient to have all the ships built in Europe, the pattern of American "heavy" frigates with sixty guns each, as opposed to thirty-two or forty-four in Europe, would give him an invaluable advantage over the Turks. Moreover, his experiences in Chile and Brazil convinced him that all these ships must be manned by English or American crews. Despite Admiral Miaoulis's efforts, it was evident that Greek seamen were quite undisciplined in battle. Nor could he rely on much support ashore. "With respect to the Greek army," General Ponsonby advised

Wellington, "it is, generally speaking, a mob; and a chief can only calculate upon keeping it together as long as he has provisions to give it or the prospect of plunder without danger." Ponsonby had no doubt of their courage, yet he saw no portent of victory so long as there was "nothing to oppose the Egyptian army but a mob".[24]

In practical terms, Cochrane suffered from interminable delays on the part of the engineer who was to supply boilers for the steamships. There were accusations and counter-accusations over alleged sharp practice by the New York builders of the two heavy frigates. Finally, as a means of preventing him ever taking up his command, he heard that he was about to be prosecuted under the Foreign Enlistment Act for his service in Chile and Brazil. Brougham warned him that "if he stayed many days longer in England, he would be arrested". On 9 November 1825, with Kitty and his children, he crossed the Channel and took up residence at Boulogne. While he waited impatiently for news of his steamships, he received another warning. He was about to be arrested by the French for having illegally detained a French brig, the *Gazelle*, during his blockade of Spanish ports on the Chilean coast. In the case of the Foreign Enlistment Act, the threat to him had not been a specific gesture of support for the Turkish cause. In France, however, he was given to understand that matters were otherwise and that there had been an understanding with Mohammed Ali of Egypt. He packed his possessions once more, and took the road from Boulogne to the sanctuary of Brussels.[25]

Then followed more sinister delays over the completion of the first steamship at Greenwich, she was the *Perseverance* of 42 horse-power. It was hinted that the contractor had been bribed by Turkish representatives in London to frustrate Cochrane's plans for naval victory. In New York, the first of the two frigates was completed but the builder, who had agreed to build both ships for £150,000, now demanded payment of £200,000 for the first one alone.[26]

Yet Cochrane's intention of commanding the Greek navy, whatever the obstacles, had a salutary effect on British diplomacy. In March 1826, the Duke of Wellington passed through Brussels on his way from London to St Petersburg. In December 1825, Czar Alexander had died and Wellington was to begin the difficult task of negotiating a satisfactory conclusion to the Greek war with his successor, Nicholas I. Britain would mediate between the Turks and the Russians to prevent war between them. She would also mediate between the Turks and Greeks to bring about a degree of independence which would satisfy Mavrocordatos and his colleagues while not being

unacceptable to Sultan Mahmoud. Neither act of mediation would be
made more credible if a powerful fleet under a British mercenary
admiral were to enter Greek waters on the side of the rebels. An
interview with Cochrane was something which Wellington could not
bring himself to ask for. Instead, he left a carefully phrased message
with the keeper of his hotel to the effect that he was not available to
see anyone, *"except Lord Cochrane"*. The hotelier, having no idea of
what the message signified, took no action. Wellington travelled on to
St Petersburg and Cochrane was spared the trouble of refusing to
abandon the Greek cause.[27]

By the following month, it was clear that Cochrane would have to
go ahead of the steamships and frigates if they were not ready.
Despite his dream of arriving with a new and powerful fleet, the military situation had deteriorated so far that his presence in command of
a single vessel would be welcome. On 13 April, the Greek deputies in
London assured him: "We may with truth assert that your lordship
is regarded by all classes of our countrymen as a Messiah, who is to
come to their deliverance." Nine days later, Missolonghi fell to
Ibrahim's army after a siege which had lasted twelve months.
Cochrane put to sea from Flushing in his little schooner, the *Unicorn*,
and slipped across the Channel to Weymouth. He went to London
and spent a day inspecting the steamships. The *Perseverance* was
virtually completed. The contractor promised that the *Enterprise*
and the *Irresistible* would be ready in a fortnight and the three
remaining ships within a month.[28]

On this understanding, Cochrane sailed at once in the *Unicorn*,
waiting in Bantry Bay only until he received a message that his
second-in-command, Captain Frank Abney Hastings, had set sail
with the *Perseverance*. Hastings had served on the *Neptune* at Trafalgar, was dismissed the service in 1819 for challenging a superior
officer to a duel, and had joined the Greeks in 1822. Following the
arrangements which had been made, Cochrane sailed to Messina,
which he reached on 12 July, and waited there for the rest of his fleet.
He waited in vain. In place of the ships he received a letter from the
contractors for the Greek loan. The builder, whom they now described
as "the evil genius that pursues us everywhere", had still not completed the vessels, "his presumption is only equalled by his incom-
petency".[29]

Cochrane was dismayed by this. He protested that with the ships
which had been ordered he would win the war for Greece within six
months. Without them, he could do little. The Turks were now

assisted not only by the Egyptian fleet but by other naval forces from Algiers. Cochrane and his schooner were becoming an object of derision even to English chroniclers of the war, notably to the contemporary historian George Finlay.

> He had been wandering about the Mediterranean in a fine English yacht, purchased for him out of the proceeds of the loan in order to accelerate his arrival in Greece, ever since the month of June 1826.[30]

In fact, he retraced his steps as far as Marseille, where he superintended the purchase and fitting out of a French corvette, the *Sauveur* his one and only warship. With this and with his schooner he arrived at the island of Poros on 19 March 1827. It was not until October that the first of his steamships, the *Perseverance*, arrived in Greek waters. Yet even during the months of frustration, he had not been entirely idle. Among the letters he wrote was one addressed to his new enemy, Mohammed Ali of Egypt, in which, with sublime impudence, he denounced the Pasha for "employing foreigners in your military and naval service" and for keeping his barbarian subjects in "wretched hovels" compared with the noble buildings of Greece. But among the insults, Cochrane also offered a hope of political salvation. Predictably in advance of his time, on this occasion by a mere half century, Cochrane suggested that Mohammed Ali might earn the thanks of all men by abandoning his system of slavery and building a Suez canal. The world would stand in grateful awe, while "distant oceans would unite, and the extremities of the globe approach at your command".[31]

But as Cochrane passed the picturesque islands and caught his first distant view of the Acropolis, now besieged by Ibrahim's army, he faced sterner and more immediate realities. The major fortresses of Greece had fallen and though the situation might be turned to advantage by cutting the sea routes to Alexandria and Constantinople, the odds were against him. The *Perseverance* had at last arrived from England, to be renamed the *Karteria*. The first of the two 60-gun frigates from America, the *Hellas*, had also arrived, though with the departure of the American crew which had brought her from New York, Cochrane was hard pressed to man the powerful ship. In general, he calculated that Admiral Miaoulis's fleet of some fifty coasting brigs and similar vessels faced a Turco-Egyptian battle squadron 135 strong. The object of steamships, as Cochrane had explained, was the speed with which they could intercept one after another of the enemy's supply convoys, and their use in "towing fire-vessels and explosion-vessels by night into ports and places where the hostile squadrons anchor on the shores of Greece". With his steamships and a few small gun-boats he offered to clear the Turks and Egyptians from the Peloponnese "in a few weeks". It was not to be. Instead, it was the Egyptians who were "purchasing steam-vessels and hiring transports under neutral flags". The ships brought provisions to Ibrahim, and returned to Alexandria laden with cargoes of women and children taken as slaves.[32]

The unity of the Greeks themselves had been further shaken by the emergence of new factions, including a "French" party led by Colonel Fabvier, now defending the Acropolis, and an "English" faction under Mavrocordatos which regarded Britain as its protector. Sir Richard Church greeted Cochrane with a brief but trenchant note.

> This unhappy country is now divided by absurd and criminal dissensions. I hope, however, that your lordship's arrival will have a happy effect, and that they will do everything in their power to be worthy of such a leader.[33]

Cochrane certainly intended that this should be the case. From Hydra on 21 March he issued a challenge to the entire nation, by quoting to them the example and words of Demosthenes, since "it would be unpardonable presumption in me to address to you other than his own words". The stern call to duty, though in the improbable intonation of a Scottish aristocrat, rang with perfect aptness on the occasion.

> If you will become your own masters, and cease each expecting to do nothing himself while his neighbour does everything for him, you will then, with God's permission, get back your own, and recover what has been lost, and punish your enemy.[34]

The manner of Cochrane's arrival had a salutary effect on the factions. Admiral Miaoulis, who scorned the type of uniform worn by most European naval officers and appeared in the red cap and voluminous blue clothes of his islanders, set the example. Deferring to Cochrane's authority at once, he volunteered to serve under his command as captain of the *Hellas*. Cochrane had already intimated that he would not take up his own command so long as the factions fought one another rather than the army of Ibrahim. This, too, had a sobering influence. On 25 March, he was able to write to Sir Richard Church, "The union of the parties is, I think, now effected."[35]

The factions met on neutral ground at Damala, on the coast opposite Poros on 7 April, as a united National Assembly. Having no building large enough for the purpose, the deputies met in the open air, choosing a lemon grove as their site. Enmities among them were not forgotten but they were, at least, suspended sufficiently long for Count Capodistrias, born in Corfu and experienced in the service of Russia, to be elected President of Greece for seven years. He had been offered the leadership of the revolution at its beginning but had mistrusted the factions and, to that extent, was an independent figure.

Capodistrias's election was the sign of unity for which Cochrane had hoped. He withdrew all reservations and, in the same lemon grove, was installed as First Admiral of Greece on 18 April. His speech and his subsequent proclamations promised that, while Greece should be free, he had every intention of "carrying the war into the enemy's country". By land, this would have been impossible but when his fleet was ready, Cochrane proposed to blockade the Dardanelles and put an end to virtually all Turkish maritime trade. It was uncertain just how far he proposed to take the war but there must have been alarm in several European capitals at the size of the conflict he envisaged in prophesying that, "The sacred banner of the Cross" should "once more wave on the dome of Saint Sophia".[36]

For the time being, it hardly seemed that the inhabitants of Constantinople needed to concern themselves over these threats. Even before Cochrane could begin naval operations with the ships available to him, his attention was taken up by the most desperate struggle of the war: the siege of Athens. The attack had begun ten months before, in June 1826. By July, the city was under siege and on 14 August it was stormed by the Arab troops. Defenders and citizens alike withdrew to the Acropolis and held out for four months. Then, in December, Fabvier and Karaiskakes had broken through Ibrahim's besiegers and reinforced the garrison. Fabvier found himself defending the hill with about a thousand troops and several hundred women and children. The Arab force amounted to 7000, including cavalry and artillery.

Strategy and psychology required equally that the siege should be raised. "The eyes of Europe are turned towards Greece," wrote Cochrane on 14 April 1827, "and on the success or failure of the measures now to be adopted depends the support of your glorious cause, or its abandonment in despair."[37]

To the south of Athens, the Greeks were still in position on either side of the Piraeus. But their intended advance to relieve the Acropolis was blocked by the hill-top convent of Saint Spiridion, which overlooked both camps. Karaiskakes, who now commanded the Greek troops outside Athens, insisted that it must first be taken. He proposed to starve the Turkish defenders into submission but this plan was abandoned when messages were smuggled from Fabvier, warning the relief force that the garrison in the Acropolis could hold out only for a few more days.

By 25 April nothing had been done towards taking Saint Spiridion except for assembling more and more Greek soldiers who seemed to break up rapidly into independent groups, each acknowledging no authority but that of its leader. Cochrane decided that his best expedient was to embark troops by night and land them in the rear of Saint Spiridion so that the strongpoint would be bypassed and the way to Athens would lie open. That afternoon, he was superintending the disembarkation of thirty more soldiers close to the Greek position. The Turks on Saint Spiridion saw this and at once began to hurry down the slope to drive the landing party back into the sea.

The marines under Cochrane's command included a thousand Hydriots who were now led by Major Gordon Urquhart, the detachment being camped on the adjoining shore. At the first sign of the Turkish threat, they hurried to Cochrane's assistance. Instinctively, he chose to turn defence into attack. Waving a telescope as his only weapon, he gathered his men together, formed them up into an orderly detachment, shouted "encouraging words" to them, and then led the assault on the Turkish troops who now stood exposed on the hillside of Saint Spiridion.

The effect of this well-coordinated and resolute attack on the Turks was spectacular. They had experienced nothing like it before at the hands of the Greeks, and their advance guard scattered and fled. At the head of the assault, Cochrane led his men into the earthworks with which the defenders of Saint Spiridion had fortified their position, overrunning them with little difficulty. He lost eight men in the course of an hour's engagement. When it was over, there were sixty Turkish bodies on the hillside and the majority of the garrison was in full flight towards Athens. No more than 200 or 300 men held the building of Saint Spiridion itself against an army of almost 10,000 Greeks.[38]

His little fleet was anchored below in the bay of Phalerum. Cochrane at once ordered the *Hellas*, captained by Admiral Miaoulis, to open a bombardment of the convent. The powerful guns of the frigate delivered one broadside after another, the smoke drifting across the sunlit waters of the bay of Phalerum, stone and débris erupting from the hillside as the shells landed, until Saint Spiridion seemed to be "only a mass of ruins". But the few remaining defenders beat off three Greek infantry assaults. Karaiskakes's men were not keen to try again, their commander writing privately, "We shall not go well with these English. I fear they will ruin us by their impatience."[39]

On 28 April, however, the two hundred or so remaining Turkish troops in Saint Spiridion had had enough of the continuing bombardment by the heavy guns of the *Hellas*. Having no hope of escape, they began to negotiate a surrender. Karaiskakes agreed that they should be allowed to march out with their arms and all the honours of war, passing through the Greek lines unmolested and returning to their own army. Cochrane withdrew the 1500 men under his own immediate command to lessen the danger of any violence between the two sides. He was standing on the deck of his schooner, the *Unicorn*, which he had armed with two carronades, when the type of scene which was all too familiar in the war was repeated once again. A Greek soldier pushed forward and snatched at the sword of one of the Turks who were marching past. The Turk resisted him and there was a struggle. Two or three of the outnumbered Turks, fearing that they were about to be lynched, fired their muskets. The Greek soldiers were already angry "at finding no prizes in the deserted convent", and at this new provocation, they opened a murderous fire upon the Turkish column. When the volleys died away, there were two hundred Turkish bodies on the plain and fewer than seventy survivors. Cochrane was relieved that he had withdrawn his own men and prevented them from joining the massacre but he condemned the atrocity as "the most horrid scene I ever beheld – a scene which freezes my blood, and which cannot be palliated by any barbarities which the Turks have committed on you".[40]

For all Cochrane's triumphs in war, they had been won with an astonishingly low casualty rate, not on his own side alone but on that of the enemy as well. Most recently, his victory over the Portuguese army and navy in Brazil was one of the most bloodless campaigns that could have been devised. It was not in his character to desert a cause at the moment of its greatest need, but after the massacre of Saint Spiridion he wrote bitterly of "the mob denominated falsely the army of Greece".[41]

Had they been pugnacious and determined, that would have been

some recompense. Yet one excuse after another was produced for not
pressing on to the relief of the Acropolis. Karaiskakes announced that
they lacked food, or ammunition, or trenching tools. To make matters
worse, on 4 May, Karaiskakes was fatally wounded in a skirmish. As
he lay dying, the Greek commander left a message for Cochrane,
urging him to carry troops across the water from the camp to Cape
Colias, closer to Athens, and make the attack from there. Cochrane
and Sir Richard Church had a plan in mind, whereby about 3000 men
would be landed there at night, advancing in darkness to seize a
height near the Temple of Zeus Olympus, close to the Acropolis. By
dark, there would be less danger from the Turkish cavalry as they
crossed the plain between Colias and Athens. Once they were in position on the height, they would either relieve the Acropolis or assist
its evacuation.

In Cochrane's version of the plan, it was indispensable that the rest
of the army on the bay of Phalerum should begin a simultaneous
covering attack to divert the Turks, but also with the aim of taking
the enemy on two sides at once, the two halves of the Greek force
linking up victoriously in Athens itself. Accordingly, at midnight on
6 May, the 3000 Greeks were embarked and under the protection of
the *Hellas* were landed at Cape Colias. Dr L. A. Gosse, a Swiss volunteer who acted as Commissary-General of the Greek Navy, accompanied Cochrane. He described the troops landing on the shore at
Colias "in a clear moonlight, and in the most perfect order".

An advance guard of two hundred picked troops, including volunteers from Europe and America, marched inland unopposed and
reached their rendezvous. They were so close, Gosse was told, that
they could hail the defenders of the Acropolis. But at the landing
place itself, it was evident that things were going badly wrong.
Instead of advancing, many commanders were ordering their men
to dig in. From the main Greek army on the other side of the water,
where the second or diversionary attack should have begun, there
was no sound. Gosse discovered one leader of men on the shore,
quietly smoking his pipe, who responded to suggestions that he should
march his men towards Athens by saying, "When they pay me I will
go." Cochrane was not in command of the troops but he was
appalled to discover that they proposed to continue digging in until
daybreak. They were still digging at 9 a.m. when the Turkish cavalry
appeared. The advance party had been obliged to withdraw from
Athens at first light and were now almost wiped out by the Turks as
they retreated. The cavalry then swept down on the beach-head,

killing some 700 of the main force and taking 240 prisoners. Two thousand survivors scrambled for the boats. "There was exhibited such a panic," wrote Gosse, "as cannot be described." Some threw themselves into the sea, others tried unavailingly to fight off the Turkish horsemen, using their muskets as clubs in hand-to-hand fighting. Cochrane had insisted on going ashore from the *Hellas* to do whatever could be done but in the turmoil it was hopeless to attempt an organised defence.

By this time too, the Turkish artillery on the hills was sweeping the plain and the shore with its fire. Cochrane fought his way back to the small boat in which Gosse was waiting for him offshore, wading out until he was neck-deep. He hurried back to the *Hellas* and there took command of the guns to silence the Turkish batteries. The evacuation of Greek survivors continued and they were then ferried back across the bay of Phalerum, where the main Greek force had watched the rout without even putting into effect its planned "diversionary" attack. On 5 June, the garrison of the Acropolis surrendered to the Turks through French mediation, and Athens was lost.[42]

Though Cochrane's experience of the land war was discouraging, he found the war at sea no more promising. He knew how much could be achieved with courage and resolution, indeed this had been shown on 20 April in an attack on the main Turkish supply port of Negroponte, as Chalcis was known. He had sent Captain Hastings in command of the steamship *Karteria* and five smaller sailing ships to seize and destroy enemy provision vessels. On the day in question, Hastings found eight ships anchored under the shore-batteries. With his own broadsides, he silenced the guns ashore, destroyed three of the merchant ships and took the other five as prizes. Encountering an armed Turkish brig, he disposed of it spectacularly with a well-aimed shot in the powder magazine. Pausing at Kumi, he put his men ashore to seize the grain store, and then returned safely to Poros with his booty.[43]

But for all this, Cochrane had only two ships on which he could rely, and even the efficiency of the crews on these was not beyond question. The first was the *Hellas*, which he had chosen as his flagship and the other was the *Karteria*, under Captain Hastings. After the ill-fated attempt to relieve the Acropolis, he left the Greek army to Sir Richard Church and set out to see what could be done to serve the cause with his two best ships.

His first aim was to relieve Castle Tornese, on the coast of the Peloponnese opposite the island of Zante, which was now under siege by Ibrahim's army. By the time that the two ships arrived, on 22 May, Castle Tornese had fallen. There were, however, two Turkish frigates off the coast and, almost instinctively, Cochrane gave chase, firing into them. To his alarm, the guns of the *Hellas* were "ill-directed" and most of the crew ignored his commands. As he wrote after the encounter, "The noise and confusion on board this ship were excessive." The frigate gave up the chase. In fairness to the crew, it was no easy matter to communicate on all subjects. Even with the Greek leaders, Cochrane was obliged to talk in French or elementary Spanish, while on most other occasions an interpreter was necessary.[44]

The day following this abortive attack, Cochrane sighted a merchant vessel flying the British flag. He stopped and boarded her, discovering that though under British colours she was manned by Turks and Ionian islanders, the latter still under British rule. But the cargo of the vessel shocked even Cochrane. The ship was packed with women and children, prisoners taken at Castle Tornese and now destined for the slave markets of Turkey and Egypt. He at once put the ship under escort for Corfu and wrote an angry letter to the British High Commissioner there, as the representative of the governing power. He described the British flag as having been "prostituted" and demanded that the Royal Navy should play its part in "enforcing obedience to the laws of justice and humanity". He sent the crew of the slave ship as prisoners to Corfu, but warned the High Commissioner that such men might well be torn to pieces, in any future incident, by "the fury of the Greeks ... bursting forth upon the violators of their countrywomen".[45]

By an irony, on the following day, Cochrane captured an armed Turkish brig. On board was part of Reshid Pasha's harem. It seems that Cochrane applied a quite different standard in the case of ladies who willingly accepted the system. With a courteous apology for having to take their ship from them, he put them ashore near Missolonghi with all their possessions.[46]

His complaints over the conduct of Greek crews continued, but he was apt to make too few allowances for them. To some extent he was in the position of Spanish naval commanders during the Napoleonic wars, when they had been obliged to man ships rapidly with crews whose lives had been spent ashore. The degree of education or sophistication among his Greek seamen was far behind that of the worst crews in his Royal Navy experience. In one ill-judged attempt to win the confidence of the men on the *Hellas*, he arranged a magic-lantern show for them. The "dissolving views" filled them with an obvious and child-like delight. Then Cochrane put on a slide of a Greek being pursued by a Turk, which melted into a picture of the Turk cutting off the Greek's head. The audience broke into wild panic, some jumping over the ship's side, others barricading themselves in the hold, from which it took many hours to coax them out.[47]

Cochrane's disillusionment, in this respect, was witnessed by Dr Gosse to whom he one day showed the loaded pistol he carried under his coat.

"See, my friend, see what it is to be a Greek admiral!"[48]

It had always been Cochrane's intention, as he promised when he accepted his commission as First Admiral, to carry the war into the enemy's homeland. Accordingly, he planned a major attack on Alexandria, where the Egyptian fleet was preparing for a final blow against Greece. Not only did he propose to destroy or capture the ships, he then planned to seize the port of Alexandria itself, as he had seized Valdivia or Maranham. The British government already feared for the safety of its subjects in Alexandria if the Egyptians discovered that Cochrane had led the Greek attack, but if Alexandria itself were in his hands, there would be no fear of reprisals.

On 11 June he assembled his squadron off Cape Saint Angelo, the south-eastern tip of the Peloponnese, for the Mediterranean crossing. Besides the *Hellas* and the corvette *Sauveur*, which he had acquired at Marseille, he had with him fourteen armed brigs and eight fire-ships. It was a slow crossing, the *Hellas* having to heave to from time to time so that the brigs could catch up, and it was on 15 June, at five in the morning, that Cochrane sighted Alexandria on the horizon. "The wind is fair for us, and our enterprise unsuspected," he told his crew, urging them to strike this one great blow against their oppressors, thereby winning Athens and setting Greece free at last. "The war is concentrated in one point of action and of time." It was an apt and succinct summary of the military situation.

He spent the rest of the day with his ships anchored just out of sight of Alexandria, while he himself prepared an explosion vessel to add to the havoc which he hoped the fire-ships would cause. There was a score of large Egyptian ships in the harbour and he ordered the attack to be made, using fire-ships, on the evening of 16 June.

It had not occurred, even to Cochrane, that there would be so few volunteers to take the fire-ships in. Eventually, he mustered enough of them to man two of the eight vessels. The *Hellas* and the *Sauveur* sailed at the head of the squadron, flying Austrian colours, Cochrane's intention being to sail into the port at once and open a bombardment of the Egyptian warships. But at the harbour entrance his crews saw the array of large Egyptian vessels, and their enthusiasm for the attack vanished. There was no alternative but to stand guard at the harbour mouth while the two available fire-ships went in, under cover of darkness, at about 8 p.m. Blazing impressively, they entered the port of Alexandria.

The success of the two *brûlots* was doubtful, one of them managed to drift alongside an Egyptian warship, which caught fire quickly and went up in flames. In terms of actual destruction it was a small recompense. But, as at the Basque Roads, the psychological effect of this was out of all proportion to the damage done. The other Egyptian ships began to head for the open sea and scatter in every direction, while the inhabitants of Alexandria, convinced that bombardment was about to follow, left their homes and fled to villages outside the city.

Unfortunately, the Greek ships assumed that the escaping Egyptian vessels were coming out against them in an organised attack, so Cochrane, in exasperation, saw most of his own squadron leading the flight. By the morning of 18 June, they were scattered over some twenty miles of the Mediterranean. With the crews of the *Hellas* and the *Sauveur* in their present mood, it was hopeless to attempt the seizure of the port. At length, Cochrane put to sea in pursuit of twenty-five warships, from Alexandria and near by, who were sailing at full speed to escape from the frigate and the corvette. After a chase of eighty miles, he had still not brought them to battle and, reluctantly, he turned to the task of rounding up his straggling navy. As a final gesture, he effected a brief landing on the Turkish coast of Asia Minor, near Phineka, seized supplies of food and water, and wrote a second contemptuous letter from conquered enemy soil to Mohammed Ali of Egypt. It was some consolation to injured pride. Despite the destruction of one Egyptian ship and the gratifying effect on enemy morale, the Alexandria expedition had been one more illustration of the apparent hopelessness of trying to win the freedom of Greece by naval warfare.[49]

It had long been evident that the outcome of the struggle between Greeks and Turks would probably be decided by the attitude of the major European powers. England, certainly, had a strong strategic interest in the area by virtue of possessing the Ionian islands. A Royal Navy squadron commanded by Sir Edward Codrington was detailed to see that neutral shipping was not exposed to Turkish interference or Greek piracy. Stratford Canning, as British ambassador at Constantinople, offered peace by negotiation. Its basis was that the Greeks should acknowledge the authority of the Sultan but that they should have internal self-government. The proposal was rejected by the Turks.

During Wellington's visit to St Petersburg, in 1826, Britain and Russia had signed a protocol agreeing to the right of the Greeks to independence, in principle. While the Turks remained intransigent and Greek resistance began to disintegrate, the representatives of France, Russia, and Britain met in London. As Cochrane returned despondently from Alexandria, the three great powers signed a treaty which pledged them to enforce the St Petersburg protocol. Greece was to have internal self-government under Turkish sovereignty. If an armistice was not agreed within a month, the forces of the signatories would intervene. As might be expected, the Greeks agreed at once to the proposed settlement, and the Turks rejected it.

In the months which followed, both sides in the war fought to be in the best position when an armistice should be imposed. Independence would mean little to the Greeks if they held nothing but a few fortified positions in the Peloponnese. As for the Turks, they had everything to gain by pushing their military frontier as far south into Greece as they could.

Cochrane's part in this final struggle was to assist the remnants of the army, under Sir Richard Church, in holding as much territory as possible in Albania and western Greece. To facilitate this, he was also to do as much damage as possible to the Turkish and Egyptian fleets which had concentrated in Navarino Bay. Navarino, almost at the south-west extremity of the Peloponnese, was a natural choice as a naval base. Some five miles across and three miles deep, it was almost landlocked by virtue of the long island of Sphacteria lying like a huge breakwater across its mouth. A narrow channel at the northern end and the wider Megalo Thouro channel at the south were overlooked by fortifications and shore-batteries. On the southern shore was Navarino itself and at the northern end the ancient city of Pylos with the palace and cave of Nestor.

One of Cochrane's first duties was to transport Sir Richard Church's army from the Gulf of Patros to Albania, to fuel the rebellion against Turkey on the Adriatic coast. He had been cruising off Navarino, which he left on 11 September, and entered the Gulf of Patras six days later. While he was waiting there for Sir Richard Church's army, H.M.S. *Philomel* appeared and her commander, Lord Ingestre, hailed the *Hellas*. He had been instructed to bring a message from Sir Edward Codrington, Commander-in-Chief in the Mediterranean. Codrington had enjoyed a distinguished naval career, as captain of the *Orion* at Trafalgar, at Cadiz, and in the Scheldt, as well as in the actions at Baltimore, Washington, and New Orleans in the war against the United States. It was now his duty to enforce the agreement of the great powers, ensuring that Ibrahim's fleet remained in Navarino Bay and that Cochrane's activities ceased. The menace of his warning to Cochrane was subdued but clearly present.

> Whereas I am informed by Sir Frederick Adam that Lord Cochrane, with the Greek fleet, is about to embark the army of General Church in the neighbourhood of Cape Papas, for the purpose of conveying them to the coast of Albania, you are hereby directed to make known to the commander of that expedition that I consider it my duty, in the present state of affairs, to prevent such a measure being carried into execution, and that I shall shortly present myself in that neighbourhood for that purpose.[50]

Novel though it might have been for Cochrane to engage a Royal Navy squadron in battle, he obeyed the command. But Captain Hastings, with the *Karteria* and the *Sauveur*, was operating independently. He did not even know of the agreement between Ibrahim and the admirals of the English, French, and Russian squadrons patrolling the area, that there should be a cessation of naval hostilities under the terms of the London treaty. The Turks had reluctantly agreed to this maritime truce when the warships of the three powers appeared in Greek waters. Captain Hastings spent an unusually fruitful week in the Gulf of Lepanto attacking a few Turkish ships which were still anchored there. He attacked them with solid shot from the *Sauveur* and red-hot shells from the *Karteria*. He destroyed seven of the Turkish ships and captured three. Then he heard of the armistice.

At Navarino, Ibrahim received news of this outrage, which had occurred on 30 September. On 1 October thirty warships broke out of the anchorage to take vengeance on Captain Hastings. But Sir Edward Codrington overtook them and escorted them back to Navarino. On the evening of 3 October, Ibrahim sent off another squadron of ships but Admiral Codrington rounded up these as well, and drove them back to the anchorage. Infuriated by this, Ibrahim sent out a punitive expedition by land to burn the villages of the Peloponnese, destroying the olive groves and the crops.

In response to this wholesale repudiation, the combined fleet of the great powers sailed for Navarino. Whether their intention was to subdue Ibrahim by a mere parade of force alone is debatable. At the head of the fleet were ten British ships under Codrington's command, followed by seven French ships under Admiral de Rigny, and eight Russian under Count Heiden. At 2 p.m. on 20 October, Codrington in H.M.S. *Asia* led them into the wider Megalo Thouro channel at the southern end of Navarino Bay. Twenty thousand Turkish troops camped on the slope above watched the billowing armada sail past. Within the shelter of the bay, the eighty-two warships of Ibrahim's fleet were anchored in a horseshoe formation. One by one, Codrington's ships came to rest close by them, without any indication of what was intended.

In the crowded anchorage, it was a Turkish soldier or seaman who fired the first, unauthorised musket shot. Other ships of the Turco-Egyptian fleet, believing that they were being attacked, joined in. There was, in Codrington's words, "a fire of musketry" which soon turned to exchanges of cannon shot. The British admiral at once gave his orders, he and de Rigny taking on the battleships, while Count Heiden's squadron dealt with the frigates and sloops. Despite the numerical superiority of Ibrahim's fleet, it was no match for the gunnery and tactics of the allied force. Codrington at once laid H.M.S. *Asia* alongside the Turkish flagship, true to the traditions of the great sea battles of the past. At almost point-blank range the broadsides of his ships tore through the hulls of the Turks and Egyptians, until the whole of Ibrahim's fleet seemed to be ablaze. The Ottoman army on the cliffs above looked on helplessly.

Even by the standard of a full-scale sea fight, the scene at Navarino was awe-inspiring. One after another, Ibrahim's battleships burnt until they blew up, sending a fountain of fire into the smoke-laden sky before the shattered hulls, according to contemporary portrayals, seemed almost to crumple into the water. As night fell, the rocks of Sphacteria reflected the fire of the ships which still burnt. On board Codrington's vessels, the crews struggled throughout the hours of darkness to keep clear of the fiery wreckage. By daybreak on 21 October, only twenty-nine of Ibraham's eighty-two ships were still afloat, though in no condition to engage an enemy. He had lost about

6000 men who were killed in action, or burnt or drowned in its after-math. To all intents, the fleet of Turkey and Egypt had been anni-hilated and the means of maintaining an army to subdue Greece was gone. Navarino was a remarkable, if lurid, example of war as the extension of diplomacy.

Cochrane's employment had virtually been taken from him. Codrington informed the Greek government that only a few corvettes and brigs had escaped the destruction. Greece might now "easily obstruct the movements of any Turkish force by sea". However, lest he should be accused of partiality, he also warned the Greeks that they were to confine their naval activities to legitimate interests within the area allotted them by the great powers. "The maritime armistice is, in fact, observed on the side of the Turks, since their fleet no longer exists. Take care of yours, for we will destroy it also, if the case requires it."[51]

The happy life of piracy to which some Greek captains turned, as soon as the menace of Ibrahim was removed, was partially checked by Codrington's warning and Cochrane's actions during the last weeks of 1827. Moreover, Codrington's instructions were to prevent the Greeks from pursuing their ambitions eastward into Turkish-held islands, or into Albania. He ordered an end to the attack on the island of Chios, which Cochrane's ships were supporting. This policy was not dictated by mere sympathy for the Turks. Codrington knew well that when peace came, Chios and Albania would probably remain under Turkish rule. It was only five years since the brutal retaliation on the inhabitants of Chios, which inspired Delacroix's great paint-ing. Whatever heroics the Greeks might accomplish, these inhabitants would afterwards be left, in Codrington's words, to "the cruel reprisals of the Turks".[52]

Under the circumstances, Cochrane judged it best to secure the position which the Greeks already held. He left at once for London, where he arrived on 19 February 1828, hoping to persuade the government to amend the Foreign Enlistment Act so that British seamen would be permitted to man the Greek warships and ensure a sufficient protection against Turkey. He had no success in this. Worse still, many of the English Philhellenes were now disillusioned with the corruption of the factions in Greece, and the steamships were still not completed. Indeed, the money for them had run short and Cochrane now donated £2000 of his own to aid the progress of the work.

After a fortnight in London, it was evident that the public mood was set against supplying further funds for Greece. Cochrane accordingly crossed to Paris to see what could be done there. On 22 March he wrote at last to Count John Capodistrias, President of Greece, reporting that no funds were to be had in either London or Paris. Soon after, he received a demand from the Greek deputies in London that he should repay all the money he had received from them for his service as First Admiral, on the grounds that by going to England and France to raise funds for Greece he had deserted his naval post. Cochrane had received a single payment of £37,000 which he invested at once in the Greek loan and used his own money to pay for such items as the completion of steamships and the costs of his foreign service. It had been agreed that he should receive a further £20,000 at the conclusion of the war, but he returned the money and asked that it should be used to assist Greek seamen and others who had suffered during the struggle against Turkey.

In the summer, the steamship *Mercury* was at last ready, and Cochrane decided to return to Greece to see what use could be made of her. On his Mediterranean journeys he was not universally applauded as the hero of democracy and liberty. Crauford Tait Ramage, the young tutor to the sons of the British consul at Naples, wrote to his mother in 1826 that the authorities of the Kingdom of the Two Sicilies were so alarmed at the air of subversion of established order which attended Cochrane, that they refused to let him land.[53]

None the less, he reached Poros at the end of September 1828, prepared to resume the fight against the Turks until they and their allies had been cleared from Greece. By now Greece was under the firm, though authoritarian, rule of Capodistrias, which was an improvement militarily. Ibrahim's troops held only a few remaining strongpoints and were soon to be driven from these by a French army under General Maison, an operation which was almost completed when Cochrane arrived.

There was, in truth, nothing left for him to do except to hand over the *Mercury* to the provisional government and spend tedious months in going through the naval accounts of the war to satisfy his masters that every payment could be justified. Had he failed to do so, payment to his subordinates was to be withheld. At last, on 4 December, Capodistrias accepted the gift of Cochrane's £20,000 and of all his rights in prizes taken during the war, adding that "the Provisional Government can engage in no warlike operation worthy of

your talents and your station". Accordingly, his employment was at
an end.[54]

The rule of Capodistrias degenerated into tyranny, culminating in
his assassination three years later. But Cochrane was no longer in
Greece to witness these events. On 20 December 1828, he left Poros
for the last time. Count Heiden, commanding the Russian squadron,
was anchored off the island in the *Azoff*. Hearing of Cochrane's
departure, he wrote to Dr Gosse to inquire whether Cochrane was still
First Admiral and what honours it would be appropriate to pay him
on his leaving Poros. Gosse replied, listing the "coldness and indifference" shown by the Greek government on Cochrane's recent
return from Paris, the failure to provide him with lodging, provisions,
or employment. At every turn he had met "the insolence of servants
of the Government".[55]

Count Heiden replied, assuring Cochrane that he might "send back
to their kennels these miserable causes of his annoyance". A Russian
corvette would be put at his disposal to take him to Malta, and the
crews of the Russian ships would man the rigging in salute as he
passed them. So it was that, in the Imperial corvette *Grimachi*, he
embarked at last for Malta. Waiting for him on his arrival there was
Admiral Sir Pulteney Malcolm, who as Captain Pulteney Malcolm
had been one of the few witnesses to support Cochrane in their evidence to the Gambier court-martial. Malcolm put a Royal Navy ship
at his disposal for the voyage to the European mainland. After a long
overland journey as well, he arrived in Paris to rejoin his family at the
beginning of March 1829.

His dedication to the ideal of democracy and the struggle for
national liberty did not require him to suppress his feelings about the
state of affairs in Greece. He wrote to the Chevalier Eynard of the
Philhellenic Committee in Paris, describing the government of Greece
as depending on "bands of undisciplined, ignorant, and lawless
savages". Such sentiments might have horrified Shelley and the
romantic Philhellenes of the early rebellion as being the rhetoric of a
reactionary. Cochrane, at least, had shed the delusion that the society
of Plato and Demosthenes, as enshrined in its literature, bore some
resemblance to the Greek culture of the 1820s. To Eynard, he suggested that the alternative to the gloomy expedient of letting the
revolution "work itself out" was to station six regiments of troops
from friendly powers there, until the return of new leaders, educated
elsewhere, or the growth of a new generation should make the country
fertile for democracy.[56]

In this mood, he returned home, reaching England in September 1829. It was widely said that he had enriched himself by speculating in the Greek loan. Hobhouse even wrote that Cochrane's aim was to "establish himself in the sovereignty of Greece". He had been paid £37,000 for his four years' service, to cover his own pay and the expenses of his campaign. He invested this sum in Greek bonds at a time when the price, like the expectations of Greek victory, stood low. If anything, it was a gesture of support quite as much as "speculation". He then used his own money for the costs of the campaign. As a partial consequence of his own exertions, the hopes for Greek freedom and the value of the bonds rose. To that extent, he made money out of them. Against this must be set the sum of £20,000, due to him at the end of the war, which he returned to the Greek government.[57]

As a mercenary admiral, it might seem that he expected too much of the Chileans, even more of the Brazilians, and far too much of the Greeks. The Chileans, at least, he felt had been trained to an acceptable level of fighting ability, the Brazilians rather less so. But Brazilian independence was a less clear-cut matter than that of Chile. It was separate government under the same royal house as that of Portugal, with a strongly pro-Portuguese faction in the "independent" government at the time of Cochrane's employment. The Greeks, demoralised as a subject race and dependent on leaders who owed part of their loyalty to other interested powers, were no better placed. Their sailors, with no tradition of naval service, drew the line between prize-taking and piracy at a different point from Cochrane. Disorganisation, made worse by a variety of languages, was a greater problem than faintheartedness. And if they seemed more cowed by their traditional conquerors, it is only fair to remember how much more easily and effectively the Turks could hold Greece than the Spanish or the Portuguese could police the distant hinterland of South America.

The truth is that whatever Cochrane's criticisms of the Greeks, however justified they might be and however valiantly he had striven for their cause, his anger was made all the more savage by knowing that, almost for the first time in his fighting career, he had accomplished less than the world expected of him. He had, however, helped to keep the struggle alive and, as a British subject fighting the Turks, traditional allies of his own country, he had assisted in involving the great powers in the conflict to the final and decisive advantage of the Greeks.

On his return from the Greek war, at the age of fifty-four, he still

had a long span of life ahead of him, almost as long as the period
from his first command of the *Speedy* until the present date. But after
all his wars in the service of other powers, there was one rather
different battle whose issue had still not been decided. It was that
battle to which he devoted his energy and determination for the next
thirty-one years, seizing whatever weapon came most easily to hand.

# 9
# See, the Conquering Hero Comes!

---

THE long remainder of Cochrane's life was devoted, in various ways, to the fight for personal justice. He had made his first moves during his temporary return from Greece in 1828 by addressing a memorial on 4 June to the one man of influence who might hear him favourably. His choice fell on the Duke of Clarence, who was then Lord High Admiral and was to succeed his brother in 1830 as "the Sailor King" or "Silly Billy", according to one's taste. At Windsor, or St James's, or Brighton, with the motherly figure of Queen Adelaide and the brood of illegitimate Fitzclarences, the court was to acquire an easy-going dowdiness which contrasted strongly with the self-conscious sophistication of George IV. As Duke and as King William, Clarence showed an amiable and simple nature, for though he could be petulant he was not vicious, and though his naval manners and country gentleman's behaviour lacked refinement, he showed a sense of justice and fair play.

To the future king, Cochrane addressed a long and impassioned protest of his innocence of the Stock Exchange fraud, referring to himself in the third person as "your memorialist". In solemn terms he insisted on this.

> He asserts it now, most solemnly, as in the presence of Almighty God, and certain he is, if every doubt be not dissipated in this world, that when summoned to enter more immediately into that Awful and Infinite Presence, he shall not fail, with his last breath, most solemnly to assert his innocence.[1]

The Duke of Clarence forwarded the memorial to the Prime Minister, the Duke of Wellington, and it was considered by the cabinet. Wellington returned a brisk reply, to the effect that the cabinet had considered it and "cannot comply with the prayer of the memorial".[2]

Cochrane left England and made no further attempt for the time being. He had never greatly admired the Wellesleys. To petition again, while Wellington was in office, would be "to debase myself in my own estimation, and, I think, in that of every man of sense and feeling". He remained abroad, in France and Italy, partly for the sake of Kitty's health. Yet there were signs that England had not forgotten him. His eldest son was introduced to the Duke of Clarence at Portsmouth, and when the Duke heard the Cochrane name, he at once offered to enter the boy at the naval academy so that the new generation might emulate its predecessor.[3]

Those who met Cochrane during his voluntary exile in Italy found his enthusiasm and his democratic belief unaltered by experience. Charles Greville encountered him at Florence in the spring of 1830.

23rd March. . . . To-night at a child's ball at Lady Williamson's, where I was introduced to Lord Cochrane, and had a great deal of talk with him; told him I thought things would explode at last in England, which he concurred in, and seemed to like the idea of it, in which we differ, owing probably to the difference of our positions; he has nothing, and I everything, to lose by such an event.

26th March. . . . Then rode to Lord Cochrane's villa, where we found them under a matted tent in the garden, going to dinner. He talks of going to Algiers to see the French attack it. He has made £100,000 by the Greek bonds. It is a pity he ever committed a robbery; he is such a fine fellow, and so shrewd and good humoured.[4]

Three months exactly after this encounter, George IV died and the Duke of Clarence became William IV. But Wellington remained Prime Minister and there was no more to be done as yet. In one of his letters, Cochrane remarked that other men who had offended the old régime were being pardoned, "But I, who protested against the forging of charts and public waste of money, have had no mercy shown!" It was on 15 November 1830 that Wellington's government resigned and a liberal Whig ministry under Lord Grey came into office. Within a few months the country was stimulated to new political enthusiasms as the Reform Bill began its first slow progress through parliament. Europe waited to see if "things would explode" or not, in Greville's terms.[5]

Cochrane returned to England with a "review" of his case prepared for publication. In Earl Grey's government, his old friend Henry

Brougham had been raised to the peerage as Lord Chancellor. Surely there was hope of justice at last. A further reason for his return was an invitation to stand as parliamentary candidate for the borough of Southwark. As the battle for reform began, Cochrane had every intention of playing his part in it.

First of all, he addressed copies of his published case to members of the cabinet and sent a copy to the King. On 12 December, he received a personal reply from Grey.

> I need not say that it would give me great satisfaction if it should be found possible to comply with the prayer of your petition. This opinion I expressed some years ago in a letter which, I believe, was communicated to you. To the sentiments expressed in that letter I refer, which, if I remember aright, acquitted you of all blame, except such as might have been incurred by inadvertence and by having suffered yourself to be led by others into measures of the consequences of which you were not sufficiently aware.[6]

Cochrane had handed the King's copy of his printed *Review* to the Home Secretary, Lord Melbourne, accompanied by a short informal petition. William handed the pamphlet back to Melbourne without comment. This was not the correct form in which a petitioner was required to present his case to the monarch.

Throughout 1831 the negotiations continued. On 25 April, Cochrane met his friend Brougham, the Lord Chancellor, at an evening party given by Lord Lansdowne. Brougham warned him ominously that there would be "a battle to fight" over his case. He also learnt that Brougham's brother was standing as candidate at Southwark. Cochrane decided to withdraw his candidacy. He had no wish to oppose Brougham's family and he thought it best not to be a parliamentary supporter of a government from whom he sought personal vindication.[7]

It mattered very little, in fact, because on 1 July, at his Paris lodging in the Rue Vaurigard, the old Earl, who disowned his son's activities two decades before, died at the age of eighty-three. Thomas Cochrane was now 10th Earl of Dundonald in succession to his father and, of course, disqualified from sitting in the House of Commons. He held the title for almost thirty years, but it was as "Cochrane" that he remained best known. His inheritance was little more than a title, and such titles were nothing in his estimation by comparison with the claim to honour and reputation.

One of Cochrane's advantages was that he had, quite simply, outlived so many of the old naval officers and politicians who were his greatest enemies. Among the new generation, he enjoyed the friendship of such political figures as Brougham, Lord John Russell, and Lansdowne. Lord Auckland, who was twice to be First Lord of the Admiralty, was another sympathiser. The press admired him, particularly the more liberal *Times*, from 1841 under the famous editorship of John Thadeus Delane. His politics, which had seemed so revolutionary and dangerous thirty years earlier, now enshrined some of the most precious beliefs of government in a more democratic age. Above all, the revelations of his adventures marked him as a great naval hero and perhaps the most brilliant naval commander of a single ship.

For all that, there were rumours that his case was not universally sympathised with. Two members of the cabinet had refused to give way. Admiralty reports on Chile were being quoted against him and when Cochrane asked the First Lord, Sir James Graham, for a chance to refute these private allegations, he was told that the contents of such records were confidential.

Kitty, as the new Countess of Dundonald, sought an interview with Lord Grey who "expressed his readiness to do all he can". But still there was "something in the way". Cochrane himself appealed once more to William IV, asking for a private audience. The King was at Brighton, where the audience was granted at the Royal Pavilion on 27 November. William listened attentively to Cochrane's claim for a chance to hear and answer whatever charges were now being privately uttered against him over the Stock Exchange affair or his service in Chile, or any other matter. He asked for a fair investigation. Whatever the King's more obvious failings, his naval experience and allegiance had given him a natural admiration for Cochrane's achievements. He promised to see that the case was "fairly looked into".[8]

The early weeks of 1832 passed, and still nothing was done. Burdett, one of the most loyal of Cochrane's friends, offered to raise a campaign in parliament over the way in which an allegedly sympathetic government was dragging its heels. But it was Kitty who went first to Lord Grey and then to the King himself. From Grey she learnt that "there are two individuals in the Cabinet who will not give in". But, even without consulting his government, William had the power to grant a free pardon and it was this for which Kitty, with Cochrane's reluctant consent, at length asked.[9]

His reluctance was a symptom of chronically sensitive pride. A pardon, he thought, implied forgiveness of an offence. But it was his claim that he had never been guilty of any offence in the first place. To the world at large, it meant simply that he had been innocent, that his innocence was now recognised, that Lord Ellenborough and all those who had sought the downfall of the hero in 1814 were now rebuked by the powers of a more enlightened age.

For the moment, the attention of the world was diverted to the momentous fate of the Reform Bill, which would extend the vote into the middle classes of society and abolish forever the corruption of rotten boroughs and their attendant political patronage. As the Bill passed the Commons for the last time, Cochrane wrote:

> It is a rare felicity for a nation to be governed by men having the liberality and justice which induce them to confer free institutions peacefully on the country; institutions which merit the gratitude of all who now exist, and will receive the unqualified applause of future generations. The page of history affords no parallel to the present event.[10]

A fortnight after the letter was written, on 2 May, the Privy Council bowed to royal command and Cochrane received his free pardon. Six days later, the public read that the new Earl of Dundonald had been restored to the Navy List, and that he was now gazetted as Rear-Admiral of the Fleet. The tables were turned with a vengeance on his dead persecutors. The Mulgraves and the Melvilles were generally consigned to oblivion; Ellenborough was soon held up to criticism by Lord Campbell's famous *Lives*; Liverpool and his creatures were subjects of derision as the weak and frightened ministries of a sick and hated king. The portait of George IV which ruled the Victorian imagination was not that of the boisterous Regent, but of Thackeray's bilious ogre in *The Four Georges*.

On the day after his appointment, Cochrane was summoned to a royal levée at St James's where, as on other occasions, "congratulations poured in from all quarters". As the reputations of his old enemies rotted and withered, it seemed that for him the promise of his own election ballad had at last come true.

> The laurels of fame, that encompass his head,
> Shall bloom when the triumphs of warfare are fled;
> For the friend of REFORM and of FREEDOM at home,
> More immortal shall make him in ages to come.[11]

The dawn of the newest and greatest reign of the nineteenth century, with Victoria's accession in 1837, saw in Cochrane every admirable quality. He was the sailor-hero, the liberator of oppressed nations, the champion of freedom in his own land, and that most appealing of popular legends – the brave man wrongly accused and condemned, to whom justice is at length done. To add to his other honours, the new King Otho of Greece had made him Grand Commander of the Order of the Saviour of Greece.

He was sixty-two years old when the Queen came to the throne and had no intention whatever of becoming a mere ornament to the naval profession. There would be wars to fight and actions of one sort or another in which the Royal Navy would be engaged. In the present interval of peace, he turned his attention to his inventions, particularly the application of steam power to naval warfare. One of the more bizarre applications was the curing of fevers among his men in tropical or sub-tropical regions. In Greece, the unfortunate Dr Gosse had contracted fever and visited Cochrane on the steamship *Mercury* while still suffering the effects. Cochrane had devised a curative bath, using steam from the ship's boilers. He lifted Gosse up and put him into the currents, making him perspire copiously. "My illness disappeared as by enchantment," wrote the surprised patient.[12]

Cochrane was far from having invented the first steamship or even having supervised its construction. But in the case of the *Rising Star*, built for Chile, he was able to claim that this steamship with its retractable paddle was among the first to cross the Atlantic and that he was responsible for its design. During the reign of William IV and the earlier years of Victoria, he turned his attention to the problem of devising a rotary engine, capable of turning a ship's paddle or propeller directly, to replace the old reciprocating engines with their simple backward and forward movement. He fitted out a little steamboat of his own, on the Thames, as a floating laboratory.

By 1834 he was already urging his invention on Sir James Graham, as First Lord of the Admiralty. Both Graham and his successor, the Earl of Minto, were sympathetic. In 1839, the Secretary to the Admiralty, Sir John Barrow, wrote to Cochrane:

I am commanded to acquaint your lordship that the opinions received of your revolving engine are favourable to the principle, and that it has not been stated that there are any insurmountable obstacles to its practical execution.[13]

But novelty did not commend itself to the officials of the Admiralty in general. In 1842, Cochrane was still trying to persuade another First Lord, the Earl of Haddington, that the Royal Navy must exploit the power of steam if its ships were to remain a match for the newer and heavier American frigates or the latest warships launched by France. He was also concerned that Royal Navy officers would continue to think in terms of blockades and the tactics of the Napoleonic wars, which were entirely outmoded by steam.

> A couple of heavy line-of-battle ships, suddenly fitted, on the outbreak of war, with adequate steam-power, would decide the successful result of a general action; and I am assured that I could show your lordship how to fit a steam-ship which, in scouring the Channel or ranging the coast, could take or destroy every steam-ship belonging to France that came within view.[14]

Haddington visited him at Portsmouth in August to inspect the work on which Cochrane had already spent £16,000 of his own money. The First Lord ordered a small steamship, the *Firefly* to be put at Cochrane's disposal. The experiments were so successful that the Admiralty decided to order the building of a frigate on the lines of Cochrane's suggestions. By the beginning of 1843 he had also patented another of his inventions, one of the earliest ship's propellers. Yet even some more sympathetic of his patrons, like Lord Minto, saw only a need for "occasional steam power" to assist the sails. A speed of five knots, to aid a ship in getting into or out of battle, or off a lee shore, was considered sufficient. Minto could not see why Cochrane should "wish to steam the *Vanguard* or the *Queen* at the rate of ten miles an hour".[15]

However, during 1844 and 1845 he was much occupied with the new steam frigate being built according to his plans and which was launched as H.M.S. *Janus* at the end of 1845. In the main, she was a success, though there were the usual deficiencies and delays which customarily seemed to try Cochrane's patience, and that patience was somewhat shorter now that he had reached his seventieth birthday.

But while much of his time was taken up by practical questions of design, or the improved construction of boilers, or other technical matters, he was obsessed as ever by the need for England to prepare for war on the basis of his own "secret plans", which he had first submitted to the Prince Regent a quarter of a century before. While William IV was still on the throne, Cochrane had gone down to

Brighton and in another audience at the Royal Pavilion tried to persuade the King of the value of his plans for gas attacks and saturation bombardment. He had not, of course, used them in Greece or
South America because he had promised the Prince Regent that they
would never be employed except in the service of his own country.
William listened, agreed that the plans had "value", and praised
Cochrane's "honourable conduct in keeping his secret so long and
under such inducements to an opposite course".[16]

Nothing more happened, and Cochrane took the matter up with his
friend Lord Lansdowne who held office in Lord Grey's government as
President of the Council. But four years later, Lansdowne would still
promise only to press the plans on the government "if the occasion
arises, which I sincerely hope it will not". At that time, in 1838, the
potential enemy was Russia, whose growing influence in Afghanistan
was seen as a challenge to British ambitions in India. But Russia, in
Lansdowne's view, would "yield to remonstrance", and there would
be no need of the secret weapons. The truth was that men like
William IV and his ministers accepted that war was an inevitable
occurrence between great nations but even in war there were certain
notions of decorum and civilisation which ought to be observed.
Other men, like Wellington, had expressed the sceptical view that
"two could play" at Cochrane's game. Cochrane answered this in a
letter to Lord Minto on 3 August 1840.[17]

> Your lordship will perceive, that "although two can play at the
> game", the one who first understands it can alone be successful.
> In the event of war, I beg to offer my endeavours to place the
> navy of France under your control, or at once effectually to
> annihilate it.[18]

"I shall bear your offer in mind," Minto replied coolly, "but there
is not the slightest chance of war."[19]

In 1846, Cochrane's friend Lord Auckland became First Lord of
the Admiralty, the post which he had held briefly in 1834. During the
intervening period he had been Governor-General of India and was
well aware that, contrary to Minto's placid assumption, Victorian
England had a very good chance of being involved in one sort of war
or another. His own experience had been of the Afghan war of 1838–
1842 and the ill-fated British march on Cabul to thwart Russian
ambitions in Afghanistan. It hardly required a tremendous feat of
imagination to foresee the war with Russia which broke out in the
following decade.

Auckland set up a secret committee, consisting of Sir Thomas Hastings, Surveyor-General of the Ordnance, Sir J. F. Burgoyne, and Lieutenant-Colonel J. S. Colquhoun. They considered Cochrane's plans under three headings: camouflage, saturation bombardment, and gas attack. Reporting confidentially to the First Lord on 16 January 1847, they agreed that the plan for the first of these should be made available to the Admiralty. The bombardment and the gas attack they thought should not even be experimented with. They had no doubt that the weapons concerned would be successful but, if used in war, "It is clear this power could not be retained exclusively by this country." And, in any case, they rejected the weapons inevitably because such devices would not "accord with the feelings and principles of civilised warfare". The details should "remain concealed" in their secret file.[20]

There was no more that Cochrane could do at the time, though he warned Auckland that the French appeared to be developing equally "uncivilised weapons" in the form of guns firing shells fast and low, annihilating any ship which attempted to approach and slaughtering her crew. "I submit that, against such batteries as these, the adoption of my plans Nos. 2 and 3 would be perfectly justifiable." [21]

Apart from improved gunnery, the French were in fact living on the lessons of the Napoleonic naval war. As Cochrane discovered, the basis of their new strategy was to avoid battles between fleets or large squadrons and trust to fast cruisers which would destroy England's commerce. The Prince de Joinville was a leading advocate of this. Cochrane had anticipated them to some extent by advising the Admiralty to think less in terms of battleships and more in terms of smaller faster boats.

"Give me a fast small steamer," he remarked, "with a heavy long-range gun in the bow, and another in the hold to fall back upon, and I would not hesitate to attack the largest ship afloat."[22]

His support for what he called a "mosquito fleet" was based upon his experience of steamships like the *Karteria* in Greece. Small and manoeuvrable vessels with well-trained crews were the answer, even though they might carry only one or two guns. His recommendation to the Admiralty was simple: "As large a gun as possible, in a vessel as small and swift as possible, and as many of them as you can put upon the sea." Lord Exmouth, who as Sir Edward Pellew was famed as commander of the *Arethusa* and later as the victor in the battle of Algiers, surveyed the plan of Cochrane's war-steamers in 1826 with astonishment.[23]

"Why," he said, "it's not only the Turkish fleet, but all the navies in the world, that you will be able to conquer with such craft as these."[24]

Despite all the interest shown in Cochrane's inventions and his secret plans, and despite his rank as flag-officer, he had not been appointed to any command. This was his own doing. In 1839 he had written to Lansdowne and to Lord Melbourne, as Prime Minister, pointing out that though he had received a free pardon, his rank as Knight Commander of the Bath had not been restored to him. If he was now recognised to be innocent of the Stock Exchange fraud, why was this not done? So long as there was any question of his guilt, he would not hold a command.

He managed to convince himself that on the marriage of Victoria and Albert, in 1840, his honours would be restored as a royal gesture. But nothing was done. Instead, he was awarded a pension for good and meritorious service, in the following year, at the age of sixty-six. When Peel became Prime Minister, Cochrane took up the matter of the Bath with him. Peel replied to him on 7 November 1844, reminding him that he had received a pardon and had been restored to the naval list.

> Adverting to that circumstance, and to the fact that thirty years have now elapsed since the charges to which the free pardon had reference were the subject of investigation before the proper judicial tribunal of the country, her Majesty's servants cannot consistently with their duty advise the Queen to reopen an inquiry into these charges.[25]

But there was now some question, soon raised memorably by Lord Chief Justice Campbell himself, as to whether Ellenborough's court had been proper or judicial in its standards. And, as Cochrane was to discover, his role as hero of the new age had attracted the admiration of the Queen and Prince Albert for his courage and loyalty. With his innate talent for publicity, he duly published a pamphlet in February 1847, *Observations on Naval Affairs*, listing his services to the navy and the evidence of injustice done to him over the Stock Exchange fraud. He had, of course, made similar appeals before but now he made them to contemporaries who regarded the rulers of England in 1814 as morally and politically alien. It happened that in June 1846 Sir Robert Peel's government had resigned over the failure to impose a Coercion Bill to maintain public order in Ireland. When Cochrane made his appeal in the following February, it was to the first specifically Liberal government under Lord John Russell, an administration which had every reason to admire Cochrane's beliefs and crusades on behalf of liberty.

Within the cabinet and the Privy Council, opinion was still divided, Cochrane's main supporters being Auckland and Lansdowne. Auckland began to consult senior naval officers, to see what support there was for Cochrane's reinstatement. Sir Thomas Byam Martin, who had been present at Government House, Portsmouth, when the Prince first announced Cochrane's degradation in 1814, warned Auckland that many officers might oppose full restoration of honours.

"Yes," said the First Lord, "I am aware of such an opinion."

But Auckland went on to praise Cochrane's "great enterprise and talent". In the event of war, it would be "highly desirable" to call upon his services. Martin agreed that the majority opinion would favour full restoration, remarking of Cochrane that "his gallantry, enterprise, and professional intelligence was acknowledged throughout the service".[26]

Even while this discussion was taking place, Lord Lansdowne, now Leader of the House of Lords, was granted an audience by the Queen in order to present Cochrane's case. Victoria listened, and then announced that "with or without the approval of her Privy Councillors, she would confer the next vacant Order of the Bath upon Lord Dundonald".[27]

Nor was this all. Cochrane received a private message from Buckingham Palace.

> Her Majesty has had conversation as to the justice of some further atonement for the injuries that have been inflicted on me, and . . . she said it was a subject of regret that such was not in her power; but should the subject be entertained by her advisers, her concurrence should not be wanting.[28]

The "atonement" which he had in mind was the repayment of the fine inflicted in 1814, as well as pay from the time of his dismissal from the navy until his reappointment by William IV. This would involve a reversal of the original verdict, an act beyond Victoria's constitutional power at that time. Yet there was no doubt of the admiration which she and Albert felt for Cochrane and his career. Lord John Russell, as Prime Minister, assured him of this in a letter of 12 May.

Your services to your country are recorded among those of the most brilliant of a war signalised by heroic achievements. I will lay before her Majesty the expression of your gratitude, and I can assure you that the Queen has sanctioned with the greatest satisfaction the advice of her ministers.[29]

The death of Admiral Sir Davige Gould soon created a vacancy in the Order. Victoria placed it at Auckland's disposal with instructions that it should be conferred upon Cochrane. On 25 May, thirty-three years after his degradation by the Prince Regent, he was gazetted for a second time as Knight Grand Cross of the Order of the Bath. Prince Albert, as Grand Master of the Order, sent him the warrant at once. Though the installation was some weeks away, Cochrane had been summoned to the Queen's birthday drawing room at St James's on 27 May. The Prince wished him to wear the cross on that occasion. He was also entitled to wear most of his foreign decorations, though his title as Marquess of Maranham was not recognised. Government policy prohibited Royal Navy officers from serving under foreign titles.[30]

On the warm May afternoon the staircases and anterooms beyond the audience chamber were crowded with the élite of Victorian society – political, military, and naval – waiting to be presented to the sovereign. With her escort of Life Guards, the young Queen appeared in her train of gold-embroidered satin, trimmed with honeysuckle and ornamented with diamonds. Among the plumes of the general staff, Prince Albert attended in the uniform of Field Marshal, as did the Duke of Cambridge, and Wellington. In this company, the tall, stooping figure of the old admiral was presented to the Queen. The Garter installation, at Buckingham Palace on 12 July, made a bizarre sequel. Prince Albert, as Grand Master of the Order, presided in the presence of the Knights Grand Cross and many inferior Crosses. Among the members was the frail figure of the Duke of Wellington. The Duke, who had so summarily dismissed Cochrane's plea for justice, while Prime Minister, that Cochrane felt it would be demeaning to petition him ever again, came slowly across and shook him by the hand, "expressing his satisfaction" at this reinstatement. Even more bizarre was the role of Lord Ellenborough, son of the famous judge, who was now called upon by Prince Albert to act as Cochrane's sponsor. It was not so much an act of reconciliation as poetic justice. The next Lord Ellenborough, in his turn, commented on his father's predicament.

Taken by surprise, he may well have preferred to act as his sponsor to causing an unseemly squabble in, or almost in, the presence of the Throne, and I do not see that any inferences can well be drawn from his conduct.[31]

To Cochrane, the most heartening thing of all was that he was not required to be knighted on this occasion. Victoria and Albert, at least, had vindicated him by confirming that his knighthood dated from its first conferment in 1809 and that Cochrane had done nothing at any time to forfeit his title.

It had always been his own contention that he could not resume active service so long as his honours were not restored. He had been promoted to Vice-Admiral in 1841 but still remained on half-pay. Now that his conditions were met, there was no reason, in principle, why Cochrane should not resume active service in the Royal Navy at the age of seventy-two. However, he had grown so accustomed to "neglect" of one sort or another that he must have been doubly surprised by a letter from Lord Auckland on 27 December 1847.

I shall shortly have to name a Commander-in-Chief for the North American and West Indian Station. Will you accept the appointment? I shall feel it to be an honour and a pleasure to have named you to it, and I am satisfied that your nomination will be agreeable to her Majesty, as it will be to the country, and, particularly, to the navy.[32]

He accepted the offer which, in effect, made him admiral of Britain's Atlantic fleet. From other admirals, from Members of Parliament, and from Delane of *The Times*, letters of congratulation reached him on the news of his appointment. They spoke of the "foul aspersions" against him having been dispelled and of the justice "to the bravery of your lordship as an officer and your goodness and honour as a man". But, gratifying though this might be, there was peace in the Atlantic and no opportunity for Cochrane to exercise the very talents which were now so widely praised. To have held such a command in 1810 would have enabled him to alter the course of the greatest war in history. To hold it in 1847 was merely a matter of courtesy.[33]

Cochrane remained commander-in-chief from the beginning of 1848 until the spring of 1851. He sailed from Plymouth on his flagship H.M.S. *Wellesley* on 25 March, and there were, of course, sufficient routine duties to occupy him. The United States was involved in war with Mexico, and Cochrane's ships were to maintain a patrol of the Gulf of Mexico in the hope that this would induce both sides to seek peace under the threat of British intervention. In general, the fleet was occupied with the protection of British fishing interests and the suppression of the slave trade.

Cochrane himself took the opportunity of reporting to Lord Auckland on various matters which caught his attention. The convict hulks should be removed from Bermuda, the defences and the dockyards of the island reorganised, proper drainage and water supplies provided. Despite his appointment to the new command, Cochrane gave the impression of a man looking about him with increasing frustration for something to do. It was in vain that Auckland assured him that even the most routine class of duties "is not without interest, and carries credit as it is performed with justice and exactness".[34]

The two men exchanged letters frequently during the first year of Cochrane's command, Auckland sending news of Chartism in England and revolution in Europe. It was on 1 January 1849 that Admiral Dundas, assistant to the First Lord, wrote to Cochrane, "It is with great regret I have to inform you of the death of Lord Auckland, after a few hours' illness." The new First Lord was Sir Francis Baring, a former Chancellor of the Exchequer, whose interest was less in the proposals and improvements suggested by Cochrane than in the making of economies wherever possible. Cochrane turned his attention to observing and noting the topography and industry of the Canadian Atlantic coast, the geology of Bermuda, and the disposition of the inhabitants of the West Indies. His journal contained a mass of observations on his travels, from Nova Scotia to Trinidad. It was in Trinidad that he saw something which impressed him more than almost any other sight during his period as commander-in-chief.[35]

Near La Brea was the famous "Pitch Lake", a bituminous expanse some three miles in circumference. The surface was a waxy brown, though Cochrane noted from the corrugations in it that the bitumen below the surface was "still on the move". His first thought was that it might in some way be used as fuel for steamships. "Our vessels would be supplied when an enemy would be almost deprived of the use of steam in these seas." Though this bitumen had been tried in laying London pavements, it had gone out of fashion and remained unexploited. Cochrane, finding too little employment under Sir Francis Baring, seized on its possibilities. He devised new uses for it and took out patents accordingly. In 1851 he was granted a patent for the use of bitumen in constructing sewers, tunnels, columns, and capitals. In 1852 there followed patents for its use in insulating wire, and in 1853 for producing a substitute for expensive gums and for laying pipes below ground. Nor was this all. He proposed to use bitumen as the basis for a grand scheme to end the pollution of the Thames. Embankments, their stones set in waterproof bitumen, were to be built out to narrow the river between Vauxhall and London Bridge. The aim would be to create a deeper and faster-flowing river which would sweep the pollution out to sea. Sewers were to be laid, running beneath the docks themselves, and were to be watertight subterranean tunnels whose pavement stones would, once again, be made waterproof by bitumen.[36]

As might be expected of Cochrane, he dealt speedily with the argument that the abolition of slavery in the West Indies had merely brought poverty to those who might otherwise have worked contentedly in servitude. There was no doubt, when he visited Jamaica, that most of those on the island were living in poverty. But the answer was simple. When he inspected the Customs House, he discovered that much of the island's food was imported and subject to a high rate of duty. Moreover, the sugar plantations employed fewer workers since emancipation, so that there was now a reservoir of surplus and unemployed labour. At the same time, the government held tracts of potentially productive land which it declined to let anyone work. The answer, in Cochrane's view, was simple enough. Let the land be given or leased to the unemployed, so that enough food might be produced to feed the starving and, indeed, to make the island self-sufficient. Even here there was a major difficulty. So many taxes were payable on the transfer of land that even workers who could afford to buy land were unable to pay the taxes as well.

> Is it reasonable to instruct the negroes in their rights as men, and open their minds to the humble ambition of acquiring spots of land, and then throw every impediment possible in the way of its gratification? I perceive by the imposts and expenses on the transfer of small properties, that a barrier almost insurmountable is raised to their acquisition by the coloured population.[37]

The unreasonableness of the situation was a primary cause of the so-called Jamaica Mutiny, five years after Cochrane's death, in which the unrest of the native population was put down with punitive zeal by the British army.

As for Cochrane's tour of duty, Sir Francis Baring wrote to him on the last day of 1850 informing him that Sir George Seymour had been appointed as his successor. It was not an unreasonable decision. Cochrane had held his command for two years and he was now seventy-five years old. Whatever the faults of the Admiralty, they could hardly be blamed for the peaceful and uneventful nature of his duty. Accordingly, he accepted the orders given him, sailing from Halifax on 14 May 1851 and arriving at Portsmouth at the beginning of June.

The summer of 1851, with the Crystal Palace rising as a monument to national self-congratulation among the trees of Hyde Park, appeared to set the seal of international agreement on peace and industry as the two goals of the latter half of the nineteenth century. The mood of peace and his own advancing age would have seemed to offer little hope to Cochrane of active service in the future. But the mood was deceptive and British public opinion on matters of war and peace had rarely been so volatile.

Even by the time that Lord Aberdeen succeeded as Prime Minister, in December 1852, whatever euphoria had survived the summer of the exhibition was dispersed by the "Eastern Question". Almost half a century earlier, in his meeting with Napoleon at Tilsit, Czar Alexander had laid claim to Turkey as falling within the Russian sphere of influence. In January and February 1853, his successor, Nicholas, argued with the British ambassador, Sir Hamilton Seymour, that the Turkish Empire was disintegrating. "We must come to an understanding," he insisted. The proposal was that Britain should take Cyprus and Egypt, leaving Russia free to dispose of the rest of the Turkish Empire.

On the one hand, Aberdeen's government was alarmed at the prospect of Russian expansion to the Adriatic and into the Middle East. On the other hand, they regarded themselves as men of peace, deterred from a major conflict by their memories of the slaughter which some of them had seen with their own eyes at Leipzig or Waterloo. In July 1853, however, Russia invaded the Turkish Danubian provinces. On 30 November, her warships sank the Black Sea squadron of the Turkish fleet without warning and at point-blank range.

Public opinion in Britain and France turned towards war. A British ultimatum of 27 February 1854 demanded the withdrawal of Russian troops from the occupied provinces of Turkey. There was no reply. On 28 March, Britain and France declared war on Russia. Their

first military aim was to reinforce the Turks by way of the Dardanelles. From this there developed the strategy of invading the Crimea,
seizing the port and arsenal of Sebastopol, and holding it as a hostage
for Russian compliance with British and French demands. In the
early spring of 1854, as the Scots Guards and a host of other famous
regiments marched through London, Portsmouth, and the dockyard
towns, en route for the troopships that would carry them to Scutari
or Varna, Cochrane turned his attention to the naval war against
Russia.

By now, of course, he was one of the very few surviving commanders who had seen active service against the French in 1793–
1815. More to the point, his mind was sharp and his ideas as logically
organised as they had ever been. Even before the declaration of war
in 1854, it was evident that the British military plan would involve
equipping and maintaining an army of some 20,000 men in a location
which, by the sailing time of most ships, would be six or eight weeks
away. The Russians need only resume a defensive position in order to
wear down the allies by a policy of attrition. Accordingly, Cochrane
wrote to the First Lord of the Admiralty, offering his secret plans as
the means of devastating the Russian defences at Sebastopol or
Cronstadt, in the Baltic, and winning the war with less effort and
infinitely less loss of life than must otherwise be the case.

The First Lord in Aberdeen's cabinet was Sir James Graham, who
had held the same post in 1834 and had been sympathetic towards
Cochrane's plans for the development of steamships in the navy. But
in 1853, when war had not even been declared, he declined to consider the use of the secret weapons. By February 1854, war was
inevitable and the Aberdeen cabinet had to discuss the appointment
of a commander-in-chief of the Baltic fleet. Britain and Russia
recalled ambassadors on 7 February and the cabinet met the next
day. The question was whether to appoint Cochrane to the important
command and the discussion was reported by the First Lord to
the Queen in his letter of the following day.

Lord Dundonald is seventy-nine years of age; and though his
energies and faculties are unbroken, and though, with his
accustomed courage, he volunteers for the Service, yet, on the
whole, there is reason to apprehend that he might deeply commit the Force under his command in some desperate enterprise,
where the chance of success would not countervail the risk of
failure and of the fatal consequences, which might ensue. Age

has not abated the adventurous spirit of this gallant officer, which no authority could restrain; and being uncontrollable it might lead to most unfortunate results. The Cabinet, on the most careful review of the entire question, decided that the appointment of Lord Dundonald was not expedient.[38]

There could hardly be a more splendid testimonial to Cochrane in old age than the fears which he inspired in Aberdeen and his ministers. His triumphs, in far more desperate enterprises, echoed through the history of half a dozen countries in the earlier nineteenth century: the *Gamo*, Fort Trinidad, the Basque Roads, Valdivia, the *Esmeralda*, and Maranham. Instead of the "risk of failure" in another such coup, thousands of men were condemned to misery and death by disease in the long siege of Sebastopol. By a quirk of the official mind, to lose 10,000 or 20,000 men in this way was a routine misfortune. To lose 5000 in action was both a defeat and a national humiliation.

Having missed the Baltic command, Cochrane pressed on with the campaign to have his secret weapons used in one form or another. He wrote to Sir James Graham on 22 July 1854, pointing out that because the allies would not be able to invade the Crimea, let alone take Sebastopol, until they had secured the Danubian provinces, the seizure of Cronstadt in the Baltic was the one swift defeat which could be inflicted on the Czar. Under cover of the clouds of gas from his "stink vessels", the port and its armament would be seized, so that "the maritime defences of Cronstadt, however strong against ordinary means of attack, may be captured, and their red-hot shot and incendiary missiles, prepared for the destruction of our ships, turned on those they protect". In its audacity, and its impudent use of the Russians' own weapons to destroy them, the plan had the unmistakable cast of Cochrane's thinking. He could not, of course, be given command of the Baltic fleet, since that had now gone to Sir Charles Napier. But he asked "unreservedly" to be allowed to accompany the attack, under the command of Napier and his deputy. "Personal acquaintance with Vice-Admiral Sir Charles Napier and Rear-Admiral Chads warrants my conviction that no feeling of rivalry could exist, save in the zealous performance of the service."[39]

Graham replied cautiously that, "The Cabinet, unaided, can form no judgment in this matter." Would Cochrane allow his plans to be put before a secret committee under Admiral Sir Thomas Byam Martin, with Sir William Parker, Admiral Berkeley, and Sir John Burgoyne as its other members? He replied at once, agreeing to

accept the committee and its decision, which was communicated to
him by Graham on 15 August 1854. The army was still disembarking
in Turkey and the extent of the disasters which it was to experience
in the following winter were, as yet, nowhere prefigured. Under
the "present circumstances", therefore, the committee had decided
that it would be "inexpedient" to use the secret weapons against
Cronstadt. But the members did not absolutely rule out their use
at any stage of the war, and the blow was judiciously softened for
Cochrane himself, as the First Lord explained.

> They do full justice to your lordship, and they expressly state
> that, if such an enterprise were to be undertaken, it could not be
> confided to fitter or abler hands than yours; for your professional
> career has been distinguished by remarkable instances of skill
> and courage, in all of which you have been the foremost to lead
> the way, and by your personal heroism you have gained an
> honourable celebrity in the naval history of this country.[40]

Cochrane noted merely that the secret committee had not expressed
any doubt of the "practicability" of his plans. Sir Charles Napier was
left to attack Cronstadt unsuccessfully with conventional weapons
and to return to England in the autumn with the reputation of failure
gathering about him. Cochrane came at once to his defence, intimat-
ing to the *Morning Post* that the weapons allowed to Napier were no
match for the Russian defences. "There is but one means to place
these parties on an equal footing, and that I confidentially laid before
the Government." In addition, he wrote again to the First Lord on 11
November, by which time the allied losses at the Alma, Balaclava,
and Inkerman casued a sober reassessment of the Crimean campaign.
There was, Cochrane conceded, a popular prejudice against elderly
admirals.

> But, my dear Sir James, were it necessary – which it is not –
> that I should place myself in an arm-chair on the poop, with
> each leg on a cushion, I will undertake to subdue every insular
> fortification at Cronstadt within four hours from the commence-
> ment of the attack.[41]

For good measure, he added that there would be no greater problem
in capturing Sebastopol. To the men who endured the hunger and
sickness of that winter, camped round the little port of Balaclava,
such a prospect was beyond credence. Sir James Graham replied

courteously that weather conditions would make further operations in the Baltic impossible until next year, while in the Crimea, "I still venture to hope that at Sebastopol our arms will be triumphant."[42]

Cochrane not only doubted the triumph but foresaw that the position of the British army in the Crimea might be in danger. He wrote to the Prime Minister, Lord Aberdeen, offering his secret weapons as the means of rescuing Lord Raglan's expeditionary force. The reply came from Sir James Graham once more, reminding Cochrane of the opinion of the secret committee. "Neither Lord Aberdeen nor I can venture to place our individual opinions in opposition to a recorded judgment of the highest authority."[43]

But in January 1855, Sir Charles Napier's command of the Baltic fleet ended. Cochrane, now approaching his eightieth birthday, at once volunteered to succeed him. He was not chosen, but as a consolation he had now been promoted to Admiral of the Fleet, though without a fleet to command. In any case, there was nothing that Aberdeen could do for him, since the government was forced to resign over the Crimean affair. Lord Palmerston became Prime Minister of a new Liberal government, with Sir Charles Wood as First Lord of the Admiralty. Cochrane swiftly offered his plans to the new administration, writing directly to Palmerston and also announcing in *The Times* on 10 March that, given eight or ten days of fine weather, the use of his plans in the Crimea "would spare thousands of lives, millions of money, great havoc and uncertainty of results". Given a free hand, he would also effect "the emancipation of Poland" and liberate "the usurped territories of Sweden".

He petitioned the House of Commons to oblige the government to use his new weapons as the means of ending the war. His reputation and popularity were now so widespread that there was a lively response from the middle-class Victorian public. One of the most forthright suggestions was that a public subscription should be raised to equip an independent force under Cochrane's command. This would be despatched to Sebastopol or Cronstadt, complete with the secret weapons, to do the job which the regular army or navy seemed unable to dispose of unaided. Cochrane refused to act in anything but an official role, yet the popular demand for a swift and successful conclusion to the war persuaded Palmerston to grant him an interview. When it had taken place, Lord Panmure wrote from the War Office to General Simpson in the Crimea, "What would you say to try Dundonald's scheme on the Malakoff? It might answer."[44]

The subject was further discussed between Panmure and Palmerston

himself during July and August 1855. Cochrane's plans were now
somewhat more elaborate than they had been in 1812, though in his
memorandum to the Prime Minister on 7 August he still favoured a
gas in which "five parts of coke effectually vaporise one part of sulphur". To take Sebastopol by this means, "Four or five hundred tons
of sulphur and two thousand tons of coke would be sufficient." He
also suggested that "a couple of thousand barrels of gas or other tar"
should be used to "mask" the fortifications on either side of the area
to be attacked.[45]

His more advanced researches involved floating naphtha on the sea,
close to Sebastopol, and "igniting it by means of a ball of potassium".
But whereas the authorities were prepared to consider the more modest
scientific weaponry offered by coke and sulphur, there was alarm at
the dangerous possibilities of the naphtha if the wind should change
at a critical moment. Cochrane was prepared to settle for whatever
was permitted and had not the least doubt that Sebastopol would be
overwhelmed in a matter of hours, after twelve months of misery
which the besieging army had endured. "There is no doubt," he
informed Palmerston, "but that the fumes will envelop all the
defences from the Malakoff to the Barracks, and even to the line-of-
battleship, *The Twelve Apostles*, at anchor in the harbour."[46]

Among all the self-congratulation of the Victorians at the way in
which the political corruption and blindness of their predecessors had
been routed, it was easy to forget that some of those predecessors
were still alive and held high office. Palmerston, though now a
Liberal Prime Minister, had once been a Lord of the Admiralty in the
very government whose corruption and cynicism Cochrane had
attacked. It might be argued that the Palmerston of 1855 was a
different man from the young Tory lord of 1807. But he had had cause
to dislike Cochrane then, and his letter to Panmure on 7 August 1855
shows a cynicism. which would have done credit to the Duke of
Portland's ministry, in which he had served almost half a century
before.

I agree with you that if Dundonald will go out himself to superin-
tend and direct the execution of his scheme, we ought to accept
his offer and try his plan. If it succeeds, it will, as you say, save a
great number of English and French lives; if it fails *in his hands*,
we shall be exempt from blame, and if we come in for a small
share of the ridicule, we can bear it, and the greater part will fall
on him.[47]

But the war in the Crimea was moving towards an independent conclusion. Sebastopol fell in September 1855 and the belligerents prepared for the Treaty of Paris, signed in the following year. The last chance for the practical demonstration of his secret weapons, or indeed for Cochrane to hold another active command in the Royal Navy, had gone for ever.

The last six years of his life were occupied equally by honours long delayed and controversies even longer established. In October 1854, besides his rank of Admiral of the Fleet, he had been appointed to the honorary command of Rear-Admiral of the United Kingdom. Characteristically, he accepted the honour only on condition that "such distinction shall not preclude my further service to the Crown and country". This was agreed. In the following month he received a letter from Prince Albert, asking that he should also consent to be elected one of the Elder Brethren of Trinity House. Cochrane replied, accepting the honour and acknowledging the "signal acts of justice and favour" which he had experienced from the Queen and her Consort. At the end of the Crimean War, the United Service Club, founded while Cochrane was in the King's Bench prison by men who were generally glad to see him there, elected him to honorary membership. He had always refused to put himself forward for election, claiming that he was too old to enjoy such associations and that, in any case, he preferred privacy to club life.[48]

He received the honours of his country graciously but, because he never over-estimated such thanks, without excessive gratitude. At eighty-one years old, it was evident to him that his life must end without any further active service or a chance to try his secret weapons in earnest. He therefore devoted himself to the last battle of all, the fight for personal justice.

It was on 26 May 1856 that he wrote to Palmerston, reminding him that though he had been restored to the Order of the Bath, his banner had not been replaced in Henry VII's Chapel at Westminster, down whose steps it had been ceremonially kicked in 1814. Moreover, though he had been restored to the navy by William IV, justice demanded that he should at least receive his half-pay for the period during which he had been wrongly dismissed. And finally, since he had been unjustly condemned in 1814, the government ought now to pay back the £1000 fine. Palmerston replied that the question of the banner was not one for the Prime Minister to deal with. There were no funds for the repayment of fines, and no precedent for making such restitution. As for the half-pay: "I find, on inquiry, that pay or half-pay has not been granted to any naval officer for any period during which he may have been out of the service."[49]

Cochrane continued to correspond with the government on these subjects, but to no effect. Technically, the state was under no obligation to him and, so far as the public was concerned, the restoration of his rank and honours marked the official acknowledgement of the injustice done him in 1814. The total of his "claim" against the British government was £5000 for the cost of his fine and legal expenses plus £4000 half-pay for the years 1814–1832.

At the same time, he was still claiming £26,000 due to him from the Chilean government and £100,000 from the government of Brazil. There was no obvious way of obtaining payment, and Cochrane might have been in danger of becoming little more than a laughing stock in his dotage. But, as usual, to draw the easiest conclusion was to underestimate him. In 1858, when he was eighty-three and his health began to fail, he retired to the house of his eldest son, Lord Thomas Cochrane, at Queen's Gate, Kensington. Even Kitty, his companion through so many years, who had seemed so much his junior at the time of their marriage, was now sixty-two years old. With the aid of a professional author, G. B. Earp, Cochrane began to put together his *Narrative of Services in the Liberation of Chili, Peru, and Brazil*. Because he employed a man who was at least a secretary and, at the most, a collaborator, Cochrane's critics were to cast doubt on the worth of his reminiscences. Tried by the test of other contemporary accounts of the same events, they emerge with credit. Indeed, their chief failing is the disproportionate amount of space devoted to the author's financial claims against the governments whom he had served.

With the publication of the *Narrative*, in 1859, and his *Autobiography of a Seaman*, whose two volumes appeared in 1859 and 1860, Cochrane's reputation blazed more brightly than ever before the mid-Victorian public. The books were written to obtain the vindication from posterity which it had been so difficult to wring from governments. As they were composed, Earp found himself undertaking more and more of the work, basing the account on Cochrane's papers and documents, supplemented by the old man's memories.

However written, the events of Cochrane's life had the supreme quality of forming a classic Victorian boys' adventure story. But while they found a ready market, in this respect, they also enhanced his prestige as one of the last living relics of the great wars against France. Wellington had died in 1852; St Vincent, Gambier, and the

other naval commanders had died long before that; even the youngest
survivors of the last battle, Waterloo, were not old men. The hero of
the *Narrative* and the *Autobiography*, though he lay dying in the
house at Queen's Gate, had first seen active service in H.M.S. *Hind*
sixty-seven years before. Even when he returned from Canada in
1851, he had been a serving officer over a period of fifty-eight years
and under the flags of four countries.

He was, in almost every respect, an ideally Victorian hero. Politically, he had served the very causes which had gained so much instinctive approval by 1860. He had fought for the freedom of those
countries which, for cultural reasons in the case of Greece and
economic ones in that of Chile or Brazil, seemed most clearly to
deserve it by Victorian standards. Conveniently overlooking his own
admiration for Napoleon, it was possible to see him as one of the
great defenders of his own country's liberty against the tyranny of
France. In his own cause, he had fought against the injustice and
oppression of the servants of George IV in a manner now thoroughly
admired by the democrats of the new age. Indeed, it would be hard
to say whether the Victorians were more concerned over his innocence of the Stock Exchange fraud or whether they merely felt that
his other qualities were so overwhelmingly sympathetic to them that
the alleged offence had long since been paid for.

The *Autobiography of a Seaman* ended with the Stock Exchange
prosecution. Cochrane had intended to continue the story of his life
in another volume but he was not to live long enough to write it.
Instead, he left the *Narrative* of his South American service as an
account of his later active career. He sent one of the first copies of
this to Prince Albert and received a reply promising that the Prince
would place "a high value" on the gift and asking that Cochrane
should inscribe the first volume in his own hand.[50]

By the autumn of 1860, the publication of the first two volumes of
the *Autobiography* had spread Cochrane's name more widely than
ever. Yet whatever the role of the books in justifying him to posterity,
they were destined to achieve little more during his lifetime. In
October, he underwent an operation in the house at Queen's Gate.
On the last day of the month he died there, a few weeks before his
eighty-fifth birthday.

His death was reported briefly at first by some papers, with promises
that it would be noticed more fully later on. It might have been
thought, perhaps, that some of them were waiting for the official

reaction of court and state before committing themselves to an un-
stinted eulogy. They had not long to wait. Whatever hesitations had
been felt on the part of Palmerston's government, Victoria and Albert
had no intention of allowing one of the last and most gallant of the
heroes of the Napoleonic wars to pass in obscurity from the scene. On
6 November, it was announced that he was to be buried among the
nation's honoured dead, in Westminster Abbey. The funeral would
take place on 14 November.

Ironically, Henry VII's Chapel at Westminster had remained a
source of annoyance to Cochrane, since Palmerston had refused to
have his banner restored there as Knight of the Bath. After it had
been ceremonially evicted from the chapel in 1814, the banner had
been retrieved from a curiosity shop. On the day before the funeral,
ignoring Palmerston, the Queen ordered that the banner and insignia
of her hero should be restored to their place in the chapel after an
absence of forty-six years.

Victorian England had raised the public funeral almost to an art of
pageantry by 1860. The cortège itself, setting out from Kensington
for the Abbey, was saluted by the tributes of the press.

> Ashes to ashes! Lay the hero down
>> Within the grey old Abbey's glorious shade.
>> In our Valhalla ne'er was worthier laid
> Since martyr first won palm, or victor crown.[51]

The ornate hearse with six black horses, plumed and caparisoned,
was followed by eight mourning coaches and a host of carriages,
bearing the Chilean and Brazilian ambassadors, admirals of the Fleet,
Brougham, the old Lord Chancellor, and men who had served under
Cochrane's command. From 11.30 a.m. until 1 p.m., the procession
passed from Kensington to Piccadilly, down St James's Street and
Parliament Street, to the Abbey. Few of those who stood in silence
along the route were old enough to recall the enthusiasm of the crusade against republican France, when Cochrane first went to sea as an
awkward midshipman in 1793. At eighty-five, he had lived more than
twice the average span of life among his contemporaries. He represented, both in age and reputation, the link which united two centuries in deeds of gallantry and honour. As at the funeral of
Wellington, eight years before, the cortège marked the end of an era.
Perhaps more haunting than the public memories was the mood
inspired by death.

A Sea-King, whose fit place had been by Blake,
    Or our own Nelson, had he been but free
    To follow glory's quest upon the sea,
Leading the conquered navies in his wake.[52]

Beyond the crowds, the Abbey doors stood open to receive the procession, the burial service sung to Purcell's chant in G minor. The coffin was borne to its place by two admirals, five captains, and the Brazilian ambassador, the choir singing an anthem specially composed by John Goss, organist of St Paul's, "O Lord God, the strength of my heart, Thou hast covered my head in the day of battle." As the mellow treble notes echoed among the vaulted stone, the words described Cochrane's fortunes in a hundred engagements with singular aptness.

The grave had been prepared in the nave of the Abbey. As the principal mourners stood round it, Brougham looked about him and said bitterly, "No cabinet minister here! No officer of state to grace this great man's funeral!"[53]

It was characteristic of Cochrane's life that it should be so, just as his great commemorative statue was built in Valparaiso rather than London, and that when guards of honour stood at his tomb they were Chilean or Brazilian, rather than the representatives of his own country. Indeed, despite the absence of Palmerston and his colleagues, Westminster Abbey was crowded for the funeral by those who, like Brougham, were at one with the words of the triumphal concluding anthem, Handel's "His body is buried in peace, but his memory shall live for ever".

By now, the tone of eulogy in the press seemed unanimous, from *The Times*, which had always befriended him under Delane's editorship, to *Punch* and the *Illustrated London News*, where his enemies were denounced as the men of "envy, obloquy, and malice", and even as, "The crawling worms that in corruption breed". Liberal England had taken up its hero's cause and turned savagely upon the weak and frightened governments of the Regency and George IV.[54]

Nowhere was the popular feeling for Cochrane more cogently summarised than in the epitaph on his tomb, ornamented by the arms of Greece, Brazil, Chile and Peru. The words were those of Sir Lyon Playfair, who was then Professor of Chemistry at Edinburgh. Cochrane is described as Earl of Dundonald, Baron Cochrane, Marquess of Maranham, Knight Commander of the Bath, and Admiral of the Fleet:

Who by the confidence which his genius, his science,
and extraordinary daring inspired,
By his heroic exertions in the cause of Freedom,
and his splendid services alike to his own country,
Greece, Brazil, Chili, and Peru,
Achieved a name illustrious throughout the world for
courage, patriotism, and chivalry.

It might be expected that the controversies of Cochrane's life would not be ended merely by his death. In the first place, of course, there was the confusion which he had caused by marrying Kitty three times. From 1861 until 1863, the House of Lords Committee of Privileges met intermittently to determine the claim of Thomas Cochrane to his father's title. There were four sons, as well as a daughter, and Thomas, the infant Tom Cochrane of the South American wars, succeeded by proving the validity of the first marriage in 1812 and, hence, his own legitimacy. In the course of investigating the claim, the committee took evidence from Kitty herself, who was now living in France for her health. For some years Cochrane himself had been convinced that France was healthier for her than England. It certainly agreed with her looks and temperament. "Met Lady Dundonald," wrote Henry Greville from Paris in 1841, "who has the remains of beauty, and a joyous laugh which begets merriment in others."[55]

Thomas Cochrane's claim to the title was duly established, but that was only the first of the battles which the 11th Earl of Dundonald had to fight. The question of whether his father had been entitled to a repayment of the 1814 fine, and half-pay as a naval officer for the period 1814–1832, was still not settled. By the will of his father, the son was bequeathed "all the monies due to me from the British Government", except for 10 per cent of the money recovered which was to be paid to Earp who had collaborated in writing Cochrane's *Narrative* and *Autobiography*. In 1864, his son applied to the Admiralty and the Home Office for the money, but the application was rejected. In 1876, Cochrane's grandson petitioned the Queen, the petition being referred to the Treasury, but without any further success. It was on 10 April 1877 that Sir Robert Anstruther and Spencer Walpole moved for a select committee to inquire into the merits of the petition. Their motion was carried and a committee set up under the Solicitor-General, Sir Hardinge Giffard, who was later to be a distinguished Lord Chancellor, as Lord Halsbury.

The select committee considered the evidence and concluded that no governments which believed Cochrane to have been guilty in 1814 would have restored his rank and honours in the manner which they had done. This was entirely logical, since he had not served the British crown between 1814 and 1832 and so could hardly have earned forgiveness for a crime which it was then believed he must have committed. In June 1876, the select committee recommended that an award of £5000 should be paid to his grandson. Cochrane himself had put his legal expenses and loss of pay at £9000, but even this recognition vindicated him by his own criteria. The Brazilian government, too, recognised that at least some of Cochrane's claims against it were justified. Of his demand for £100,000, a settlement of £40,000 was duly made.[56]

Unfortunately, the satisfaction among Cochrane's descendants was matched by outrage among those of Lord Ellenborough, who now regarded their famous ancestor as having been slandered in the basest manner, libelled by Cochrane in the *Autobiography* and by Lord Campbell in his *Lives of the Chief Justices*, and unfairly dealt with by the House of Commons and its select committee. Accordingly, Ellenborough's grandson, Edward Downes Law, employed a barrister, J. B. Atlay, to write *The Trial of Lord Cochrane before Lord Ellenborough*. The book, which appeared in 1897, confirmed that the truth of the Stock Exchange case was, ultimately, beyond proof or disproof. However, in view of the way in which Atlay was employed to write the entire book, there is a certain irony in the dismissal of Cochrane's autobiography on the grounds that he wrote it with Earp's assistance. The squabble continued until 1914, when Ellenborough's grandson himself wrote and published *The Guilt of Lord Cochrane in 1814* to celebrate the centenary of the Stock Exchange trial.

Of Cochrane's immediate family, Kitty died five years after him, in Boulogne in 1865, at the age of sixty-nine. His heir, Thomas Barnes Cochrane, lived to see payment made by order of parliament in 1876, in recognition of his father's unrequited services. The 11th Earl of Dundonald had chosen the army as his career and took part in the China wars. The grandson, Douglas Cochrane, earned considerable military fame as 12th Earl of Dundonald, reaching the rank of Major-General after the South African war of 1899–1901, in which he was mentioned in despatches six times. After being promoted to Lieutenant-General, he emerged from retirement to command the 2nd Life Guards in the First World War. He was the last of his line who overlapped Cochrane's own life, having been born in 1852 and succeeded to the title on the death of the 11th Earl in 1885.

Shortly before his death, the *Athenaeum* summarised Cochrane's attraction for the Victorians by remarking, "Everything about Lord Dundonald's career is strange and romantic. . . . He inherited an earldom – and a gold watch. . . . He was liker Nelson than any other officer of his generation." The world at large was familiar with the imposing figure of the old sailor, "a broad-built Scotchman, rather seared than conquered by age, with hairs of snowy white, and a face in which intellect still beams through sorrow and struggle, and the marks of eighty years of active life". His great height, somewhat reduced by a pronounced stoop, was still "commanding". The Victorians found in him the manners of a more elegant age, "good old-fashioned courtesy colouring the whole man, his gestures, and speech".[57]

As Cochrane himself had remarked, without having "a particle of romance" in his character, he was destined to become one of the most romantic warriors of his day. It was perhaps inevitable that he should be so described in a period later summed up by the literary catch-phrase of "the Romantic Revival". In the heroics of warfare, as well as in his attachment to a new ideal of democracy, he was as much a part of that culture as Byron or Scott. He mirrored the qualities of action and drama which Scott portrayed in fiction, while sharing the Philhellenism and democratic enthusiasm which moved both Byron and Shelley. His admiration for the greatest romantic hero, Napoleon, and his particular distaste for the Wellesleys and all their works reflects a sympathy with the prevailing intellectual fashion. Indeed, there seems an almost Byronic grandeur in the plan to free the famous prisoner of St Helena and set him on the throne of a great South American Empire.

The extremes of Cochrane's character embraced the contraries of amiability and pertinacity, generosity and extreme touchiness. He was master of surprise in naval warfare, yet victim of an extraordinary degree of naïveté in dealing with governments of every complexion. With a handful of ships, he could liberate half a continent, but his attempts to win a degree of political freedom for his own countrymen led to his repeated humiliation in the House of Commons. In his financial dealings, conditioned by the long memory of the "res angusta domi", he speculated unhesitatingly to increase his fortune and hounded British and foreign governments for every penny which he considered they might owe him. But while he seemed unremittingly mercenary, he was unpredictably generous. He gave or returned money, as in the case of the Greek government, with the appearance of caring nothing for it. In many of his campaigns on behalf of nations fighting for their independence, he gave more than he received.

"He is such a fine fellow," wrote Charles Greville in 1830, "and so shrewd and good humoured." Since Greville also believed him guilty of the Stock Exchange fraud, there is no reason to regard the judgement as mere flattery. A quarter of a century before, Mary Russell Mitford, observing the young captain of the *Speedy* had found him, most of all, "gentle, quiet, mild". As a matter of disposition, he seems indeed to belong to the eighteenth century rather than to its successor and to display those qualities of courtesy and benevolence which were recognised by it in the phenomenon of "the Good-Natured Man".[58]

But if this was the countenance which Cochrane presented to those with whom he had no quarrel, he was an implacable enemy to his opponents. Even in his old age, there was no mellowing and no sense in which past antagonisms were forgotten. In his eighties, he fought with embittered resolve to clear his name and to destroy the reputations of men like Ellenborough for the injury they had done him almost half a century before. It mattered little that most men by this time believed him innocent, or that those who remained in doubt none the less regarded any suspicion against him as insignificant by comparison with the numerous deeds of honour and gallantry which stood to his credit. As Cardinal Manning once remarked of Cardinal Newman, Cochrane was "a good hater". It mattered nothing, for example, that St Vincent had been one of the best naval commanders of his day, nor that he was a vigorous opponent of the same naval corruption which Cochrane attacked. He had put himself beyond the pale by his treatment of the brash commander of the *Speedy*. Even fifty-eight years later there was no forgiveness for this.[59]

Whether in personal conflict or general battle, Cochrane was interested in nothing but absolute victory. In naval politics or legal quarrels this was notoriously difficult to achieve. He was an artist in war, whether in the split-second annihilation of French cavalry at Port Vendre by a turning broadside from the *Imperieuse*, or in the concept of instant and total triumph offered to the Prince Regent in 1812, by virtue of the famous secret weapons. Yet in English public life, complete and demonstrable victories, of the sort represented by the *Gamo* or the *Esmeralda* in war, eluded him.

Underlying his skill in war, and even his private amiability, was an embarrassing quickness to resent injury either to his reputation or his purse. He found the servants of the Admiralty, and those of the Greek or South American governments, difficult to deal with. However Cochrane's own prickliness could make him one of the most awkward partners. He might be an artist in war, but his repeated threats to resign his command and leave the stage of combat suggested, more specifically, a prima donna. Nor did he show great tolerance of the Brazilian or Greek crews who found themselves manning a vessel which was unfamiliar to them. It happened that the best Royal Navy crews had long experience of the sea, in peace and war, while those of many other nations had not. Cochrane made too few allowances for this, perhaps, but he was never guilty of mere chauvinism. As he wrote to Lord Haddington at the Admiralty: "I am not one of those, my lord, who deem it advantageous to act on the belief that one Englishman can beat two Frenchmen." In his own case, it happened that he had beaten the French, or beaten them off, on every occasion but one, when the *Speedy* was trapped by three battleships off Alicante in 1802. But that occasion remained in his mind, combining with wider experience to safeguard him from the comfortable nationalistic myths generated by legends of Trafalgar or Waterloo.[60]

The day to day chores of commanding a larger fleet seem to have been uncongenial to him and to have brought out his less admirable traits. In battle, as his tactics against the Portuguese off Bahia established, he could lead such formations with a flair worthy of his single-ship actions. As the commander of a single ship, he was supreme. Since Drake and the Elizabethans, no man could rival the successive achievements of the *Speedy*, the *Pallas*, the *Imperieuse*, the *O'Higgins*, and the *Pedro Primiero*. His plans for gas attacks on the enemy coast or saturation bombardment from his "temporary mortar" vessels might have altered the course of the Napoleonic and Crimean wars dramatically, or might have ended in fiasco. None the less, England had a weapon of equal potential in Cochrane himself. Armed with the conventional force of two or three frigates and a regiment or two of troops, his destruction of French commerce, communications, and supplies might have given England a decisive initiative in the most important theatre of the earlier war.

The Victorian reading public, no less than those who had heard the first news of his astonishing victories, found in him a hero of almost

Byronic individualism. He had, as the *Athenaeum* termed it, "a mixture of rapid calculation with supreme daring". From the viewpoint of a liberal historian, Justin McCarthy observed, "Cochrane's true place was on his quarter-deck; his opportunity came in the extreme moment of danger. . . . His gift was that which wrenches success out of the very jaws of failure." He was the swashbuckling commander whose triumphs were half the result of tactical genius, and half the outcome of a practical joke played on his enemies. Then he was the valiant young lord eloping with an impecunious beauty at the cost of fortune and reputation. He was even the wrongly-imprisoned fighter, scaling the walls of his gaol, in Malta or the King's Bench, to set himself at liberty. It seemed hardly relevant that he was deeply interested in Stock Exchange speculation, and that his democratic sympathies were accompanied by the acceptance of the gallows, the press gang, and the lash as necessary evils. In this, as in his old-fashioned anti-Catholicism, he was a child of his own time, not of his admirers.[61]

By the time of his death, the great question of the Stock Exchange fraud seemed easily disposed of. "It is impossible to read the old Earl's narrative of this affair without indignation," said the *Athenaeum*. Ellenborough's conduct was condemned by two Lord Chancellors, by Campbell in his *Lives of the Chief Justices*, and by Brougham in *Historical Sketches of Statesmen who flourished in the Reign of George III*. The conduct of the judge was condemned in the *Modern State Trials* and even the *Quarterly Review* paused to brand Ellenborough for his "monstrous attempt to tinge the ermine of justice with the colour of party". Of Cochrane's Victorian sympathisers, Justin McCarthy treated his hero's enemies with some lenience, remarking that Cochrane had been "the victim of cruel, although not surely intentional, injustice". It was left to *The Times*, in Cochrane's obituary, to suggest the motive for such injustice, when it admitted that Cochrane was "everything which a man in office would dislike".[62]

He was a Radical, whereas those were the palmy days of Toryism. He was outspoken, whereas officials admire reticence and discretion. He was resolute in exposing abuses, and therefore constantly creating trouble. He was impracticable – a term still in favour for describing inconvenient excellence; and he had a strong spirit of independence – a quality which as very recent controversies have shown is singularly obnoxious to the official mind.[63]

It would have appeared unseemly in such an obituary to recall the zeal with which Cochrane also pursued the dead objects of his hate, including St Vincent, Gambier, Croker, and Ellenborough.

When all the arguments over prize money, promotion, political corruption, and the famous trial of 1814 were exhausted, it was to Cochrane as buccaneer that the Victorian press returned. He had, as *The Times* reminded its readers, held the French and Spanish at bay, seized fifty or more of their ships, including a xebec-class frigate, and defied three of their battleships with the diminutive *Speedy*, a vessel "about half as big as the smallest steam-tug now borne on the effective list of the navy". He seemed a more human figure than Nelson, a fit companion for Sir Francis Drake, and a man whose personal courage was dazzling. He escaped the worst that his enemies might have done to him through a brilliance of improvisation and a degree of daring which was beyond anything that his opponents in battle thought possible. William Miller, watching him at moments of extreme peril in the South American wars, saw an example of sang-froid which he would remember for the rest of his life. Marryat and his companions in the Mediterranean and the Bay of Biscay delighted in the piratical gaiety and untiring impudence with which Cochrane faced the odds against him. To his men, he was not a commander but a leader. One favourite Victorian anecdote, repeated from the *Naval Chronicle*, described how the boat crew of the *Imperieuse*, facing an apparently impregnable French shore-battery, replied when Cochrane suggested they might care to postpone the attack: "No, my lord! We can do it, if you go!"[64]

This was the stuff of which legends were woven, duly enshrined for the youth of late Victorian England in such schoolboy bestsellers as Macmillan's "English Men of Action" series. The baroque elegance of Nelsonian or Napoleonic battlefleets was a borrowed memory to Chilean guards of honour who still paid homage at Cochrane's tomb in Westminster Abbey. His Victorian admirers looked in vain for public memorial sculpture. But in the new democratic medium of mass publication, including Marryat's fictionalised accounts of Fort Trinidad and the Basque Roads, where his courage was commemorated, he won the tribute which had been denied him in monuments and statuary. In literature, at least, his flawless audacity and casual valour lit the dark canvas of suffering, where the futile misery of the Walcheren expedition or the long ordeal of the Peninsula haunted the public mind. There was one other name which was persistently coupled with Cochrane's, not necessarily to his own disadvantage, as the opinion of the contemporary historian Sir Archibald Alison showed.

> Lord Cochrane was, after the death of Nelson, the greatest naval commander of that age of glory. Equal to his great predecessor in personal gallantry, enthusiastic ardour, and devotion to his country, he was perhaps his superior in original genius, inventive power, and inexhaustible resources.[65]

That Nelson's reputation should have stood in the least danger from Cochrane's during the nineteenth century seems remarkable. In a longer perspective of history, however, it is possible to see them as worthy contenders for the fame which posterity bestows upon the supreme romantic hero.

# Notes

SOURCES referred to in the notes are fully described in the bibliography. The following abbreviations are used in the notes themselves.

*Autobiography:* Thomas Cochrane, 10th Earl of Dundonald, *Autobiography of a Seaman* (2nd edition), 1860
Cochrane, *Narrative:* Thomas Cochrane, 10th Earl of Dundonald, *Narrative of Services in the Liberation of Chili, Peru, and Brazil,* 1859
*Life:* Thomas, 11th Earl of Dundonald and H. R. Fox Bourne, *The Life of Thomas, Lord Cochrane, 10th Earl of Dundonald,* 1869
*Court-Martial: Minutes of a Court-Martial holden on board H.M.S. Gladiator . . . on the Trial of the Right Honourable James, Lord Gambier,* 1809

Footnotes are usually given at the end of a paragraph to identify the material on which the paragraph or sequence of paragraphs is based. However, in order not to burden the narrative with an inordinate number of notes, groups of sources are sometimes cited together under one reference. So far as possible, they are cited in the order in which the material appears in the narrative.

## PREFACE

1. *Times,* 2 November 1860.
2. *Creevey,* ed. John Gore, 1948, p. 119n.; Doris Langley Moore, *The Late Lord Byron,* 1961, pp. 119 and 192; J. W. Fortescue, *Dundonald,* 1895, p. 215.

## 1. THE LORDS OF CULROSS

1. *Autobiography,* I, 43.
2. David Beveridge, *Between the Ochils and the Forth,* 1888, pp. 31, 162.
3. *The Earl of Dundonald's Answer to the Mis-statements contained in the Life of the late T. Coutts, Esq.,* 1822, p. 5; Gilbert Burnet, *History of his own Time,* 1724–1734, I, 634.
4. *Edinburgh Review,* CXVIII (1833), 242–243.
5. John, Baron Campbell, *Lives of the Lord Chancellors,* 1856–1857, VII, 319.
6. Archibald Cochrane, 9th Earl of Dundonald, *Memorial and Petition to the East India Company,* 1786, *passim.*

7. Basil Cochrane, *An Inquiry into the Conduct of the Commissioners for Victualling His Majesty's Navy*, 1823, p. 5.
8. Basil Cochrane, *An Historical Digest of the Reports of the Commission appointed to inquire into Abuses in the Public Departments of Government*, 1824, pp. 46–48; Basil Cochrane, *An Exposé of the Conduct of the Victualling Board*, 1824, p. 57.
9. Andrew Cochrane-Johnstone, *Defence of the Honourable Andrew Cochrane-Johnstone*, 1806, p. ii; A. Aspinall (ed.) *Correspondence of George, Prince of Wales, 1770–1812*, 1963–1971, V, 372-375.
10. Archibald Cochrane, 9th Earl of Dundonald, *Description of the Estate and Abbey of Culross*, 1793, pp. 72–74.
11. *ibid.*, p. 55.
12. National Library of Scotland, MS. 5379 (British Tar Company), ff. 3–4.
13. *ibid.*, ff. 5–7; *Autobiography*. I, 39.
14. *Autobiography*, I, 45.
15. *ibid.*, I, 45.
16. National Library of Scotland, MS. 5379, ff. 16–18.
17. E. G. Twitchett, *Life of a Seaman*, 1931, p. 10.
18. *Autobiography*, I, 46–47.
19. *ibid.*, I, 47.
20. Bernard de Lacombe, *Talleyrand the Man*, 1910, p. 31.
21. *ibid.*, pp. 31–32.
22. *Historical Manuscripts Commission: Fortescue Manuscripts*, 1894, II, 301–302.
23. Lacombe, *Talleyrand the Man*, p. 15.
24. *Historical Manuscripts Commission: Fortescue Manuscripts* II, 371–372.
25. *ibid.*, 372–373.
26. William James, *The Naval History of Great Britain*, 1902, I, 50.
27. *Historical Manuscripts Commission: Fortescue Manuscripts*, II, 378.
28. Abraham Crawford, *Reminiscences of a Naval Officer during the late War*, 1851, II, 32–36.
29. William Richardson, *A Mariner of England*, 1908, p. 277; Crawford, *Reminiscences of a Naval Officer*, I, 128–129; James, *Naval History of Great Britain*, I, 314.
30. John Wilson Croker, *Correspondence and Diaries of John Wilson Croker*, 1885, I, 47–49; *Letters of the Earl of St Vincent*, 1922–1927, II, 179–180, 217–218, 247–248, 313–314.
31. Croker, *Correspondence and Diaries*, I, 33–34.
32. Crawford, *Reminiscences of a Naval Officer*, I, 103–107.
33. Thomas Hodgskin, *An Essay on Naval Discipline*, 1813, pp. 97–98.
34. *Life and Letters of Captain Marryat*, 1872, I, 158.
35. Fortescue, *Dundonald*, p. 34.
36. W. V. Anson, *The Life of John Jervis, Admiral Lord St Vincent*, 1913, pp. 161–162; H. G. Thursfield (ed.) *Five Naval Journals*, 1951, p. 105.
37. Richardson, *A Mariner of England*, pp. 178, 180.

38. *ibid.*, pp. 186–187.
39. Hodgskin, *Essay on Naval Discipline*, pp. 110–111; Edward Giffard, *Deeds of Naval Daring*, 1852, pp. 120–124.
40. Richardson, *A Mariner of England*, p. 44; David Howarth, *Trafalgar*, 1969, pp 21–22.
41. Anson, *Life of St Vincent*, p. 138; Richardson, *A Mariner of England*, pp. 125–127.
42. *Letters of St Vincent*, II, 431n.; Edward Pelham Brenton, *Life and Correspondence of John, Earl of St Vincent*, 1838, II, 159, 160, 190.
43. *Letters of St Vincent*, II, 475.
44. *ibid* , II, 449.
45. *Parliamentary Debates*, XVI, 1006–1011.

## 2. STEERING TO GLORY

1. *Autobiography*, I, 51.
2. *ibid.*, I, 51–52.
3. Thursfield, *Five Naval Journals*, p. 226.
4. *Autobiography*, I, 52.
5. Crawford, *Reminiscences of a Naval Officer*, I, 219–221.
6. *Autobiography*, I, 70–72.
7. *ibid.*, I, 73.
8. W. H. Smyth, *The Life and Services of Captain Philip Beaver*, 1829, pp. 122–124.
9. *Autobiography*, I, 77–78.
10. *ibid.*, I, 78–79; Twitchett, *Life of a Seaman*, pp. 31–32; Christopher Lloyd, *Lord Cochrane*, 1947, p. 10.
11. *Autobiography*, I, 80; Twitchett, *Life of a Seaman*, p. 32.
12. *Autobiography*, I, 88–89.
13. *ibid.*, I, 89–90.
14. *ibid.*, I, 94–95.
15. *ibid.*, I, 93–94.
16. *ibid.*, I, 95.
17. *ibid.*, I, 98.
18. *ibid.*, I, 100–102.
19. *ibid.*, I, 107.
20. *ibid.*, 103–105.
21. *ibid.*, I, 110–112; *Naval Chronicle*, VI (1801), 151; E. P. Brenton, *Naval History of Great Britain*, 1823–1825, III, 30.
22. *Autobiography*, I, 116; *Naval Chronicle*, XXII (1809), 6; Brenton, *Naval History*, IV, 25.
23. Brenton, *St Vincent*, II, 80–81.
24. *Autobiography*, I, 146–147.
25. *ibid.*, I, 147–150.
26. *ibid.*, I, 124, 146.
27. Clements Markham (ed.) *Selections from the Correspondence of Admiral John Markham*, 1904, p. 11.

28. *Autobiography*, I, 124–127.
29. *ibid.*, I, 130.
30. Lewis Gibbs, *Sheridan*, 1947, p. 214; Jasper Ridley, *Lord Palmerston*, 1970, p. 16.


### 3. "A SINK OF CORRUPTION"

1. Twitchett, *Life of a Seaman*, p. 155.
2. *Autobiography*, I, 163.
3. Anson, *Life of St Vincent*, p. 91.
4. *Autobiography*, I, 153.
5. *Letters of St Vincent*, II, 14–15, 17, 182–183.
6. J. S. Tucker, *Memoirs of the Earl of St Vincent*, 1844, II, 150.
7. William James, *Old Oak: The Life of John Jervis, Earl of St Vincent*, 1950, p. 184; *Letters of St Vincent*, II, 451n.
8. Cf. *England and Napoleon in 1803: Being the Despatches of Lord Whitworth and others*, ed. Oscar Browning (Royal Historical Society), 1887.
9. *Diary and Correspondence of Charles Abbot, Lord Colchester*, 1861, I, 469–471.
10. Cf. *Sir Andrew Snape Hamond v. Messrs. Brents Shipbuilders*, 23 February 1804.
11. *Letters of St Vincent*, II, 25.
12. *Autobiography*, I, 165.
13. *Letters of St Vincent*, II, 337.
14. *Autobiography*, I, 166.
15. *ibid.*, I, 166.
16. *ibid.*, I, 166.
17. Crawford, *Reminiscences of a Naval Officer*, I, 144–159.
18. George Keith Elphinstone, Viscount Keith, *The Keith Papers*, ed. Christopher Lloyd, 1955, III, 190–191; Lloyd, *Lord Cochrane*, p. 28, *Selections from the Correspondence of Admiral Markham*, p. 153.
19. *Letters of St Vincent*, II, 68–71.
20. Gibbs, *Sheridan*, p. 217.
21. Joseph Farington, *The Farington Diary*, ed. James Greig, 1922–1928, V, 59, 163.
22. 29 *State Trials*, 549–1482.
23. *Autobiography*, I, 174; *Naval Chronicle*. XIII (1805), 328–329.
24. *Naval Chronicle*, XIII (1805), 358; *Autobiography*, I, 176.
25. *Autobiography*, I, 176.
26. *ibid.*, I, 176–178.
27. *ibid.*, I, 178–179.
28. *Defence of the Honourable Andrew Cochrane-Johnstone*, p. 157.
29. *Cobbett's Weekly Political Register*, IX (1806), 968.
30. *ibid.*, IX (1806), 970.
31. *Naval Chronicle*, XXII (1809), 18.
32. *Autobiography*, I, 179.

33. *ibid.*, I 179; *Cobbett's Weekly Political Register*, IX (1806), 971.
34. *Autobiography*, I, 180.
35. *ibid.*, I, 183–184.
36. *ibid.*, I, 185–186.
37. *ibid.*, I, 187–188.
38. *ibid.*, I, 188–193; *Naval Chronicle*, XV (1806), 317.
39. G. E. Cockayne, *The Complete Peerage*, 1910–1959, IV, 530.
40. Lloyd, *Lord Cochrane*, p. 38.
41. *Autobiography*, I, 193, 195–201; *Naval Chronicle*, XVI (1806), 75–76.
42. *Autobiography*, I, 203.
43. *ibid.*, I, 203–204.
44. *ibid.*, I, 205.
45. *ibid.*, I, 208–209.
46. *Correspondence and Diaries of John Wilson Croker*, I, 2–4.
47. *Creevey*, ed. John Gore, 1948, p. 191.
48. P.R.O., Adm. 51/2462 (7 January 1809); *Life and Letters of Captain Marryat*, ed. Florence Marryat, 1872, I, 28.
49. *Life and Letters of Captain Marryat*, I, 231–234.
50. *ibid.*, I, 17; *Autobiography*, I, 210–211.
51. *Life and Letters of Captain Marryat*, I, 18.
52. *ibid.*, I, 18.
53. *ibid.*, I, 17–18; *Autobiography*, I, 211–212.
54. *Life and Letters of Captain Marryat*, I, 18.
55. *ibid.*, I, 19–20.
56. *ibid.*, I, 20–22; *Autobiography*, I, 212–213; *Naval Chronicle* XVII (1807), 167.
57. *Autobiography*, I, 226–233; *Parliamentary Debates*, IX, 754–760, 765–768.
58. *Autobiography*, I, 227.
59. *Letters of Richard Brinsley Sheridan*, ed. Cecil Price, 1966, III, 8.
60. M. W. Patterson, *Sir Francis Burdett and his Times*, 1931, I, 218; *Henry Crabb Robinson on Books and their Writers*, ed. Edith J. Morley, 1938, I, 61; British Museum Add. MS. 27,838 f. 107.
61. *Autobiography*, I, 215–216.
62. Add. MS. 27,838 f. 109.
63. *ibid.*, f. 173.
64. *ibid.*, ff. 117, 132.
65. British Museum Add. MS. 27,850, f. 71.
66. Add. MS. 27,838 f. 61.
67. *ibid.*, ff. 111, 134.
68. *ibid.*, f. 147.
69. *ibid.*, f. 173.
70. *Pilot*, 7 May 1807.
71. *Times*, 13 May 1807.
72. Add. MS. 27,850 f. 80.
73. *Autobiography*, I, 222–225; *Parliamentary Debates*, IX, 745–746, 738*–739*.

74. *Autobiography*, I, 226–233; *Parliamentary Debates*, IX, 754–760 and 765–768.


## 4. "EXCESSIVE USE OF POWDER AND SHOT"

1. *Edinburgh Review*, X (1807), 19; *Parliamentary Debates*, X, 692–694, 708–709, 1182.
2. *Parliamentary Debates*, XII, 25, 46 ff.; *Morning Chronicle*, 21 January 1809; British Museum Add. MS. 37,888 ff. 44–45, 102, 104.
3. Twitchett, *Life of a Seaman*, 90–91.
4. *Life and Letters of Captain Marryat*, I, 24–28; *Autobiography*, I, 234–236.
5. Christopher Lloyd, *Captain Marryat and the Old Navy*, 1939, p. 54.
6. *Autobiography*, I, 238.
7. *Life and Letters of Captain Marryat*, I, 42–46; *Autobiography*, I, 242–244.
8. *Autobiography*, I, 254–256.
9. *ibid.*, I, 257–260; *Life and Letters of Captain Marryat*, I, 46.
10. *Autobiography*, I, 261–266; *Life and Letters of Captain Marryat*, I, 46; *Naval Chronicle*, XX (1808), 327.
11. *Autobiography*, I, 267.
12. P.R.O., Adm. 51/2462 (24 August 1808); *Autobiography*, I, 270.
13. *Autobiography*, I, 270–274; *Life and Letters of Captain Marryat*, I, 46–48.
14. *Memoir of the Life and Services of Vice-Admiral Sir Jahleel Brenton*, ed. Henry Raikes, 1846, pp. 337–338; P.R.O., Adm. 51/2462 (7–10 September 1808); *Autobiography*, I, 279–281.
15. *Life*, II, 361n.
16. *Autobiography*, I, 288, 321–322.
17. *ibid.*, I, 283–284.
18. *ibid.*, I, 294–312; *Life and Letters of Captain Marryat*, I, 50–51; Frederick Marryat, *Frank Mildmay: or The Naval Officer*, ed. W. L. Courtney, pp. 76–80.
19. Marryat, *Frank Mildmay*, pp. 82–83.
20. *Life and Letters of Captain Marryat*, I, 51; *Autobiography*, I, 313–316.
21. *Naval Chronicle*, XXI (1809), 195, 260.
22. *Autobiography*, I, 336–337.
23. *ibid.*, I, 335.
24. *Naval Chronicle*, XXI (1809), 372–373.
25. *Selections from the Correspondence of Admiral John Markham*, p. 50; Thomas Hood, *The Poetical Works of Thomas Hood*, 1862–1863, II, 430.


## 5. IN THE FACE OF THE ENEMY

1. James, *Naval History of Great Britain*, IV, 390–393.
2. *The Farington Diary*, V, 176.

3. *Autobiography*, I, 340–342; *Court-Martial*, p. 115.
4. *Autobiography*, I, 342–343.
5. *ibid.*, I, 343–346.
6. *ibid.*, I, 346–348.
7. *Court-Martial*, pp. 115, 119.
8. *ibid.*, p. 22.
9. *The Yale Edition of Horace Walpole's Correspondence*, ed. W. S. Lewis, XXV (1971), 12.
10. *Autobiography*, I, 356–359; *The Farington Diary*, V, 173; *Memorials Personal and Historical of Admiral Lord Gambier*, ed. Georgiana, Lady Chatterton, 1861, II, 97n.
11. *Autobiography*, I, 361–362.
12. *ibid.*, I, 361, 363.
13. Richardson, *A Mariner of England*, pp. 243–244.
14. *Letters and Papers of Sir Thomas Byam Martin*, ed. Sir Richard Vesey Hamilton, 1898–1903, III, 314.
15. *Autobiography*, I, 370–371.
16. *Letters and Papers of Sir Thomas Byam Martin*, III, 316–317.
17. *Autobiography*, I, 375; Marryat, *Frank Mildmay*, p. 127.
18. *Autobiography*, I, 377; *Life and Letters of Captain Marryat*, I, 67; Marryat, *Frank Mildmay*, pp. 127–128; Twitchett, *Life of a Seaman*, p. 134.
19. *Letters and Papers of Sir Thomas Byam Martin*, III, 317; *Autobiography*, I, 378; James, *Naval History of Great Britain*, IV, 406.
20. *Autobiography*, I, 378.
21. Richardson. *A Mariner of England*, p. 247; *Autobiography*, I, 379.
22. *Court-Martial*, pp. 215–216.
23. *Letters and Papers of Sir Thomas Byam Martin*, III, 317.
24. *ibid.*, III, 319.
25. *Court-Martial*, p. 272.
26. *ibid.*, p. 39; *Autobiography*, I, 381.
27. *Court-Martial*, p. 39.
28. *Autobiography*, I, 383.
29. Richardson, *A Mariner of England*, p. 248.
30. *Autobiography*, I, 384.
31. *ibid.*, I, 385.
32. *ibid.*, I, 384.
33. *ibid.*, I, 386.
34. *ibid.*, I 386–387.
35. Marryat, *Frank Mildmay*, p. 130.
36. *Letters and Papers of Sir Thomas Byam Martin*, III, 321.
37. *Autobiography*, I, 392.
38. *Court-Martial*, p. 192.
39. *Autobiography*, I, 394–396.
40. *ibid.*, I, 396–397.
41. *Court-Martial*, pp. 5–7.
42. Add. MS. 27,838 f. 173.

43. *ibid.*, f. 173.
44. *Court-Martial*, p. 6.
45. *ibid.*, p. 6.
46. *ibid.*, p. 8.
47. *Autobiography*, I, 403.
48. *ibid.*, I, 403–404.
49. *ibid.*, I, 404–405.
50. *Life*, II, 368; Fortescue, *Dundonald*, p. 212; *Selections from the Correspondence of Admiral John Markham*, pp. 47–48.
51. William Beckford, *Life at Fonthill 1807–1822*, ed. Boyd Alexander, 1957, p. 124.
52. *Naval Chronicle*, XXI (1809), 371; XXII (1809), 1, 16.
53. *Court-Martial*, p. iii.
54. *ibid.*, pp. 10–15.
55. *ibid.*, p. iv.
56. John McArthur, *A Treatise of the Principles and Practice of Naval Courts-Martial*, 1792, pp. xxxv–xlii.
57. *Court-Martial*, p. 2.
58. James, *Naval History of Great Britain*, IV, 425; *Court-Martial*, p. 36.
59. *Court-Martial*, pp. 52–57, 70.
60. *ibid.*, p. 42.
61. *ibid.*, pp. 27–28.
62. *ibid.*, pp. 152–153.
63. *ibid.*, p. 198.
64. *ibid.*, pp. 198–204, 222.
65. *ibid.*, pp. 151, 229–230, 233–234.
66. *ibid.*, pp. 242–243.
67. *Memorials of Admiral Lord Gambier*, II, 328.
68. *ibid.*, II, 328, 330.
69. *ibid.*, II, 342.
70. Barry O'Meara, *Napoleon in Exile*, 1822, II, 291.
71. *Parliamentary Debates*, XV, 219–247; *Autobiography*, II, 125.

## 6. "ANNOUNCE LORD COCHRANE'S DEGRADATION"

1. *Autobiography*, II, 159.
2. British Museum Add. MS. 41,083 f. 166.
3. *ibid.*, f. 166.
4. *ibid.*, ff. 171–172.
5. *ibid.*, f. 167.
6. *ibid.*, f. 167.
7. *ibid.*, f. 167.
8. *ibid.*, ff. 167, 173.
9. Fortescue, *Dundonald*, p. 94.
10. *Autobiography*, II, 236.
11. Robert Graves, *Goodbye To All That*, 1929, pp. 198–199.
12. *Creevey*, ed. John Gore, p. 90.

13. *Creevey*, pp. 90–91; *Correspondence and Diaries of John Wilson Croker*, I, 126.
14. Add MS. 41,083 ff. 176–177, 183; *The Keith Papers*, III, 316.
15. *Life*, II, 249–250.
16. Add. MS. 41,083 f. 190.
17. Add. MS. 37,888 ff. 44–45.
18. Add. MS. 41,083 f. 192.
19. *Autobiography*, II, 167–169.
20. *ibid.*, II, 168–180.
21. *ibid.*, II, 269.
22. *ibid.*, II, 270; *House of Lords Sessions Papers: Dundonald Peerage Claim*, 1861–1863, p. 58.
23. *House of Lords Sessions Papers: Dundonald Peerage Claim*, p. 58.
24. *ibid.*, pp. 58–60.
25. *Autobiography*, II, 271.
26. Patterson, *Sir Francis Burdett*, I, 242.
27. *ibid.*, I, 255–257.
28. Add, MS. 27,850 ff. 188, 189.
29. *ibid* , f. 199.
30. *ibid.*, f. 200.
31. Patterson, *Sir Francis Burdett*, I, 270–274.
32. Samuel Bamford, *Passages in the Life of a Radical*, 1844, I, 25–26.
33. *ibid.*, I, 26–27.
34. *Autobiography*, II, 142–143; *Parliamentary Debates*, XVI, 1006–1011.
35. *Autobiography*, II, 145–146; *Parliamentary Debates*, XVI, 1017.
36. *Autobiography*, II, 146.
37. *Times*, 18 February 1814.
38. William C. Townsend, *Modern State Trials*, 1850, II, 29.
39. *Autobiography*, II, 330–331.
40. *Times*, 22 February 1814.
41. J. B. Atlay, *The Trial of Lord Cochrane before Lord Ellenborough*, 1897, p. 16.
42. *Autobiography*, II, 422–425.
43. Aspinall, *Correspondence of George, Prince of Wales*, VIII, 416.
44. Townsend, *Modern State Trials*, II, 4.
45. *Autobiography*, II, 334; Atlay, *Trial of Lord Cochrane*, pp. 40–42.
46. Leigh Hunt, *Autobiography*, 1850, II, 134.
47. Thomas Moore, *Poetical Works*, 1840–1841, III, 109.
48. Atlay, *Trial of Lord Cochrane*, pp. 68–84.
49. *ibid.*, p. 141.
50. *Autobiography*, II, 355–358, 361.
51. Townsend, *Modern State Trials*, II, 45.
52. Atlay, *Trial of Lord Cochrane*, pp. 42–43, 55, 185–186; Townsend, *Modern State Trials*, II, 50–51.
53. Atlay, *Trial of Lord Cochrane*, p. 155n.
54. Townsend, *Modern State Trials*, II, 5, 90.
55. *ibid.*, II, 92–93.

56. *Autobiography*, II, 353.
57. P.R.O., K.B. 28/461/5 and 6; *Parliamentary Debates*, XXVIII, 538–606; *Autobiography*, II, 370–371; Townsend, *Modern State Trials*, II, 9, 110n.
58. Townsend, *Modern State Trials*, II, 94–103.
59. Fortescue, *Dundonald*, p. 101.
60. *Letters and Papers of Sir Thomas Byam Martin*, III, 198–199.
61. A. G. L'Estrange, *The Life of Mary Russell Mitford*, 1870, I, 271.
62. Townsend, *Modern State Trials*, II, 7.
63. *Letters of Richard Brinsley Sheridan*, III, 192.
64. *Autobiography*, II, 383–384.
65. 17 *State Trials*, 297–618.
66. *Autobiography*, II, 392–394.
67. *Life*, I, 51–54.
68. *ibid.*, I 55–56.
69. *ibid.*, I, 57–59.
70. *ibid.*, I, 70–71.
71. *Autobiography*, II, 399.
72. *Lord Cochrane's Reasons for Escaping: The Trial of Lord Cochrane at Guildford*, 1816, pp. 9, 11, 16.
73. *Parliamentary Debates*, XXXI, 1074–1080.
74. *ibid.*, XXXII, 1145–1208; *Life*, I, 78–81.
75. John, Baron Campbell, *Lives of the Chief Justices*, 1849–1857, III, 219.
76. *ibid.*, III, 219.
77. *Life*, I, 84–99.
78. Bamford, *Passages in the Life of a Radical*, I, 20.
79. *Life*, I, 111–116; *Parliamentary Debates*, XXXV, 78–99.
80. *Life*, I, 118–119.
81. Add. MS. 41,083 ff. 198–210; *Case Submitted to the Consideration of the Navy and the Public*, 1817, p. 19.
82. *Life*, I, 127–130.
83. Add. MS. 41,083 ff. 217–220.
84. *The Earl of Dundonald's Answer to the Mis-statements contained in the Life of the late T. Coutts, Esq.*, 1822, p. 4.
85. *Life*, I, 131–136; *Parliamentary Debates*, XXXVIII, 1149.
86. Warren Tute, *Cochrane*, 1965, p. 175.

## 7. THE DEVIL'S ADMIRAL

1. W. B. Stevenson, *A Historical and Descriptive Narrative of Twenty Years' Residence in South America*, 1825, III, 159–161; *Memoirs of General Miller*, ed. John Miller, 1829, I, 207–208.
2. *Memoirs of General Miller*, I, 208–209; Stevenson, *Historical and Descriptive Narrative*, I, 308.
3. *Memoirs of General Miller*, I, 207.
4. Cochrane, *Narrative*, I, 4–5.

5. *ibid.*, I, 6.
6. *ibid.*, I, 9–11.
7. *ibid.*, I, 12–14; *Life*, I, 158.
8. Cochrane, *Narrative*, I, 23–24.
9. *ibid.*, I, 34–36; *Memoirs of General Miller*, I, 240.
10. Cochrane, *Narrative*, I, 37–39; Stevenson, *Historical and Descriptive Narrative*, III, 216–217; *Memoirs of General Miller*, I, 242–244.
11. Cochrane, *Narrative*, I, 39–46; Stevenson, *Historical and Descriptive Narrative*, III, 217–221; *Memoirs of General Miller*, I, 245–255.
12. Cochrane, *Narrative*, I, 54.
13. *ibid.*, I, 68.
14. Stevenson, *Historical and Descriptive Narrative*, III, 279–280.
15. Cochrane, *Narrative*, I, 77.
16. Tute, *Cochrane*, p. 176.
17. Cochrane, *Narrative*, I, 78–79.
18. *Memoirs of General Miller*, I, 282.
19. Stevenson, *Historical and Descriptive Narrative*, III, 289–290.
20. Cochrane, *Narrative*, I, 83–94; Stevenson, *Historical and Descriptive Narrative*, III, 290–300; *Memoirs of General Miller*, I, 283–285.
21. *Life*, I, 189.
22. *ibid.*, I, 193.
23. Stevenson, *Historical and Descriptive Narrative*, III, 307–319.
24. Cochrane, *Narrative*, I, 22.
25. *ibid.*, I, 22.
26. I, 22.
27. *ibid.*, I, 94–95.
28. *ibid.*, I, 104–105; Stevenson, *Historical and Descriptive Narrative*, III, 321–322.
29. *Memoirs of General Miller*, I, 298.
30. Cochrane, *Narrative*, I, 115–117.
31. *ibid.*, I, 117–118.
32. *ibid.*, I, 127–128; Stevenson, *Historical and Descriptive Narrative*, III, 352–355.
33. Cochrane, *Narrative*, I, 155–158; Stevenson, *Historical and Descriptive Narrative*, III, 385–388.
34. Cochrane, *Narrative*, I, 232–237.
35. *ibid.*, I, 271–286.
36. *ibid.*, I, 251.

## 8. UNDER TWO FLAGS

1. Cochrane, *Narrative*, II, 7–8.
2. *ibid.*, II, 8.
3. *ibid.*, II, 8.
4. *ibid.*, II, 14.
5. *ibid.*, II, 10–12.
6. *ibid.*, II, 27.

7. *ibid.*, II, 27–29.
8. *ibid.*, II, 29–32, 34.
9. *ibid.*, II, 40–46.
10. *ibid.*, II, 48–59.
11. *ibid.*, II, 60–84.
12. *ibid.*, II, 102.
13. *ibid.*, II, 105–108; *Life*, I, 254.
14. Cochrane, *Narrative*, II, 110–111.
15. *ibid.*, II, 139–142.
16. *ibid.*, II, 147–156.
17. *ibid.*, II, 157–168.
18. *ibid.*, II, 179–252.
19. *Life*, I, 264–265; *Parliamentary Debates: New Series*, XI, 1477–1478.
20. *Life*, I, 327.
21. *ibid.*, I, 326.
22. *ibid.*, I, 320.
23. P. B. Shelley, *Complete Poetical Works*, ed. Thomas Hutchinson, 1914, p. 443.
24. *Life*, I, 379.
25. *ibid.*, I, 329.
26. *ibid.*, I, 362n.
27. *ibid.*, I, 346–347.
28. *ibid.*, I, 353.
29. *ibid.*, I, 358.
30. George Finlay, *History of the Greek Revolution*, 1861, II, 137.
31. *Life*, II, 97–99.
32. *ibid.*, I, 349, II, 97.
33. *ibid.*, II, 19.
34. *ibid.*, II, 16.
35. *ibid.*, II, 20.
36. *ibid.*, II, 30.
37. *ibid.*, II, 36–37.
38. *ibid.*, II, 48–49.
39. *ibid.*, II. 50, 54.
40. *ibid.*, II, 55–57.
41. *ibid.*, II, 61.
42. *ibid.*, II, 68–72.
43. *ibid.*, II, 37.
44. *ibid.*, II, 85.
45. *ibid.*, II, 85–87.
46. *ibid.*, II, 87–88.
47. *ibid.*, II, 103.
48. *ibid.*, II, 117.
49. *ibid.*, II, 92–97.
50. *ibid.*, II, 126–127.
51. *ibid.*, II, 133, 137.
52. *ibid.*, II, 137.

53. Crauford Tait Ramage, *Ramage in South Italy*, ed. Edith Clay, 1965, p. 204.
54. *Life*, II, 178–179.
55. *ibid.*, II, 186–188.
56. *ibid.*, II, 193.
57. MS. Journals of John Cam Hobhouse, Baron Broughton, 18 August 1825.

## 9. SEE, THE CONQUERING HERO COMES!

1. *Life*, II, 203.
2. *ibid.*, II, 206.
3. *ibid.*, II, 207; Add. MS. 41,083 f. 211.
4. *The Greville Memoirs*, ed. Lytton Strachey and Roger Fulford, 1938, I, 398–399.
5. *Life*, II, 207–208.
6. *ibid.*, II, 210.
7. *ibid.*, II, 213.
8. *ibid.*, II, 214–215.
9. *ibid.*, II, 217.
10. *ibid.*, II, 219n.
11. Add. MS. 27,838 f. 173.
12. *Life*, II, 222–223n.
13. *ibid.*, II, 227: Cf. British Museum Add. MS. 38,781 ff. 68–69, "The Steam Engine Simplified, By the Earl of Dundonald, 1833", an argument on behalf of "revolving engines".
14. *Life*, II, 230–231.
15. *ibid.*, II, 238.
16. *ibid.*, II, 247–248.
17. *ibid.*, II, 249.
18. *ibid.*, II, 250.
19. *ibid.*, II, 250.
20. *ibid.*, II, 257–258.
21. *ibid.*, II, 260.
22. *ibid.*, II, 270.
23. *ibid.*, II, 271–272.
24. *ibid.*, II, 272.
25. *ibid.*, II, 278.
26. *Letters and Papers of Sir Thomas Byam Martin*, III, 198.
27. *Life*, II, 284.
28. *ibid.*, II, 284.
29. *ibid.*, II, 285.
30. *Times*, 28 May 1847.
31. Ellenborough, Edward Law, 3rd Baron, *The Guilt of Lord Cochrane in 1814*, 1914, pp. 237–238.
32. *Life*, II, 289–290.
33. *ibid.*, II, 291–293.

34. *ibid.*, II, 295.
35. *ibid.*, II, 305.
36. *ibid.*, II, 318, 334–335n.
37. *ibid.*, II, 325.
38. *Letters of Queen Victoria, 1837–1861*, ed. A. C. Benson and Viscount Esher, 1908, III, 9.
39. *Life*, II, 339.
40. *ibid.*, II, 340–341.
41. *ibid.*, II, 343.
42. *ibid.*, II, 344.
43. *ibid.*, II, 345.
44. *The Panmure Papers*, ed. Sir George Douglas and Sir George Dalhousie Ramsay, 1908, I, 308.
45. *ibid.*, I, 341.
46. *ibid.*, I, 342.
47. *ibid.*, I 340.
48. *Life*, II, 355–356.
49. *ibid.*, II, 358.
50. *ibid.*, II, 360n.
51. *Punch*, XXXIX (1860), 203 (24 November).
52. *Times*, 15 November 1860; *Punch*, XXXIX (1860), 203 (24 November).
53 *Life*, II, 362.
54. *Times*, 2 November 1860; *Punch*, XXXIX (1860), 203; *Illustrated London News*, 17 November 1860.
55. *Leaves from the Diary of Henry Greville*, ed. Viscountess Enfield, 1883–1904, I, 149.
56. *Parliamentary Debates: Third Series*, CCXXXIII, 857–877; *Report from the Select Committee on Lord Cochrane's Petition*, 1877, *passim*.
57. *Athenaeum*, 17 December 1859; Cockayne, *Complete Peerage*, IV, 530.
58. *The Greville Memoirs*, ed. Lytton Strachey and Roger Fulford, I, 399.
59. Lytton Strachey, *Eminent Victorians*, 1918, p. 108.
60. *Life*, II, 230.
61. *Athenaeum*, 17 December 1859; Justin McCarthy, *A History of Our Own Times*, 1905, II, 233.
62. *Athenaeum*, 17 December 1859; Campbell, *Lives of the Chief Justices*, III, 218–220; Henry, Baron Brougham, *Historical Sketches of Statesmen who flourished in the Time of George III: Third Series*, 1843, pp. 219–222; Townsend, *Modern State Trials*, II, 3–5; *Quarterly Review*, LXVI (1840), 612; McCarthy, *History of Our Own Times*, II, 232–233; *Times*, 2 November 1860.
63. *Times*, 2 November 1860.
64. *Times*, 2 November 1860; *Naval Chronicle*, XXXII (1814), 201; Fortescue, *Dundonald*, pp. 226–227.
65. Archibald Alison, *History of Europe*, 1833–1842, VII, 650.

# Bibliography

THE second section of the following bibliography contains those periodical publications which have been used as general sources for the period of Cochrane's life, or for other periods specified in the footnotes. Where a specific article from a journal has been used, this will be found listed in the third section of the bibliography.

In the third section of the bibliography, books written at the instigation of such men as Cochrane or Gambier, or as part of their campaigns, and which otherwise appear anonymously, have been listed with their own publications. The place of publication of all books in this section is London, unless otherwise specified.

## 1. MANUSCRIPT SOURCES

British Museum:
    Add. MS. 27,850 (Place papers)
    Add. MS. 27,838 (Place papers)
    Add. MS. 27,840 (Place papers)
    Add. MS. 34,459 (Auckland papers)
    Add. MS. 36,461 (Hobhouse papers)
    Add. MS. 36,464 (Hobhouse papers)
    Add. MS. 36,544 (Church papers)
    Add. MS 37,888 (Windham papers)
    Add. MS. 38,781 (Stephenson papers)
    Add. MS. 41,083 (Melville papers)
Public Record Office:
    K.B. 28/461 (King's Bench Indictments)
    Adm. 51/1554 (Log of the *Pallas*)
    Adm. 51/1624 (Log of the *Pallas*)
    Adm. 51/2462 (Log of the *Imperieuse*)
    Adm. 1/5632 (Crimean papers)
National Library of Scotland:
    MS. 5379 (British Tar Company)

## 2. PERIODICAL PUBLICATIONS

Annual Register
Athenaeum
Bell's Universal Advertiser
Champion
Chronique de Paris
Cobbett's Weekly Political Register
Courier
Edinburgh Review
Examiner
Gentleman's Magazine
Illustrated London News
Independent Whig

Morning Chronicle
Morning Post
Naval and Military Gazette
Naval Chronicle
Parliamentary Debates
Pilot
Punch
Quarterly Review
Times
True Briton
United Service Gazette

## 3. BOOKS AND ARTICLES

Abbot, Charles, Baron Colchester, *Diary and Correspondence of Charles Abbot, Lord Colchester*, 3 vols., 1861.

Alison, Archibald, *History of Europe*, 10 vols., Edinburgh and London, 1833–1842.

Anson, W. V., *The Life of John Jervis, Admiral Lord St Vincent*, 1913.

Aspinall, A. (ed.) *Correspondence of George, Prince of Wales, 1770–1812*, 8 vols., 1963–1971.

Atlay, J. B., *The Trial of Lord Cochrane before Lord Ellenborough*, 1897.

Bamford, Samuel, *Passages in the Life of a Radical*, 2 vols., 1844.

Beckford, William, *Life at Fonthill 1807–1822*, ed. Boyd Alexander, 1957.

Berenger, Charles Random de, *The Noble Stock-Jobber*, 1816.

Beveridge, David, *Between the Ochils and the Forth*, Edinburgh and London, 1888.

Bird, Anthony, *The Damnable Duke of Cumberland*, 1966.

Brenton, Edward Pelham, *Life and Correspondence of John, Earl of St Vincent*, 2 vols., 1838.

Brenton, Edward Pelham, *Naval History of Great Britain*, 5 vols., 1823–25.

Brenton, Jahleel, *Memoir of the Life and Services of Vice-Admiral Sir Jahleel Brenton*, ed. Henry Raikes, 1846.

Brialmont, M., and Gleig, G. R., *Life of Arthur, Duke of Wellington*, 5 vols., 1860.

Brougham, Henry, Baron, *Historical Sketches of Statesmen who flourished in the Time of George III: Second Series*, 1839; *Third Series*, 1843.

Browning, Oscar (ed.), *England and Napoleon in 1803: Being the Despatches of Lord Whitworth and others* (Royal Historical Society), 1887.

Burdett, Sir Francis, *Accurate Report of the Proceedings of the Friends of Reform*, 1809.

Burnet, Gilbert, *History of his own Time*, 2 vols., 1724–1734.

Calcott, Maria Graham, Lady, *Journal of a Residence in Chili*, 1824.

Caldeclough, A., *Travels in South America*, 2 vols., 1825.

*Calumnious Aspersions in the Report of the Sub-Committee of the Stock Exchange exposed and refuted*, 1814.

Campbell, John, Baron, *Lives of the Lord Chancellors*, 10 vols., 1856–1857.

Campbell, John, Baron, *Lives of the Chief Justices*, 3 vols., 1849–1857.

Cecil, Lord David, *Lord M.*, 1954.

Clarke, Mary Ann, *The Rival Princes: or, A Faithful Narrative of Facts*, 1810.

Clow, Archibald, and Nan L., "Lord Dundonald", *Economic History Review*, XII (1942), 47–58.

Cochrane, Archibald, 9th Earl of Dundonald, *Account of the Qualities and Uses of Coal Tar*, 1785.

Cochrane, Archibald, 9th Earl of Dundonald, *Description of the Estate and Abbey of Culross*, Edinburgh, 1793.

Cochrane, Archibald, 9th Earl of Dundonald, *Directions for Extracting Gum from the Lichen or Tree Moss*, Glasgow, 1801.

Cochrane, Archibald, 9th Earl of Dundonald, *The Earl of Dundonald's Answer to the Mis-statements contained in the Life of the late T. Coutts, Esq.*, 1822.

Cochrane, Archibald, 9th Earl of Dundonald, *Introduction to and Contents of an Intended Publication* (On the exporting of textiles), 1806.

Cochrane, Archibald, 9th Earl of Dundonald, *Letters by the Earl of Dundonald on Making Bread from Potatoes*, Edinburgh, 1791.

Cochrane, Archibald, 9th Earl of Dundonald, *Memorial and Petition to the Honourable the Directors of the East India Company*, 1786.

Cochrane, Archibald, 9th Earl of Dundonald, *A New Year's Gift. Recommended to the Perusal of Persons desirous of promoting Domestic Economy*, 1798.

Cochrane, Archibald, 9th Earl of Dundonald, *The Present State of the Manufacture of Salt explained*, 1785.

Cochrane, Archibald, 9th Earl of Dundonald, *Thoughts on the Manufacture and Trade of Salt*, Edinburgh, 1784.

Cochrane, Archibald, 9th Earl of Dundonald, *A Treatise shewing the Intimate Connection that subsists between Agriculture and Chemistry*, 1795.

Cochrane, Basil, *An Exposé of the Conduct of the Victualling Board to the Honourable Basil Cochrane*, 1824.

Cochrane, Basil, *An Historical Digest of the Reports of the Commissioners appointed to Inquire into Abuses in the Public Departments of Government*, 1824.

Cochrane, Basil, *An Improvement in the Mode of Administering the Vapour Bath*, 1809.

Cochrane, Basil, *An Inquiry into the Conduct of the Commissioners for Victualling His Majesty's Navy*, 1823.

Cochrane, Basil, *Observations upon the System pursued by the Victualling Department*, 1821.

Cochrane, John, *A Reply to the Quarterly Review*, 1861.

Cochrane, Thomas, 10th Earl of Dundonald, *An Address from Lord Cochrane to the Electors of Westminster*, 1815.

Cochrane, Thomas, 10th Earl of Dundonald, *The Answer of Lord Cochrane to the Address of the Electors of Westminster*, 1817.

Cochrane, Thomas, 10th Earl of Dundonald, *The Autobiography of a Seaman*, 2 vols., 1860 (2nd edition, 1860).

Cochrane, Thomas, 10th Earl of Dundonald, *Brief Extracts from the Memorandum of the Earl of Dundonald on the Use, Properties, and Products of the Bitumen and Petroleum of Trinidad*, 1857.

Cochrane, Thomas, 10th Earl of Dundonald, *Case Submitted to the Consideration of His Royal Highness the Prince Regent, the Admiral of the Fleet and the Privy Council*, 1817.

Cochrane, Thomas, 10th Earl of Dundonald, *Case Submitted to the Consideration of the Navy and the Public*, 1817.

Cochrane, Thomas, 10th Earl of Dundonald, *Correspondence entre deux Philhellènes* (Letters of Cochrane and Louis-André Gosse), Paris and Geneva, 1919.

Cochrane, Thomas, 10th Earl of Dundonald, *A Letter to Lord Ellenborough*, 1815.

Cochrane, Thomas, 10th Earl of Dundonald, *A Letter to the Electors of Westminster on the Case of Lord Cochrane*, 1814.

Cochrane, Thomas, 10th Earl of Dundonald, *The Life and Eminent Services of the gallant Lord Cochrane*, 1815.

Cochrane, Thomas, 10th Earl of Dundonald, *Lord Cochrane's Farewell Address to the Electors of Westminster*, 1818.

Cochrane, Thomas, 10th Earl of Dundonald, *Lord Cochrane's Reasons for Escaping: The Trial of Lord Cochrane at Guildford*, 1816.

Cochrane, Thomas, 10th Earl of Dundonald, *Narrative of Services in the Liberation of Chili, Peru, and Brazil*, 2 vols., 1859.

Cochrane, Thomas, 10th Earl of Dundonald, *Notes on the Mineralogy, Government and Conditions of the British West India Islands and North-American Maritime Colonies*, 1851.

Cochrane, Thomas, 10th Earl of Dundonald, *Observations on Naval Affairs*, 1847.

Cochrane, Thomas, 10th Earl of Dundonald, *Review of the Case of Lord Cochrane*, 1830.

Cochrane, Thomas, 10th Earl of Dundonald, *A Second Letter to the Electors of Westminster on the Nomination of Lord Cochrane*, 1814.

Cochrane, Thomas, 10th Earl of Dundonald, *To the Merchants of England and other Nations trading to the Pacific*, 1823.

Cochrane, Thomas Barnes, 11th Earl of Dundonald, and Bourne, H. R. Fox, *The Life of Thomas, Lord Cochrane, 10th Earl of Dundonald*, 2 vols., 1869.

Cochrane-Johnstone, Andrew, *Correspondence between Colonel Cochrane-Johnstone and the Departments of the Commander-in-Chief and the Judge Advocate General*, 1805.

Cochrane-Johnstone, Andrew, *Defence of the Honourable Andrew Cochrane-Johnstone*, Edinburgh, 1806.

Cockayne, G. E., *The Complete Peerage*, 12 vols., 1910–1959.

Codrington, Sir Edward, *Piracy in the Levant*, ed. C. G. Pitcairn Jones (Navy Records Society), 1934.

Collingwood, Cuthbert, Baron, *A Selection from the Public and Private Correspondence of Vice-Admiral Lord Collingwood*, 1828.

*Complete Collection of State Trials*, ed. William Cobbett, T. B. Howell, T. J. Howell, and D. Jardine, 34 vols., 1809–1828.

Coutts, Thomas, *Life of the late Thomas Coutts, with Biographical and Entertaining Anecdotes of his first Wife, by a Person of the First Respectability*, 1819 (2nd edition, 1822).

Crawford, Abraham, *Reminiscences of a Naval Officer during the late War*, 2 vols., 1851.

Creevey, Thomas, *The Creevey Papers*, ed. Sir Herbert Maxwell, 2 vols., 1903.

Creevey, Thomas, *Creevey*, ed. John Gore, 1948.

Croker, John Wilson, *Correspondence and Diaries of John Wilson Croker*, ed. Louis J. Jennings, 3 vols., 1885.

Croker, John Wilson, *The Croker Papers*, ed. Bernard Pool, 1967.

Devereux, Roy, *John London Macadam*, 1937.

Ellenborough, John Law, 3rd Baron, *The Guilt of Lord Cochrane in 1814*, 1914.

*False Swearing No Perjury, when Subservient to State Purposes!!!* [Broadsheet] 1815.

Farington, Joseph, *The Farington Diary*, ed. James Greig, 8 vols., 1922–1928.

Finlay, George, *History of the Greek Revolution*, 2 vols., 1861.

Fortescue, J. W., *Dundonald*, 1895.

Galloway, R. H., *Refutation of Calumnious Statements*, 1871.

Gambier, James, Baron, *Memorials Personal and Historical of Admiral Lord Gambier*, ed. Georgiana, Lady Chatterton, 2 vols., 1861.

Gambier, James, Baron, *Minutes of a Court-Martial holden on board H.M.S. Gladiator*, 1809.

Gaskell, Elizabeth, *Life of Charlotte Brontë*, 2 vols. 1857.

Gibbs, Lewis, *Sheridan*, 1947.

Giffard, Edward, *Deeds of Naval Daring*, 1852.

Gordon, Thomas, *History of the Greek Revolution*, 2 vols., 1832.

Graves, Robert, *Goodbye To All That*, 1929.

Greville, Charles, *The Greville Memoirs, 1814-1860*, ed. Lytton Strachey and Roger Fulford, 8 vols., 1938.

Greville, Henry, *Leaves from the Diary of Henry Greville*, ed., Viscountess Enfield, 4 vols., 1883–1904.

Gronow, Rees Howell, *Reminiscences and Recollections of Captain Gronow*, ed. John Raymond, 1964.

*Historical Manuscripts Commission. The Manuscripts of J. B. Fortescue, Esq., at Dropmore*, Vol. II, 1894.

Hodgskin, Thomas, *An Essay on Naval Discipline*, 1813.

Hogan, Denis, *An Appeal to the Public and a Farewell Address to the Army*, 1808.

Hood, Thomas, *Poetical Works of Thomas Hood*, 7 vols., 1862–1863.

Horner, Francis, *Memoirs and Correspondence*, 2 vols., 1843.

*House of Lords Sessions Papers: Dundonald Claim of Peerage. Evidence and Documents*, 1861–1863.

Howarth, David, *Trafalgar: The Nelson Touch*, 1969.

Hunt, James Leigh, *Autobiography*, 3 vols., 1850.

James, William, *The Naval History of Great Britain*, 6 vols. 1902.

James, William, *Old Oak: The Life of John Jervis, Earl of St Vincent*, 1950.

Jervis, John, Earl of St Vincent, *Letters of Admiral of the Fleet the Earl of St Vincent, whilst First Lord of the Admiralty, 1801–1804*, ed. David Bonner Smith, 2 vols. (Navy Records Society), 1922–1927.

Keith, George Keith Elphinstone, Viscount, *The Keith Papers*, Vol. III, ed. Christopher Lloyd (Navy Records Society), 1955.

Kinglake, Alexander, *The Invasion of the Crimea*, 8 vols. 1863–1887.

Lacombe, Bernard de, *Talleyrand the Man*, tr. A. D'Alberti, 1910.

L'Estrange, A. G., *The Life of Mary Russell Mitford*, 3 vols., 1870.

Lloyd, Christopher, *Lord Cochrane*, 1947.

Lloyd, Christopher, *Captain Marryat and the Old Navy*, 1939.

Lockhart, John Gibson, *Memoirs of Sir Walter Scott*, 5 vols., 1900.

Longford, Elizabeth, *Wellington: The Years of the Sword*, 1969.

Longford, Elizabeth, *Wellington: Pillar of State*, 1972.

McArthur, John, *A Treatise of the Principles and Practice of Naval Courts-Martial*, 1792.

McCarthy, Justin, *A History of Our Own Times*, 3 vols, 1905.

McCabe, Joseph, *Talleyrand: A Biographical Study*, 1906.

[McGilchrist, John,] *The Life and Daring Exploits of Lord Dundonald*, 1861.

McRae, Alexander, *A Disclosure of the Hoax practised upon the Stock Exchange*, 1815.

Maine, René, *Trafalgar: Napoleon's Naval Waterloo*, tr. Rita Eldon and B. W. Robinson, 1957.

Mallalieu, J. P. W., *Extraordinary Seaman*, 1957.

Markham, Admiral John, *Selections from the Correspondence of Admiral John Markham*, ed. Sir Clements Markham (Navy Records Society), 1904.

Marryat, Frederick, *Frank Mildmay: or, The Naval Officer*, ed. W. L. Courtney, n.d.

Marryat, Frederick, *Life and Letters of Captain Marryat*, ed. Florence Marryat, 2 vols., 1872.

Martin, Kingsley, *The Triumph of Lord Palmerston*, 1963.

Martin, Sir Theodore, *Life of His Royal Highness the Prince Consort*, 5 vols., 1875–1877.

Martin, Sir Thomas Byam, *Letters and Papers of Sir Thomas Byam Martin*, ed. Sir Richard Vesey Hamilton, 3 vols. (Navy Records Society), 1898–1903.

Miers, John, *Travels in Chile and La Plata*, 2 vols., 1826.

Miller, William, *Memoirs of General Miller*, ed. John Miller, 2 vols., 1829.

Moore, Doris Langley, *The Late Lord Byron*, 1961.

Moore, Thomas, *Poetical Works*, 10 vols., 1840–1841.

O'Meara, Barry, *Napoleon in Exile*, 2 vols., 1822.

Panmure, Fox Maule, Baron Panmure and Earl of Dalhousie, *The Panmure Papers*, ed. Sir George Douglas and Sir George Dalhousie Ramsay, 2 vols., 1908.

Parker, C. S., *Life of Sir James Graham*, 2 vols., 1907.

Patterson, M. W., *Sir Francis Burdett and his Times*, 2 vols., 1931.

Quennell, Peter, *Byron in Italy*, 1941.

Ramage, Crauford Tait, *Ramage in South Italy*, ed. Edith Clay, 1965.

*Report from the Select Committee on Lord Cochrane's Petition*, 1877.

Richardson, William, *A Mariner of England*, ed. Spencer Childers, 1908.

Ridley, Jasper, *Lord Palmerston*, 1970.

Roberts, Michael, *The Whig Party 1807–1812*, 1939.

Robinson, Henry Crabb, *Diary, Reminiscences, and Correspondence*, ed. Thomas Sadler, 3 vols., 1869.

Robinson, Henry Crabb, *Henry Crabb Robinson on Books and their Writers*, ed. Edith J. Morley, 3 vols., 1938.

Roe, Robert, *An Answer to a Pamphlet published by the Earl of Dundonald, entitled Thoughts on the Manufacture and Trade of Salt*, 1786.

Shelley, Percy Bysshe, *Poetical Works*, ed. Thomas Hutchinson, 1914.

Sheridan, Richard Brinsley, *Letters of Richard Brinsley Sheridan*, ed. Cecil Price, 3 vols., Oxford, 1966.

Sinclair, Archibald, *Reminiscences of the Discipline, Customs and Usages in the Royal Navy*, n.d. [1857].

Sitwell, Sacheverell, and Bamford, Francis, *Edinburgh*, 1938.

Smyth, W. H., *The Life and Services of Captain Philip Beaver*, 1829.

Spinney, David, *Rodney*, 1969.

Stevenson, W. B., *A Historical and Descriptive Narrative of Twenty Years' Residence in South America*, 3 vols, 1825.

Strachey, Lytton, *Eminent Victorians*, 1918.

Thursfield, H. G. (ed.) *Five Naval Journals 1789–1817* (Navy Records Society), 1951.

Townsend, William C., *Modern State Trials*, 2 vols., 1850.

Tucker, J. S., *Memoirs of the Earl of St Vincent*, 2 vols., 1844.

Tute, Warren, *Cochrane*, 1965.

Twitchett, E. G., *Life of a Seaman*, 1931.

Urquart, David, *Views of the late Lord Dundonald on the Invasion of England*, 1860.

Victoria, Queen, *The Letters of Queen Victoria, 1837–1861*, ed. A. C. Benson and Viscount Esher, 3 vols., 1908.

Wallas, Graham, *The Life of Francis Place 1771–1854*, 1898.
Walpole, Horace, *Yale Edition of Horace Walpole's Correspondence*, ed.
  W. S. Lewis, Vol. XXV, 1971.
Warner, Oliver, *Trafalgar*, 1959.
Ziegler, Philip, *William IV*, 1971.

# Index